The Princeton Review®

MW00576008

SAT®
ELITE 2400

The Staff of The Princeton Review

PrincetonReview.com

PENGUIN RANDOM HOUSE

The Princeton Review, Inc.
24 Prime Parkway, Suite 201
Natick, MA 01760
E-mail: editorialsupport@review.com

Terms of Service: The Princeton Review Online Companion Tools
("Student Tools") for retail books are available for only the two most
recent editions of that book. Student Tools may be activated only twice
per eligible book purchased for two consecutive 12-month periods, for a
total of 24 months of access. Activation of Student Tools more than twice
per book is in direct violation of these Terms of Service and may result in
discontinuation of access to Student Tools Services.

ISBN: 978-0-8041-2553-6
eBook ISBN: 978-0-8041-2554-3
ISSN: 2373-9622

SAT is a registered trademark of the College Board, which does not spon-
sor or endorse this product.

The Princeton Review is not affiliated with Princeton University.

Editor: Selena Coppock
Production Editor: Kathy Carter
Production Artists: Deborah Silvestrini

Printed in the United States of America on partially recycled paper.

10 9 8 7 6 5 4 3 2 1

Editorial
Rob Franek, Senior VP, Publisher
Casey Cornelius, VP Content Development
Mary Beth Garrick, Director of Production
Selena Coppock, Managing Editor
Calvin Cato, Editor
Colleen Day, Editor
Aaron Riccio, Editor
Meave Shelton, Editor
Orion McBean, Editorial Assistant

Random House Publishing Team
Tom Russell, Publisher
Alison Stoltzfus, Publishing Manager
Melinda Ackell, Associate Managing Editor
Ellen Reed, Production Manager
Kristin Lindner, Production Supervisor
Andrea Lau, Designer

Contributors

Project Manager
Claudia Landgrover

Authors
Clarissa Constantine
Brian Becker
Steve Voigt
Lisa Mayo

Reviewers
Alice Swan
Teresa Schuberg

National Content Director, High School Programs
Jonathan Chiu

Contents

...So Much More Online!

More Learning...

- Online practice drills for additional elite SAT preparation
- Useful information about SAT scores, college admissions, score improvement, and the upcoming changes to the SAT

...then College!

- Detailed profiles for hundreds of colleges help you find the school that is right for you
- Information about financial aid and scholarships
- Dozens of Top 10 ranking lists including Quality of Professors, Worst Campus Food, Most Beautiful Campus, Party Schools, Diverse Student Population, and tons more from our annually revised *Best Colleges* guide

Register your book now!

- Go to PrincetonReview.com
- You'll see a Welcome page where you should register your book using the ISBN printed on the back cover of your book, right underneath the price. It's a 13 digit number, starting with "978." Type this number into the window.
- Next you will see a Sign Up/Sign In page where you will type in your E-mail address (username) and choose a password.
- Now you're good to go!

PrincetonReview.com

Part I
Orientation

Chapter 1
Introduction to the SAT

The pursuit of a perfect or near-perfect SAT score is an impressive goal. Achieving that goal requires a thorough command of the material and strategies specific to the SAT. To begin your quest, learn everything you can about the test. This chapter presents an overview of the SAT, advice about when to take it, and how to report your scores.

WELCOME

So you think you can score a 2250 or better? We're all for it. The Princeton Review supports all students who want to do their best. We've written this book specifically for students who are in a position to score at the very highest levels. We believe that to achieve a perfect or near-perfect score, you have to know as much as possible about the test itself and, more importantly, know yourself.

You may know all of the basic facts about the SAT already, but even if you think you do, we encourage you to read through this chapter to be sure you know every single thing you can about the test you're going to conquer.

FUN FACTS ABOUT THE SAT

All of the content review and strategies we teach in the following lessons are based on the specific structure and format of the SAT. Before you can beat the test, you have to know how it's built.

Structure

The SAT consists of three main sections: Math, Reading, and Writing. Each of these main sections is also broken into three smaller sections. The table below shows the distribution of these sections.

Math	18 questions 25 minutes	20 questions 25 minutes	16 questions 20 minutes
Reading	23–25 questions 25 minutes	23–25 questions 25 minutes	18–19 questions 20 minutes
Writing	Essay 25 minutes	35 questions 25 minutes	14 questions 10 minutes

There is also an "experimental" section, which looks like one of the other sections, but is unscored. Add it all up and you have ten sections and three and a half hours of test taking. Whew!

Here are some more useful facts:

- The essay section is always first.
- The 10-minute grammar section is always last.
- All the other sections can vary in order, so you can't predict the precise order of sections in advance.

Scoring

Each section of the SAT is scored on a scale of 200–800, so a perfect score is 2400.

Content

In Parts II–IV, we'll thoroughly review the content and strategies you need for each of the three main sections. Here is a brief overview of each section.

Math

The Math section features 54 questions. Most are multiple choice, but the 18-question section contains ten "grid in" questions for which you bubble in a numerical answer. Each section has an order of difficulty, as follows.

- In the 20-question section, the first 6–7 questions are easy, the next 6–7 are medium, and the rest are difficult.
- In the 18-question section, questions 1–8 are multiple choice, so questions 1–3 are easy, 4–6 are medium, and 7–8 are difficult. Questions 9–18 are grid ins, so 9–11 are easy, 12–15 are medium, and 16–18 are difficult.
- In the 16-question section, the first 5–6 are easy, the next 5-6 are medium, and the rest are difficult.

Content on the Math section is drawn from arithmetic, pre-algebra, elementary algebra, intermediate algebra, plane geometry, and coordinate geometry. No trigonometry, calculus, or other advanced topics are tested.

Reading

The Reading section contains 67 questions. Each Reading section begins with sentence completions, which are always presented in order of difficulty. The 25-minute sections will always have four questions on short reading (usually a paragraph or two), followed by longer passages with more questions. Passage-based questions are *never* presented in order of difficulty; the order of questions is chronological.

Writing

The Writing section consists of a 25-minute essay and 49 multiple-choice questions. The essay is graded on a scale of 1–6 by two different graders for a total score of 2–12. This score is worth about 30% of your total Writing (200–800) score.

The 25-minute Writing section has 35 questions, broken into three parts: Improving Sentences, Error ID, and Improving Paragraphs. Each of the first two parts has order of difficulty, just like the Math sections. The Improving Paragraphs is similar to a reading passage, so the order of questions is chronological, not according to difficulty.

THE SAT SCHEDULE

In the United States, the SAT is offered seven times a year: October, November, December, January, March, May, and June. The March test is not offered in international locations.

Take the SAT when your schedule best allows. Many high scorers take their first SAT in the fall of their junior year. If you have more commitments in the fall from sports, plays, or clubs, then plan to take your first SAT in the winter or spring.

Many high school counselors advise waiting to take the SAT until spring because students may be unfamiliar with some of the more difficult material before then. Students in an honors track, however, will have covered all of the content by the end of sophomore year at the latest. Even if you aren't in an honors track, there are relatively few concepts that will be unfamiliar to you. We recommend taking your first SAT as early as your schedule allows.

Changes To The SAT
The College Board recently announced that the SAT will be undergoing some changes. The Redesigned SAT is expected to debut in March of 2016. For updates, visit PrincetonReview.com/SATchanges.

REGISTERING FOR THE SAT

Go to collegeboard.com and create a student account. At collegeboard.com, you can view test dates, fees, and registration deadlines. You can research the requirements and processes to apply for extended time or other accommodations, register for the test, view your scores, and order score reports.

You can contact College Board customer service by phone at 866-756-7346 (or 609-882-4118 for international callers), but you cannot sign up for the test by phone if you are taking it for the first time.

Test Security
As part of the registration process, you have to upload or mail a photograph that will be printed on your admissions ticket. On test day, you have to take the ticket and acceptable photo identification with you.

Registration Tips

You have options for SAT score reports, copies of your test, and cancellation. We have recommendations on each.

Score Reports

When you register, supply the codes for any schools on your application list. If you want to add more schools to your list later, you certainly can. Since colleges are interested only in your highest scores, there is no benefit to withholding any scores from prospective colleges.

Test Information Release

If you take the SAT in October, January, or May, we recommend you sign up for the Question and Answer Service when you register. Six to eight weeks after the test, you'll receive a copy of the test and your answers. This service costs an additional fee and is available only for the dates above. You can order the Question and Answer Service up to five months after the test date, but it's easier to order at the time you register. It's a great tool to help you prepare for your next SAT.

How Many Times Should You Take the SAT?

We will be thrilled if you review the content in this book, take the SAT for the first time, and earn the score you seek. If you don't hit your target score the first time, take it again. In fact, we recommend that you enter the process planning to take the SAT two or three times. Nerves and anxiety can be unpredictable catalysts, and for many students, the first experience can seem harder than what you've seen in practice. Perception is reality, so we won't waste your time explaining that it only *seems* harder and different. That's why we recommend taking your first SAT as soon as your schedule allows. Get that first experience with a real test over with as soon as possible, and leave yourself enough time to take the test again. Subsequent administrations won't seem nearly as hard and daunting as the first.

While no one wants to take the SAT more than three times, it's not out of the question if you haven't reached the score you need. Just make sure you consider what you will do differently before taking the test again. Dedicate yourself to trying new strategies that you first thought you didn't need.

Score Cancellation

You have the option to cancel your scores, either immediately (at the testing center) or soon after the exam. Usually, you should use this option only under extreme circumstances—you were violently ill, there was a punk band rehearsing in the next classroom, or something equally dramatic. Don't cancel your scores just because you feel like you had a bad day; you can always take the test again, and it's good to have a starting point to compare subsequent tests to. If you *really* feel you must cancel your scores, you have until 11:59 P.M. (EST) on the Wednesday after the exam. See the College Board website for more information.

HOW TO PREPARE FOR THE SAT

The following lessons cover the content and strategies for the Math, Reading, and Writing sections. Review all lessons, even in the subjects that you think you already have targeted as your strengths. We want to make sure you're thoroughly prepared, and we'll risk boring you a tad to cover content you may know. But we won't waste your time. All of the content and strategies we cover are necessary.

As we noted above, the easiest path to your best score is to maximize your strengths. Find every point that you can from your strengths even as you acquire new skills and strategies to improve your weaknesses.

Practice, Practice, Practice

To achieve a great SAT score, you have to practice a lot! We recommend that you practice with both real SAT tests and Princeton Review practice tests.

The College Board publishes *The Official SAT Study Guide, 2nd Edition*. We think this book is well worth the price for the three real tests it contains (and seven additional tests that are very close to the real thing). A free, previously administered real practice test is also available on the College Board website.

For more practice materials, The Princeton Review publishes *11 Practice Tests for the SAT and PSAT*. We also publish additional practice material in *Cracking the SAT, Math Workout for the SAT,* and *Reading and Writing Workout for the SAT*. In addition, we recommend contacting your local Princeton Review office to investigate free practice test dates and follow up sessions. Visit princetonreview.com for more information.

TEST TAKER, KNOW THYSELF

To earn a perfect or near-perfect score on the SAT, it's not enough to know everything about the test. You also need to know yourself. Identify your own strengths and weaknesses. Don't try to make yourself something you're not. You do not need to be a master of every subject to earn a top score on the SAT. You do need to be a master test taker. Stop the part of your brain that wants to do the question the *right* way. All that matters is that you get it right. *How* you get the question right doesn't matter. So don't waste time trying to make yourself into the math or reading genius you thought you needed to be.

Read more in the next chapter about the overall strategies, and read through all the lessons in individual subjects that follow. Be willing to tweak what you already do well, and be willing to try entirely new approaches for what you don't do well.

Summary

o Knowing the structure of the SAT is the first step to mastering the test.

o Take your first SAT as soon as your schedule allows.

o Order the Question and Answer Service if it's available for your test date.

o Plan to take the SAT 2–3 times.

o Take the SAT again if you do not achieve the best score you've hit in practice.

o Know your options about score reporting and cancellation.

o Practice on real SATs as much as possible.

o Use Princeton Review practice materials to supplement your practice.

Chapter 2
Strategy, Pacing, and Scoring

To earn a perfect or near-perfect SAT score, you need strategies specific to the SAT. In this chapter, we'll provide an overview of the universal strategies. Each section of the SAT demands a specific approach, and even the most universal strategies vary in their applications. In Parts II–IV, we'll discuss these strategies in greater detail customized to the Math, Reading, and Writing sections.

THE BASIC APPROACH

The SAT is different from the tests you take in school, and, therefore, you need to approach the SAT differently. The Princeton Review's strategies are not arbitrary. To be effective, strategies have to be based on the SAT and not just any old test.

Enemy #1: Time

Consider the structure of one of the 25-minute Reading sections. You have 25 minutes to answer 24 questions. That's just about one minute per question, plus you have to read the passages as well. Time is your enemy on the SAT, and you have to use it wisely and be aware of how that time pressure can bring out your worst instincts as a test taker.

Enemy #2: Yourself

There is something particularly evil about tests like the SAT. The skills you've been rewarded for throughout your academic career can easily work against you. You've been taught since you started school to follow directions, go in order, and finish everything. But treating the SAT the same way you would a school test won't necessarily earn you a perfect or near-perfect score.

On the other hand, treating the SAT as a scary, alien beast can leave our brains blank and useless and can lead to irrational, self-defeating behavior. When you pick up a #2 pencil, you tend to leave your common sense at the door. Test nerves and anxieties can make you misread a question, commit a careless error, see something that isn't there, blind you to what is there, talk you into a bad answer, and worst of all, convince you to spend good time after bad.

Work Smarter, Not Harder

When you're already answering most questions correctly, it can be difficult to change your approach. But to answer nearly *every* question correctly, you have to do something different. You can't just work harder. Instead, you have to work smarter. Know what isn't working. Be open-minded about changing your approach. Know what to tweak and what to replace wholesale. Know when to abandon one approach and try another.

The following is an introduction to the general strategies to use on the SAT. In Parts II–IV we'll discuss how these strategies are customized for each section on the SAT.

SAT STRATEGIES

Pacing

The biggest mistake many high scorers make is to spend too *little* time on the easy and medium questions, and too *much* time on the hard ones. That might seem backward—the hard questions are hard (duh), so you need to spend as much time as possible on them, right?

The problem with this approach is that if you rush through the easy and medium questions, you are almost certain to make a few careless mistakes, which will have a devastating impact on your score. If you want to score in the high 700s on a section, you can't afford *any* careless mistakes. So here's the first step toward improving your score: *slow down* and spend enough time (but not a minute more) on the easy and medium questions to get *every* one of them right. With practice, you should have enough time for the hard questions as well, but you've got to get the easy and medium questions right first.

Personal Order of Difficulty (POOD)

Most of the questions on the SAT are presented in order of difficulty, but there are exceptions (reading passages and improving paragraphs). And even when there is a clear order of difficulty, you may find some medium questions to be difficult, and you might sail through some of the hard questions. So, don't be a slave to the order of the test. Create your own Personal Order of Difficulty (POOD). If you're stumped by a question, circle it and come back later. Do all the questions that are easy and medium *for you*, and save the hardest ones for last.

Process of Elimination (POE)

Multiple-choice questions offer one great advantage: They provide the correct answer right there on the page. Of course, they hide the correct answer amidst four incorrect answers. However, it's often easier to spot the wrong answers than it is to identify the right ones, particularly when you apply a smart Process of Elimination (POE).

> ### The Best Way to Bubble In
> Work a page at a time, circling your answers right in the booklet. Transfer a page worth of answers to the bubble sheet at one time. It's better to stay focused on working questions than to disrupt your concentration to find where you left off on the scantron. If you do this, you'll become more accurate at both tasks.

POE is a powerful strategy on the SAT. For some question types, you'll always use POE rather than wasting time trying to figure out the answer on your own. For other questions, you'll use POE when you're stuck. The SAT hides the correct answer behind wrong ones, but when you cross off just one or two wrong answers, the correct answer can become more obvious, sometimes jumping right off the page.

POOD, Pacing, and POE all work together to help you get right as many questions as possible.

Use Your Pencil

You own the test booklet, and you should write where and when it helps you. Use your pencil to literally cross off wrong answers on the page.

Scoring

There are two types of scores on the SAT: raw and scaled. Your raw score on the SAT is the number of questions you got right, minus a fraction of the number that you got wrong (except on the grid-ins, which have no guessing penalty). Every time you answer an SAT question correctly, you get 1 raw point. Every time you leave an SAT question blank, you get 0 raw points. Every time you answer an SAT question incorrectly, ETS subtracts 1/4 of a raw point if the question is multiple choice, or nothing if it is grid-in.

Yes, for grid-in questions, nothing is deducted for an incorrect answer. That means that an incorrect answer is no worse for your score than a question left blank. And, by the same token, a blank is just as costly as an error. Therefor, you should be very aggressive in answering grid-in questions. Don't leave a grid-in question blank just because you're worried that the answer you've found may not be correct. ETS's scoring computers treat incorrect answers and blanks exactly the same for grid-ins. If you have arrived at an answer, you have a shot at earning points, and if you have a shot at earning points, you should take it.

To get an idea of how your raw score is converted into a scaled score, take a look at the table below, based on a recent SAT (the conversion grid varies slightly with each test, but this one is pretty typical).

Critical Reading			
Raw Score	Scaled Score	Raw Score	Scaled Score
67	800	31	500
66	800	30	490
65	800	29	490
64	780	28	480
63	760	27	470
62	750	26	470
61	730	25	460
60	720	24	460
59	710	23	450
58	700	22	440
57	690	21	440
56	680	20	430
55	670	19	420
54	660	18	420
53	650	17	410
52	640	16	400
51	630	15	400
50	630	14	390
49	620	13	380
48	610	12	380
47	600	11	370
46	600	10	360
45	590	9	350
44	580	8	340
43	580	7	330
42	570	6	320
41	560	5	310
40	560	4	300
39	550	3	280
38	540	2	270
37	540	1	250
36	530	0	230
35	520	−1	210
34	520	−2	200
33	510	−3	200
32	510	& below	

Math			
Raw Score	Scaled Score	Raw Score	Scaled Score
54	800	25	490
53	790	24	490
52	760	23	480
51	740	22	470
50	720	21	470
49	710	20	460
48	700	19	450
47	690	18	440
46	680	17	430
45	670	16	430
44	660	15	420
43	650	14	410
42	640	13	400
41	630	12	390
40	620	11	390
39	610	10	380
38	600	9	370
37	590	8	360
36	580	7	350
35	570	6	340
34	570	5	330
33	560	4	310
32	550	3	300
31	540	2	290
30	530	1	270
29	520	0	250
28	520	−1	230
27	510	−2	210
26	500	−3	200
		& below	

Writing Multiple Choice			
Raw Score	Scaled Score	Raw Score	Scaled Score
49	80	22	47
48	80	21	46
47	77	20	45
46	75	19	44
45	73	18	43
44	71	17	42
43	69	16	42
42	68	15	41
41	66	14	40
40	65	13	39
39	63	12	38
38	62	11	37
37	61	10	36
36	60	9	35
35	59	8	34
34	58	7	33
33	57	6	32
32	56	5	31
31	55	4	30
30	54	3	28
29	53	2	27
28	52	1	25
27	51	0	23
26	50	−1	21
25	49	−2	20
24	49	−3	20
23	48	& below	

You should use the scoring table above to set goals for yourself. For example, if your goal for your next practice test is 780 on the Reading section, you can skip 3 questions, or you can answer all the questions and get at most two wrong. If that's a lot better than you've done on previous tests, then it's probably not a realistic goal at this point. Make sure you set a goal that you can actually achieve, and don't set a higher goal until you've achieved the first one.

Should You Guess?

Consider what happens if you guess on five questions. There are five answer choices, so the laws of probability suggest that on average you will get one question right, which will give you one point. You will lose a quarter point for each wrong answer, so your raw score will be…zero! That's the purpose of the guessing penalty—to neutralize the effect of guessing.

However, what if you could eliminate at least one answer choice on every question? Then, the laws of probability suggest that you would benefit by guessing. Therefore, you should *never* guess unless you can eliminate at least one answer choice.

Before guessing, always ask yourself two questions:

- Do I need to answer this question to hit my goal score?
- Can I eliminate at least one answer?

If the answer to both of these questions is yes, then go ahead and guess. Otherwise, leave the question blank.

BE RUTHLESS

The worst mistake a test taker can make is to throw good time after bad. You read a question, don't understand it, so you read it again. And again. If you stare at it really hard, you know you're going to just *see* it. And you can't move on, because really, after spending all that time it would be a waste not to keep at it, right?

Wrong. You can't let one tough question drag you down, and you can't let your worst instincts tempt you into self-defeating behavior. Instead, the surest way to earn a great SAT score is to follow our advice.

- Use the techniques and strategies in the lessons to work efficiently and *accurately* through the questions. Set a goal right now of zero careless mistakes.
- Know when to move on. If you're stuck, come back later.
- Guess *only* if you need the question to achieve your goal score, *and* you can eliminate at least one answer.

In Parts II-IV, you'll learn how POOD, Pacing, and POE work in each section.

Summary

○   Don't let your own worst instincts work against you on the SAT. Work Smarter, Not Harder.

○   Identify your own Personal Order of Difficulty (POOD). Don't be a slave to the order of the test.

○   Pace yourself. Don't rush through easy and medium questions only to make careless errors.

○   Use Process of Elimination (POE) to save time, when you're stuck, or when you're out of time.

○   If time does run out, consider guessing, if you need the question *and* you can eliminate at least one answer choice.

○   Be Ruthless. If one strategy isn't working, switch immediately to another.

126

Part II
Math

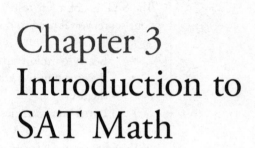

Chapter 3
Introduction to
SAT Math

If you're aiming for the highest score on the SAT, you probably already have a broad range of math skills. In fact, you probably already know the math required to answer almost every question on the typical SAT Math section. So why aren't you already scoring an 800?

You may be surprised to learn that what's holding you back is *not* content knowledge. Students who score in the high 600s have roughly the same amount of mathematical knowledge as those who score an 800. Knowing more math is not the key—you've likely already learned every concept that's on the Math test.

The problem is that on the SAT, the questions are not so much difficult as tricky. The SAT is not a fair test; in fact, the test writers are out to get you! To improve your score, you'll need to do three things:

- Learn to avoid traps and eliminate careless errors.
- Become familiar with the types of questions that always appear on the SAT.
- Learn our strategies for recognizing and defeating these questions.

In this chapter, we'll focus on the first of these points; in later chapters, we'll cover the other two.

Avoiding Traps and Careless Errors

If you want to score a 750 or higher on the math section, you can't afford to make *any* careless errors. The first thing to do is to slow down! This might seem counterintuitive. In order to score an 800 you must answer every single math question correctly. But it doesn't matter if you get all the hardest questions right, if you throw it all away on a few silly mistakes on easier questions. Set a goal *right now* that you will have zero careless mistakes from now on.

To avoid careless mistakes, burn this acronym into your brain: RTFQ. This stands for Read The Full Question. Consider the following question:

Example 1:

At which coordinates does the graph of $2y - x = 6$ intersect the x-axis?

(A) (0,3)

(B) (0,6)

(C) (−6,0)

(D) $\left(\frac{1}{2}, 0\right)$

(E) (6,0)

$$2(0) - x = 6$$
$$-x = 6$$
$$x = -6$$

This problem is a fairly typical medium math question. The majority of high scorers will expect to get it right. However, did you catch the trap? Read the full question one more time. Which intercept are you looking for? Your math classes in high school have likely conditioned you to put this equation into the format $y = mx + b$, where b represents the y-intercept. If you did not read the question carefully and simply converted the equation to this format, you could easily fall for answer choice (A). However, the question is asking for the coordinates when $y = 0$. RTFQ! Slow down. Take a few extra seconds between reading the question and starting to solve it. Make sure you know exactly what you are looking for.

A closely related skill is Process of Elimination (POE). Focus on the word "process." This implies an action on your part. POE is not something that occurs in your head. You have a pencil; make sure that you use it to cross off wrong answers. Let's consider the above problem one more time. Assume that you read the question carefully and you caught that the question was about the x-intercept. Use POE to cross off any answer choices that represent y-intercepts:

Example 2:

At what coordinates does the graph of $2y - x = 6$ intersect the x-axis?

(A) ~~(0,3)~~

(B) ~~(0,6)~~

(C) (−6,0)

(D) $\left(\dfrac{1}{2}, 0\right)$

(E) (6,0)

Notice how this simple technique allows you to avoid falling for the obvious traps. However, there are some less obvious traps as well. Answer choice (D) has the right y-coordinate, but the x-coordinate is actually the slope. Answer choice (E) has the correct number, but the wrong sign. Get rid of all the traps, and you're left with only one answer:

Example 3:

At what coordinates does the graph of $2y - x = 6$ intersect the x-axis?

(A) ~~(0,3)~~

(B) ~~(0,6)~~

(C) (−6,0)

(D) ~~$\left(\dfrac{1}{2}, 0\right)$~~

(E) ~~(6,0)~~

The moral of the story is that the SAT is full of traps. Making sure to RTFQ and using your pencil to cross off bad answer choices can improve your score right now, just by helping you avoid careless mistakes.

Try the following questions, chock-full of typical, nasty SAT traps. To get the most out of the drill, don't just do the questions; instead, see if you can spot the traps in the questions and answers. When you're done, check out each explanation of how to crack it. Let's dive in.

——————○——————

1. The population of a certain town increased by 20% in one year. The following year, the town's population decreased by 20%. What was the net effect on the town's population over two years?

   (A) It increased by 44%.
   (B) It increased by 40%.
   (C) It was unchanged.
   (D) It decreased by 4%.
   (E) It decreased by 10%.

Here's How to Crack It

The main trap answer in this question is (C). Many students will be tempted to think that the 20% increase is cancelled out by the 20% decrease. This just goes to show that on the SAT, if you arrive at an answer by simply thinking for a few seconds, that answer is probably wrong. To see why, use some real numbers. Let's say the population was originally 100. A year later, it will be 20% higher, or 120. The population then decreases by 20%, so take 20% of 120 and subtract from the total: $120 - (0.20)(120) = 96$. The population has decreased by 4%, so the correct answer is (D).

——————○——————

——————○——————

2. The least possible sum of three positive odd integers is s. What is the least possible sum of three positive integers that are each greater than s ?

   (A) 15
   (B) 24
   (C) 33
   (D) 36
   (E) 39

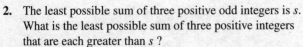

Here's How to Crack It

This question is about reading carefully. On the SAT, you must not only read every word in the question, you must also avoid adding words that aren't there! To find s, we need to add up the three smallest positive odd integers, so $1 + 3 + 5 = 9$. Then, we need to add up the next three integers that are greater than 9, so $10 + 11 + 12 = 33$, and the correct answer is (C). If you imagined that the question was asking for *odd* integers greater than s, you probably chose (E). If you ignored the word *odd* at the beginning, you may have chosen (B). For every reading mistake you are likely to make, the SAT has a trap answer waiting, so read carefully.

Don's travel expenses

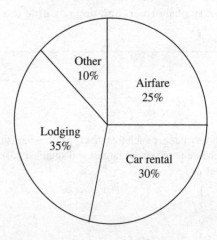

3. The pie chart above shows how Don spent $360 on a recent business trip. The amount Don spent on car rental was only a portion of the total cost of the car rental, because he shared the cost of the car equally with three other people. What was the total cost of the car rental?

   (A) $108
   (B) $270
   (C) $324
   (D) $360
   (E) $432

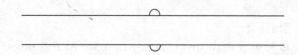

Here's How to Crack It

To find what Don spent on car rental, take 30% of $360: $(0.30)(\$360) = \$108$. Notice that this number is answer choice (A). Partial answers often appear on the SAT. To find the correct answer, we need to multiply by four, because Don shared with three other people, so $(4)(\$108) = \$432$, and the correct answer is (E). The most common mistake on this question is to multiply by three, which would lead you to pick (C). Watch out for traps; they're everywhere!

---

4. When 39 is divided by positive integer n, the remainder is 3. How many possible values are there for n?

(A) 5
(B) 6
(C) 7
(D) 8
(E) 9

$$\begin{array}{r} 39 \\ - 3 \\ \hline 36 \end{array}$$

$1, 2, 3, 4, 6, 9, 12, 18, 36$

Here's How to Crack It

The remainder is 3, so n must divide evenly into 36. At this point, you might be tempted to add up the factors of 36 (1, 2, 3, 4, 6, 9, 12, 18, 36) and pick (E). If you omitted 1, 36, or both, you might have picked (C) or (D). However, the three smallest factors (1, 2, 3) will not result in a remainder of 3, so the correct answer is (B). On the SAT, be wary of shortcuts and don't assume too much.

5. If j is any integer such that $4 < \sqrt{j} < 9$, what is the difference between the largest and smallest possible values of j?

(A) 1
(B) 3
(C) 39
(D) 63
(E) 65

$16 < j < 81$

$17 \leq j \leq 80$

$80 - 17 = 63$

Here's How to Crack It

First, square each element of the inequality to get $16 < j < 81$. You may be tempted to simply subtract here: $81 - 16 = 65$. But j is an integer that is *between* these values, so the largest and smallest values for j are 80 and 17, respectively. Therefore, $80 - 17 = 63$, and the correct answer is (D). If you didn't square the inequality, you may have picked (B). If you took the positive square root of the inequality, you may have chosen (A).

TIME MANAGEMENT

You might be wondering at this point how you are supposed to incorporate this advice. Slow down! Use your pencil more! You may think that these techniques will leave you with less precious time for those tricky math questions. However, consider how little time it will actually take to cross off incorrect answer choices with your pencil. If you eliminate incorrect answer choices immediately as they are identified, the time spent is negligible. Reading the Full Question can also seem more time consuming than skimming the question quickly and beginning work as soon as possible, but, in reality, reading each question carefully and looking for traps often saves time. Students who do this work each problem more efficiently: They understand the question more quickly and are able to apply smart strategies without losing precious seconds rereading each problem. Time management is certainly important. Following are a few techniques you can use to maximize your time.

Order of Difficulty: Still Personal, Even For High Scorers

Why should a high-scoring student care about the order of difficulty on the SAT Math section? If you've got the math skills to do all—or at least, almost all—of the questions on the SAT Math section, you may think the best approach for you is to dive straight in and do the questions in order. That's not necessarily the best approach, though.

The questions on the Math section are presented in Order of Difficulty (OOD), so the easier questions tend to be earlier in a section, and the harder questions tend to be later. The Math OOD is helpful for planning how you will attack each section. However, just because the test writers think a question is easy (or hard) doesn't mean it's easy (or hard) *for you*. It's possible you will find the last question on a section to be surprisingly easy; conversely, you may find one in the middle to be excruciatingly difficult.

So, remember to use Personal Order of Difficulty (POOD). To maximize your efficiency, don't linger too long on any one question. Do every question that you understand immediately. If you're not sure how to work a question, or if it just seems like it will be too time consuming, skip it for now.

Once you have reached the end of the section, go back to the ones you skipped. You will now have more time to decipher their meaning and work through to the answer without worrying about other questions that you haven't gotten to yet. Consider the following scenarios for solving for *x*.

Example 4:

(1) $x + 4 > 7$

(2) $2x = 8$

(3) $x^3 + 3x^2 + 3x + 1$

(4) $\dfrac{x}{4} = 3$

Assume that you have poorly managed your time and you only have two minutes to work these four questions. What would be the advantage of passing over question (3)? Perhaps you could solve it if you had enough time. However, compared to the other three questions, it is much more challenging and time consuming. If you worked questions (1), (2), and (4), you could then use all of the remaining time you had to puzzle out question (3). If you allowed yourself to get bogged down in solving question (3), you might not have any time left to answer question (4).

Using POOD has two major advantages. First, you will be less likely to either skip or have to rush through easier questions because you wasted too much time on hard ones. Second, since this is a timed test, longer or harder problems can cause your anxiety to build, which might affect your performance on other questions. Saving those tough questions for last will allow you to work more smoothly, efficiently, and confidently through the section.

Smart Bubbling Saves Time

As previously mentioned, you should bubble by page. The least efficient way to bubble is question by question. Consider how many precious seconds are ticking away as you constantly jump back and forth between the test book and your answer sheet. The most efficient strategy is to work every single problem on one page. Circle the answers in your test book and cross off all of the other ones. Then, before you turn the page, bubble in those answers. The only exception to this technique is at the very end of a section: If time is running low, and you're down to the last two or three questions, you should bubble one question at a time, so you don't get stuck when time is called.

A Note on Calculators

Most common calculators are allowed on the SAT. Some exceptions include:

• Laptops
• Calculators with a QWERTY keyboard
• Cell-phone calculators

If you aren't sure whether your calculator is allowed, check the College Board website (www.sat.collegeboard.org/register/calculator-policy).

Your calculator can definitely come in handy for complicated calculations; to be efficient on the test, you'll want to make the best use of it. But be careful! Some questions are designed with "calculator traps" in mind—careless errors the test writers know you might make when you just dive into a problem with your calculator.

Example 5:

Given the function $f(x) = 5x^2 - x - 7$, what is $f(-4)$?

(A) −91
(B) −83
(C) 69
(D) 77
(E) 397

[handwritten:]
$5(-4)^2 - (-4) - 7$
$5(16) + 4 - 7$
$80 + 4 - 7$
$84 - 7 = 77$

This problem can be solved manually or with the calculator—whichever you prefer! But if you use a calculator, be careful with that (−4). What you punch into your calculator should look something like this:

$$5(-4)^2 - (-4) - 7$$

When working with negative numbers or fractions, make doubly sure that you use parentheses. If you don't, a lot of weird stuff can happen, and unfortunately all of the weird, wrong stuff that can happen is reflected in the wrong answer choices. If you ran this equation and found 77, choice (D), you got the right answer. If not, go back and figure out where you made your calculator mistake.

Types of Calculators

Throughout the rest of the Math chapters, we occasionally discuss ways to solve calculator-friendly questions in an accurate and manageable way. We'll show how to solve the problem on a TI-83, because that is the most commonly used calculator in U.S. high schools. If you don't plan to use a TI-83 on the test, we recommend you make sure your calculator is acceptable for use on the test and that it can do the following:

- handle positive, negative, and fractional exponents
- use parentheses
- graph simple functions
- convert fractions to decimals and vice versa
- change a linear equation into $y = mx + b$ format

> Use your calculator, but use it wisely. Be careful with negative numbers and fractions and parentheses.

Working Smarter

The techniques and strategies in this book are not that hard to learn, but they will not be second nature to you. Make sure that you focus on putting them into practice. Your goal is to internalize every strategy in this book. When you have internalized a concept, you no longer consciously think about what to do. You simply do it. Think about some of the example equations above. Were you able to look at some of them and immediately know what the answer was without consciously thinking about the math? If so, then you have successfully internalized the concepts necessary to manipulate basic equations when solving for x. Test prep is no different!

Successfully incorporating these techniques requires two things: practice and review. Many of the techniques you will learn from these pages may initially seem awkward. You may even ask yourself why you should try something new if you can already solve the problem another way. This is a valid question; however, at its core it reveals the distinction between a technique and content knowledge. A technique is a transferable skill that you can use on a variety of questions. Content knowledge, while certainly useful, is not necessarily equally applicable to all test questions. Techniques are.

Mastering new skills requires practice. Think about learning a new sport. Your coach explains how to perform an action, such as spiking a volleyball or making a lay-up. You easily comprehend what is being said. "No problem," you think. However, there is a big difference between understanding a concept and having the necessary coordination to complete it. This analogy is comparable to testing techniques. Much of what you read in this manual will seem easy, such as using POE as described above. Only practice, however, will make crossing off wrong answers *every time* second nature to you.

The second reason you should try something different is more pragmatic: if you could hit your goal score already, you wouldn't be reading this book! Do not merely skip to the practice questions and try to work them the old way. Even if you think your way is easier, practice the techniques. Remember that working many practice problems will reinforce all the techniques you currently use. This includes bad habits. Practicing math problems without attempting anything new will never improve your score. It is often said that insanity is doing the same thing over and over again but expecting different results. Do not drive yourself crazy with meaningless practice. Apply what you learn in these pages to every single question you work. You will be pleased with the results.

Finally, review your work. Do not simply tally up your points and pat yourself on the back. Every question missed is a learning opportunity. On every question you miss, you should ask what happened. Did you have the necessary content knowledge? Did you miss an opportunity to use a new technique? Did you rush and miss a keyword? Did you not correctly apply process of elimination? For every problem, you can identify a reason that you missed it. Over time, you will begin to see patterns emerging. For example, you might notice that you tend to rush through all algebra problems and therefore have more careless errors. The beauty of test prep is once you know what you are doing wrong, that problem will vanish. You will be on guard against making the same mistakes in the future.

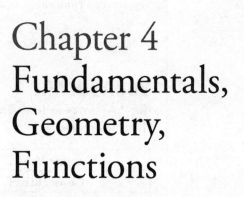

Chapter 4
Fundamentals,
Geometry,
Functions

INTRODUCTION

This chapter will focus on the fundamental question types of the SAT Math section. While there are many legitimate shortcuts that can be made and will be discussed below, ultimately you will simply need to solve many of the questions on the SAT. This chapter will begin with a discussion of math vocabulary words and concepts that appear throughout the SAT. Then we will show you how the SAT uses those vocabulary words to lead students astray. Next, we will discuss geometry and functions and the many ways that they can be presented on the SAT. Finally, the chapter will conclude with several drills where you can hone the skills you learned from this chapter.

VOCABULARY

The SAT loves to test vocabulary words. Make sure you're familiar with all of these definitions:

Absolute Value:	The distance from zero on the number line
Consecutive:	In increasing order
Difference:	The result of subtraction
Digits:	The integers 0 through 9
Distinct:	Different
Divisible:	An integer can be divided by another integer evenly, with no fraction or decimal left over
Even:	Divisible by 2
Exponent/Power:	A number that indicates how many times to multiply a base by itself
Factors:	Integers that multiply together to make a given product
Integers:	All real numbers other than decimals or fractions
Irrational:	A number that can be expressed as a decimal but not a fraction
Multiple:	The product of an integer and another integer
Negative:	Less than 0
Non-negative:	Zero or positive
Non-positive:	Zero or negative
Odd:	NOT divisible by 2
Positive:	Greater than 0
Prime:	A number that has exactly two distinct factors: 1 and itself (1 is not prime)
Product:	The result of multiplication
Quotient:	The result of division

Real:	Any non-imaginary number (including zero, all positive and negative integers, fractions, decimals, roots, and irrational numbers)
Rational:	A number that can be expressed as the ratio of two other numbers (a fraction)
Reciprocal:	The inverse of a number—flip the numerator and the denominator.
Remainder:	The number left over in long division when a number is not evenly divisible by another number
Sum:	The result of addition

MATH FUNDAMENTALS

As we discussed in the introduction, it's very important to Read the Full Question (RTFQ)! Many common errors occur because students miss a key word, rather than not knowing how to work a problem. Consider the following question.

1. If x, y, and z are distinct positive integers and sum to 66, which of the following could be the greatest possible value for x ?

(A) 21
(B) 22
(C) 23
(D) 63
(E) 64

Here's How to Crack It

First, underline the key vocabulary words in this problem: ***distinct***, ***positive***, and ***integer***. The problem says that they ***sum*** to 66. Finally, RTFQ! Notice that you are looking for the "greatest possible value for x." Now, use Process of Elimination (POE). In (A). If x is 21, then $y + z$ must sum to 45. Therefore, y could be 22, and z could be 23. Eliminate (A). Answer choice (B) is a trap for the student who simply divides 66 by 3 to get an average value of 22. Eliminate (B). Now, consider (C). Be very careful here! If x is 23, then $y + z = 43$, so y could be 21 and z could be 22. However, there is nothing in the problem that says the numbers have to be *consecutive*, so eliminate (C) and try (D). If x is 63, then $y + z = 3$. These have to be distinct, positive integers, but that is OK since one of the variables could be 2 and the other could be 1. Now consider choice (E). If x were 64, then $y + z = 2$, so y and z would each be 1. Since the variables must be *distinct* integers, you must eliminate (E). Therefore, the credited response is (D).

Odd and even numbers are also commonly tested on the SAT. There are a few basic addition and multiplication rules with odds and evens that you need to know. These relationships are summarized in the table below.

Relationship	Result
Odd ± Odd	Even
Even ± Even	Even
Odd ± Even	Odd
Odd × Odd	Odd
Odd × Even	Even
Even × Even	Even

As you can see, it is much easier to produce an even number than an odd number. As a result, the SAT will often ask how to produce an odd number. These concepts are often presented on the SAT using variables. Consider the following example.

2. If x and y are odd integers and z is an even integer, which of the following must be odd?

(A) $z(x+z) - y$
(B) $y(x+y) - z$
(C) xyz
(D) $xz-z$
(E) $yz-z$

Here's How to Crack It

Let's compare these using the table. Look at (A). The variable z is even. An even number multiplied by anything produces and even number. Since y is odd, we have even minus odd. This will always produce an odd number. Answer (A) is correct. However, let's make sure by eliminating the remaining answer choices. The variable y is odd in answer (B), but the two values in the parentheses are also both odd. According to the table, you will always arrive at an even number when you sum two odds. This makes the multiplication even. An even number minus an even number is always even. In answer (C), we have an odd times an odd times an even. This combination will always be even. Answers (D) and (E) look different, but they are testing the exact same concept. In the multiplied pair, you see an odd times an even which is even. Even minus even will always be even.

If you find it hard to remember all of these rules, there's a simpler way to tackle the problem: substitute numbers for the variables. This is called Plugging In, and we'll discuss it more thoroughly in the next chapter. The technique is straightforward and intuitive. Since x and y are odd, let's say $x = 3$, $y = 5$. Since z is even, we'll say $z = 2$. Now plug these values into the answers, like this:

(A) $2(3 + 2) - 5 = 5$
(B) $5(3 + 5) - 2 = 38$
(C) $(3)(5)(2) = 30$
(D) $(3)(2) - 2 = 4$
(E) $(5)(2) - 2 = 8$

Since only (A) is odd, that's our answer.

Plugging In is an extremely useful technique. Use it any time you forget the rules, are unsure of an answer, or just find it easier to do so.

Like evens and odds, negative and positive numbers are associated with special rules. A *positive* number is any number greater than zero, while a *negative* number is less than zero. The most common rule that the SAT tests is that a negative times a negative is positive, but a positive times a negative (in any order) will be negative. This concept is often combined with exponent rules. For example, $(-1)^2 = 1$ because $-1 \times -1 = 1$. However, $(-1)^3 = -1$ since $-1 \times -1 \times -1 = -1$. Remember that a negative number raised to an odd power will always be negative.

Let's consider a similar question to the one above. Some other important concepts have to do with adding and subtracting negative and positive numbers. A negative number added to a positive number will result in a smaller sum than the original positive number. A negative number subtracted from a positive number will result in a greater number than the original positive number. A negative number added to another negative number will result in a smaller (more negative) value. A negative number subtracted from another negative number will result in a number greater than the first negative number. This information is summarized below.

Operation	Result
Positive + Negative	< Positive
Positive − Negative	> Positive
Negative + Negative	Smaller Negative
Negative − Negative	Greater Than Original
Negative × Negative	Positive
Negative × Positive	Negative
(Negative)$^{\text{Even Exponent}}$	Positive
(Negative)$^{\text{Odd Exponent}}$	Negative

3. If x and y are negative integers and z is a positive integer, which of the following must be negative?

(A) $x(x+y) - y$
(B) $y(x+y) - x$
(C) xyz
(D) $xz+y$
(E) $yz-x$

Here's How to Crack It

This is a much trickier problem than Example 2. We cannot assume anything about the relative values of x, y, or z. However, let's apply the positive and negative rules to analyzing this problem. Begin with answer (A). The value in the parentheses must be negative. A negative times a negative will then be positive. Finally, a positive minus a negative will result in a larger positive, so eliminate (A). The same logic must be true of answer (B), so eliminate it. In (C), we have a negative times a negative times a positive. This will result in a positive number, so eliminate it. Answer (D) starts with a negative times a positive, which results in a negative number. We then add a negative to another negative, resulting in a smaller negative number. Answer (D) looks good. Answer (E) is a bit trickier. We start with a negative times a positive, resulting in a negative value. However, we then are subtracting a negative number from a negative. This will result in a value greater than the first negative value. If x is greater than yz, the result will be negative, but if x is less than yz, the result will be positive. Therefore, while (E) *could* be negative, only answer (D) *must* be negative.

You can solve this problem just as well with Plugging In, but the approach from the previous problem will have to modified slightly. Let's say $x = -2$, $y = -3$, and $z = 2$. Here's what we get:

(A) $-2(-2 +(-3)) - (-3) = 13$
(B) $-3(-2 + (-3)) - (-2) = 17$
(C) $(-2)(-3)(2) = 12$
(D) $(-2)(2) + (-3) = -7$
(E) $(-3)(2) - (-2) = -4$

Notice that we have two answers that are negative. We're looking for the one that *must* be negative, so cross off (A), (B), and (C). Now, let's change the numbers. It often pays to question your assumptions in this type of problem. For example, you may have assumed that the numbers have to be distinct, but it doesn't actually *say* this in the problem. So, we could say x and y are both -1, and $z = 1$. Now let's try the last two answers again:

(D) $(-1)(1) + (-1) = -2$
(E) $(-1)(1) - (-1) = 0$

This time, only (D) is negative, so that's the correct answer.

Tackle the Try It Drill below and apply what you have learned thus far.

TRY IT DRILL 1

See Chapter 7 for complete answers and explanations.

1. $x^2 < 4$
   $0 < y^3 < 25$

   If x and y are integers that satisfy the above inequalities, how many distinct possible values are there for $x + y$?

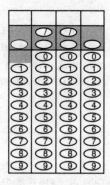

2. If a is an odd integer, how many odd integers are there between $a + 2$ and $a + 11$, inclusive?

   (A) 4
   (B) 5
   (C) 6
   (D) 7
   (E) 9

3. In the three-digit number $1K9$, K represents a digit. If $1K9$ is divisible by 7, what is the remainder when $1K5$ is divided by 7?

   (A) 1
   (B) 2
   (C) 3
   (D) 4
   (E) 5

GEOMETRY

Beating tough geometry problems is all about putting together puzzle pieces. Many students struggle with geometry because, unlike algebra, they cannot see the end result as easily. If this is you, try to think of geometry as a puzzle. First, you find the corner pieces. Next, you build the edges. Finally, you finish the interior. Geometry is the same way. There are three steps to beating any geometry problem:

- If there's no figure, draw your own.
- Write any information from the problem directly on the figure.
- Write down any formulas you need, and add in any information from the problem.
- If a figure is noted as not drawn to scale, re-draw it.

Always start by drawing the figure if one is not provided. Next, label the figure with all the information that you know. Last, always write down any formulas you need. These steps are comparable to finding the corner and edge pieces of a puzzle. Once these are in place, you will often be able to see what the next step is. Consider the following.

---

4. A square is inscribed in a circle with a circumference of 8π. What is the area of the square?

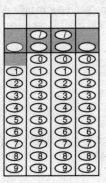

Here's How to Crack It

At first glance this may seem to be a very challenging problem. Don't panic. Instead, begin by drawing the figure:

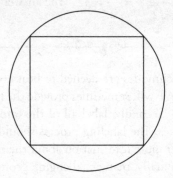

Now, label the figure. The only information that the problem provides is the circumference of the circle, which is 8π. Now, write down formulas. The problem asks for the area of the square. The formula for the area of a square is $A = s^2$, where A is the area of the square and s is the length of each side. To solve this problem, you need to somehow find the length of one of the sides of the square. Next, since the problem provided the circumference, write that down as well: $C = \pi d$ (or $C = 2\pi r$). Put the information from the problem into this equation to find that $8\pi = \pi d$, so the diameter is 8. Now, add this information to the figure. A diameter is any line segment that extends from one edge of a circle to another while passing through the center of a circle. Be sure to add the information to the figure in a way that helps with the square:

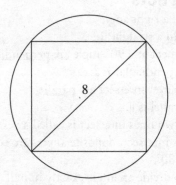

As you can see from this figure, the diameter of the circle is the same distance as the diagonal of the square. Whenever a square is bisected, two special right triangles are formed with angle measures of 45-45-90. The side lengths of this triangle are fixed as well into the following ratio: $s:s:s\sqrt{2}$, where s are the legs of the triangle and $s\sqrt{2}$ is the hypotenuse. Use this ratio to solve for s: $s\sqrt{2} = 8$ so $s = \dfrac{8}{\sqrt{2}}$.

Congratulations, you have finally found the last piece of the puzzle you needed. At the beginning of this example, you determined that in order to find the area of the square, you needed the length of the sides. Finish the problem by solving for the area of the square: $s^2 = \left(\dfrac{8}{\sqrt{2}} \right)^2 = \dfrac{64}{2} = 32$. The answer is 32.

To review, three basic techniques are needed to beat every geometry question. A figure is necessary; the SAT will sometimes provide the figure and sometimes force you to create your own. Secondly, label all of the information that the problem gives you about the figure. The labeling process should continue throughout the problem. As you discover more information about the problem, be sure to continue labeling your figure. Finally, many challenging geometry questions appear unsolvable at first glance. To avoid the panic that this feeling may cause, write down formulas for every measurement mentioned in the problem. Writing down the formulas will ensure that you do not make math errors, will give you a goal, will give you some starting math to do, and will often lead you directly to the solution.

Since formulas are so important, the following pages will list and review the different formulas that will appear on the SAT. Each section is followed by a "Try It Drill" that will challenge you to apply the basic approach to geometry while using the facts you just reviewed.

Angle and Line Facts
- There are 90° in a right angle.
- There are 180° in a straight line.
- Two lines that meet at a 90° angle are <u>perpendicular</u>.
- The sign for perpendicular is ⊥ .
- Two lines that never intersect are <u>parallel</u>.
- The sign for parallel is ‖.
- A point where two lines intersect is called a vertex (plural: vertices).
- When two lines intersect, opposite angles are equal and adjacent angles sum to 180°.
- Bisect means to divide an angle exactly in half.
- A line has no width and extends infinitely in both directions.
- On the SAT, if something looks like a straight line, it is actually straight.
- On the SAT, if a line appears to pass through a point, then it does actually pass through that point.
- A line segment is part of a line that has two endpoints.

TRY IT DRILL 2

See Chapter 7 for complete answers and explanations.

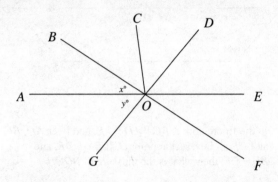

1. In the figure above, lines *AE*, *BF,* and *DG* all intersect at vertex *O*. If $x + y = 70$ and if line *CO* bisects angle *BOD*, then what is the measure of angle *BOC* ?

   (A) 20°
   (B) 40°
   (C) 60°
   (D) 55°
   (E) 75°

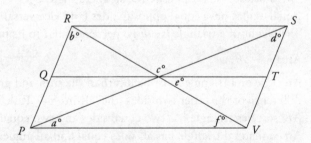

2. In the figure above, *RS* ∥ *QT* ∥ *PV*. Which of the following must equal 180° ?

   (A) $a + b + c$
   (B) $a + c + e$
   (C) $b + c + d$
   (D) $c + e + f$
   (E) $d + e + f$

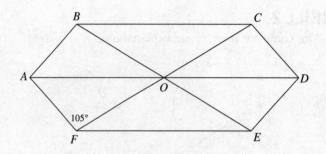

3. In the figure above, *BC* ∥ *AD* ∥ *FE*, and lines *AD, BE,* and *CF* all intersect at point *O*. If *BA* ⊥ *AF*, and *BE* = *CF*, then what is the measure of *BOC* ?

(A) 75
(B) 90
(C) 105
(D) 120
(E) 135

Triangle Facts

- There are 180 degrees in a triangle.
- The longest side is opposite the largest angle.
- The shortest side is opposite the smallest angle.
- Equal angles have equal opposite sides (and vice versa).
- The height of a triangle is *always* perpendicular to its base.
- Area = $\frac{1}{2}bh$.
- Any side of a triangle must be less than the sum and greater than the difference of the other two sides (the "Third Side Rule").
- An isosceles triangle has two equal sides and two equal angles.
- An equilateral triangle has all sides equal and all angles equal.
- If a triangle has a 90 degree angle, use the Pythagorean Theorem, or $a^2 + b^2 = c^2$, to find the length of the third side.
- Similar triangles have the same angle measurements but different side lengths.
- If two triangles are similar, then their sides have the same proportion: $\frac{A_1}{B_1} = \frac{A_2}{B_2}$ where *A* and *B* are corresponding sides.
- In a special right triangle with angles 30-60-90 degrees, the sides are in the fixed proportion of $x - x\sqrt{3} - 2x$. This special triangle is half of an equilateral triangle.
- In a right isosceles triangle, the angles measure 45-45-90 degrees and the sides are in a fixed proportion of $x\text{-}x\text{-}x\sqrt{2}$. This special right triangle is half of a square.
- On the SAT, the following special right triangles commonly appear: 3-4-5; 6-8-10; 5-12-13.

TRY IT DRILL 3

See Chapter 7 for complete answers and explanations.

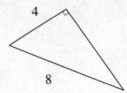

1. What is the area of the triangle above?

   (A) 8

   (B) 16

   (C) $8\sqrt{3}$

   (D) 32

   (E) $16\sqrt{3}$

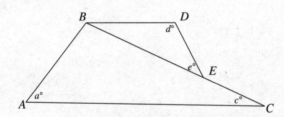

NOTE: Figure not drawn to scale.

2. In the figure above, $a = e = 50$, $c = 30$, and $d = 100$. If $BE = \dfrac{2}{3}AC$, then which of the following is equal to AB?

   (A) $\dfrac{2}{3}DE$

   (B) $\dfrac{3}{2}$

   (C) $\dfrac{3}{2}DE$

   (D) $2BD$

   (E) $2DE$

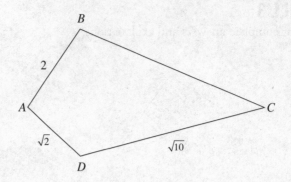

3. In the figure above, line segments AC and BD are perpendicular and intersect at point O (not shown). If $AO = DO$, then what is the ratio of the area of triangle ACD to the area of triangle ABC ?

(A) 1 to $\sqrt{3}$

(B) 1 to 2

(C) 1 to 3

(D) $\sqrt{3}$ to 1

(E) 2 to 1

Circle Facts

- There are 360 degrees in a circle.
- A radius r is the distance of *any* line that extends from the center of the circle to a point on its edge.
- All radii in a circle are equal.
- The straight line distance from one point on the circle to another, passing through the center, is the diameter (d).
- The diameter is the longest possible line in the circle.
- The diameter is twice the radius.
- A chord is any line segment from one point on the edge of a circle to another.
- The diameter is the longest possible chord.
- Circumference is the distance around the circle.
- Circumference = πd or $2\pi r$.
- An arc is any portion of the circumference.
- Arc measure is proportional to the size of its interior angle.
- The formula for the area of circle is $A = \pi r^2$.
- A sector is any portion of the area of a circle that is bounded by two radii and an arc.
- The sector area is proportional to the central angle measure.

- In order to find an arc length or a sector area, use the following formula: $\dfrac{part}{whole} = \dfrac{central\ angle}{360°} = \dfrac{sector}{\pi r^2} = \dfrac{arc}{\pi d}$.

- Any line that is tangent to a circle is perpendicular to the radius of the circle at the point where the radius and the tangent line intersect.

TRY IT DRILL 4

See Chapter 7 for complete answers and explanations.

1. A homeowner is buying a circular rug for a square room that has an area of 144 square feet. If the homeowner wants the rug to be centered in the room with 1 foot of space between the edge of the rug and any wall, which of the following is closest to the largest possible area of the circular rug, in square feet?

    (A)   40
    (B)   50
    (C)   80
    (D)   100
    (E)   160

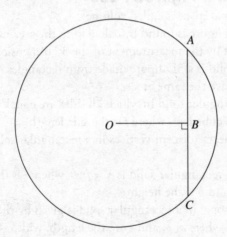

2. In the figure above, A and C are points on the circumference of circle O. If the area of the circle is 64π and the measure of minor arc AC is 4π, then what is the length of line segment BO ?

    (A) 4

    (B) $4\sqrt{2}$

    (C) 8

    (D) $8\sqrt{2}$

    (E) It cannot be determined.

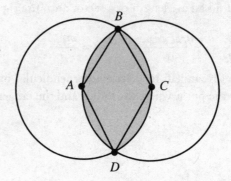

3. In the figure above, A and C are the centers of the circles and B and D are the points of intersection. If the perimeter of the shaded region is 40π, what is the perimeter of quadrilateral $ABCD$?

(A) 40
(B) 60
(C) 80
(D) 120
(E) 144

Three Dimensional Figures Facts

- Three dimensional space is called volume.
- The volume of a figure is found by calculating the area of one side and multiplying that by the measurement of the 3rd dimension.
- A rectangular solid is a 3D figure made from rectangles in which opposite faces have the same areas.
- A cube is a rectangular solid in which all sides are equal.
- The volume of a cube is s^3, where s is the side length.
- A line that connects adjacent vertices in a rectangular solid is called an "edge."
- The volume of a rectangular solid is $V = lwh$, where l is the length, w is the width, and h is the height.
- The longest diagonal in a rectangular solid is given by the formula $a^2 + b^2 + c^2 = d^2$, where a, b, and c are the length, width, and height.
- A right circular cylinder is a figure in which the base and top are circles and the sides are perpendicular to the base.
- The volume of a right circular cylinder is $V = \pi r^2 h$, where r is the radius of the circular base, and h is the height of the cylindrical side.
- Three dimensional questions on the SAT are relatively rare, but each SAT Math test typically includes at least one.
- If the test asks for a rarely seen volume measure, such as that of a cone or sphere, the test will provide the formula to you.

TRY IT DRILL 5

See Chapter 7 for complete answers and explanations.

1. The radius of right circular cylinder A is half of that of right circular cylinder B. Cylinder A has a volume of 100π cubic centimeters and a height of 4 centimeters. If the volume of cylinder B is 200π cubic centimeters, what is the height of cylinder B?

```
┌───┬───┬───┬───┐
│   │ ⊘ │ ⊘ │   │
│ ⊘ │ ⊘ │ ⊘ │ ⊘ │
│   │ ⓪ │ ⓪ │ ⓪ │
│ ① │ ① │ ① │ ① │
│ ② │ ② │ ② │ ② │
│ ③ │ ③ │ ③ │ ③ │
│ ④ │ ④ │ ④ │ ④ │
│ ⑤ │ ⑤ │ ⑤ │ ⑤ │
│ ⑥ │ ⑥ │ ⑥ │ ⑥ │
│ ⑦ │ ⑦ │ ⑦ │ ⑦ │
│ ⑧ │ ⑧ │ ⑧ │ ⑧ │
│ ⑨ │ ⑨ │ ⑨ │ ⑨ │
└───┴───┴───┴───┘
```

2. A right circular cone and a right circular cylinder have equal heights and the volume of the cylinder is twice that of the cone. What is the radius of the cylinder if the base radius of the cone is 3 cm and the volume of the cone is 18π cm³? (The volume of a cone with base radius r and height h is $\frac{1}{3}\pi r^2 h$)

(A) 1

(B) $\sqrt{2}$

(C) 2

(D) $2\sqrt{3}$

(E) $\sqrt{6}$

2. A cube with a volume of 64 cubic inches is inscribed in a sphere so that all vertices of the cube touch the sphere. What is the volume, in cubic inches, of the sphere? (The volume of a sphere with volume V and radius r is $V = \frac{4}{3}\pi r^3$)

(A) $16\pi\sqrt{3}$

(B) $32\pi\sqrt{3}$

(C) $64\pi\sqrt{3}$

(D) $128\pi\sqrt{3}$

(E) $256\pi\sqrt{3}$

Basic Coordinate Geometry Facts

- The coordinate plane is a system of two perpendicular axes used to describe the position of a point (x, y).
- The x-axis is the horizontal axis of the coordinate plane.
- The y-axis is the vertical axis of the coordinate plane.
- The origin is the intersection of the x and y axes and has the coordinates $(0, 0)$.
- Point locations within the coordinate plane are written as (x, y) where x denotes the horizontal distance from the origin and y denotes the vertical distance from the origin.
- The y-intercept is the coordinate at which a line or a function intersects the y-axis. Therefore the value of x for the y-intercept will always be zero and will take the form $(0, y)$.
- The x-intercept is the coordinate(s) at which a function intersects the x-axis. Therefore, the value of y for the x-intercept will always be zero and will take the form $(x, 0)$. These values are also known as solutions or roots of the function.
- Slope is defined as the ratio of vertical change to horizontal change, or $\dfrac{rise}{run}$.
- Slope can always be calculated with two sets of points from the same line, using the formula $m = \dfrac{y_2 - y_1}{x_2 - x_1}$, where m is the slope value, (x_2, y_2) is one point, and (x_1, y_1) is another.
- The slope-intercept form of the equation of the line is $y = mx + b$, where m is the slope, and b is the y-intercept. Both of these values are constants. In this formula, x and y are coordinate values of any point on that line.
- Parallel lines have identical slopes.
- Perpendicular lines have slopes that are negative reciprocals of one another.

Advanced Coordinate Geometry Facts

- A parabola is a graph of a quadratic equation in the *xy*-coordinate plane. The general form of the equation is $y = ax^2 + bx + c$.
- Parabolas are symmetrical around an axis of symmetry and have a single vertex on the axis of symmetry.
- If *a* is positive, the graph opens upward. If *a* is negative, the graph opens downward. When *a* is positive, increasing its value makes a parabola steeper; If *a* is negative, decreasing its value also makes a parabola steeper. It may be helpful to think of *a* as analogous to slope.
- Changing the value of *b* shifts the parabola's axis of symmetry left or right, in the *opposite* direction. So, a negative value for *b* means that the axis of symmetry is positive, and vice versa.
- *c* is the *y*-intercept of the parabola. For example, if *c* = 2, the the coordinates of the *y*-intercept are (0, 2).
- The *y*-coordinate of any point can be found by putting the *x* value into the standard equation and solving for *y*.
- Parabolas also can be written using the standard form of the equation: $y = a(x - h)^2 + k$, where *a*, *h*, and *k* are constants.
- The vertex of the parabola in this form is (*h*, *k*).

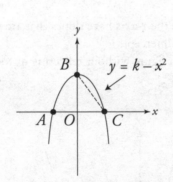

1. The figure above shows the graph of the parabola $y = k - x^2$, where *k* is a constant. If the coordinates of point *A* are (–2, 0), what is the length of line segment *BC* ?

   (A) $\sqrt{5}$

   (B) $2\sqrt{5}$

   (C) 6

   (D) $5\sqrt{2}$

   (E) 12

Here's How to Crack It

The parabola $y = k - x^2$ is centered on the y-axis, so if the coordinates of A are $(-2,0)$, the coordinates of C must be $(2, 0)$. Whenever you have a point on a graph, you can plug it into the equation to find a missing piece. So, plug in $(2, 0)$ to find k: $0 = k - 2^2$, therefore $k = 4$. This tells that the coordinates of B are $(0, 4)$. To find the length of BC, you don't need the distance formula: just draw a right triangle and use the Pythagorean theorem. The legs of the triangle are 2 and 4, so $2^2 + 4^2 = (BC)^2$, and $BC = \sqrt{20} = 2\sqrt{5}$. The correct answer is (B).

Reflection and Transformation Facts

*   Rotation means turning a line or function around a point called the center of rotation.
*   Reflecting a line or a function means creating a mirror image of the graph or function around the line of reflection.
*   Lines reflected across the x-axis have slopes that are negatives of each other (*not* negative reciprocals) and y-intercepts that are negatives of each other.
*   Lines reflected across the y-axis have slopes that are negatives of each other but the same y-intercept.
*   A translation moves a figure without reflecting or rotating it. See the examples below:

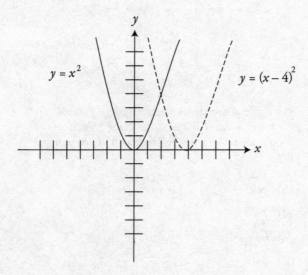

In this example, the graph is translated to the right by adjusting the *x*-coordinate value. If a number is inside the parentheses with the *x*-value, then the graph shifts the number of units opposite the direction of the sign.

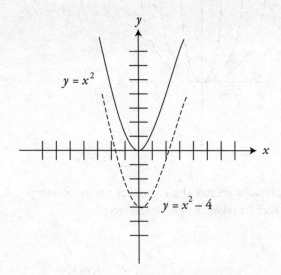

In the example above the graph is translated down 4 units. Notice that a translation on the *y*-axis is outside the parentheses and the shift matches the value of the sign.

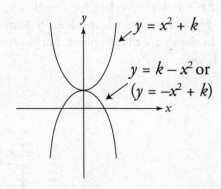

Putting a negative sign in front of x^2 flips the parabola upside down.

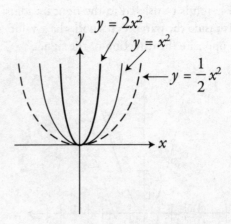

Multiplying x by a constant greater than 1 makes the graph steeper. Conversely, a constant between 0 and 1 makes the graph less steep.

Functions

There are two types of functions that you will see on the SAT. The first type is very similar to coordinate geometry and often overlaps significantly with the material discussed earlier. These are often called linear functions. Essentially, a function acts like a machine. A function produces a y-value whenever you put in an x value. A function can have multiple x values for a single y-value, but a function can never have multiple y-values for a single x-value. In other words, a function can move up and down in the xy-coordinate plane, but it can never double back on itself. See the figures below:

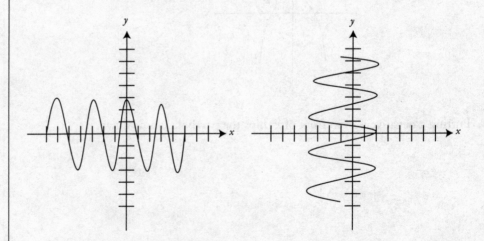

The figure on the left is a function, while the figure on the right is not a function. If you can draw a vertical line that touches more than one point on the graph, it's not a function (this is called the "vertical line test").

Function notation is slightly different from coordinate geometry notation. The y-value is usually written as $f(x)$. In other words $f(x) = y$. The value (x) represents all the possible x-values for the function. The f alone is not a variable and should not be solved for. It merely denotes the name of the function. If there are multiple functions on a graph, then they are usually denoted using an alphabetical pattern: $f(x)$, $g(x)$, $h(x)$... As long as you are comfortable following directions, functions should not pose too many issues for you. Consider the following example:

Example 5:

> The function $f(x)$ is defined by $f(x) = 3x^2 - 1$. If p is a positive integer, and $4f(p) = 428$, then what is the value of p?

Begin by simplifying to the basic function by dividing both sides by 4, so $f(p) = 107$. Next since $f(p) = f(x)$ with a value of p, substitute the given equation for $f(p)$: $3p^2 - 1 = 107$. Now, solve for p: $3p^2 = 108$, $p^2 = 36$, so $p = 6$.

Function questions on the SAT may also require you to process information from charts and graphs. Since $f(x)$ represents the y-coordinate and x represents the x-coordinate, functions can also be understood as a form of point notation. Consider in the following two examples how function notation can be used to represent coordinate graphs.

Example 6:

> If $f(x)$ is a linear function such that $f(1) = 5$ and $f(-1) = 9$, then what is the slope of the graph of $y = f(x)$?

As mentioned in an earlier question, don't get confused by the terminology. A linear function is just a line. Since $f(x) = y$, $f(1) = 5$ can be read as "the function $f(x)$ has a y value of 5 when x is 1." In other words, this is just the point $(1, 5)$. The second pair can be read in the same way: "the function $f(x)$ has a y value of 9 when x is -1," which is the point $(-1, 9)$. With two points on a line, use the slope formula to find that $m = -2$.

Harder functions may require you to interpret graphical data for find an x or a y value. Consider the following example:

Example 7:

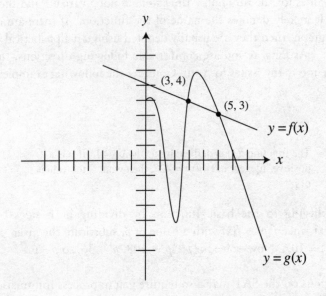

The figure above shows the graphs of the functions
$y = f(x)$ and $y = g(x)$. Which of the following describes
all the values of x for which $g(x) \geq f(x)$?

This question is asking you to find all of the values for x for which the line $g(x)$ is above (greater than) the line $f(x)$. The values range from 3 to 5 or $3 \leq x \leq 5$. Trap answers on the SAT would include the y-values or would confuse greater than and less than.

Unusual Functions

The final topic that this chapter will cover is unusual functions. Any weird (non-standard) symbol in a math equation is also a function. As with the $f(x)$ notation, the key to answering these questions is following directions. It may help to think of strange symbol functions as mathematical "follow the leader." Figure out the rules of the function and then follow directions. Consider the following example.

8. For all positive integers n, let $n\odot$ be defined as the difference of square roots of the integers from n to 1, inclusive. For example, $5\odot = \sqrt{5} - \sqrt{4} - \sqrt{3} - \sqrt{2} - \sqrt{1}$. Which of the following is equal to 3?

(A) $3\odot$
(B) $4\odot$
(C) $9\odot$
(D) $9\odot - 6\odot$
(E) $9\odot - 8\odot$

Here's How to Crack It

This is a very tricky problem, so it is helpful to work backwards through the answer choices to explain how the function works. First, pay close attention to the definition of the function. The variable n is a positive integer. Now, consider answer choice (A). Since $n\odot = 3\odot$, then n must be 3. From the directions in the problem, $3\odot = \sqrt{3} - \sqrt{2} - \sqrt{1}$. This does not equal 3. In answer choice (B), $4\odot = \sqrt{4} - \sqrt{3} - \sqrt{2} - \sqrt{1}$. This simplifies into $2 - \sqrt{3} - \sqrt{2} - \sqrt{1}$, which does not equal 3 either. In choice (C), $9\odot = \sqrt{9} - \sqrt{8} - ... - \sqrt{1}$, which still doesn't work. Now look at choice (D). This choice subtracts the lowest six values from the function, leaving only the three highest values:: $\sqrt{9} - \sqrt{8} - \sqrt{7} ... - \sqrt{1} - \left(\sqrt{6} - \sqrt{5} - \sqrt{4} ... - \sqrt{1}\right) = \sqrt{9} - \sqrt{8} - \sqrt{7}$. This is not the answer, but you can probably see now why the answer is (E). Since we are subtracting the lowest eight values, only the highest value remains, and $\sqrt{9} = 3$, so the correct answer is (E).

Chapter 5
Alternative
Approaches

Scoring a 750 or higher on the SAT Math section requires near perfection. Hardly a single problem can be skipped or answered incorrectly. One of the major challenges is developing the necessary flexibility to deal with every type of problem that the SAT might throw at you. Memorizing the many different equations and formulas needed is one way of beating these problems. However, there are hundreds of formulas, so the task of memorization is arduous. Additionally, you must ask yourself what you will do if you can't remember the correct formula for a problem. If you are ever stumped on the SAT, you may not hit the score you want.

As a result, it is vital that you develop alternative strategies for dealing with challenging questions. A successful alternative strategy should do several things: 1) it should guarantee the correct answer; 2) it should be as fast as or faster than applying the "correct" algebraic formula; and 3) it should be applicable to numerous situations.

This chapter will cover two alternative techniques for approaching challenging questions—Plugging In and ballparking.

PLUGGING IN

Speed and accuracy are a vital combination for acing the Math section of the SAT. If you had only thirty seconds left on the Math section, which of the following two questions would you rather have:

1. A customer walks into a convenience store to purchase two candy bars valued at 50 cents apiece. If he pays with a ten dollar bill, how much change will he receive?

    (A) $5
    (B) $6
    (C) $7
    (D) $8
    (E) $9

2. A customer walks into a convenience store to purchase b bars of candy valued at c cents apiece. If he pays d dollars, which of the following expressions represents his change, in dollars?

    (A) $d - bc$

    (B) $bc - d$

    (C) $db - c$

    (D) $\dfrac{bc}{100} - d$

    (E) $d - \dfrac{bc}{100}$

Without a doubt, you would rather do the first problem, but why? The two problems are nearly identical! They cover the same topic and require the same math. What aspect of these problems makes number two so much more challenging? The answer, of course, is the presence of variables. Even if you're really good at algebra, numbers are easier to work with. As a result, the first problem is very straightforward, despite the need to convert from cents to dollars in order to solve for the change. Algebra, on the other hand, is not as intuitive.

By the way, did you get (E) for both questions? If not, come back and try the second one after you've completed this section!

Fortunately, it is possible to eliminate the need to use algebra on many SAT questions. This strategy is called Plugging In. Consider the following problem:

Example 1:

The sum of $x + y$ is equivalent to which of the following expressions:

(A) $3x + 3y$

(B) $\dfrac{x}{3} + \dfrac{3}{y}$

(C) $3x^2 - 3y^2$

(D) $(x + 3) - (y + 3)$

(E) $(x + 3) - (3 - y)$

Instead of looking at each answer choice and trying to decide if it is valid, try Plugging In. Begin by assigning a value for each of the variables. For example, let $x = 3$ and $y = 2$. Now plug those numbers into the original equation: $x + y$ becomes $3 + 2 = 5$. Since the number 5 is the "solution" to the equation in the question, what must be true of the correct answer? The correct answer must also equal 5 when using the values you created for x and y. Think of this solution as a *target* that you are trying to hit. Now, insert those values into the problem:

(A) $3(3) + 3(2) = 9 + 6 = 15.$ This doesn't match your target, so eliminate it.

(B) $\dfrac{3}{3} + \dfrac{3}{2} = 1 + 1.5 = 2.5$ This doesn't match your target, so eliminate it.

(C) $3(3)^2 - 3(2)^2 = 3(9) - 3(4) = 27 - 12 = 15$ This doesn't match your target, so eliminate it.

(D) $(3 + 3) - (2 + 3) = 6 - 5 = 1$ This doesn't match your target, so eliminate it.

(E) $(3 + 3) - (3 - 2) = 6 - 1 = 5$ This matches, so it is the correct answer.

Consider the speed at which it is possible to move through this problem. Since arithmetic is so much more intuitive than algebra, most of these answers were probably obviously incorrect as soon as you Plugged In. Also, ask yourself which method is more error prone: using knowledge of algebraic principles and number theory in your head, or doing some basic arithmetic on paper?

Plugging In can be used for any and every question that has variables in the answer choices. Just follow these steps:

1. Choose a number for the variables in the equation.
2. Solve the problem using arithmetic. Circle the solution: This is your *target* number.
3. Plug In the numbers you substituted for variables into each answer choice.
4. The answer choice that matches your target is the correct answer. Be sure to check all five answers.

Now try another:

────────────○────────────

2. If $x - 6, = r$, what does $x^2 - 36$ equal, in terms of r ?

    (A) $(r + 6)^2$
    (B) $(r - 6)^2$
    (C) $r^2 + 6r$
    (D) $r^2 + 12r$
    (E) $r^2 - 6r$

Here's How to Crack It

This is a tricky problem, and you may be stumped by the algebra or make a careless mistake, so Plug In instead. The first step is to choose values for the variables. Since there are two variables that are related, Plug In numbers that make the math as simple as possible. Let's say $x = 8$. Then $8 - 6 = 2$, so $r = 2$. Now solve the problem: $8^2 - 36 = 28$, so 28 is the target. Now, Plug In $r = 2$ into each of the answer choices; the correct answer will equal 28.

(A)	$(2 + 6)^2 = 64$	This doesn't match your target, so eliminate it.
(B)	$(2 - 6)^2 = 16$	This doesn't match your target, so eliminate it.

(C) $2^2 + 6(2) = 16$ This doesn't match your target, so
                                      eliminate it.

(D) $2^2 + 12(2) = 28$ This matches your target, but check
                                      all five answers!

(E) $2^2 - 6(2) = -8$ This doesn't match your target, so
                                      eliminate it.

Therefore, the answer is (A).

When plugging in, be careful which numbers you choose. Take a look at the next problem, and consider what would happen if you Plug In $b = 1$.

---

3. If $a = b^2$ and $b = m^{\frac{1}{3}}$, what is a^3 in terms of m?

    (A) m

    (B) $\sqrt[3]{\dfrac{1}{m}}$

    (C) m^2

    (D) $\sqrt[3]{m}$

    (E) m^3

Here's How to Crack It

If $b = 1$, then $b^2 = 1$, so $a = 1$, therefore $m^{\frac{1}{3}} = \sqrt[3]{m} = 1$ and $m = 1$. So if you Plug In using 1, then your target is also 1. Now try the answer choices.

(A) $m = 1$ This matches your target.

(B) $\sqrt[3]{\dfrac{1}{1}}$ This matches your target.

(C) $1^2 = 1$ This matches your target.

(D) $\sqrt[3]{1} = 1$ This matches your target.

(E) $1^3 = 1$ This matches your target.

By Plugging In the number 1 for your value, no answer choices were eliminated. In basic terms, avoid numbers that either have unusual properties (such as 0 or 1), or that might make the math more challenging. The acronym **FROZEN** is useful for remembering which numbers to avoid:

F = fractions
R = repeating the same value (such as x and y are both 2)
O = one
Z = zero
E = extreme (numbers that are very large or that are very small)
N = negatives

Let's try this question again. We'll avoid the **FROZEN** numbers and pick values that make the math as simple as possible. In this question, it's easiest to start by working backwards. Since you are taking the third root of m, pick a number that is the cube of an integer, such as 8. If $m = 8$, then $b = 2$ and $a = 2^2 = 4$. The question asks for a^3, so our target is $4^3 = 64$. Now try the answer choices.

(A) $m = 8$ — This doesn't match your target, so eliminate it.

(B) $\sqrt[3]{\dfrac{1}{8}} = \dfrac{1}{2}$ — This doesn't match your target, so eliminate it.

(C) $8^2 = 64$ — This matches your target, but check all five answers!

(D) $\sqrt[3]{8} = 2$ — This doesn't match your target, so eliminate it.

(E) $8^3 = 512$ — This doesn't match your target, so eliminate it.

Therefore, the answer is (C).

———————————————○———————————————

As you can see, Plugging In is a powerful technique for improving both speed and accuracy on challenging problems. Two more examples below will deal with the nuances of Plugging In.

The hallmark for recognizing a Plugging In question is variables in the answer choices and an urge to solve algebra equations. Typically, choosing a number for those variables is the most straightforward method. However, there could be some problems with variables for which you don't plug in directly for the variable.

4. The price of a dress after it was reduced by 60 percent is x dollars. What was the original price, in terms of x, of the dress?

(A) $1.40x$
(B) $1.60x$
(C) $2.40x$
(D) $2.50x$
(E) $3.00x$

Here's How to Crack It

Normally, we start by Plugging In for the variable. Here, however, it is hard to see what the original price should be if you plug in directly for x. For example, make $x = \$50$. The target value of the original price is not easy to calculate. In situations such as this one, find another value from the problem that you can Plug In for. Remember that the goal of the Plugging In technique is to make the math of the problem easier. Ask yourself what piece of information from the problem would make this question easier to deal with. What about the original price of the dress? If this was known, then the math would be simpler. Go ahead and Plug In a value for the price of the dress.

Since the problem deals with percentages, use either 10 or 100 to make the math straightforward. Set the original price of the dress as $100. Now, reduce that by 60% to find the new price of $40, which is x. By Plugging In for the unknown element, you have both a value for x and a target answer of $100. Now check each answer choice:

$1.40(40) = \$56$	This doesn't match your target, so eliminate it.
$1.60(40) = \$64$	This doesn't match your target, so eliminate it.
$2.40(40) = \$96$	This doesn't match your target, so eliminate it.
$2.50(40) = \$100$	This matches your target, but check (E).
$3.00(40) = \$120$	This doesn't match your target, so eliminate it.

Many of the more challenging number theory questions on the SAT are phrased as MUST BE or COULD BE questions. Plugging In will work on these questions as well; however, be careful about the meaning of MUST BE. This means that the correct answer choice will work in all cases, regardless of the value that is chosen. As a result, be prepared to Plug In more than once on MUST BE and COULD BE questions until only one answer choice remains.

5. If $x < y$ then which of the following must be true?

(A) $x < 0$
(B) $y > 0$
(C) $xy > 0$
(D) $x - y < 0$
(E) $x^2 < y^2$

Here's How to Crack It

As with all Plugging In questions, begin by choosing easy numbers that satisfy the rules of question. For example, $x = 2$ and $y = 3$. Now check each of the answers.

(A)	$2 < 0$	Since your x and y satisfy the equation, this is not true, so eliminate it.
(B)	$3 > 0$	This is currently true.
(C)	$2(3) > 0$	This is currently true.
(D)	$2 - 3 < 0$	This is currently true.
(E)	$4 < 9$	This is currently true.

Even though the values you chose for x and y were valid, you were only able to eliminate one answer choice. This is not unusual when plugging in "normal" values for x and y. Remember the FROZEN numbers that we said to avoid? The phrase "must be" includes all possible situations as defined by the equation. Therefore, if $x < y$ the correct answer will be valid even if you plug in a fraction, a repeating number, a one, a zero, an extreme, or a negative. Choose one of the FROZEN numbers and Plug In again. FROZEN numbers can even be mixed and matched: for example, a negative fraction. A quick reminder though: you must choose two values that work in the original problem. For example, in this situation, you cannot make x greater than (or equal to) y.

Try Plugging In again, using a negative value for x and zero for y: so $x = -2$ and $y = 0$. Since (A) has been eliminated already, check only the remaining answers:

(A)		Already eliminated
(B)	$0 > 0$	Not true, so eliminate it.
(C)	$-2(0) > 0$	Not true, so eliminate it.
(D)	$-2 - 0 < 0$	Still true; keep moving.
(E)	$(-2)^2 < (0)^2$	Not true, so eliminate it.

Therefore, the answer must be (D).

While Plugging In is most common on multiple choice problems, it can sometimes work on grid-ins as well.

6. If $\dfrac{a}{b-2}=\dfrac{3}{4}$ and $\dfrac{b}{c}=\dfrac{2}{3}$, what is the value of $c-2a$?

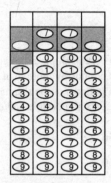

Here's How to Crack It

Let's pick some numbers. If $a = 3$, then $b - 2 = 4$, so $b = 6$. Then, $\dfrac{6}{c}=\dfrac{2}{3}$, so $c = 9$. Now let's find the answer: The question asks for the value of $c - 2a$, so $9 - 2(3) = 3$. It's that easy!

Ultimately, the Plugging In technique is useful for improving both speed and accuracy on challenging algebra questions. In order to get the score you want, you must have a method for ensuring that you can answer nearly every question, no matter how difficult it may first appear. Plugging In can help you save time, and give you options when other methods fail you.

Here are a few Plugging In questions for you to try. Read the explanations when you are finished, to be sure you are applying the Plugging In strategy correctly.

TRY IT DRILL 1

See Chapter 7 for complete answers and explanations.

1. If x is a single digit prime number greater than 2, which of the following must also be prime?

   (A) $x-1$
   (B) $x+2$
   (C) $3x-2$
   (D) $4x+1$
   (E) $5x-4$

2. The weight of a certain shipment of apples may not deviate from 50 pounds by more than 5 pounds. If W is the weight, in pounds, of the shipment, which of the following represents all possible values of W?

   (A) $|W-5| \le 50$

   (A) $|W-5| \ge 50$

   (A) $|W-50| \le 5$

   (A) $|W-50| \ge 5$

   (A) $|W-45| \le 10$

3. The wholesale price of a boat is x dollars. At an auction, the boat sells for y percent more than the wholesale price. Don later purchases the boat at z percent below the auction price. Which of the following expressions represents the price, in dollars, that Don paid for the boat?

   (A) $x\left(1+\dfrac{y}{100}\right)\left(1-\dfrac{z}{100}\right)$

   (A) $x\left(\dfrac{y}{100}\right)\left(\dfrac{z}{100}\right)$

   (A) $x\left(\dfrac{yz}{100}\right)$

   (A) $x+\dfrac{xy}{100}-\dfrac{xz}{100}$

   (A) $x\left(\dfrac{xy}{100}-\dfrac{xz}{100}\right)$

4. If a, b, c, and d are consecutive odd integers, such that $0 < a < b < c < d$, what is $d^2 - a^2$ in terms of b?

   (A) $12b+12$
   (B) $12b-12$
   (C) $6b+6$
   (D) $12b$
   (E) $6b+12$

5. Which of the following expressions is equivalent to

$$3^{2x} \times 27^{\frac{1}{2}x} \text{ ?}$$

(A) 3^x

(B) $3^{\frac{7}{2}x}$

(C) $3^{\frac{9}{2}x}$

(D) $3^{\frac{13}{2}x}$

(E) 3^{7x}

Algebra is not the only topic that can be sidestepped on the SAT. Geometry problems have similar features that can be used to speed up and improve accuracy. The most important concept to realize about geometry figures on the SAT is that they are drawn to scale (unless stated otherwise). In other words, you can trust the appearance of geometry figures. The only exception to this rule is when the figure includes the note "not to scale."

A ballpark number is a rough estimate. The logic of ballparking on the SAT is straightforward: if you can trust the figure, you can use the information that the problem provides to make an educated guess about the answer. A few examples will highlight this.

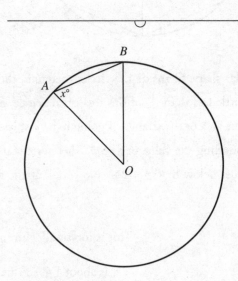

In the figure above, O is the center of the circle and $x = 67.5°$. If the area of the circle is 64π, then what is the area of triangle ABO?

(A) 12

(B) $16\sqrt{2}$

(C) 12

(D) 16

(E) $32\sqrt{2}$

Here's How to Crack It

This is a tricky question. If you're not sure how to solve it, or you think you might not have time, consider ballparking instead. Also, you can use ballparking to eliminate trap answers before beginning to actually solve a problem.

The first step of ballparking is to generate a rough estimate of what value you are looking for. The figure is drawn to scale, so carve up the circle into multiple triangles of the same size as the one in the problem. Use your pencil to extend the lines of triangle ABO into diameters. Then keep adding lines until you have filled up the circle, like so:

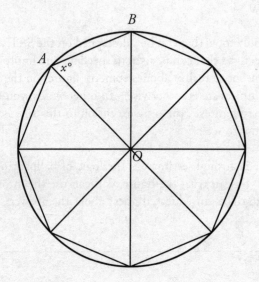

Eight triangles of similar shape fit inside the circle; therefore, the area of the triangle is going to be a little less than $\frac{1}{8}$ of the area of the circle. Since the area of the circle is 64π, then the area of the triangle is going to be just less than 8π. Continue ballparking by rounding the value of π to 3. Therefore, you need an answer choice whose value is just below $8 \times 3 = 24$. Now look at the answers and use POE aggressively:

(A)	12	This is too small, eliminate it.
(B)	$16\sqrt{2}$	$\sqrt{2}$ is about 1.4, so this is about 22.4. It's close, so keep it!
(C)	12π	This is too large, so eliminate it.
(D)	16π	This is too large, so eliminate it.
(E)	$32\sqrt{2}$	This is too large, so eliminate it.

Therefore, the answer is (B).

Ballparking can be much faster than solving on challenging geometry questions. When you ballpark, you can either use your calculator, or just estimate the value of common geometry numbers such as π, $\sqrt{2}$, and $\sqrt{3}$. It is likely that you already know that $\pi \cong 3$. Here is a handy trick for remembering the values of $\sqrt{2}$ and $\sqrt{3}$. The second month is February, and the holiday in February is Valentine's Day on February 14: 2 = 14 or $\sqrt{2}$ = 1.4. Likewise, the third month is March, and the holiday in March is St. Patrick's Day on March 17th: 3 = 17 or $\sqrt{3}$ = 1.7.

Let's tackle another one.

7. A square is inscribed in a circle. If a point within the circle is randomly chosen, what is the probability that the point will <u>not</u> be within the square?

    (A) $\dfrac{\pi}{2}$

    (B) π

    (C) $\dfrac{2-\pi}{\pi}$

    (D) $\dfrac{\pi-2}{\pi}$

    (E) 2π

Here's How to Crack It

This is another question that might be too difficult, or too time-consuming, to solve. Instead, consider ballparking. Begin by drawing the figure:

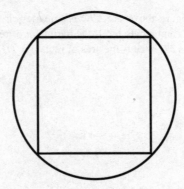

Now estimate. How much of the figure is taken up by the square? Certainly more than half; two-thirds might be a good estimate. Therefore, one-third of the area is <u>not</u> taken up by the square, and the probability of choosing a point that is inside the circle, but outside the square, is one-third.

Now tackle the answer choices either with your calculator or by estimating. (A) ≅ 1.55, which is not even close (and technically impossible, since any probability is always a number from 0 to 1). For the same reason, we can eliminate (B), (C), and (E). That leaves only (D), which is indeed close to one-third, as the correct answer.

○

Here are a few questions for you to attempt. Try ballparking all of them, even if you think you know how to solve them Be sure to read the explanations when you are finished.

TRY IT DRILL 2
See Chapter 7 for complete answers and explanations.

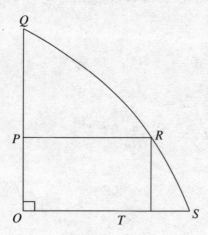

1. In the figure above, arc $\overarc{QRS}$ is a quarter-circle with center O and length 6π. If the perimeter of rectangle $OPRT$ is 32, what is the area of rectangle $OPRT$?

   (A) 12π
   (B) 16π
   (C) 48
   (D) 56
   (E) 64

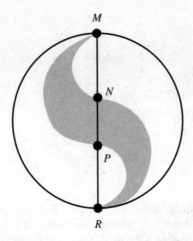

2. In the figure above, *MR* is the diameter of the large circle, and *MN*, *MP*, *NP*, and *NR* are the diameters of semicircles. If *MR* = 12, and *MN* = *NP* = *PR*, what is the area of the shaded region?

(A)   6π
(B)   10π
(C)   12π
(D)   16π
(E)   24π

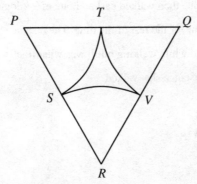

3. In the figure above, *PQR* is an equilateral triangle with a perimeter of 12. Points *S*, *T*, and *V* are the midpoints of the sides of the triangle, and arcs $\overset{\frown}{ST}$, $\overset{\frown}{TV}$, and $\overset{\frown}{VS}$ are centered at points *P*, *Q*, and *R*, respectively. What is the perimeter of the region bounded by the darkened arcs?

(A)   6

(B)   2π

(C) $8 - \dfrac{2\pi}{3}$

(D)   π + 3

(E) $8 + \dfrac{2\pi}{3}$

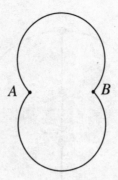

4. In the figure above, two identical 300 arcs intersect at points *A* and *B*. If each arc is a portion of a circle with radius 6, what is the total area of the figure?

(A) 60π

(B) 72π

(C) $30\pi + 9\sqrt{3}$

(D) $60\pi + 18\sqrt{3}$

(E) $60\pi + 36\sqrt{3}$

5. On a backpacking trip, Jane started by walking north at a rate of 6 kilometers per hour for $\frac{3}{8}$ of her total walking time. She then walked east at a rate of 3 kilometers per hour for the rest of the time. The distance that Jane covered while walking north was what fraction of the total distance she walked?

(A) $\frac{1}{8}$

(B) $\frac{1}{3}$

(C) $\frac{3}{8}$

(D) $\frac{5}{11}$

(E) $\frac{6}{11}$

Now that you've gained familiarity with both Plugging in and ballparking, try one more drill to fine-tune your mastery of these techniques. Since there are more opportunities to Plug In than to ballpark on the SAT, this drill contains more Plugging In questions, but both types are covered. Make sure you identify the appropriate technique and then use it.

CONCLUSION

Alternative strategies are essential for achieving the highest scores. The sheer number of geometry and algebraic equations precludes most students from being able to memorize and recall every single possible formula that might be needed for this test. As a result, many high scoring students are perpetually disappointed because they always seem to have at least a few questions per test that they cannot work.

As discussed above, an ideal alternative strategy will enable you to find the correct answer in the same amount of time or less than that required to work the problem algebraically. Plugging In by choosing a number is one of these alternative methods. A thorough understanding of Plugging In gives you a way to handle algebra problems even when you don't know exactly how to work them. Additionally, on hard number theory questions, Plugging In can often be faster, since you are dealing with concrete numbers rather than abstract theory.

Whenever you plug in, begin by choosing a number and solving the original problem. The arithmetic solution to the problem is the target value. The correct answer choice will match this value. When choosing numbers, remember the goal of Plugging In is to make your math fast and accurate. Therefore, always choose numbers that work well in the problem and avoid the FROZEN numbers, which have unusual properties.

Ballparking is another alternative strategy for dealing with challenging geometry questions. Unless stated otherwise, the figures on the SAT are always drawn to scale. As a result, they can be trusted to narrow in on the correct answer choice whenever you either are short on time or knowledge, and can also help you eliminate trap answers before you begin working a problem. Use the figures to eliminate implausible answer choices first. Often two or three of the answers will be clearly wrong. If you are stuck between two or more answer choices, make an assumption about the relative size of the figure you are solving for and eliminate the less likely answer.

Chapter 6
Word Problems and
Other Hot Topics

On the SAT, word problems can present some special difficulties. The test writers love these problems because there is a host of ways that they can lead you into traps. This chapter presents the most effective strategies for avoiding these traps, and covers the topics that are most likely to trip you up on hard problems.

Use Bite-Sized Pieces

The first step in conquering word problems is to break the question into bite-sized pieces. After you Read The Full Question (RTFQ), go back to the beginning. As soon the problem gives you something to do, do it! Let's use the question below as an example.

1. In a woodworker's toolbox, there are one-half as many chisels as gouges, and one-third as many planes as chisels. If there are 60 tools in the toolbox, and there are no tools other than chisels, gouges, or planes, how many chisels and gouges are in the toolbox?

   (A) 6
   (B) 12
   (C) 18
   (D) 36
   (E) 54

Here's How to Crack It

Remember to Read The Full Question (RTFQ) first, and underline what the question is asking for. Now go back to the beginning and take it one bite-sized piece at a time.

> In a woodworker's toolbox, there are one-half as many chisels as gouges…

We could tackle this piece of information by saying that gouges = x and chisels = $\frac{1}{2}x$. Now tackle the next bite-sized piece.

> …and one-third as many planes as chisels.

Since chisels were $\frac{1}{2}x$, planes must be $\frac{1}{2}x \bullet \frac{1}{3} = \frac{1}{6}x$. Move on to another bite sized piece.

> If there are 60 tools in the toolbox, and there are no tools other than chisels, gouges, or planes…

Now we can say that $x + \frac{1}{2}x + \frac{1}{6}x = 60$, so $\frac{5}{3}x = 60$ and $x = 36$.

Finally, reread what the question is asking for.

…how many chisels and gouges are in the toolbox?

Notice that the question is <u>not</u> asking for x, but rather for $x + \frac{1}{2}x$, which equals 54, so the correct answer is (E).

Using bite-sized pieces will help you break problems into a series of simple, manageable steps, improving both your accuracy and efficiency.

Start with the Easiest Piece

The example above was relatively easy because it presented the pieces in a logical order. But this won't always happen on hard SAT questions. One of the test-writers' favorite tricks is to mix up the logical order, hiding the most useful information near the end of the problem. Take a look at the next example.

2. *ABCD* is a four-digit integer, in which *A*, *B*, *C*, and *D* represent distinct digits. The following rules are used to form *ABCD*.

   1. *B* is equal to the sum of *A*, *C*, and *D*.
   2. *C* is three less than *A*.
   3. *A* is six more than *D*.

What is the four-digit integer?

Here's How to Crack It

After you RTFQ, think about where to start. The 1st rule isn't very helpful; there are too many possibilities. The 3rd rule, on the other hand, is a good place to start. Remember that digits are integers from 0 to 9, so there aren't very many possibilities for A. Suppose that $D = 1$; then add six to get $A = 7$. You might want to organize the information in a table. Remember, bite-sized pieces.

A	B	C	D
7	?	?	1

Moving to the 2nd rule, C is three less than A, so $C = 4$.

A	B	C	D
7	?	4	1

Now tackle the 1st rule. Since B is the sum of the other three digits $B = 11$. But a digit can't be greater than 9, so this won't work; we need to start with a smaller value for D. The only possibility left is zero! If $D = 0$, then $A = 6$.

A	B	C	D
6	?	?	0

If $A = 6$, $C = 3$.

A	B	C	D
6	?	3	0

Finally, $B = 6 + 3 + 0 = 9$.

A	B	C	D
6	9	3	0

Therefore, the correct answer is 6,930.

To summarize: Break the problem into bite-sized pieces, and start with the easiest piece, which is not necessarily the first piece of the word problem.

Plug In The Answers (PITA)

In the previous chapter, we saw how useful it is to Plug In whenever there are variables in the answer choices. A closely related technique is Plugging In The Answers (PITA for short). When the answers contain numbers rather than variables, see if you can Plug In The Answers! Let's look at an example.

4. A cargo ship currently holds two-thirds of its maximum capacity by weight. If seven tons of cargo were added to the ship, it would hold three-fourths of its maximum capacity. What is the maximum capacity, in tons, of the ship?

(A) 42
(B) 48
(C) 60
(D) 84
(E) 96

To Plug In The Answers, follow these three simple steps:

1. Label the Answers. This will help you avoid careless mistakes and traps.
2. Start with (C). If it's not correct, you'll often be able to tell whether to go up or down, so you'll only need to check three answers at most.
3. Work through the problem in bite-sized pieces. Look for some condition in the problem that tells you whether the answer is correct. Stop when you find the right answer.

Here's How to Crack It

Let's give it a try. First, label the answers. In this case the answers represent the maximum capacity of the ship, so write something like "max" over the answers. Then start with (C) and work through the problem in bite-sized pieces. We need to find two-thirds of 60, which is 40. Then we need to add 7 more tons, so we have 47. Finally, is 47 three-fourths of 60? No, 45 is three-fourths of 60, so (C) is incorrect. Here's what your work should look like so far:

4. A cargo ship currently holds two-thirds of its maximum capacity by weight. If seven tons of cargo were added to the ship, it would hold three-fourths of its maximum capacity. What is the maximum capacity, in tons, of the ship?

Max.	$\frac{2}{3}$	$\frac{2}{3}+7$	$=\frac{3}{4}$?
(A) 42			
(B) 48			
(C) 60	40	47	No
(D) 84			
(E) 96			

Which answer should we try next? In (C), adding 7 tons had too large of an effect—we overshot the goal of three-quarter's capacity. We need to "dilute" the effect of adding 7 tons by starting with a larger number, so let's try (D) (or just choose a direction and see whether the result is closer or farther away from the answer you want). Two-thirds of 84 is 56. Add 7 more tons and we have 63. Is 63 equal to three-fourths of 84? Yes it is, so (D) the correct answer. Here's what your work should look like:

4. A cargo ship currently holds two-thirds of its maximum capacity by weight. If seven tons of cargo were added to the ship, it would hold three-fourths of its maximum capacity. What is the maximum capacity, in tons, of the ship?

Max. $\qquad \frac{2}{3} \cdot \qquad \frac{2}{3}+7 \quad = \frac{3}{4}$?

(A) 42
(B) 48
(C) 60 $\qquad$ 40 $\qquad$ 47 $\qquad$ No
(D) 84 $\qquad$ 56 $\qquad$ 63 $\qquad$ Yes
(E) 96

Unlike Plugging In your own number, when you Plug In The Answers, you don't need to check all five answers—there is only one correct answer, so stop as soon as you find it.

Let's try a more difficult problem.

5. During the 93 days of summer, the number of tourists at a certain resort can be modeled by the function $n(d) = \frac{1}{5}d^2 - 14d + c$, where c is a constant and $n(d)$ represents the number of visitors on day number d for $1 \le d \le 93$. The number of visitors on day number 20 was equal to the number of visitors on what number day?

(A) 40
(B) 50
(C) 60
(D) 70
(E) 75

Here's How to Crack It

This problem is tougher than the last, but it can be beaten by the same approach. Start by labeling the answers; they represent the number of a day (for example, the 30th day, the 40th day, etc.). Now work the problem in bite size pieces. First, we need to know the number of visitors on the 20th day, so plug 20 into the function: $n(20) = \frac{1}{5}(20)^2 - 14(20) + c$. This simplifies to $-200 + c$. What's c? We don't know, so we can either just leave it, or we could plug in our own number for c. Either approach will work. For simplicity's sake, let's leave it and say the total we're looking for is $-200 + c$.

Now tackle the answer choices, starting with (C). Plug 60 into the function: $n(60) = \frac{1}{5}(60)^2 - 14(60) + c$. This simplifies to $-120 + c$, which is too big, so (C) is incorrect. Now try (B). Plugging 50 into the function, you get $n(50) = \frac{1}{5}(50)^2 - 14(50) + c$, which simplifies to $-200 + c$. Success! (B) is the correct answer.

As you can see, it usually pays to start with (C) because if it's not the correct answer, we can often tell which direction to go. However, there is one exception to this rule. When a question asks for the *least* (or *greatest*) value, start with the least (or greatest) answer choice. Let's try an example.

---

6. Harriet has 21 marbles, each of which is either red, green, or blue. If she has fewer green marbles than red marbles, and fewer blue marbles than green marbles, what is the greatest number of green marbles Harriet could have?

(A) 6
(B) 7
(C) 8
(D) 9
(E) 10

Here's How to Crack It

Since this question is asking for the *greatest* number, we should start with (E). First, label the answers "green." You should also make columns for red and blue.

To maximize the number of green marbles, we need to minimize the number of red and blue marbles. Since there must be more red marbles than green, there would have to be at least 11 red marbles in (E), which leaves no room for blue marbles. Therefore, (E) is too large. Let's try (D). If there are 9 green marbles, there could be 10 red marbles, leaving 2 blue marbles. Therefore, (D) is correct. Your work for this problem should look something like this:

6. Harriet has 21 marbles, each of which is either red, green, or blue. If she has fewer green marbles than red marbles, and fewer blue marbles than green marbles, what is the greatest number of green marbles Harriet could have?

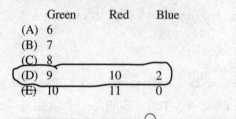

	Green	Red	Blue
(A)	6		
(B)	7		
(C)	8		
(D)	9	10	2
(E)	10	11	0

As you can see, PITA is a very useful strategy that can save you time, and bail you out when you don't know how to solve a question. Remember, when you PITA, do the following:

1. Label the answers.
2. Start with (C) (unless the question asks for the least/greatest value.
3. Work through the problem in bite-sized pieces. Stop when you find the correct answer.

To practice Plugging In The Answers, try the drill below.

TRY IT DRILL 1

See Chapter 7 for complete answers and explanations.

1. Three consecutive even integers are such that the square of the smallest is equal to twice the largest. Which of the following could be the largest of the three integers?

    (A) 2
    (B) 4
    (C) 6
    (D) 10
    (E) 16

2. Mrs. Johnson earns $60 more per week than does Mr. Johnson. If three-fifths of Mrs. Johnson's weekly salary is equal to two-thirds of Mr. Johnson's weekly salary, how much do the Johnsons earn together in one week?

(A) $540
(B) $600
(C) $780
(D)   960
(E) $1,140

3. If a and c are positive integers such that $\dfrac{2}{5}a = b$ and $b = \dfrac{3c^2}{4}$, what is the least possible value of a ?

(A) 30
(B) 36
(C) 42
(D) 48
(E) 60

HOT TOPICS

You may not realize it, but the SAT is pretty predictable. The test writers like to recycle the same old topics, year after year. Below are some the SAT's greatest hits, with some helpful strategies to get you through these questions.

Percent

With percent questions, it's often helpful to translate English to math. The following terms come up frequently, so make sure you know how to translate them.

English	Math
percent (%)	divide by 100
of	multiply
is	equals
what, what number, some number	x (or any variable)

Let's try an example.

---

1. An auto dealer conducting an inventory found that 40 percent of his vehicles were trucks, and 30 percent of the trucks had four-wheel drive. If 14 of the trucks did <u>not</u> have four-wheel drive, how many of the vehicles were not trucks?

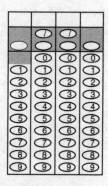

Here's How to Crack It

Remember to use bite-sized pieces. The statement "40 percent of his vehicles were trucks, and 30 percent of the trucks had four-wheel drive" can be translated as $\frac{40}{100} \times \frac{30}{100} = \frac{12}{100}$, so 12% of the vehicles were trucks with four-wheel drive. Therefore, 28% of his vehicles were trucks *without* four-wheel drive. Now, 28% of what equals 14? You can translate this to an equation: $\frac{28}{100}x = 14$. Or if you prefer, set up a proportion: $\frac{28}{100} = \frac{14}{x}$. Either way, solve to find that $x = 50$. This is the total number of vehicles, but remember, RTFQ! We want to know how many vehicles are not trucks. Since 40% <u>are</u> trucks, 60% are not, so $\frac{60}{100}(50) = 30$. The correct answer is 30.

Another great tip for percent problems is to Plug In 100 on any questions that have a variable. Let's try another example.

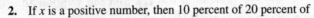

2. If x is a positive number, then 10 percent of 20 percent of $\frac{x}{5}$ is equal to what percent of x ?

   (A) 0.1%
   (B) 0.4%
   (C) 1%
   (D) 2%
   (E) 4%

Here's How to Crack It

To make this problem easier, let's say $x = 100$. Then, the statement "10 percent of 20 percent of $\frac{x}{5}$" becomes $\frac{10}{100} \times \frac{20}{100} \times \frac{100}{5} = 0.4$. Now, 0.4 is what percent of 100? Well, that's the beauty of Plugging In 100! Percent means "out of 100," so the answer is 0.4, or (B).

Mean, Median, and Mode

Average (also called "arithmetic mean") is one of the SAT's favorite subjects. Fortunately, we've invented a great tool for handling average problems, called the average pie.

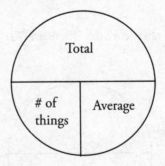

In any average calculation, three components are involved: The total, the number of things, and the average. What makes the average pie so useful is that it represents, in easy-to-read form, the following three versions of the calculation.

$$\frac{\text{Total}}{\text{\# of things}} = \text{Average} \qquad \frac{\text{Total}}{\text{Average}} = \text{\# of things} \qquad \text{\# of things} \times \text{Average} = \text{Total}$$

Any time you have two of the components, you can easily find the third by using the pie. Just think of the horizontal bar as a division symbol, and the vertical bar as a multiplication symbol. Let's look at a sample question.

―――――――――――○―――――――――――

3. The average (arithmetic mean) weight of five gold bars is 9 pounds. After two more bars are added, the average weight increases to 11 pounds. What is the average weight, in pounds, of the two bars that were added?

(A) 13
(B) 14
(C) 15
(D) 16
(E) 17

Here's How to Crack It

Start with the first (bite-sized) sentence. The number of things is 5 and the average is 9, so multiply to find the total and fill in the pie.

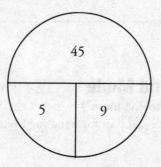

Now do the same for the next sentence. There are 7 things, and the average is 11, so the total is 77.

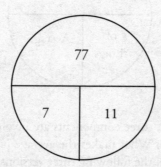

Finally, to tackle the last sentence, make a new pie. There are two things, and the total is $77 - 45 = 32$, so divide to get the average, which is 16, and the correct answer is (D).

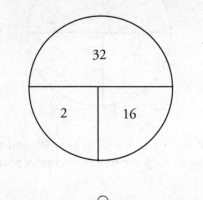

Along with average, the SAT likes to throw in the related concepts of median and mode. Just remember that median is the middle number of an ordered list, and mode is the number (or numbers) that occurs most often in an ordered list. Try a question.

[1, 3, 9, 10, 17]

4. A list of five numbers is shown above. A new list of seven numbers is to be formed from the list above by repeating one number, using the remaining numbers once each, and adding one additional number. If the mean and median of the new list is 9, which of the following CANNOT be the mode?

(A) 1
(B) 3
(C) 9
(D) 10
(E) 17

Here's How to Crack It

This is a tough question, so you need to be organized. You know that the mean (average) of the new list is 9, so make a pie and fill it in.

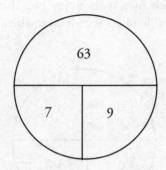

Since the original total is $1 + 3 + 9 + 10 + 17 = 40$, and the new total has to be 63 in order for the mean to be 9, the repeated number plus the new number must equal 23.

You also know that the median is 9, so draw 7 spots and put 9 in the middle.

__   __   __   9   __   __   __

Now, PITA! Start with (C). If the mode is 9, that means the repeated number must be 9. We need to add 23, so the new number is $23 - 9 = 14$. Fill in your list:

1   3   9   9   10   14   17

The median is still 9, so (C) checks out, which means it's <u>NOT</u> the answer.

Which answer should we try next? It's hard to tell, so if you're not sure, pick a direction and go! Let's try (D). If the mode is 10, that's the number we repeat, so the new number is $23 - 10 = 13$. Now fill in the list again.

1   3   9   10   10   13   17

This time, the median is 10, but since the question states that the median is 9, 10 cannot be the mode, and the correct answer is (D).

———————————○———————————

One of the keys to mean, median, and mode questions is to stay organized. Using the average pie and writing everything down will help you to avoid overlooking important pieces of the puzzle.

Counting and Probability

When a question asks how many ways there are to put things in an order, use your pencil! Draw a slot for each element in the problem, and fill in the number of options for each slot.

---

5. Five cyclists are competing in a race. If there are no ties, and all cyclists finish the race, in how many different orders could the five cyclists finish?

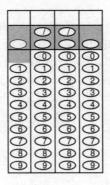

Here's How to Crack It

Draw five slots, representing first through fifth place. Any of the cyclists could win, so there are five options for the first slot. Since *someone* wins, there are only four options for the second slot, and so on. Here's what your diagram looks like:

$$\underline{5} \quad \underline{4} \quad \underline{3} \quad \underline{2} \quad \underline{1}$$

All you have to do is multiply the possibilities, so $5 \times 4 \times 3 \times 2 \times 1 = 120$.

On some counting questions, restrictions will be placed on some of the slots. When this happens, tackle the restricted slots first.

6. How many four-digit even integers are there in which each digit is prime and no digits are repeated?

(A) 6
(B) 12
(C) 18
(D) 24
(E) 36

Here's How to Crack It

Start by listing out the prime digits: 2, 3, 5, and 7. Remember, 1 is not prime. Next, make 4 slots for the digits. The restricted spot is the units (or "ones") digit. Since the number must be even, the units digit can only be 2, so there is just one option for that spot. Now fill in the remaining spots, and multiply. Your diagram should look like this:

$$\underline{3} \times \underline{2} \times \underline{1} \times \underline{1} = 6$$

There are six possibilities, so the correct answer is (A).

———————————◯———————————

If you found this question at all confusing, or were unsure of how to go about it, consider listing out the possibilities instead. Very often in these questions, the right answer is small enough that you can list out the options in less than a minute. In this case, the number can only start with 3, 5, or 7, so list all the the possibilities that start with 3, then with 5, etc. Here they are:

> 3572
> 3752
> 5372
> 5732
> 7352
> 7532

Now that wasn't so bad, was it?

Probability questions are often related to counting questions. Here's the basic definition of probability:

$$\text{Probability} = \frac{\text{number of desired options}}{\text{number of possible options}}$$

Let's try a question.

7. A six-sided die with the faces numbered one through six is rolled three times, and the results of the three rolls are added together. What is the probability that the sum of the three rolls is less than five?

(A) $\dfrac{1}{216}$

(B) $\dfrac{1}{108}$

(C) $\dfrac{1}{54}$

(D) $\dfrac{1}{36}$

(E) $\dfrac{1}{27}$

Here's How to Crack It

Start with the easy part of probability—the denominator. For each of the three rolls, there are six options, so the denominator is $6 \times 6 \times 6 = 216$. The numerator is trickier. Since the sum must be less than five, the sum can only be 3 or 4. Before you read any further, try listing out all the possible ways to get a sum of 3 or 4.

Finished? Here's what you should have:

1, 1, 1
2, 1, 1
1, 2, 1
1, 1, 2

Since there is one way to get a sum of 3, and three ways to get a sum of 4, the probability is $\dfrac{4}{216} = \dfrac{1}{54}$, and the correct answer is (C).

Sequences

Like several of the topics in this chapter, the most important thing with SAT sequences is to be organized. If a question asks you about the first six terms of a sequence, make slots for each term and label them. Like this:

$$1^{st} \qquad 2^{nd} \qquad 3^{rd} \qquad 4^{th} \qquad 5^{th} \qquad 6^{th}$$

___ \qquad ___ \qquad ___ \qquad ___ \qquad ___ \qquad ___

It also helps to look for patterns that will make the question easier. Let's try an example.

$$2^{-9}, 2^{-9} + 2^{-9}, 2^{-9} + 2^{-9} + 2^{-9}, \ldots$$

8. The first term in the sequence above is 2^{-9}, and each term after the first is 2^{-9} more than the previous term. Which term of the sequence has a value of 2^{-6}?

   (A) 3rd
   (B) 4th
   (C) 6th
   (D) 8th
   (E) 9th

Here's How to Crack It

Start by making a diagram like the one above. Always map out at least one more term than the test gives you; the test writers deliberately try to give you too few terms to spot a pattern. Then, see if you can find a pattern. Ask yourself: Is there a simpler way to write the 2nd, 3rd, and later terms? In fact, there is. We could write the 2nd term as 2×2^{-9}, the 3rd as 3×2^{-9}, the 4th as 4×2^{-9}, and so on. Next, since the question is about exponents, think about your exponent rules. When the base numbers are the same, we multiply by adding the exponents (for example $3^4 \times 3^5 = 3^9$). If we rewrite the 4th term as $2^2 \times 2^{-9}$, then we can add the exponents to get 2^{-7}. Now we're onto something! If we keep going, the 8th term will be $8 \times 2^{-9} = 2^3 \times 2^{-9} = 2^{-6}$. The correct answer is (D).

For the next question, see if you can spot the appropriate strategy to use.

$$\frac{1}{j}, \frac{1}{2}, \frac{j}{4}, \dots$$

9. In the sequence shown above, the first term is $\frac{1}{j}$ for all values of j greater than 2. Each term after the first is equal to the preceding term multiplied by a constant. Which of the following, in terms of j, is equal to the sixth term of the sequence?

(A) $\dfrac{j^2}{8}$

(B) $\dfrac{j^2}{16}$

(C) $\dfrac{j^3}{16}$

(D) $\dfrac{j^3}{32}$

(E) $\dfrac{j^4}{32}$

Here's How to Crack It

If you used Plugging In on this question, you spotted the smart strategy!

Since $j > 2$, let's see what happens if we pick $j = 3$. Then, the first three terms are $\frac{1}{3}$, $\frac{1}{2}$, and $\frac{3}{4}$. It's not easy to spot the relationship between these numbers. Is each term really the preceding term multiplied by a constant? It's hard to tell, so let's pick a number that makes the math easier. If $j = 4$, then the first three terms are $\frac{1}{4}$, $\frac{1}{2}$, and 1. Now we can see the relationship: Each term is double the previous term. Armed with this knowledge, you should make a diagram for the first six terms.

1st	2nd	3rd	4th	5th	6th
$\dfrac{1}{4}$	$\dfrac{1}{2}$	1	2	4	8

The sixth term is 8, so that's our target. Now plug $j = 4$ into the answers, and pick the one that equals 8; it's (E).

Equations

Although Plugging In and PITA are extremely valuable strategies, once in a while you just have to write equations and solve. This often happens near the end of the grid-in section. When you're faced with this situation, translate the word problem carefully, and pay close attention to what the problem is asking for. Let's try an example.

---

10. Two rival cell-phone companies have different rate structures. Company X charges a flat rate of $0.15 per minute. Company Y charges $0.25 per minute for the first five minutes, and $0.10 for each minute after the first five. If a call costs the same amount with either plan, how long, in minutes, does that call last?

Here's How to Crack It

Let's break this down into bite-sized pieces. We'll say that $x =$ the number of minutes. A call with the company X costs $0.15x$. A call with company Y costs—be careful here—$5(0.25) + 0.1(x - 5)$. The two calls cost the same amount, so set them equal to each other and solve; you should get $x = 15$, so the correct answer is 15.

Sometimes a question will require two variables, so you'll need to write two equations. Try the next question.

11. On Saturday, Abeke participated in a long-distance race. After the race, he learned that 11 more runners finished before him than finished after him. He also learned that the total number of runners who finished the race was four times the number of runners who finished after him. How many runners finished the race before Abeke did?

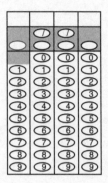

Here's How to Crack It

When we first discussed bite-sized pieces, we said that the test writers will often hide the most useful information near the end of a problem. That's definitely the case here. The second sentence is much easier to handle than the first, so let's deal with it first. But even before that, draw a map or picture of the problem! The total is four times the number who finished after Abeke. Let's say the total = t, and the number who finished after Abeke = x. Therefore, $t = 4x$. Now let's translate the first sentence. If x runners finished after Abeke, then $x + 11$ finished before him, and the total number is $x + (x + 11) + 1$ (we have to count Abeke), which simplifies to $2x + 12$. Now we can write a second equation: $t = 2x + 12$. From the first equation, substitute $4x$ for t in the second equation, so now you have $4x = 2x + 12$. Solve this to get $x = 6$.

Wait! Stop! Don't forget to RTFQ! The question asks how many runners finished *before* Abeke, which is $x + 11$, so the correct answer is $6 + 11 = 17$. No matter how pleased you are when you've solved a question, don't forget to READ THE FULL QUESTION.

Chapter 7
Math Drills:
Answers and
Explanations

CHAPTER 4—FUNDAMENTALS, GEOMETRY, FUNCTIONS

Try It Drill 1

1. **4**   Question 1 deals with the basic properties of integers as they are squared or cubed. Any squared value will be positive, so x can be either negative or positive. On the other hand, y can only be positive, since its cube is positive (a cubed negative number will always result in a negative). Remember to RTFQ! The question asks for **distinct** values of $x + y$. Start by writing down all possible values for x and y. Since x^2 is less than 4, the only possible values for x are -1, -1, 0, and 1. Since y^3 is less than 25 but greater than zero, the possible values for y are 1 and 2.

Since there are three values for x and two for y, you might assume the answer is $3 \times 2 = 6$. But like most easy short cuts on the SAT, this is a trap. Write it out! Sum the values systematically:

$$-1 + 1 = 0$$
$$-1 + 2 = 1$$
$$0 + 1 = 1$$
$$0 + 2 = 2$$
$$1 + 1 = 2$$
$$1 + 2 = 3$$

Since the distinct values of $x + y$ are 0, 1, 2, and 3, the answer is 4.

2. **B**   This is a good opportunity to Plug In. Suppose $a = 3$. Then the question becomes "how many odd integers are between 5 and 14, inclusive?" List them: 5, 7, 9, 11, and 13.

3. **C**   It is important to realize that K is a digit, not a variable. There are several ways to tackle this problem. One way is to actually find a value for K. "Divisible" means a remainder of zero, so use your calculator to try multiples of 7 until you find one that ends with 9. You'll find that $7 \times 17 = 119$, so $K = 1$. Now you just need to find the remainder when 115 is divided by 7 (K could also be 8, because $7 \times 27 = 189$, but the process would be the same).

A slightly more direct route is to realize that that if $1K9$ has a remainder of zero, then $1K8$ has a remainder of 6, $1K7$ has a remainder of 5, and so on. Either way, the answer is (C).

Try It Drill 2

1. **D** There are several ways to solve this one. Here is an efficient way. Line *BF* has 180 degrees. Since *x* + *y* = 70 degrees, then angle *GOF* must be 110 degrees. Since opposite angles are congruent, angle *BOD* is also 110 degrees. Finally, since line *CO* bisects this angle, angle *BOC* is half this size, or 55 degrees.

2. **B** To tackle this problem efficiently, try penciling in every angle that's equal. Like this:

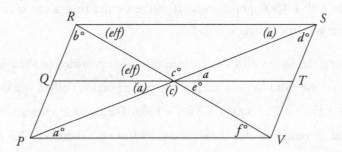

   Note that angles *e* and *f* are also equal, as indicated above. Now we can clearly see that *a*, *c*, and either *e* or *f* make up straight line *QT*. Therefore, the correct answer is (B).

3. **D** This one is tricky. Draw in lines BF and CE. Since lines *BE* and *CF* are equal lengths, *BCEF* must be a rectangle. The diagonals of a rectangle intersect at their midpoints, so point *O* is actually the midpoint of *BE* and *CF*. Therefore, *BO* = *FO* = *CO* = *EO*. Since *AD* intersects point *O* and is parallel to *BC* and *EF*, it must bisect ∠*BOF*, so angles *BOA* and *FOA* must be congruent, which also means that angles *BAO* and *FAO* are also congruent. Since ∠*BAF* is 90°, angles *BAO* and *FAO* must be 45° each. There are 180° in a triangle, so angles *BOA* and *FOA* are each 30°. Finally, there are 180 degrees in a line, so ∠*BOA* + ∠*FOA* + ∠*BOC* = 180°, so ∠*BOC* − 30° − 30° = 120° or answer choice (D).

Try It Drill 3

1. **C** Don't let the diagram throw you. The base of a triangle is always perpendicular to its height. The long way to solve this is to use the Pythagorean Theorem to find the length of the third side: $4^2 + b^2 = 8^2$, so $b^2 = 48$ and $b = 4\sqrt{3}$. Now, put this into the area formula for a triangle: $\frac{1}{2}(4)(4\sqrt{3}) = 8\sqrt{3}$.

   The faster way to solve is to recognize that this is a 30-60-90 right triangle. Since two sides of a right triangle determine the third side, any right triangle in which the hypotenuse is twice one of the legs *must* be a 30-60-90 right triangle. If you recognize this, it can save you some time on calculations. Either way, the answer is (C).

2. **C** Begin by labeling the figure with all of the information provided in the problem. Next, find the angle measure for the third angle in each of the two triangles. When you do so, you will find that $a = e = 50$, $c = \angle EBD = 30$, and $d = \angle ABC = 100$. The two triangles are similar. It may help to redraw the smaller triangle so that the similar sides line up. Therefore, side AB corresponds to DE and AC corresponds to BE. Begin by using process of elimination to narrow your answer choices. The question asks about side AB, and only side DE corresponds to AB, so eliminate (B) and (D). Next, note that AB is longer than DE, so eliminate (A). To solve, use the information given: $BE = \frac{2}{3}AC$. Since this will be true of any corresponding pairs of sides, $DE = \frac{2}{3}AB$. Manipulate this equation by multiplying both sides by $\frac{3}{2}$ to get $\frac{3}{2}DE = AB$, which is answer choice (C).

3. **A** Start by drawing line segments AC and BD, label their intersection as O. Since AO and DO are the same lengths, $\angle AOD$ is a 45-45-90 right triangle (*any* right triangle with two legs that are the same is automatically a 45-45-90). Since the hypotenuse is $\sqrt{2}$, $AO = DO = 1$. See the figure below:

   As mentioned two questions ago, any right triangle in which the hypotenuse is twice on of the legs must be a 30-60-90 right triangle, so BO is $\sqrt{3}$. Now, use the Pythagorean Theorem to find the length of OC, which is 3. Next, use the area formula of a triangle to find the area of triangles ABC and ACD. Area of $ABC = \frac{1}{2}(\sqrt{3})(4) = 2\sqrt{3}$ and area of $ACD = \frac{1}{2}(1)(4) = 2$. Finally, set this into a ratio, being careful to match the order asked in the question: Area of ACD to area of ABC, so 2 to $2\sqrt{3}$, which reduces to 1 to $\sqrt{3}$. The correct answer is (A).

Try It Drill 4

1. **C** Begin by drawing the figure described. The room is square and has an area of 144 ft². Since the area of a square is s^2, then each side of the room measures 12ft. Next, draw the circular rug in the center of the room. Be sure to leave 1 foot of space between the rug and each wall. The figure should now appear similar to the one below:

   Since there is 1 foot of space on each side, the diameter of the rug must be 10ft and the radius 5ft. The area of a circle is $A = \pi r^2$, so $A = 5^2\pi$ or 25π. This translates to an actual value of about 78.5 square feet, but we're looking for the closest answer, which is (C).

2. **B** Begin by drawing lines AO and CO in order to highlight the minor arc distance better:

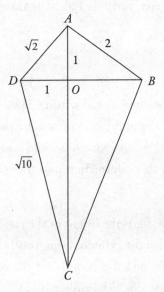

   Since the problem mentions the area of the circle, write down the formula $A = \pi r^2 = 64\pi$. Therefore, $r = 8$, which is the distance of AO and CO. The problem mentions an arc length, so calculate the circumference: $C = 2\pi r = 16\pi$. Now, use a proportion to find the measure of central angle AOC:

   $\dfrac{x}{360°} = \dfrac{4\pi}{16\pi}$ where x is the central angle measure. Central angle AOC is 90°, which is bisected by line segment BO. Therefore, there are two 45-45-90 triangles. The hypotenuse AO is 8, so use the properties of a 45-45-90 triangle to find that BO is $\dfrac{8}{\sqrt{2}} = 4\sqrt{2}$. The answer is (B).

3.   **D**   This is a tricky problem. However, always begin by labeling what is known. Any line from the center of a circle to a point on the circle is a radius. Therefore, in order to find the perimeter of *ABCD*, you need to find the radii of circles *A* and *C*. First, draw line segment *AC*. Since *A* and *C* are the centers of the circle, but also lie on the circumference of the other circle, these two circles must be identical. See the figure below:

All radii are equal, so the shaded region is formed from two equilateral triangles. Work with only one of the two circles. Start by halving the perimeter to 20π. Since there are two equilateral triangles, $\angle BAD$ must be 120°, or one-third of the full circle. Knowing this, we can set up a proportion to find the radius: $\dfrac{\text{inscribed angle}}{360} = \dfrac{\text{arc}}{\text{Circumference}}$, so $\dfrac{120}{360} = \dfrac{20\pi}{2\pi r}$. Solving, we *get* $r = 30$. Multiply by 4 to get the perimeter, which is 120. The answer is (D).

Try It Drill 5

1.   **2**   Begin by drawing the figure, labeling it, and writing down the volume formula for a right circular cylinder: $V = \pi r^2 h$. Now, put the information from the problem into the formula: $100\pi = \pi r^2(4)$ and solve for *r*; you should get $r = 5$. Now draw and label cylinder *B*. The radius of *B* is twice that of *A*, so $r = 10$. Now, put this information into the volume formula and solve for the height: $200\pi = \pi 10^2 h$, so $h = 2$.

2.   **E**   The first thing you should solve for is the height of the cone: $18\pi = \dfrac{1}{3}\pi(3)^2 h$ so $18\pi = 3\pi h$. Therefore, $h = 6$. Now draw and label the cylinder using this information. The volume of the cylinder is twice that of the cone or 36π and the formula for the volume of a cylinder is $V = \pi r^2 h$. Thus, $36\pi = \pi r^2(6)$, and $r^2 = 6$, and $r = \sqrt{6}$. The answer is (E).

3.   **B**   You are given the volume of the cube, so start there. $V = s^3$, so $64 = s^3$ and $s = 4$. The longest diagonal of the cube will be the diameter of the sphere, so find the diagonal using the "super-Pythagorean" formula: $a^2 + b^2 + c^2 = d^2$. Since this is a cube, all the sides are the same, so $4^2 + 4^2 + 4^2 + d^2$, and $d = \sqrt{48} = 4\sqrt{3}$ (if you don't want to simplify roots, you can just convert to decimals on your calculator). Divide by two to find the radius, which is $2\sqrt{3}$. Now plug that into the formula given in the problem: $V = \dfrac{4}{3}\pi r^3 = \dfrac{4}{3}\pi\left(2\sqrt{3}\right)^3 = 32\pi\sqrt{3}$.

CHAPTER 5—ALTERNATIVE APPROACHES

Try It Drill 1

1. **C** With "must be" style questions, be prepared to Plug In more than once. Begin by choosing a single digit prime number greater than 2. There are only three possible options for x: 3, 5, and 7. An ugly SAT twist on this question is that if you choose $x = 3$ (the most obvious choice), all of the answer choices are prime. Begin with a less obvious choice, such as $x = 5$. Now, check each answer choice. Answer choice (A) becomes $5 - 1$, or 4, which is not prime, answer choice (D) becomes $4(5) + 1$ which is not prime, and answer (E) becomes $5(5) - 4$ which is not prime. Eliminate these three answers. Now, repeat the process with $x = 7$, checking only the remaining answers. Answer (B) becomes $7 + 2$ which is not prime, so eliminate this. Only answer choice (C) is prime with all three single digit prime numbers greater than 2. The answer is (C).

2. **C** Range questions such as this one can be very challenging. Unfortunately, Plugging In on range questions can also be tricky. It may help to consider the logic of a range. Acceptable weights for the shipment will all fall within the range. Weights that are too big or too small cannot be in this range. Always begin by choosing a value in the range: $W = 50$ and check the answers. Answer (B) and (D) are invalid. Since $W = 50$ is within the range, eliminate these two answers. Checking the remaining answers is more challenging. Remember that *only* acceptable weights should make the inequality true, so now plug in an unacceptable number, $W = 40$. This number is outside of the shipment range, so the inequality should be false. Check (A). The inequality is true, so (A) is *not* the correct answer. Check (C). An invalid number does not work, so this one looks good. Finally, check (E). Again, the inequality is true; therefore, answer (E) is incorrect. Eliminate it. The answer is (C).

3. **A** Don't panic with labor-intensive problems such as this. Instead, get rid of the algebra by Plugging In. Also, don't worry about making the numbers realistic. Set the price of the boat as $x = 100$ since this number works well with percentages. Make the markup at auction $y = 20$ and the discount $x = 10$. Now use these numbers to find the price of the boat. Since the markup is 20%, the auction price of the boat is $120. Don later purchased the boat for 10% off. 10% of $120 is $12, so the final purchase price is $108. This is the target number. Now plug those numbers into a calculator: Answer (A) is the only one that matches your target. The answer is (A).

4. **A** Choose numbers that work within the bounds of this problem. Let $a = 3$, $b = 5$, $c = 7$, and $d = 9$. Now, calculate the target: $9^2 - 3^2 = 81 - 9 = 72$. Finally, Plug In $b = 5$ to the answer choices. Only choice (A) matches the target.

5. **B** Challenging exponent questions are among some of the fastest questions on the SAT when you use Plugging In. Set $x = 2$ and run the numbers through the calculator: $3^4 \times 27^1 = 2187$. This is the target. Now, Plug In $x = 2$ to the answers. Only answer (B) matches this target.

Try It Drill 2

1. **D** Start by finding $\overline{OQ}$ and $\overline{OS}$. If the length of the quarter-circle is 6π, then the circumference of the circle would be 24π, and the radius would be 12, so $\overline{OQ} = \overline{OS} = 12$. We also know that the length plus the width of *OPRS* is half the perimeter, or 16. At this point, if you are stuck, use a little POE. There is no good reason π should be part of the answer, so eliminate (A) and (B). Now try to ballpark. $\overline{PR}$ looks like it's nearly as long as $\overline{OS}$ so let's estimate $\overline{PR} = 11$. $\overline{OP}$ looks like it's a bit less than half of $\overline{OQ}$, so let's estimate that $\overline{OP} = 5$. The area would then be $(11)(5) = 55$, which is very close to (D), which is in fact the right answer.

   Suppose you had chosen 10 and 6 as your numbers. Then, your estimate of the area would be 60, which is exactly half way between (D) and (E). What should you do? You should pick one. Always guess if you can eliminate answer choices.

   To actually solve this question is quite difficult and time consuming. To start, let's draw in diagonal $\overline{OR}$. Since it's a radius of the quarter-circle, $\overline{OR} = 12$. Let's also refer to the base and height of *OPRS* as *a* and *b*. We know that $a^2 + b^2 = 12^2 = 144$. We also know that $a + b = 16$, so we can make use of a common quadratic and say that $(a + b)^2 = 16^2 = 256$ Expanding this quadratic gives $a^2 + 2ab + b^2 = 256$. Subtracting $a^2 + b^2$, we get $2ab = 112$. Since *ab* is the area, divide by 2 to get $ab = 56$. The actual lengths of *a* and *b* are irrational numbers, so if you get stuck trying to find them, you could end up wasting a lot of time. Ballparking is probably the best approach for this problem.

2. **C** If the diameter of the largest circle is 12, the radius is 6, and the total area is 36π. If you get stuck after this, it's time to ballpark. The figure looks like it consists of three approximately equal parts, so it's reasonable to guess that the shaded region is $\dfrac{36\pi}{3} = 12\pi$. This is the correct answer. (B) and (C) are quite close, so if you can't decide, pick one!

   To solve this question, isolate the left half of the figure. If we subtract the semicircle with diameter *MN* from the semicircle with diameter *MP*, we will have half of the shaded region. *MP* = 8, so the radius is 4, and the area of the larger semicircle is $\dfrac{\pi(4)^2}{2} = 8\pi$. *MN* = 4, so the radius is 2, and the area of the smaller semicircle is $\dfrac{\pi(2)^2}{2} = 2\pi$. Subtract: $8\pi - 2\pi = 6\pi$. Wait! That's only one of the two shaded areas, so if you picked (A), you forgot to multiply by two. This is the sort of careless error that ballparking can help you avoid.

3. **B** The perimeter of *PQR* is 12, so the sides are 4. If you don't know what to do next, try ballparking. Start by drawing: connect points *S*, *T*, and *V* with straight lines. You can probably see that this divides the figure into 4 identical equilateral triangles, each with a side length of 2. Since the perimeter of triangle *STV* = 6, the perimeter of the shaded region must be a little more than 6. Therefore, eliminate (A) (too small) and (B) (too big). For the remaining answers, use your calculator, or estimate ($\pi \cong 3.1$) to get an approximate value. (B) $\cong$ 6.2, (C) $\cong$ 5.93, and (D) $\cong$ 6.1. Eliminate (C), leaving (B) and (D). If you're not sure which to pick, consider the form the answer should take. The arcs are just portions of a circle, so π + 3 doesn't make sense. Eliminate (D), leaving (B), which is the correct answer.

To solve this question takes some work. First, pencil in the angles in the corners of *PQR* – it's an equilateral triangle, so the angles are all 60°. Therefore, each arc is $\dfrac{60}{360} = \dfrac{1}{6}$ of a circle, and the sum of the three arcs is equal to $\dfrac{3}{6} = \dfrac{1}{2}$ of a circle. The radius of the circle is 2, so the circumference is 4π, and half of that is 2π.

4. **D** This is a very tough problem to solve, so consider ballparking. We have two overlapping circles and each has an area of 36π, so the total area must be less than 72π. How much less? Try drawing in the rest of the circles, like this:

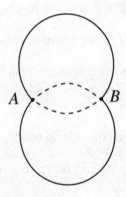

It looks like we have one complete circle and about $\dfrac{7}{8}$ of another. Throw that into your calculator : $36\pi + \dfrac{7}{8}(36\pi) \cong 212$. Now tackle the answer choices. (A) is too small. We know (B) is wrong, because it's the sum of the areas of the two circles. (C) is too small, and (E) is too large. That leaves only (D), which is the correct answer.

To solve the question, you will need to divide up the figure like this:

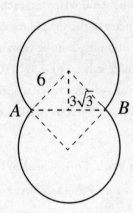

Above line segment AB is a sector that is $\frac{300}{360} = \frac{5}{6}$ of a circle, plus an equilateral triangle. The area of the sector is $\frac{5}{6}(\pi 6^2) = 30\pi$. To find the area of the equilateral triangle, draw in the height, dividing the triangle into a pair of 30-60-90 right triangles, each with sides of 3, $3\sqrt{3}$, and 6. The base of the equilateral triangle is 6, and the height is $3\sqrt{3}$, so the area is $\frac{1}{2}(6)\left(3\sqrt{3}\right) = 9\sqrt{3}$. Therefore, the area of the top half of the figure is $30\pi + 9\sqrt{3}$. Don't forget to multiply by two. This is a treacherous problem with many traps, so even if you end up solving it, a quick ballpark at the outset will help to keep you out of trouble.

5. E   This is not a geometry problem, but the principles of ballparking can still be applied. Jane spends a little less than half her time walking a *lot* faster, so it stands to reason that she would cover more than half the total distance at the faster speed. Another way to look at this is that if she spent half as much time walking at 6 k.p.h. as she did walking 3 k.p.h., the two speeds would balance out, and she would cover the same distance at both speeds. But if that were the case, she would spend $\frac{1}{3}$ of her time walking at the faster speed. Since she spends more than $\frac{1}{3}$ of her time walking fast, she will cover more than half the distance at the faster speed. Notice that only (E) is a fraction greater than $\frac{1}{2}$, so (E) is the only possible answer.

If you want to solve this question exactly, you can use the formula rate × time = distance. Let's say her total time is x. At the beginning, her distance is $6 \times \frac{3}{8}x = \frac{18}{8}x$. For the second part, her distance is $3 \times \dfrac{5}{8}x = \dfrac{15}{8}x$. Therefore, her total distance is $\dfrac{18}{8}x = \dfrac{15}{8}x = \dfrac{33}{8}x$. To find the answer,

divide $\dfrac{18}{8}x$ by $\dfrac{33}{8}x$ to get $\dfrac{6}{11}$.

Alternatively, you could Plug In on this problem. Suppose Jane's total walking time is 6 hours.

First, she walks 3 hours at 6 k.p.h. for a distance of $3 \times 6 = 18$ kilometers. Next, she walks 5 hours

at 3 k.p.h. for a distance of $5 \times 3 = 15$ kilometers. Her total distance was $18 + 15 = 33$; the north-

bound part of the trip was $\dfrac{18}{33} = \dfrac{6}{11}$. Either Plugging In or Ballparking works great here; the worst

strategy is the one you learned in math class. Remember, the goal is to get the question right by the

easiest method.

CHAPTER 6—WORD PROBLEMS AND OTHER HOT TOPICS

Try It Drill 1

1. **A** Start with answer choice (C). If the largest integer is 6, the middle integer is 4, and the smallest is 2. Now check: is $2^2 = 2 \times 6$? No, so move on.

    In this question, it is difficult to tell whether to try (B) or (D) next. That's OK; pick a direction and go! If you make a mistake, it won't take that long to check the other answers. Eventually you will get to (A), where the middle integer is zero and the smallest is –2. Now check: is $(-2)^2 = 2 \times 2$? Yes, so the correct answer is (A).

2. **E** In this question, you may need to mix a bit of basic algebra with Plugging In The Answers. Start with (C). If the Johnsons earn $780, we need to find what each of them earns. Let's say Mr. Johnson's earnings are x. Then, Mrs. Johnson's are $x + 60$, so $2x + 60 = 780$ and $x = 360$. Therefore, Mr. Johnson earns $360, and Mrs. Johnson earns $420. Now, does $\dfrac{3}{5}(420) = \dfrac{2}{3}(360)$? No, so (C) is incorrect. Keep trying until you get to (E). If the Johnson's earn $1,140, then $2x + 60 = 1,140$ and $x = 540$, so Mr. Johnson earns $540 and Mrs. Johnson earns $600. Now check again: does $\dfrac{3}{5}(600) = \dfrac{2}{3}(540)$? Yes it does, so the correct answer is (E).

3. **A** Since this question is asking for the *least* possible value, we should start with (A). If $a = 30$, then

$\dfrac{2}{5}(30) = 12 = b$, and $12 = \dfrac{3c^2}{4}$, so $c^2 = 16$, and c (which must be positive) is 4. The question speci-

fies that a and c must be positive integers, and they are, so answer choice (A) works, and there is no

need to check any other answers.

Chapter 8
Math Test 1

Directions: For this section, solve each problem and decide which is the best of the choices given. Fill in the corresponding circle on the answer sheet. You may use any available space for scratchwork.

 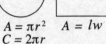 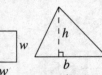 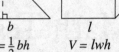
1. If the integer p is 2 less than a factor of 12, then p is the cube of an integer.

   The statement above is true for all of the following values of p EXCEPT

   (A) −8
   (B) −1
   (C)   0
   (D)   1
   (E)   8

2. If $m \leq n$, which of the following must be true?

   (A) $m - n > 1$
   (B) $mn \geq 1$
   (C) $n - m \leq 1$
   (D) $m + n \geq 0$
   (E) $m + n \leq 0$

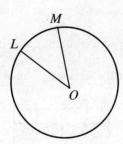

3. In the figure above, O is the center of the circle and the diameter (not shown) has a length of y. If the area of sector LMO is 9π and represents $\dfrac{1}{9}$ of the area of the entire circle, what is the circumference of circle O, in terms of y?

   (A) $\dfrac{y\pi}{2}$

   (B) $y^2\pi$

   (C) $2y\pi$

   (D) $y\pi$

   (E) $\dfrac{y2\pi}{2}$

4. A store reduces the price of a pair of shoes by 15 percent. If the sale price is r dollars, which of the following is the closest approximation of the original price, in dollars, of the shoes, in terms of r?

   (A) $0.85r$
   (B) $0.87r$
   (C) $1.10r$
   (D) $1.15r$
   (E) $1.18r$

5. An athletic trainer coaches only athletes who play football, baseball, and soccer. In a certain month, 3 football players were coached for every 7 baseball players, and 6 soccer players were coached for every football player. If the total number of athletes coached that month was between 375 and 400, how many soccer players were coached?

   (A)   42
   (B)   72
   (C)   98
   (D)   252
   (E)   392

6. Which of the following expressions is equivalent to $4^{2y} \cdot 8^{y}$?

   (A) 2^{3y}
   (B) 2^{5y}
   (C) 2^{7y}
   (D) 4^{3y}
   (E) $4^{3(y^2)}$

7. Scott takes three times longer to pack 12 boxes than Jean takes to pack 7 boxes. What is the ratio of Scott's average packing rate to Jean's average packing rate?

   (A) 2:3
   (B) 4:7
   (C) 7:4
   (D) 7:12
   (E) 7:24

8. The function *f* is defined by $f(x) = 4x + 3$. If $3 \bullet f(r) = 93$, what is the value of *r* ?

9. Let the function *f* be defined by $f(x) = \dfrac{(x^2 - x)}{x}$, where $x \neq 0$. If $f(y) > 10$, what is one possible value of *y* ?

10. A jar contains glass beads of equivalent weights. If 47 glass beads have a total weight of 3.2 ounces, and the maximum capacity of the jar is 4 pounds, how many glass beads can the jar hold? (16 ounces = 1 pound)

11. Two circles, with centers *A* and *B*, respectively, are tangent at Point *C*. The circumference of Circle *A* is 24π, and the distance between Points *A* and *B* is 15. How many times larger than the area of Circle *B* is the area of Circle *A*?

Chapter 9
Math Test 2

Directions: For this section, solve each problem and decide which is the best of the choices given. Fill in the corresponding circle on the answer sheet. You may use any available space for scratchwork.

Reference Information

$A = \pi r^2$
$C = 2\pi r$

$A = lw$

$A = \frac{1}{2}bh$

$V = lwh$

$V = \pi r^2 h$

$c^2 = a^2 + b^2$

Special Right Triangles

The number of degrees of arc in a circle is 360.

The sum of the measures in degrees of the angles of a triangle is 180.

1. At a school field day, Jonah, Vanessa, Keegan, and Samantha will compete in the 100-yard dash. If there are no ties, and there are no other runners in the race, in how many different orders can they finish?

(A) 4
(B) 8
(C) 10
(D) 16
(E) 24

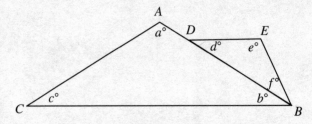

Note: Figure not drawn to scale.

2. In the figure above, point D is on side $\overline{AB}$ of $\triangle ABC$. If $b = f = 30$, $a = 100$, $d = 50$, $\overline{AD} = \frac{1}{3}\overline{AB}$, and $\overline{BE} = \frac{1}{2}\overline{AB}$, which of the following is equal to $\overline{BC}$?

(A) $2\overline{AD}$

(B) $2\overline{AB}$

(C) $4\overline{AD}$

(D) $\overline{AB}\sqrt{2}$

(E) $\overline{AB}\sqrt{3}$

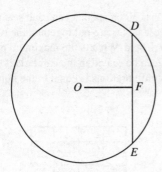

3. In the figure above, the circle has center O and area 169π. The midpoint of $\overline{DE}$ is F, and $\overline{OF} = 12$. What is the length of $\overline{DE}$?

(A)   5
(B)   10
(C)   12
(D)   13
(E)   26

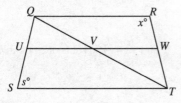

Note: Figure not drawn to scale.

4. In the figure above, $\overline{QR} \parallel \overline{UW} \parallel \overline{ST}$ and $\overline{QV} = \overline{UV}$. If the measure of $\angle QVW$ is 122°, what is the value of $\angle S$?

(A)   29
(B)   58
(C)   61
(D)   116
(E)   122

5. If r is the smallest prime number, which of the following could also be a prime number?

(A) $2r$
(B) $3r$
(C) $r + 2$
(D) $r + 3$
(E) $r + 4$

6. A plane is tangent to the sphere with center O at point P. How many radii of the sphere are parallel to the plane?

(A)   None
(B)   One
(C)   Two
(D)   Three
(E)   More than three

7. In a certain community organization, there are 12 volunteers on the fundraising committee and 10 volunteers on the safety committee. There are a total of 15 volunteers. Of those students, how many are on both committees?

(A) 2
(B) 3
(C) 5
(D) 7
(E) 15

8. In a high school play, 6 students will be chosen to play 6 different roles, with each student playing only one role. How many different assignments of students to roles are possible?

9. A cafeteria has 30 tables that can each seat up to 6 people. If two of these tables are put together, the two tables can seat 10 people. What is the maximum number of people that can be seated in the cafeteria if the number of 10-people configurations is equal to the number of 6-people configurations?

10. If $\dfrac{a}{b+2} = \dfrac{3}{5}$ and $\dfrac{b}{c} = \dfrac{2}{3}$, what is one possible value of $2b - c$?

11. When 47 is divided by positive integer x, the remainder is 5. How many values of x are possible?

Chapter 10
Math Tests:
Answers and
Explanations

MATH TEST 1

1. **E** This question is an ideal candidate to tackle with Plugging In The Answers, but because it hasn't given a value to match in the question, you don't need to start with answer choice (C). Start with answer choice (A), and work through the answers to identify which ones, if any, are 2 less than a factor of 12. Remember that negative numbers can be factors, too, so (A) and (B) both satisfy the first part of the statement. (C) and (D) are each also 2 less than a factor of 12, meaning they can be eliminated, too. That leaves you with only answer choice (E).

2. **C** With variables in the question and variables in the answers, you should plug in on this question. Also, because it asks what MUST BE true, you should be prepared to plug in more than once. So if $m = 2$ and $n = 3$, answer choice (A) is $2 - 3 > 1$, which is false. Answer choice (B) is $2 \times 3 \geq 1$, which is true, so leave it in. (C) is $2 - 3 \leq 1$, which is true, so leave it in. (D) equals $2 + 3 \geq 0$, which is true, so leave it in. (E) is $2 + 3 \leq 0$, which is false, so eliminate it. Now choose two different numbers. Pay particular attention to the ways they're trying to trick you: Try Plugging In the same value for both integers, or try a negative number or zero since there are no restrictions on what kind of values you can plug in. Let's say both m and n equal 0. (B) equals $0 \times 0 \geq 1$, which is false. Eliminate (B). (C) becomes $0 - 0 \leq 1$, which is true, so leave it. (D) becomes $0 + 0 \geq 0$, which is true again, so leave it. Now try negative values, like $m = -6$ and $n = 0$. Answer (C) is true, with $-6 - 0 \leq 1$. Leave it. (D) says $-6 + 0 \geq 0$, which is not true, so get rid of it. Your answer is (C).

3. **D** Variables in the question and variables in the answers indicate that you should Plug In. But the question also gives information to work with, so pay attention to those details. Remember the proportional aspect of circles:

$$\frac{\text{part}}{\text{whole}} = \frac{\theta}{360} = \frac{\text{arc}}{\text{circumference}} = \frac{\text{sector area}}{\text{total area}}$$

Since the area of the sector is 9π and is also $\frac{1}{9}$ of the entire circle, set up the following proportion:

$$\frac{1}{9} = \frac{9\pi}{x}$$

That means the area is 81π. Using the area formula, solve for the radius: That proves the radius is equal to 9, and the circumference ($C = 2\pi r$) is 18π, which is the target. Pay careful attention to the fact that the question says that y is the diameter, which must be 18. Plug 18 into the answer choices, and (D) is the only one that matches.

4. **E** Variables in the question and answers mean to Plug In! Since the question deals with percents, start with $100 for the original price of the shoes. The price is reduced 15%, which means it is now $85, or r. The question is asking for the original price, which makes $100 the target. Plug $85 into the answer choices to find the one that comes closest to $100. Answer (D) is $97.75 and (E) is $100.30. (E) is closer, and is therefore the closest approximation.

5. **D**   Use the Ratio Box to keep your information organized. The first relationship given is 3 football players for every 7 baseball players, so enter those values into the Ratio line. The next piece says 6 soccer players for every football player; since you've already put 3 in for football players, you can't just put in 6 for soccer. Set up a proportion: $\dfrac{6 \text{ soccer}}{1 \text{ football}} = \dfrac{x \text{ soccer}}{3 \text{ football}}$, and you'll find that you should actually enter 18 on the ratio line under Soccer.

Next, add all the numbers on the Ratio line (3 + 7 + 18 = 28) and enter that under the Total on the Ratio line. The next piece of information given is that the total actual number of players coached in the month was between 375 and 400, so you'll have to do a bit of ballparking to determine your multiplier. The Total on the Ratio line (28) is pretty close to 30, and to get from 30 to at least 375 you'll have to multiply by at least 11 or 12. Try 12, and see what your actual number becomes: 28 × 12 = 336; that's not big enough, so try 13 or 14: 28 × 13 = 364, which isn't quite big enough. 28 × 14 = 392, which is exactly what you're looking for. Write 14 in every space on the Multiplier line.

Now, don't go crazy doing all the math to figure out how many athletes in each sport were trained! The question asks only about how many soccer players were coached, so only do what you need to answer the question! The correct answer is (D).

FOOTBALL	BASEBALL	SOCCER	TOTAL
3	7	18	28
14	14	14	14
		252	392

6. **C**   Anytime a question asks you to manipulate exponents, remember that exponent rules apply only to the expressions with the same base, so start by converting each expression into the same base. Both 4 and 8 are powers of 2, so you should get

$$4^{2y} \cdot 8^y = (2^2)^{2y} \cdot (2^3)^y = 2^{4y} \cdot 2^{3y} = 2^{7y}$$

7. **B**   One of the ways ETS (the people who administer the SAT), makes questions challenging is by combining multiple concepts into one problem. This question is a ratio question, but there's also information missing, and it asks for the ratio of their averages, not their time or actual number of boxes packed. Start by Plugging In for the missing information so you can actually work with values. The missing information is the amount of time it takes each of them to pack different numbers of boxes. So, say Jean takes 2 hours to pack 4 boxes; if it takes Scott three times longer to pack his 10 boxes, that means it takes him 6 hours.

Next use a Rate Pie (the same thing as an Average Pie, but with Distance/Work on the top, Time on the bottom left and Rate on the bottom right) to determine their individual rates:

Scott:

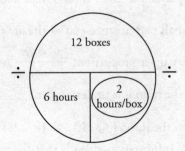

Jean:

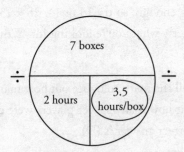

The last step is to find the ratio of Scott's average to Jean's average. Currently, it looks like 2:3.5, but it's unusual for ETS to put decimals in average questions, so you'll need to convert that into whole numbers: 4:7, which is answer choice (B). Notice that (C) is a trap answer: it reverses the ratio, so read the question carefully!

8. 7   Start by dividing $3 \cdot f(r) = 93$ by 3 to get to the value of $f(r)$, 31. Now set the original function equal to 31 and solve:

$$f(x) = 4x + 3$$
$$f(r) = 4r + 3$$
$$31 = 4r + 3$$
$$\underline{-3 \quad\quad -3}$$
$$\frac{28}{4} = \frac{4r}{4}$$
$$7 = r$$

9.   **12 (any value larger than 11)**

You have variables, so Plug In! Start out with $y = 5$ to see what you get. $25 - 5$ is 20, divided by 5 is 4: that doesn't meet the requirement that the function needs to be larger than 10. Try plugging in 10, which yields 9—closer! Try again with 11, which gives you EXACTLY 10. Be careful, though;

the question said the function must be LARGER than 10, so y cannot be equal to 11. That's enough information, though, to know that anything larger than 11 will satisfy the condition, so you can answer with any value larger than 11.

10. **940** Solve this using proportions. $\dfrac{16 \text{ ounces}}{1 \text{ pound}} = \dfrac{x \text{ ounces}}{3 \text{ pounds}}$ will tell you that the capacity of the jar is

64 ounces. Next, $\dfrac{47 \text{ cookies}}{3.2 \text{ ounces}} = \dfrac{x \text{ cookies}}{64 \text{ ounces}}$ allows you to determine that the jar can accommodate

940 cookies.

11. **16** Remember the three steps for Geometry:

1 – Draw the figure
2 – Label the info
3 – Write the formula(s)

Step 1: Draw two circles that touch in exactly one point; label the center of one circle A and the other B, and the point where they touch is C.

Step 2: Draw a line from A to B, and mark its length of 15. Also note that the circumference of Circle A is 24π.

Step 3: Write your formulas for circumference and area: $C = 2\pi r$ or $C = \pi d$. $A = \pi r^2$.

Solve for the radius of Circle A: $24\pi = 2\pi r$, or $r = 12$. Label this on Circle A. That means the radius of Circle B is 3.

Next, solve for the area of both circles:

Circle A	Circle B
$A = \pi r^2 = \pi(12^2) = 144\pi$	$A = \pi r^2 = \pi(3^2) = 9\pi$

The question asks how much larger the area of Circle A is than the area of Circle B, so divide $\dfrac{144\pi}{9\pi} = 16$. So the area of Circle A is 16 times larger than the area of Circle B.

MATH TEST 2

1.   **E**   "How many different" is an indicator that this is an arrangements question. Write out the number of spaces you're filling:

_____   _____   _____   _____

How many of the four runners could potentially finish first? 4. Put that in the first space.

___4__   _____   _____   _____

Once one student passes the finish line, how many students are left who could potentially finish second? 3. Then how many are left who could finish third? 2. And that leaves only one to finish last. Multiply all the values together, and get 24 different orders in which they can finish, which is answer choice (E).

$$\underline{4} \times \underline{3} \times \underline{2} \times \underline{1} = 24$$

2.   **C**   Remember the three steps for Geometry:

1 – Draw the figure
2 – Label the info
3 – Write the formula(s)

Step 1 – They've given you a figure, so you don't need to draw anything.

Step 2 – Write in the information they've given you: $b = f = 30$, $a = 100$, $d = 50$. If you continue to determine all of the angle measurements, you'll find that these are two similar triangles.

Step 3 – Write the formula(s). There aren't actually any formulas that you need to solve this question (apart from the basic formulas for the sum of angles in a triangle and for similar triangles).

Once you recognize the similar triangles, the next step is to Plug In for the unknown lengths of the sides they've given in the question: $\overline{AD} = \frac{1}{3}\,\overline{AB}$. Plug in 2 for $\overline{AD}$, which means that $\overline{AB}$ is 6, $\overline{BD}$ is 4, and $\overline{BE}$ is 3. Next, use a proportion to determine $\overline{BC}$: $\frac{\overline{AB}}{\overline{EB}} = \frac{\overline{BC}}{\overline{BD}}$ or, $\frac{6}{3} = \frac{\overline{BC}}{4}$. So $\overline{BC} = 8$. That's the target.

Now go back to the answers and Plug In the appropriate side lengths to determine which answer choices match 8, and only answer (C) does.

3.   **B**   Remember the three steps for Geometry:

   1 – Draw the figure
   2 – Label the info
   3 – Write the formula(s)

   Step 1 – A figure is already provided.

   Step 2 – Label $\overline{OF}$ = 12, and identify that $\overline{DF}$ and $\overline{DE}$ are congruent.

   Step 3 – Write the formula for area of a circle, since that's what they've provided. $A = \pi r^2$. Solve to find $r = 13$. The radius isn't drawn in, so draw in either $\overline{OD}$ or $\overline{OE}$. You will now see that you have a right triangle with one leg of 12 and a hypotenuse of 13, which should trigger your memory of Special Right Triangles: 5-12-13. That means that both $\overline{DF}$ and $\overline{EF}$ are 5. Be careful as you read the question: it's asking for $\overline{DE}$, which is 10, *not* $\overline{DF}$ or $\overline{EF}$, which are each 5 . The credited response is (B).

4.   **C**   Anytime you see parallel lines, you need to be thinking about the angles they create. Extend the parallel lines so the angles are easier to see. If $\angle QVW$ is 122°, then $\angle QVU$ is 58°. The question also says that $QV = UV$, so you know that the angles across from those sides are equal; with 180° in a triangle, and 58° already accounted for, that means VQU and VUQ are both 61°. Then, using parallel lines, you can determine that angle s will also be equal to 61°, or answer (C).

5.   **D**   The key to nailing this question is to remember that 2 is the smallest prime number. 1 is NOT considered prime. So Plug In 2 for each answer choice, and (D) is the only choice that results in a prime number.

6.   **E**   Remember the three steps for Geometry:

   1 – Draw the figure
   2 – Label the info
   3 – Write the formula(s)

   Step 1 – Draw the figure – this is the most challenging step of the question – sketch it the best you can. Draw a circle, and a vertical line, as if you were looking at it in two dimensions instead of three.

   Step 2 – There's no info to label.

   Step 3 – There are also no formulas to write.

Once you have a circle sketched with a vertical line tangent to it, look at the drawing as if you're looking straight down at a ball leaning up against a wall. If you slice the ball right down the middle on a plane that is parallel to the wall, you would have an infinite number of radii on the plane you just cut. So, the answer is (E), more than three.

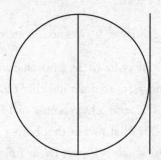

7. **D** You'll need the Group Formula to solve this question:

Total = Group 1 + Group 2 – Both + Neither

Fill in the information you know:

15 = 12 + 10 – B + 0

Remember, the question gave no indication of any volunteers other than those on the fundraising and safety committees, so the 'Neither' category would equal zero.

Solve, and you find that there are 7 volunteers who serve on both committees, or answer choice (D).

8. **720** "How many different" is an indicator that this is an arrangements question. Give yourself 6 spaces to fill, and ask yourself how many students can fill each space:

How many students could be assigned to the first role? 6

After one is assigned to the first role, how many are left to fill the second? 5

After that student is assigned, how many are left to fill the third? 4

Continue this thought process, and then multiply: 6 × 5 × 4 × 3 × 2 × 1 = 720.

9. **160** The tricky part here is that the question indicates that the number of CONFIGURATIONS is equal. You can use a Ratio Box again to determine how many configurations you'll have. In the Ratio Box, you'll have a column for the 6-seat configurations, and a column for the 10-seat configurations. You'll have one table for each of the 6-seat groups, and 2 tables for each of the 10-seat groups, so put a '1' and a '2' in each column, respectively, on the Ratio line. If you add those together, you'll have a total of 3, and then your multiplier would be 10 to get a total of 30 tables.

6-seat Configuration	10-seat Configuration	Total
1 table	2 tables	3
10	10	10
10	20	30

This tells you that you have ten 6-seat configurations and ten 10-seat configurations. So you'd have $10 \times 6 + 10 \times 10 = 160$.

10.   4   Variables in the question mean you should consider Plugging In. You could start by making $a = 3$ and $b = 3$, but then things get sticky when you go to the second equation. So, reformat the equation to $\dfrac{a}{b+2} = \dfrac{6}{10}$. Now, you can see that $a = 6$ and $b = 8$ would work. This makes things a lot easier when you go to the second equation: $\dfrac{8}{c} = \dfrac{2}{3}$. Solve, and you find that $c = 12$. Next, solve for what the question is actually asking:

11.   5   A variable in the question means to Plug In—but remember to pay attention to the constraints presented in the question. Also, be methodical as you Plug In so you can identify any patterns that may arise.

In order to have a remainder of 5 when 47 is divided by x, x must be a factor of 42. So, list the factors of 42:

1   42
2   21
3   14
6   7

Now, plug those in for x, and determine whether that results in a remainder of 5:

47 ÷ 1 = 47   R0 No
47 ÷ 2 = 23   R1 No
47 ÷ 3 = 15   R2 No
47 ÷ 6 = 7   R5 Yes!
47 ÷ 7 = 6   R5 Yes!
47 ÷ 14 = 3   R5 Yes!
47 ÷ 21 = 2   R5 Yes!
47 ÷ 42 = 1   R5 Yes!

That means there are 5 values of x that will produce a remainder of 5 when 47 is divided by x.

Part III
Reading

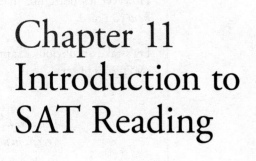

Chapter 11
Introduction to
SAT Reading

INTRODUCTION

When you read a book or watch a movie, you're typically able to make a choice. The questions you may typically ask yourself when checking the bookstore shelves or the movie listings may not only be, "*What* would I like see or read?" but also, whether you realize it or not, "*How* would I like to see or read?"

You are actually reading all the time, and *how* you read can take a tremendous number of forms. The basics are always the same: You know how to read English, the letters combine to make words, and those words make sentences and paragraphs. Somehow in the middle of all of it, meaning is dumped into your brain. However it's not quite that simple because ultimately *what* you read determines *how* you read.

Let's take an obvious example. What do you do differently when you read these two pieces of text?

1.   *Tomorrow, and tomorrow, and tomorrow,*
        Creeps in this petty pace from day to day
        To the last syllable of recorded time,
        And all our yesterdays have lighted fools
        The way to dusty death. Out, out, brief candle!

2.   *I saw Lisa the other day lol she told me the funniest thing oh and what are you doing this Fri?*

It's safe to say that we're looking at two very different things here. The first comes from Shakespeare's *Macbeth*, and the second comes from a text message.

One big difference in your approach is that you're more likely to read the first example much more carefully because you'll likely be reading it in an English class. Its language is unfamiliar, so understanding it is the first basic hurdle. Once you get through to a basic understanding of the words, there's the question of meaning. You might look at the repetition of the word "tomorrow" or try to find the referents for "this petty pace" or "brief candle." You could spend a lifetime reading these lines, as many scholars have, and find something new or newly meaningful each time.

You'll use a much different skill set on the other text. There's no reason to look at how the language is used here. The weird non-grammar of the passage isn't really worthy of attention either. This text message is all content, and all the basic information you need to receive from it is right there. You'll never have a reason to read it again.

So that's a pretty obvious example. Shakespeare requires a different kind of reading from that of a text message. The point is not that one is better than the other (do you think your friends would want to text you anymore if you subjected all their text messages to intense literary scrutiny?). They're just different.

Now how about the Shakespeare passage in different contexts? How, for example, would it change the way you read if

1. You read the "Tomorrow, and tomorrow, and tomorrow" speech in a class
2. You read the "Tomorrow, and tomorrow, and tomorrow" speech on an English test

We've already thought about how you'd read in the first instance. Now, in the second, you're reading the same speech, but this time you have to read it on a test.

There are a number of things you'd have to do differently this time. For one, you'll probably have to answer some question about the text: You may be asked to analyze the language or literary devices, you may be asked to identify the speaker (Macbeth!), or you may be asked to tie the passage to some theme or larger question you discussed in class. The point, though, is that you're asked to be a more active participant in your reading than you were initially, and that's going to change how you read. There's also the fact that you'll have to read on a timed test, that you'll probably already be familiar with the passage, and that you're much more likely to *assess* than to *understand*.

You often apply these different styles of reading without even realizing it. One of the keys to success on the most difficult passages of the SAT is to be aware of what you do when you read. When you read a passage about a topic that's not of particular interest to you, you might skim, assume, match words in the passage and the answer choices, and spend far too much time along the way. The best way to beat the SAT at its own game, to really crack the SAT, is to understand the peculiarities of SAT Reading and how it differs from other reading you do in school and out. The students who knock the SAT out of the park are those who have the self-awareness necessary to avoid the SAT's traps.

GENRES OF READING

We are all familiar with the ideas of genres in writing—romance, horror, and sci-fi are just three of the most popular. However, becoming a good, self-conscious reader is about realizing that there are genres of *reading* as well. What you're trained to do in your English classes is something we could call the genre of *Literary Reading*.

If you like to read, or if you do particularly well in your English classes, then you're probably already very proficient at Literary Reading. Above all, this genre is characterized by sophisticated interpretations. The papers that you write in high-school or college English classes require creative but convincing readings of the meanings of particular texts. There are some basic aspects on which everyone has to agree—plot, characters, narrative voice—but beyond that, the rein is relatively free. In many classes, you are actually *encouraged* to come up with your own interpretation, and you are evaluated on your ability to interpret a text in a personal way. This is why some people still love to read novels in their spare time. Two people may read the same novel but have totally different reactions to it because literary reading is rooted in a kind of personalization. The students who do best in English classes, and those who go on to become English majors, are those who forge the closest personal connections to the material that they read, and are not necessarily those who understand the text in the most "correct" way. The best English students, in other words, are those who have mastered the genre of Literary Reading.

The Genre of SAT Reading

There's a simple reason that the best readers in an English class are not necessarily the best readers on an SAT: Literary Reading and SAT Reading are two different genres of reading. They require different skill sets.

It helps to remember what a standardized test is. Essentially, ETS needs to be able to promise that everyone—regardless of race, gender, region, or family income—can read a question and have an equal shot at getting the correct answer. If the SAT were testing Literary Reading, everyone would come up with a different answer, and the test would be impossible to score because it would no longer be standardized.

As a result, SAT Reading is much more characterized by *understanding* than by *interpretation*. Interpretation is personal to the reader. Understanding is all about what the text says. This is good news because it means that everything you'll need to answer the questions will be right in front of you in the text, but it also means that you have to stop approaching it the same way you've been trained to approach reading in your English classes all along.

Reading for understanding is tough! Let's take a paragraph from an SAT passage about the studio-recording device Auto-Tune:

> The first major hit to popularize Auto-Tune was Cher's "Believe," which was released in 1998. Since that time, the vocal pitch corrector has become almost a staple of popular
> *Line* music. A 2011 study said that 95% of Top 40 radio hits that
> 5 year had used Auto-Tune to one degree or another. The technology is clearly here to stay, though its effects on the present and future of popular music are hotly debated. While some have argued that the new technology has opened up new possibilities for popular music, others have responded that
> 10 the technology has ripped music from its roots, creating an industry built on computer enhancement rather than musical talent.

This is part of a larger essay, but let's think for a moment about how we might answer a question about it on the SAT.

1. In this paragraph, what is the author's main point about Auto-Tune?

    (A) The technology was useful in the late 1990s, but it is no longer useful.
    (B) The technology has changed popular music for the worse.
    (C) Popular music is now dominated by poor singers whose voices are modified.
    (D) The technology has shifted popular music's focus away from musical talent.
    (E) Popular music has been influenced by the introduction of Auto-Tune technology.

While this question seems fairly straightforward, it can actually be very difficult if you apply your Literary Reading skills. In Literary Reading, the major question is typically, "What does the author *mean*?" or "What is the author suggesting?" You can take those questions in a number of directions.

You could say, for example, that choice (A) is the correct answer because the author singles out Cher's "Believe," thus implying that this was an innovative use of Auto-Tune technology. The later discussion of the widespread use of the technology could also be said to imply that the author believes that Cher's use of Auto-Tune inspired many imitators and that popular music is now watered-down and dull.

But does the author actually *say* any of this?

How about choice (B)? The author clearly suggests that Auto-Tune is changing popular music, and he cites some critics who suggest that it is ruining music. We might say that the author is implying his own critique of Auto-Tune in giving more space to Auto-Tune's detractors than to its supporters.

But, again, even with all these smart reasons, can we actually choose this as our correct answer?

As for choice (C), the author does cite a statistic (the 2011 study) that indicates that popular music is now dominated by Auto-Tune. Because Auto-Tune does modify the voices of singers, couldn't we say that these singers must be poor? Seems logical, but is it definitely true?

Choice (D) comes directly from the author's own words in the last sentence, and as with the other answer choices, we might be able to see how this would be the author's own implied position. We might feel this way ourselves, actually, and it might seem like any mention of Auto-Tune implies a critique. But it's not the main point.

In the end, however, only choice (E) is actually *stated* in the passage, so it is the only possible correct answer. We can even point to the lines that make it correct (*A 2011 study said that 95% of Top 40 radio hits that year had used Auto-Tune to one degree or another. The technology is clearly here to stay*). No intense thinking or reasoning required.

This demonstrates the cornerstone of the genre of SAT Reading; correct answers are always rooted firmly in the text and are based on what the author *actually says*, not what the author *could be perceived to say*. There will always be a word or phrase that offers direct, irrefutable support for the correct answer. If you find yourself *reasoning* rather than *identifying*, be careful!

So here's the thing that SAT will never admit but that is absolutely true, particularly for students like you who do well in school and are shooting for Reading scores in the 700s.

> Thinking is not rewarded on the SAT. All the things that make you an interesting, well-rounded person can actually hurt you on this test.

We can debate the merits of this approach all day long, and we can express our indignation that we're subjected to such a silly, inhuman test. However whether the test is better, worse, or equal to what you learn in school doesn't change the basic fact: SAT Reading is a genre of reading that will not change, but you can learn and perfect the skills necessary to master it.

So the first rule of the SAT Reading genre is as follows:

> Read to understand, not to assess. Read for information, not interpretation.

Rhetorical Devices: Reading for Structure

In your English classes, you spend a lot of time learning about literary devices. Sometimes the SAT will ask you to identify these devices, but they are typically pretty basic, and those types of questions show up infrequently—maybe once a test.

In the SAT Reading genre, however, you'll be rewarded much more frequently for looking at the general movement and structure of the passages. In other words, look at not only *what* the author says but also *how* the structure of the passage helps him or her to say it. Let's have a look at a sample from a recent PSAT passage about online education:

> Whatever its negative implications, online education is no longer something we can choose to ignore. Thirty-two percent of higher-education students now take at least one
> Line class online, and the percentage that takes two or more is
> 5 not much lower. Even for courses that are not taught purely online, as many as 70% of instructors say that online learning is critical to their long-term teaching strategies. Though our initial response may be one of panic, things are not so revolutionarily bad as they might seem. Online education
> 10 certainly has its benefits. (77% of instructors rank online courses nearly as high as face-to-face courses in terms of learning effectiveness.) And the belief that online education must necessarily be a diluted form of the "real thing" is simply misguided conservatism. The "real thing," after all,
> 15 had its own set of problems long before online education came along, and while students may be truant or distracted during online courses, they are just as likely to be so in face-to-face courses.
> The online education model is not only less expensive
> 20 and more convenient than traditional educational models, it's also—like so much else in the culture today—excitingly multifaceted. Imagine an online physics course. A basic unit on mechanics will give you not just a sheet of formulas and a list of problems but also interactive games with mini-labs,
> 25 links to outside sources for extra help, and online chats with TAs and professors. For traditional educators, the risk of online education is not that it doesn't teach the material but that it teaches too much material and floods students with so many stimuli and so much information that they end up
> 30 learning nothing at all.

There are only two paragraphs here, but this passage still has a relatively straight-forward movement from beginning to end:

It begins by stating that online education is *no longer something we can choose to ignore* and then goes on to cite some statistics about its prominence. From this idea of prominence, the passage then takes up how online education is perceived, beginning with the sentence *Though our initial response may be one of panic…*, suggesting that in fact online education may be just as good as or better than live education. The last paragraph does away with objection and gives reasons that online education is effective.

In short, the movement of the passage can be summed up this way:

1. Prominence of online education
2. Surprising effectiveness of online education
3. New benefits of online education

Getting a sense of the rhetorical skeleton of a passage like this can be tremendously effective not just for main idea questions but for confusing detail questions.

Here's one from the same PSAT.

45. The author of Passage 2 most likely thinks of face-to-face education as

(A) collaborative and able to incorporate many media
(B) the last hope for aspiring professionals
(C) an outmoded way of relaying information
(D) exclusive to those who can afford it
(E) susceptible to compromising influences

Face-to-face education comes up at the end of the first paragraph, which is the point at which the author is discussing the *surprising effectiveness of online education*. He must therefore mention *face-to-face education* in the context of this discussion of effectiveness, so choices (A), (B), and (D) can be eliminated because they discuss some other aspect. Then, between choices (C) and (E), choice (E) is an overstatement of the author's actual point and goes beyond the information in the passage. Even if you got down to only choices (C) and (E), your chances of guessing were still 50% on what is actually a very difficult question.

Now let's try to answer a question with *only* this structural outline. One of the passages on a recent PSAT has this basic structure (organized by paragraph):

1. Catalina moves to a new place.
2. She makes a close friend.
3. The friend convinces her to come to a political protest.
4. Catalina is flattered and excited.
5. Catalina goes to many more protests throughout her life

Even though this passage comes from a prose-fictional source, the structural analysis can still be very effective because stories, too, have a clear movement and structure, and the words within those stories advance that structure.

Let's look at three different questions from this passage. We don't have the passage, so let's just use the basic analysis given above.

38. The primary purpose of Clara's various questions in the third paragraph is to

(A) encourage Catalina to join her at the protest
(B) interrogate Catalina about her childhood
(C) spark a political dialogue with Catalina
(D) force Catalina to change her political views
(E) test whether Catalina is able to protest

This question references the third paragraph, in which we said *The friend convinces her to come to a political protest.* From this idea alone, we can see that the answer must be choice (A). Only choices (A) and (E) even mention the protest, and choice (E) goes against the description.

> **40.** The repetition of the word "really" in the first sentence of the fourth paragraph serves to emphasize Catalina's
>
> (A) consternation
> (B) astonishment
> (C) misanthropy
> (D) befuddlement
> (E) dishonesty
>
> **41.** The fourth paragraph represents Catalina as
>
> (A) hopeful
> (B) suspicious
> (C) deceptive
> (D) apathetic
> (E) thoughtful

Both of these questions ask about the same part of the passage, the fourth paragraph, which details how *Catalina is flattered and excited.* With only this description, we are much less likely to get caught in the trap answer choices. Catalina's feelings are positive, which makes (B) the only possible answer to question 40 and eliminates choices (B), (C), and (D) from question 41. Then, choice (A) agrees more with *flattered and excited* than does choice (E).

Reading for rhetoric and structure can save you from having to read the same lines and sentences over and over. If you have a sense of the passage's big picture, the small details of it should fall into place.

So the second rule of the SAT Reading genre is the following:

> Find the movement and organization of the passage. Read for structure.

Answer Support and Selective Close Reading

As we will see in future chapters, it's usually not a good idea to read every word of an SAT passage. It's best to let the questions guide you through the passage. Read the parts of the text that will get you the most points. Who cares about the rest?

But when you do read, make sure you are reading carefully. *Every answer on this test will have specific support within the passage,* but sometimes that support can hide in particular words or phrases. If you're skimming too quickly, you may miss these words or phrases altogether.

Take this selection from a recent PSAT.

> Daddy was seeing an awful lot of his new friend. One of the rooms in his house was all of a sudden full of her stuff; neither Sarah nor her brother was allowed in there anymore.
> *Line* It had started with a few dinners and shopping trips, and now
> 5 it seemed that their father's friend basically lived in the house and was shifting around some furniture that had been in place for as long as Sarah could remember.

34. The phrases "an awful lot" and "all of a sudden" help to emphasize Sarah's

    (A) disapproval of her father's new girlfriend
    (B) apathy toward her personal space being invaded
    (C) wish that things could be as they once were
    (D) unwillingness to accept a new person into her life
    (E) surprise at a new development in her father's home

This question asks you to do exactly the kind of close reading that you should always do. Another way of asking the question would be, *Why does the author use the phrases "an awful lot" and "all of a sudden"?* One way to test the effectiveness of language is to take the language in the question out of the passage.

So the first two lines would change to this:

> *Daddy was seeing a lot of his new friend. One of the rooms in his house was full of her stuff.*

Now compare that to what it actually says:

> *Daddy was seeing an awful lot of his new friend. One of the rooms in his house was all of a sudden full of her stuff.*

Notice how the original lines add Sarah's voice to the third-person narration. Phrases like *an awful lot* and *all of a sudden*, in other words, come from Sarah herself, and they help to emphasize her surprise at how quickly things are moving between her father and his "new friend." Of the answer choices listed, choice (E) best captures the use of these terms.

Let's try a slightly more difficult passage.

> To take one example, the name "Iraq" is not quite
> as applicable to all its citizens as the names "France,"
> "Portugal," or "The United States" are in their own regions.
> *Line* For many Westerners, nationality is a given and ultimately
> 5 trumps the more local identifications of town, city, or
> state. In Iraq, as the Bush administration learned, religious
> distinctions are more meaningful than national similarities.
> Approximately 65% of those living in Iraq are Shia Muslims,
> but does this make it a Shia country? To an extent, maybe,
> 10 but Sunni Muslims represent a powerful and vocal minority,
> and the northern regions of Iraq comprise a semi-autonomous
> region of a third group, the Kurds. The Western notions of
> nation-above-all and religious coexistence can't maintain
> in this and other countries because the value systems have
> 15 developed so independently of these notions.

12. What does the first sentence suggest about name of the nation of Iraq?

   (A) The name of the country comes from the region in which the majority of Shias live.
   (B) The name of the country has less significance in Iraq than it does in other countries.
   (C) The name of the country does not apply to most citizens, who therefore frequently disregard the name.
   (D) The name of the country comes from the same early language from which many European-nation names are derived.
   (E) The name of the country refers to an area that does not include the region of Kurdistan.

In this sentence, notice the difference that the words "quite as" make. Without them, the sentence would read as follows: *To take one example, the name "Iraq" is not applicable to all citizens…* Without the "quite as," therefore, this sentence is much more extreme, and the answer might be choice (C) or (E). As it is, though, the only answer that can work is choice (B).

Let's try another.

13. According to the author, how do Westerners identify with the towns, cities, or state in which they live?

(A) These local identifications play some role, but the idea of belonging to a nation is more important.

(B) These local identifications hold some importance but are trumped by religious identifications.

(C) These local identifications are most important in European countries such as France and Portugal.

(D) These local identifications matter only for Westerners who have once lived in the Middle East.

(E) These local identifications are less important than both religious and national identifications.

The correct answer here is choice (A), but choices (B), (C), (E) each contain some compelling parts, particularly if you have not read the passage closely. Choices (B) and (E) contain the words *religious identification*; choice (C) contains the names *France and Portugal;* choice (D) contains the word *Westerners*. While all of these words may have appeared in the initial passage, the answer choices rearrange the words to say things that the passage doesn't say. Use the context clues if you're not sure what terms like *trumps* and *given* mean in this particular context. The sentences surrounding this one define those words specifically. Again, these passages can't really presume any outside knowledge at all, so anything that seems especially difficult or complicated will be defined in the passage itself. When you read, do so carefully, and make sure that you've read enough to know what the passage is saying.

In future chapters, we will discuss our particular approach to reading passages, but if you're looking for the very highest scores on this test, remember the SAT Reading is a genre of reading with its own particular set of rules.

Summary

- o Read to understand, not to assess. Read for information, not interpretation.

- o Find the movement and organization of the passage. Read for structure.

- o When you do read, read carefully and read enough.

Chapter 12
Sentence
Completions

SENTENCE COMPLETIONS

Before you start the bulk of the real "reading" on the SAT, you'll be asked to fill in a few blanks. Sounds easy, right? Well, it can be if you've got all the tools you need.

These fill-in-the-blank questions are called Sentence Completions, and they rely almost entirely on the strength of your vocabulary. Particularly if you are looking to get the highest scores on the SAT, it is essential that you get all or most of the Sentence Completions correct.

> Sentence Completions Facts
> - There will be a total of 19 Sentence Completion questions on the SAT.
> - Sentence Completions come at the beginning of each Critical Reading section.
> - Sentence Completion questions are arranged more or less in order of difficulty within each section: Earlier questions are easier than later ones, often because of the level of vocabulary used.

The Reading passages on the SAT can throw you all kinds of curveballs, and SAT can ask some occasionally bizarre, frequently ambiguous questions about passages that are vaguely interesting at best and crushingly dull at worst. No matter how good you are at SAT Reading, you can't avoid these curveballs.

Sentence Completions, however, are much more straightforward. Succeeding on these questions requires you to follow one very basic principle.

> Learn as many vocabulary words as you can before the test.

We've got a technique that can help you on all Sentence Completion questions, but that technique can take you only so far if you don't have the vocabulary to back it up.

The Basic Approach

Try this Sentence Completion question:

> 1. Maria was ------- when Elias asked her to the prom.
>
>   (A) thrilled
>   (B) disgusted
>   (C) confused
>   (D) impatient
>   (E) uninterested

So what's the answer? If you're confused, there's a reason. This question doesn't have an answer! Literally any of those answer choices could work. Any of these words *sound* good in this context, but that's not quite enough.

Let's see if this rewrite of the question fixes the problem.

> 1. After waiting eagerly for him to do so, Maria was ------- when Elias asked her to the prom.
>
>   (A) thrilled
>   (B) disgusted
>   (C) confused
>   (D) impatient
>   (E) uninterested

Now the answer has to be (A). The words *waiting eagerly* tell us that Maria wanted Elias to ask her to the prom, so she must have been *thrilled* when he did.

The rewritten version of the sentence contains a **clue**, which tells you what the word in the blank should *mean*. Almost every Sentence Completion question will have a clue. Find it, and you'll be on the right track to the answer. Sound isn't enough: The *clue* is what matters, because it's all about what the word *means*.

To that end, here is a basic approach that will help you find clues and stay focused on the *meaning* of the word, rather than get distracted by the way things sound. The basic approach is as follows:

1. **Cover the answers**. Don't get distracted by the words that ETS gives you. Look for clues and triggers, and figure out what kind of word *must* go in the blank.
2. **Speak for yourself**. Pick your own word that could go in the blank. Make sure your choice is informed by the clue. It doesn't have to be a fancy word, just something that works in the context. If you have to, at least put a symbol in to represent what you're thinking: ☺, ☹, $$ are perfectly fine, if you can't come up with anything else.
3. **Use POE and guess aggressively**. Once you've chosen your own word, try to find the answer that matches it most closely. You should be able to eliminate at least one answer (even more if you've got a solid vocabulary), which will enable you to guess more effectively.

Now, let's add another twist to the sentence. We'll just change one word and add another this time and see if it changes anything.

1. Although she had waited eagerly for him to do so, Maria was ------- when Elias finally asked her to the prom.

   (A) thrilled
   (B) disgusted
   (C) confused
   (D) impatient
   (E) uninterested

The clue in this sentence remains the same as it did in the first time: *waiting eagerly*. But the answer is no longer (A) because of the new word at the beginning of the sentence: *although*. This is what we call a **trigger**. Triggers don't show up in every sentence, but when they do, they indicate what direction the sentence is going to go. In this case, *although* operates as an *opposite-direction trigger* because it reverses the meaning of the clue. Now, our answer must mean something contrary to *waiting eagerly*, or choice (E). Choice (B) presents a contrast, but the word *disgusted* is not substantiated by any clue.

Triggers can be subtle, but the meaning of the word in the blank often hinges on them. Here's a chart with a list of common triggers on the SAT:

Trigger Words	
Same Direction	*Change Direction*
Because	Although/though
And	However
Since	Yet
In fact	But
Colon (:)	Rather
Semicolon (;)	In contrast to
Thus	Despite
So	Even though
Also	Unlike
As well as	Instead

The SAT can also introduce what we call time triggers, which aren't quite as obvious as some of the major trigger words but can have just as much influence on the meaning of a sentence.

1. At first, Maria was waiting eagerly for him to do so; since then, she has become very ------- with Elias, who still hasn't asked her to the prom.

   (A) thrilled
   (B) disgusted
   (C) confused
   (D) impatient
   (E) uninterested

Here's How to Crack It

The sentence has changed a bit here, but the answer choices are still the same. This time, though, our triggers come in the form of the time words *at first* and *since then*, which are opposite-direction triggers by implying a contrast between now (*since then*) and then (*at first*). The clue is still *waiting eagerly*, but this time, the answer must be choice (D), which takes the triggers into account. If you were leaning toward choice (B), be careful! Maria might be disgusted with Elias, but there's nothing in the sentence to indicate specifically that she is!

Time Triggers indicate either a change in direction (old vs. new, healthy vs. sick) or a change in intensity (sad vs. depressed, important vs. urgent). Pay attention to words like *once, eventually, before, after,* or any others that indicate there has been a change over time.

Two Blanks... A Technique So Nice, You Do It Twice

Here's the approach for tackling two-blank Sentence Completions questions:

1. **Cover the answers.**
2. **Decide which blank is easier to figure out.** One blank will usually have a more obvious clue, which will make it easier to tackle the next step.
3. **Using clues and triggers, fill in a word for that blank.** Same idea as with one-blank Sentence Completions questions.
4. **Eliminate the entire answer choice if one word doesn't fit.** As in, use your pencil to cross out the whole thing, so you don't confuse yourself when you do the second blank.
5. **Repeat steps 3 & 4.**

Let's go back to our friends Maria and Elias. Remember to cover your answers!

1. Maria was so -------, just frankly confused, when Elias asked her to the prom, especially after she heard him ------- with a friend as to whether he should ask her or not.

   (A) perplexed…conspiring
   (B) befuddled…deliberating
   (C) bewildered…complaining
   (D) uninterested…debating
   (E) thrilled…prevaricating

Here's How to Crack It

We're going to use the same technique we used above. We're just going to do it twice this time.

Take the blanks one at a time. Pick the one that seems easier, and fill in your own word. In this sentence, the first blank has the more obvious clue (*just frankly confused*), so we'll start there. We need a word that means something like *confused*, so we can eliminate choices (D) and (E). Remember to cross out the entirety of both answer choices!

Then, the second blank needs to mean something like *discussing*, because she heard him doing this with a friend about an apparent dilemma. Choices (A), (B), and (C) are all that remain, so the fact that *debating* (choice (D)) would work is irrelevant. Of the remaining three possibilities for the second blank, only choice (B), *deliberating*, can work, so our answer is (B).

While you're more likely to see these two-blank questions as those of medium or hard difficulty, they're actually twice as easy with this technique. With this technique, after all, there's no need to know the meaning of the word *prevaricating* (though of course you know that it means *speaking or acting in an evasive way*).

Whether you're dealing with one blank or two, be on the lookout for these clues and triggers in future exercises. We will make sure to point them out in our explanations. Learning the clues and triggers is one of the keys to beating SAT at its own game.

ALL THE VOCABULARY!

Another major key to nailing the Critical Reading section, of course, is vocabulary. If you are hovering around 650 or 700 on SAT Reading, then your vocabulary is probably pretty solid already. In order to make sure that you can eke out all the extra points you need, though, here's all the vocabulary you'll ever need on the SAT (or pretty much any other standardized test for that matter).

The first list is what we call our Hit Parade, or the 250 most common words on the SAT. We've included definitions to help you along.

HIT PARADE ALPHABETICAL LIST

abase	to lower in rank, prestige, or esteem
abstruse	difficult to understand
acumen	quickness, accuracy, and keenness of judgment or insight
adroit	dexterous; deft
aesthetic	having to do with the appreciation of beauty
affable	easygoing; friendly
alacrity	cheerful willingness; eagerness
alleviate	to ease a pain or a burden
altruism	unselfish concern for the welfare of others; selflessness
amalgam	a combination of diverse elements; a mixture
ambiguous	open to more than one interpretation
ambivalent	simultaneously feeling opposing feelings; uncertain
amiable	friendly and agreeable in disposition; good-natured and likable
anachronistic	the representation of someone as existing or something as happening in other than chronological, proper, or historical order
apathetic	feeling or showing little emotion
arboreal	relating to or resembling a tree
arcane	known or understood by only a few
archaic	characteristic of an earlier period; old-fashioned
ascertain	to discover with certainty, as through examination or experimentation
assimilate	incorporated and absorbed into the mind; made similar; caused to resemble
astute	shrewd; clever
augment	to make (something already developed or well under way) greater, as in size, extent, or quantity
aural	of, relating to, or perceived by the ear

austere	without decoration; strict
autonomy	independence; self-determination; self-government or the right of self-government
averse	strongly disinclined
banal	drearily commonplace and often predictable; trite
belie	to picture falsely; misrepresent
belligerent	inclined or eager to fight; hostile or aggressive
beneficial	producing or promoting a favorable result; advantageous
benign	kind and gentle
bolster	to buoy up or hearten; to support or prop up
bombastic	given to pompous speech or writing
brevity	the quality or state of being brief in duration
burgeon	to grow and flourish; to put forth new buds, leaves, or greenery; sprout
cacophony	jarring, discordant sound; dissonance
cajole	to urge with gentle and repeated appeals, teasing, or flattery
callous	emotionally hardened; unfeeling
candid	characterized by openness and sincerity of expression; unreservedly straightforward
cantankerous	ill-tempered and quarrelsome; disagreeable
capricious	impulsive and unpredictable
castigate	to inflict severe punishment on
cathartic	causing relaxation after an emotional outburst
censure	to criticize severely; blame
chicanery	a trick; deception by trickery
circumscribe	to draw a circle around; to restrict
circumspect	heedful of circumstances and potential consequences; prudent
clandestine	done secretly, especially to deceive; surreptitious
complement	something that completes, makes up a whole, or brings to perfection
conciliatory	appeasing; soothing; pleasant
concord	agreement (antonym: discord)
concur	to agree; to be of the same opinion
conjecture	inference or judgment based on inconclusive or incomplete evidence; guesswork
conspicuous	easy to notice; obvious (antonym: inconspicuous)
contentious	quarrelsome
contiguous	sharing an edge or boundary; touching
convoluted	intricate; complex

copious	plentiful; having a large quantity
cosmopolitan	so sophisticated as to be at home in all parts of the world or conversant with many spheres of interest; pertinent or common to the whole world
credible	capable of being believed; plausible
curative	something that cures; a remedy
dearth	a scarce supply; a lack
debacle	a sudden, disastrous collapse, downfall, or defeat; a rout
debilitate	to sap the strength or energy of; enervate
debunk	to expose or ridicule falseness, shams, or exaggerated claims
defunct	having ceased to exist or live
deleterious	having a harmful effect
demure	modest and reserved in manner or behavior
denounce	to condemn openly as being evil or reprehensible
deride	to speak of or treat with contemptuous mirth
derivative	a by-product
derogatory	tending or intending to belittle
didactic	intended to instruct
diffidence	timidity or shyness
dilatory	habitually late
diligent	marked by painstaking effort; hard-working
dirge	a funeral hymn or lament
disaffected	having lost faith or loyalty; discontent
disparage	to speak of in a slighting way or negatively; to belittle
disseminate	to scatter widely, as in sowing seed
distend	to swell out or expand from or as if from internal pressure
docile	ready and willing to be taught; teachable
dogmatic	stubbornly adhering to insufficiently proved beliefs
dubious	doubtful; of unlikely authenticity
duplicitous	given to or marked by deliberate deceptiveness in behavior or speech
ebullience	intense enthusiasm
eclectic	made up of a variety of sources or styles
effrontery	brazen boldness; presumptuousness
effusive	showing excessive emotion; overflowing
embellish	to make beautiful by ornamenting; to decorate
eminent	distinguished; prominent
empathetic	identification with and understanding of another's situation, feelings, and motives

enigma	one that is puzzling, ambiguous, or inexplicable; a riddle
ephemeral	lasting for only a brief time
epitome	a representative or example of a class or type
equivocal	open to two or more interpretations and often intended to mislead; ambiguous (antonym: unequivocal)
eradicate	to get rid of as if by tearing it up by the roots; abolish
erratic	having no fixed or regular course; wandering
erudition	deep, extensive learning
esoteric	intended for or understood by only a particular group
euphemism	the act or an example of substituting a mild, indirect, or vague term for one considered harsh, blunt, or offensive
exacerbate	to increase the severity, violence, or bitterness of; aggravate
exonerate	to free from blame
exorbitant	exceeding all bounds, as of custom or fairness
expedient	appropriate to a purpose; speedy
extol	to praise highly
extraneous	irrelevant
extrapolate	to infer or estimate by extending or projecting known information
exuberant	full of unrestrained enthusiasm or joy
fabricate	to make in order to deceive
fallacy	a false notion
fastidious	possessing careful attention to detail; difficult to please
felicitous	admirably suited; apt
flag (v.)	to decline in vigor or strength; to hang limply; droop
flagrant	extremely or deliberately shocking or noticeable
flippant	marked by disrespectful levity or casualness; pert
gaffe	a clumsy social error; a faux pas
grandiose	characterized by greatness of scope or intent; grand
gratuitous	given freely; unearned; unwarranted
hackneyed	worn-out through overuse; trite
idiosyncrasy	a structural or behavioral characteristic peculiar to an individual or group
ignominy	great personal dishonor or humiliation
impetuous	characterized by sudden and forceful energy or emotion; impulsive and passionate
impetus	an impelling force; an impulse
impugn	to attack as false or questionable
incoherent	lacking cohesion, connection, or harmony
incongruous	lacking in harmony; incompatible

incontrovertible	indisputable; not open to question
indict	to accuse of wrongdoing; charge
ingenuous	lacking in cunning, guile, or worldliness; artless (antonym: disingenuous)
innocuous	having no adverse effect; harmless
inscrutable	difficult to fathom or understand; impenetrable
insinuate	to introduce or otherwise convey gradually and insidiously
insipid	uninteresting; unchallenging
insolent	insulting in manner or speech
insular	suggestive of the isolated life of an island; narrow or provincial
intransigence	refusing to moderate a position, especially an extreme position; uncompromising
inundate	to overwhelm as if with a flood; to swamp
invocation	to call on (a higher power) for assistance, support, or inspiration
jaded	worn out; wearied
jocular	characterized by or given to joking
juxtapose	to place side by side, especially for comparison or contrast
laudatory	giving praise
lavish	characterized by or produced with extravagance and abundance
litigious	tending to engage in lawsuits
loquacious	very talkative
lucid	easily understood; clear
lugubrious	mournful, dismal, or gloomy, especially to an exaggerated or ludicrous degree
magnanimous	courageously noble in mind and heart
mar	to inflict damage, especially disfiguring damage, on
maverick	one who is independent and resists adherence to a group
mendacious	lying; untruthful
mercenary	motivated solely by a desire for monetary or material gain (adjective); a professional soldier (noun)
meticulous	extremely careful and precise
modicum	a small, moderate, or token amount
multifarious	having great variety; diverse
multiplicity	the state of being various or manifold
nefarious	infamous by way of being extremely wicked
novel	fresh; original; new

obsequious	full of or exhibiting servile compliance; fawning
obstinate	stubbornly adhering to an opinion or a course of action
onerous	troublesome or oppressive; burdensome
opulent	exhibiting a display of great wealth
ornate	elaborately decorated
orthodox	adhering to the accepted or traditional and established faith, especially in religion
palliative	relieving or soothing the symptoms of a disease or disorder without effecting a cure
parity	equality, as in amount, status, or value (antonym: disparity)
partisan	devoted to or biased in support of a party, group, or cause
paucity	smallness of number; fewness
pedantic	characterized by a narrow, often ostentatious concern for book learning and formal rules
pejorative	describing words or phrases that belittle or speak negatively of someone
penchant	a definite liking; a strong inclination
pernicious	tending to cause death or serious injury; deadly
perspicacious	having or showing penetrating mental discernment; clear-sighted
philanthropic	humanitarian; benevolent
placid	calm or quiet; undisturbed by tumult or disorder
portent	an indication of something important or calamitous about to occur; an omen
potentate	one who has the power and position to rule over others; a monarch
pragmatic	practical
precocious	manifesting or characterized by unusually early development or maturity, especially in mental aptitude
prescience	knowledge of actions or events before they occur; foresight
prodigious	enormous
profundity	great depth of intellect, feeling, or meaning
proliferate	to grow or increase rapidly
prolific	very productive; producing great quantities
prosaic	unimaginative; dull
prospectus	a formal summary of a proposed venture or project
quell	to put down forcibly; suppress
quiescent	being quiet, still, or at rest; inactive
rancorous	hateful; marked by deep-seated ill-will
raze	to level to the ground; demolish

reciprocate	to mutually take or give
reclusive	seeking or preferring seclusion or isolation
rectitude	moral uprightness; righteousness
redolent	having or emitting fragrance; aromatic; suggestive, reminiscent
redouble	to become twice as great
redundant	needlessly wordy or repetitive in expression
relinquish	to retire from; give up or abandon
remiss	lax in attending to duty; negligent
renounce	to give up (a title, for example), especially by formal announcement
repudiate	to reject the validity or authority of
repugnant	arousing disgust or aversion; offensive or repulsive
reticent	inclined to keep one's thoughts, feelings, and personal affairs to oneself
rhetoric	the art of using language effectively and persuasively
rudimentary	of or relating to basic facts or principles; elementary; being in the earliest stages of development
sanctimonious	feigning piety or righteousness
sanguine	of a healthy reddish color; ruddy; cheerfully confident; optimistic
scintillating	brilliant
scrupulous	principled, having a strong sense of right and wrong; conscientious and exacting
solicitous	anxious or concerned
sonorous	producing a deep or full sound
soporific	inducing or tending to induce sleep
specious	having the ring of truth or plausibility but actually not true
sporadic	occurring at irregular intervals; having no pattern or order in time
squander	to spend wastefully or extravagantly; dissipate
squelch	to crush by or as if by trampling; squash
staid	unemotional; serious
stratify	to form, arrange, or deposit in layers
strident	loud, harsh, grating, or shrill; discordant
stymie	to thwart; stump
substantiate	to support with proof or evidence; verify
subterfuge	a deceptive stratagem or device
supercilious	disdainful; haughty; arrogant
superfluous	extra; unnecessary

supplant	to usurp the place of, especially through intrigue or underhanded tactics
surreptitious	done by secretive means
sycophant	a servile self-seeker who attempts to win favor by flattering influential people
synergy	the interaction of two or more agents or forces so that their combined effect is greater than the sum of their individual effects
tangential	merely touching or slightly connected; only superficially relevant
temperate	moderate in degree or quality; restrained (antonym: intemperate)
temporal	of, relating to, or limited by time
tenacity	persistence
tenuous	having little substance or strength; shaky
therapeutic	having or exhibiting healing powers
transient	passing away with time; passing from one place to another
tumultuous	noisy and disorderly
ubiquitous	being or seeming to be everywhere at the same time; omnipresent
vacillate	to sway from one side to the other; oscillate
vapid	lacking liveliness, animation, or interest; dull
variegated	having streaks, marks, or patches of a different color or colors; varicolored
veracity	adherence to the truth; truthfulness
verdant	green with vegetation; covered with green growth
vex	to annoy or bother; to perplex
vicarious	felt or undergone as if one were taking part in the experience or feelings of another
vigilant	on the alert; watchful
vignette	a short scene or incident, as from a movie
vindicate	to free from blame
vindictive	disposed to seek revenge; revengeful; spiteful
vituperative	using, containing, or marked by harshly abusive censure
whimsical	subject to erratic behavior; unpredictable

If you were fortunate enough to take Latin or Greek in school, then you've got a stronger vocabulary background than you may realize. Many of the words we use today descend from these languages, formed from *roots* that have retained their original meanings. In the next few pages, we'll give you a big list of the Latin and Greek roots that show up on the SAT and some of the words that use those roots.

You probably already know many of these roots, but some may surprise you. As you read through this list, try to write one or two words that use the roots in question.

MASTER ROOT LIST

a-	negative prefix	de-	away from/opposite, of
ab-	away from/negative prefix	dec/deci-	ten
ac/acr-	sharp	dent-	teeth
ad/at-	to, toward	derm-	skin
amb-	go/walk	desc-	down
ambi-	both/mixed	dext-	dexterity, ability
ami/amo-	love	di-	two, apart, split
an/anti-	against	dic/dict-	say, tell
andr-	human, male	dign/dain-	worth
anim-	life, spirit	digt-	finger, digit
ante-	before	dis-	apart from, not
anthr-	human	domi-	rule over
apt/ept-	skill, ability	dorm-	sleep
arbo-	tree	duc/dul-	lead
arch-	rule, over	dys-	faulty, bad
aud-	sound	e/ex/ej-	out, outward
auto-	self	en/em-	into
bell/belli-	war	epi-	upon
ben/bono-	good	equ/equi-	equal
bi-	two	esce-	becoming
bio/bios-	life	eu-	good, pleasant
bra-	arm	extr-	outside, beyond, additional
carn-	meat, flesh	fac/fic/fig-	do, make
cent-	hundred	fer/ferr-	strong, iron-like
chron-	time	fid-	faithful
circ/circu-	around	fort-	strong
cis/cise-	cut	fract-	break, split
cli-	lean	frat-	brother
clu/clo/cla	close, shut	fren-	highly energetic
co/com/con	with, together	gen-	birth, creation, kind, type
contr-	against	geo-	earth
cred-	believe	gno/kno-	know
culp-	blame	grand-	big
cur/cour-	run (a course)	graph-	write

grat-	grateful	nounce-	call
gress-	step	nox/nec-	harmful
gust-	taste	ob-	against
gyn-	female	olfac-	smell
hemi-	half, split part	ology-	study of
her/hes-	stick (on)	omni-	all, every
herb-	plant	ory-	place of
hetero-	different, mixed	pac/pax/plac-	peace, pleasing
hex/sex-	six	pan	all, everywhere
homo-	same	par	equal
hyd/hydr-	water	para-	beyond
hyper-	over, beyond	path-	feeling, emotion
hypo-	under, insufficient	patr-	father
il-	not	pen/pend-	weight
im-	not, into	pent-	five
in-	not, into	peri-	around
inter-	between	pet/pec-	small
intra-	within	phil-	love, high regard
itis-	inflammation, infection	phob-	fear
ium-	place, building of	phon-	sound
jeu/ju-	play, youthful	pod/ped-	foot
jaun-	yellow	pon/pos-	place, put
lab/labo-	work	port-	carry
laud-	praise	post-	after
lav-	wash	poten-	power, influence
lev-	rise	pre-	before
log/loqui-	to speak	pro-	for
lu/luc/lum-	light	prox-	near
mag/magna-	great	pseudo-	false
mal-	bad	pug-	fighting
man/manu-	hand	quad-	four
mar/mer-	sea	qui-	quiet
matr-	mother	quint-	five
met/meter	measure	re-	again
meta	more, beyond	schi-	split
mic/micro-	tiny	sci/scien	knowledge
mill-	thousand	scop-	see
mis-	wrong, bad	scrib/scrip-	write
mit-	send	sec/sequ-	follow, come after
mob/mobi-	moving	sed/sid-	sit, be still
mor/mort-	death	solo-	alone
morph-	change (shape)	son/soni-	sound
mut-	change, alter	soro-	sister
nat/natu-	natural, birth	spec/spic-	see, look
neg-	negative	sta/sti-	still, unmoving
neo/nov-	new	sua-	smooth
noct-	night	sub-	under
nom/nym-	name	super-	beyond, greater than
non/not-	negative prefix	syn/sym	bring together

tact-	touch	us/ut-	use
tech/techn-	tools	val/vale-	value, feel
tele-	at a distance	vend-	sell
temp-	time	ver/vera/veri-	true
ten/tend-	hold	verd-	green
terr-	earth, ground	verge-	boundary, together
tox-	harmful, poisonous	verse-	turn
tract-	pull	vete-	experienced
trans-	across	vi/vit/viv-	alive
trep-	fear, anxiety	vid/vis-	see
tri-	three	voc-	call, talk
un-	not	vor-	eat, consume
uni/uno-	one		

ROOTS DRILL

Here are a few words that use Latin or Greek roots. Define the words, identify which roots they use, and explain the function of the root within the word. Some have more than one root. (Answers can be found in Chapter 15.)

1. Acrimonious _____

2. Ambidextrous _____

3. Androgynous _____

4. Anteroom _____

5. Arboreal _____

6. Embrace _____

7. Circumscribe _____

8. Exculpate _____

9. Dermatology _____

10. Dormant _____

11. Fraternize _____

12. Herbivorous _____

13. Homophone _____

14. Ingratiate _____

15. Hypothermia _____

16. Lavish _____

17. Loquacious _____

18. Matrilineal _____

19. Misogynist _____

20. Olfaction _____

21. Paragraph _____

22. Potentate _____

23. Proximity _____

24. Pseudonym _____

25. Schism _____

26. Trepidation _____

27. Verdure _____

28. Veteran _____

29. Vociferous _____

30. Voracious _____

This next list is what we call our Vocabulary Master List. It gives every word we've ever seen on an SAT. If you memorize this list, you'll be unstoppable on even the most difficult questions!

This is a very long list, so try to take it in chunks. We recommend that you start with the words you've heard before. Make sure you have precise definitions for each, and look out for roots from the Master List. Once you've managed that first bunch, start moving on to the others. Invest in the biggest pack of blank flash cards you can find! You'll need them!

Everyone studies vocabulary differently, but when you are making flashcards, however you choose to make them, make sure you've got the word, a definition, and a sentence that uses the word correctly.

TOO MUCH IS NEVER ENOUGH: THE MONSTER LIST

So you've mastered all 250 words in the Hit Parade, have you? If so, onward and upward! Here is a list of an additional 400+ words that have appeared on SATs in the past three years. While they are less common than the Hit Parade words, these words—once mastered—will give you an even bigger leg up on the SAT.

abate	bravado	decried	excise
aberration	buttress	defamation	exculpate
abjure	cadent	deferment	exemplar
abridge	calumny	deleterious	expedient
acrid	capacious	delineation	expropriation
acrimony	catalyst	deluge	facetious
adept	cavort	demagogue	facile
affectation	chicanery	demurral	faction
aghast	chronic	denigrated	feign
agnostic	circuitous	denude	felicitous
allocate	circumvent	depravity	fiasco
anomaly	cloying	depreciatory	finagle
antipathy	coerced	derelict	flotilla
antiseptic	cogent	dilapidated	flourish
antithesis	commodity	dilettante	foible
apportionment	compendious	din	foppish
approbation	complacence	disarming	fortitude
appropriate (v.)	complicity	disincline	founder
apt	condone	disinterested	frivolous
arable	conferred	disjointed	fulsome
archipelago	conflagration	dispatch	furtiveness
arid	congenial	dispensation	futile
ascetic	conglomeration	disperse	gaffe
aspersion	conjure	disputation	gaiety
atrophy	conscript	distillation	gait
attenuate	consonance	divisive	gallantry
audacious	contiguous	doctrinaire	galled
avant-garde	convergence	doggerel	galvanize
avarice	convivial	dormant	garish
averse	corollary	dour	garner
balm	corpulence	effacement	garrulous
baneful	corroborate	empirical	gaunt
barrage	courtier	encumbrance	gibe
bellicose	culpability	endemic	gregarious
benefactor	cumulative	enervated	guileless
benevolent	curtail	epitaph	haranguing
blandish	dalliance	equanimity	harbinger
blatant	daunting	equivocal	hermetic
brandish	decorous	eschew	heterogeneity

histrionic
holistic
hubris
iconoclast
illicit
immaterial
immutable
imperious
impervious
impetus
imprudent
inane
inchoate
incisive
inconspicuous
incredulous
indigence
indigenous
indiscriminate
indolence
indomitable
induction
industrious
ineffable
inexorable
infamous
infelicity
ingenious
ingénue
innate
insidious
insolvent
instigation
insurrection
intermittent
interpolated
invective
invidious
iridescent
irreproachable
irresolute
itinerant
knave
labyrinth
laconic
lament
languid

latency
lethargic
libelous
lilt
lionize
lithe
lurid
machination
magisterial
malevolence
malicious
malign
manifesto
mediate
mélange
mire
mirth
miser
missive
mitigate
monotonous
motley
mundane
munificent
myopic
naïveté
nebulous
negate
nominal
nonchalance
notoriety
obstreperous
obtuse
occlusion
odoriferous
officious
opacity
oscillate
ossified
ostensible
ostentation
pallid
panacea
pander
panoramic
paradigm
paragon

parity
pathos
patronage
pedagogical
pedestrian
pensiveness
penurious
peripheral
perjure
perpetuate
perquisite
petulant
phlegmatic
pillory
placebo
plasticity
plaudit
plebian
plenitude
pluralistic
polarize
portent
posthumous
potentate
precarious
precedent
precept
precipitous
preclude
predilection
preeminent
premeditated
preponderance
prerogative
prescience
prevaricate
prodigious
profligate
profusion
propensity
punctilious
pundit
pungency
quagmire
quandary
querulous
quixotic

rambunctious
rapport
rapture
raucous
recalcitrant
recessive
recommence
recrimination
redoubtable
refute
relegate
remuneration
reparation
repartee
repertory
reprieve
requite
resolute
respite
resplendent
retraction
retroactive
risqué
rousing
ruffian
sacrosanct
sagacious
salient
sallow
salutary
salvo
sate
savant
scarce
scourge
scuttle
seditious
sedulous
serpentine
sibilant
slander
solace
somber
sophomoric
spate
spurious
spurned

squalid
stark
staunch
stoic
stolid
subversive
succinct
succulent
sullen
sumptuous
supple
surfeit
surmise
tacit
tactile
tangible
taut
teem
temper
tempest
temporal
temporize
tenet

terse
thwart
toady
topography
tortuous
touchstone
tractable
transitory
treacle
tremulous
trenchant
tribulation
trove
truculence
tryst
turpitude
ubiquitous
unalloyed
unctuous
unflagging
unscrupulous
unstinting
urbane

usurp
valor
vehemence
venal
verbatim
verdant
virtuoso
virulence
vitiate
vivacious
vociferous
voluminous
voracious
wane
warrant
wary
watershed
wax
wheedle
winnow
wistful
zenith

TRY IT DRILL 1

Complete answers and explanations can be found in Chapter 15.

1. Like monks who study complex texts and ideas endlessly, some comic book collectors have a truly ------- knowledge of Spiderman and Batman.

   (A) trivial (B) pedagogical (C) sacrosanct
   (D) erudite (E) sanctimonious

2. The tension in the room was -------: although we couldn't see it, we could feel it as if it were a physical presence in the room.

   (A) fabricated (B) palpable (C) perspicacious
   (D) close (E) invisible

3. Few things are quite so ------- as love of one's country in the United States: if you don't have it, you're often treated like a heretic.

   (A) political (B) sacrosanct (C) underwhelming
   (D) patriotic (E) nationalistic

4. Feeling an extra amount of ------- from his audience tonight, the comedian wondered if he had done something to ------- them.

   (A) condescension . . entertain
   (B) antipathy . . alienate
   (C) misanthropy . . despise
   (D) frigidity . . amuse
   (E) drollery . . dissuade

5. Although overstatement and ------- can occasionally be funny and apropos, most authors find that the more subtle ------- are the more technically sophisticated parts of a piece of writing.

   (A) humor . . details
   (B) exaggeration . . paragraphs
   (C) rhetoric . . orations
   (D) loquaciousness . . reminiscences
   (E) hyperbole . . nuances

6. Before World War II, many European governments took an attitude of ------- toward Hitler, allowing him to take what he wanted in hopes that he would not start war.

   (A) bellicosity (B) cacophony (C) pugnacity
   (D) antipathy (E) appeasement

7. The factory's main goal in mass production was -------: no product that came out of the factory should be any better or worse than the others.

   (A) excellence (B) differentiation (C) mediocrity
   (D) plentitude (E) uniformity

8. The professor's argument simply couldn't be -------: the only evidence he had was his own intuition.

   (A) articulated (B) disproven (C) educational
   (D) esoteric (E) substantiated

9. Although typically not one to wear ------- clothes, Gretchen could not resist the bright orange summer dress, which had so much more ------- than all her others.

   (A) temperate . . style
   (B) gaudy . . flair
   (C) chic . . modishness
   (D) cosmopolitan . . drabness
   (E) elegant . . averageness

10. The music critic ------- the idea to his readers that the true ------- in the orchestra was the second violinist rather than the first, who was usually considered the real master.

    (A) disproved . . savant
    (B) presented . . harmony
    (C) dismantled . . maestro
    (D) promulgated . . virtuoso
    (E) articulated . . amateur

TRY IT DRILL 2

Complete answers and explanations can be found in Chapter 15.

1. Tired of living a ------- existence at school, Martha decided to audition for the school play in hopes that she could get a little more attention.

   (A) recondite (B) miserable (C) prolific
   (D) quotidian (E) peripatetic

2. The weatherman's prediction of a ------- weekend seemed to lack a certain amount of ------- after such a cold week.

   (A) tropical . . incredulousness
   (B) temperate . . skepticism
   (C) subzero . . authority
   (D) balmy . . veracity
   (E) gelid . . probability

3. Louis C.K. works ------- on his stand-up comedy: in addition to writing his new hour-long specials every year, he also writes, directs, and stars in his own TV show.

   (A) reluctantly (B) effortlessly (C) hilariously
   (D) methodically (E) indefatigably

4. The rollercoaster at first seemed rather -------, but after we rode it a few times, we no longer felt that it was so dangerous.

   (A) precarious (B) old-fashioned (C) slapdash
   (D) anachronistic (E) antiquated

5. The most popular politicians are those who can ------- the partisan gridlock and get things done.

   (A) transcend (B) prejudice (C) deconstruct
   (D) dismiss (E) disparage

6. Unlike the businessowner's employees, who praise him almost to the point of excess, his stockholders are less likely to be so -------.

   (A) complementary (B) fulsome (C) guarded
   (D) economical (E) dismissive

7. The set of common interests and laid-back attitudes led to lots of ------- among employees, meaning that the few conflicts that there were could be ------- quickly and maturely, as among friends.

   (A) rancor . . escalated
   (B) indifference . . ignored
   (C) amicability . . personalized
   (D) ambivalence . . forgotten
   (E) collegiality . . resolved

8. One difficulty of learning another language lies in keeping track of secondary word definitions, especially those that may be insulting to native speakers: you have to be careful that the word you're ------- doesn't have another ------- meaning.

   (A) employing . . pejorative
   (B) articulating . . poetic
   (C) defining . . prosaic
   (D) speaking . . insignificant
   (E) bellowing . . quiet

9. The startup company was near shutting its doors for good when the truly ------- influx of cash came from a new investor.

   (A) meager (B) affluent (C) providential
   (D) unrequested (E) immaterial

10. As someone who always showed up on time and acted in a professional way, Harleen was always described as -------.

    (A) prim (B) lackadaisical (C) punctilious
    (D) enervating (E) ambivalent

TRY IT DRILL 3

Complete answers and explanations can be found in Chapter 15.

1. Many pet owners worry that they will never be able to tame their ------- pets because of the ------- wildness of any wild animal.

   (A) pliable . . voracious
   (B) mulish . . adapted
   (C) intransigent . . inherent
   (D) docile . . learned
   (E) recalcitrant . . liberating

2. Convincing though they were at times, many of Nietzsche's arguments were simply -------: he would present an extreme version of his own views in order to shake people out of their own complacent beliefs.

   (A) polemical (B) rhetorical (C) pedantic
      (D) incoherent (E) unconvincing

3. Some of the best comedic actors are -------: they do their best work making things up on the spot, not tied to a script.

   (A) ambivalent (B) improvisational (C) hyperbolic
      (D) equivocal (E) studious

4. In class, Gary was particularly interesting when discussing ------- issues, showing that he had read a great deal about religious and spiritual topics.

   (A) erudite (B) dogmatic (C) planetary
      (D) topical (E) metaphysical

5. James suspected that New Orleans would be filled with carousing partiers when he visited during Mardi Gras, and he soon saw that all these fears of ------- had come true.

   (A) insurrection (B) diffidence (C) sanctimony
      (D) debauchery (E) circumscription

6. We thought the fortune teller's remarks were totally misguided, but the way things have turned out, her remarks were incredibly -------.

   (A) prescient (B) psychic (C) controversial
      (D) deleterious (E) euphemistic

7. The hill was so -------, so incredibly steep, that Steve could barely look down it without becoming nauseous.

   (A) temperate (B) verdant (C) craggy
      (D) vertiginous (E) remote

8. As a satirist, H.L. Mencken had a wit that was often -------: those who faced his sharp criticisms often wondered whether he was poking fun at them or slandering them.

   (A) inhumane (B) parodic (C) balanced
      (D) acerbic (E) churlish

9. With bitterly cold temperatures in the winter, Minnesota's weather can be -------, as it is characterized by heavy snowfall and ------- air.

   (A) extreme . . temperate
   (B) precipitate . . sere
   (C) clement . . freezing
   (D) unforgiving . . lukewarm
   (E) inhospitable . . frigid

10. While many employees of the company boast of their own -------, their low productivity and frequent procrastination ------- this self-assessment.

   (A) satisfaction . . undermine
   (B) assiduousness . . belie
   (C) thoroughness . . underline
   (D) mastery . . corroborate
   (E) ingenuity . . articulate

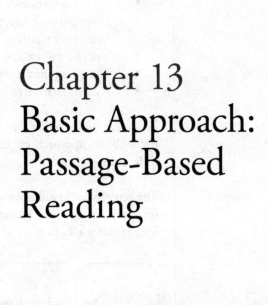

Chapter 13
Basic Approach:
Passage-Based
Reading

BASIC APPROACH—PASSAGE-BASED READING

In the Introduction, we talked about the genre of SAT reading. This should have clarified what the SAT is expecting you to do. In this chapter, we're going to discuss The Princeton Review's basic approach for attacking this peculiar genre.

Even for good readers, SAT Reading can be really tough. The difficulty can be summarized like this:

- There's not enough time to read the passage and work the questions.
- Large parts of each passage don't seem to matter, so it's impossible to focus your reading.
- You end up reading a ton of stuff you don't need.
- The questions are written in a confusing way.
- It often seems like more than one answer can work.

We know what makes the SAT Reading section tough. That's why we've come up with an approach to these reading passages that can address all of these difficulties.

The centerpiece of our approach will come as a relief. This section is a time-crunch for everyone, so here's our most important piece of advice. It'll save you three or four minutes a section.

> Don't read the passage until you know what you're looking for.

Think about it. Typically, you'll read the whole passage and then go to the questions, forget everything you just read, and read the whole passage again. Why not cut out that first step entirely? After all, you aren't scored on your ability to read quickly or to understand every aspect of the passage, as you might be in an English class. On SAT Reading, you get points for answering questions, so you'll want to get to those questions as quickly as possible and let them frame how you read.

To that end, we've come up with a Basic Approach for Long Reading passages that we can adapt for the other types of reading as well.

1. **Read the blurb.** The blurb may be only a sentence or two long, but it shouldn't be skipped. The blurb will tell you what the passage is about.
2. **Select and understand a question.** Skip any confusing or time-consuming questions and do the questions that you understand first.
3. **Mark the reference window.** Most answers will be located within a small portion of the passage. Find that portion and read it carefully.

4. **Predict the answer.** As with Sentence Completions, put the answer in your own words before you work the answer choices.
5. **POE.** Find your answer by eliminating four bad answers.

Let's look at these steps one-by-one, and then we'll see why this is such an effective strategy.

Step One: Read the Blurb

The blurb is easy to ignore. It's usually a sentence or two long, and none of the questions will ask directly about it. Still, the blurb situates you within the passage. Because you won't be reading the passage in its entirety, the blurb may be the closest you get to a statement of the main idea.

We'll work the Basic Approach through an SAT-style reading passage. We'll take it in chunks in exactly the way that we advise that you do on the test. It may feel like you're making a real leap of faith here, but you'll see that our technique contains everything you need.

So, first things first, let's check out the blurb:

This passage, adapted from a short story, presents an 11-year-old girl, Sarah, her father, and her brother.

This blurb is only a sentence long, but it contains a good deal more than you may suspect. We know it's focused on a young girl and that the two other main characters will be her father and her brother. If we wanted to go out on a limb, we might guess that this is somehow about how this family interacts or why the girl's mother is no longer in the picture.

Caveat: Skimming the Passage

Some people can benefit from a minute-or-two-long skim of the passage here. We have found that many students work a little better with skipping the passage, but if you can use your skimming time wisely (if you can do something other than just stare blankly at the passage for two minutes), go for it.

We're trying to give you a method that is based on an economical use of your time. If you can make a minute-long skim count, or if it makes you feel more secure to do it, by all means do so.

We're flexible on whether you skim or skip the passage, because ultimately, the most important step in the Basic Approach is the next one. After all, the SAT is not testing you on how you read the passage. The SAT is testing you on how you answer questions.

Step Two: Select and Understand a Question

Your first impulse might be to try to do the questions in order. Remember, though, just because the SAT presents the questions to you in a certain order, that doesn't mean you have to *do* them in that order.

The students who perform best on the SAT are those who can make the test their own. We call this strategy POOD, or Personal Order of Difficulty, and because Reading has no Order of Difficulty, POOD is even more important.

Now, remember how little you've done on this passage so far. Maybe you've skimmed for a minute or so, but more than likely, you've read only the blurb. Do you think you're ready to answer a question like this one?

1. The passage as a whole suggests that Sarah wishes that, in her family's life, she were

    (A) somewhere else
    (B) away at school
    (C) more involved
    (D) getting married
    (E) her brother's age

Absolutely not! This question asks about "the passage as a whole," but we haven't read a single line of it yet. Let's skip this question and come back to it when we've got a better sense of how the passage works.

2. In lines 1-2, the phrases "an awful lot" and "all of a sudden" help to emphasize Sarah's

    (A) disapproval of her father's new girlfriend
    (B) apathy toward her personal space being invaded
    (C) wish that things could be as they once were
    (D) unwillingness to accept a new person into her life
    (E) surprise at a new development in her father's home

This is more like it. The question guides us to a particular part of the passage and to two specific quotations within that part. This is a question we can tackle, and the question itself tells us what we need to read.

Let's make sure we understand the question first. Notice that this one doesn't contain a question mark. Let's turn it into a question that we can actually answer. Something like this would work:

Why does the passage use phrases such as "an awful lot" and "all of a sudden"? What do these phrases tell us about Sarah?

Now that we've got questions we can answer, and we know where to look for them in the passage. When you are selecting questions, take these things into account:

- **Line and paragraph references.** Both of these have the obvious advantage of directing you to the part of the passage that you need.
- **Lead words.** These are words that will "lead" you back to particular parts of the passage. Look in particular for proper nouns, italics, years and dates, or words in quotations—basically, anything you can scan for easily in the passage.
- **Chronology.** The SAT presents questions more or less in chronological order of the passage. If you do the questions in chronological order, you may find that you can read through the passage in a targeted way.
- **Shortness of questions and answers.** Shorter questions and answers are usually easier on the SAT. There's less information to manage, and you can pay more particular attention to the words.

Once you've picked your questions in a good order, it's time to go to the passage.

Step Three: Mark the Reference Window

Now that you know what you're looking for, you're ready to read. Mark the reference window you need, and read carefully. You've got enough time to do so, and you want to make sure you can pay attention to all the words you're reading.

For this question, a safe reference window includes the two sentences given in the question and another for context. Here's that window:

> Daddy was seeing an awful lot of his new friend. One
> of the rooms in his house was all of a sudden full of her
> stuff; neither Sarah nor her brother was allowed in there
> Line anymore. It had started with a few dinners and shopping
> 5 trips, and now it seemed that their father's friend
> basically lived in the house, and she was even shifting
> around some furniture that had been in place for as long
> as Sarah could remember.

The question asks about the phrases "an awful lot" and "all of a sudden." The best support comes from the third sentence: *now it seemed that their father's friend basically lived in the house, even shifting around some furniture that had been in place for as long as Sarah could remember.* Sarah seems surprised by the suddenness of this transformation, but we can't tell whether she's approving or disapproving of it.

It turns out that this a great question to start. It's got a nice, small window, and we're now right in the heart of the story.

Step Four: Predict the Answer

Now that we've read our reference window, let's try to answer the question ourselves. Remember, we rewrote it like this:

Why does the passage use phrases like "an awful lot" and "all of a sudden"? What do these phrases tell us about Sarah?

Given what we know so far, it seems that the phrases "an awful lot" and "all of a sudden" tell us that Sarah is surprised at her father's new girlfriend. The sentences don't tell us whether she feels positively or negatively toward this girlfriend, only that she's surprised. So if we could answer those questions in the simplest way possible, we could write something like this: *Sarah is surprised.*

Step Five: POE

Now, let's go back to the question and try to eliminate bad answers.

> 2. In lines 1-2, the phrases "an awful lot" and "all of a sudden" help to emphasize Sarah's
>
>   (A) disapproval of her father's new girlfriend
>   (B) apathy toward her personal space being invaded
>   (C) wish that things could be as they once were
>   (D) unwillingness to accept a new person into her life
>   (E) surprise at a new development in her father's home

Because we've already predicted an answer, this question becomes significantly easier! Given the answer we came up with (*Sarah is surprised*), we won't be distracted by the others, and the answer must be choice (E).

Sometimes you won't be able to guess the answer with such precision, so make sure you're using POE aggressively, and above all, *don't think!* Strange as it is to say, thinking can be your enemy on the SAT. Any of these answers could be *plausible* in an English class, and your English teacher might encourage you to come up with your own interpretation. However, in the SAT genre of reading that we discussed in the Introduction, thinking and interpreting can get you in big trouble.

When eliminating answers, remember that **a correct answer must have support in the passage.**

The SAT can throw you a few curveballs, so be on the lookout for three special kinds of trap answers:

- **Not mentioned.** Choice (B) is a good example of this trap. Usually at least one of the answers in a set of answer choices will be totally out of left field. Don't let it tempt you!
- **Extreme language.** Choice (A) is a good example of this trap. It takes what we saw in the window and overstates it. Be on the lookout for extreme words such as *only, always, never,* or any strongly worded statements.
- **Half-right, half-wrong.** Choices (C) and (D) are good examples of this trap. These answers have some correct elements, but every word in the answer choice must be correct.

Put It All Together

We've already read the blurb, now let's pick another question or two to tackle. Here are two that would be good candidates to do next:

3. In lines 25-26, "Bride?" primarily serves to suggest that Sarah

(A) cannot hear Tess over the noisy car
(B) is unaware of a planned future event
(C) is acting like she does not know any words
(D) resists the idea of having Tess as a mother
(E) refuses to pay attention when Tess talks to her

4. The questions in lines 43-45 ("How … play?") primarily serve to

(A) set up the scene in the next paragraph
(B) name specific topics of discussion
(C) demonstrate the depths of the disagreement
(D) suggest Sarah's continued exclusion
(E) create suspense in a reader who wants to know the answers

Step Two: Select and Understand a Question

Which of these two questions would be a better option to do first? Both contain line references, but question #3 references an earlier section of the passage, and it asks about a smaller window of text. Let's do that one first.

If we translate the question into our own words, we could ask it like this:

Why does Sarah wonder at the word "Bride"?

Let's read the passage and find out.

Step Three: Mark the Reference Window

This question comes at the end of a paragraph, so let's read a few lines before it. Here's the relevant window (Tess, by the way, is Sarah's father's girlfriend):

> And eventually there was talk of "your new mommy" and
> 20 Tess's very old parents introduced themselves as "grandma
> and grandpa." Sarah and her brother had not been warned
> that these things were happening: they just happened. And on
> one Thursday afternoon, Tess picked Sarah up after school
> to take her shopping for a junior bridesmaid's dress. Sarah
> 25 watched out the window as they drove to the mall: "Bride?"

Notice the continuity with the previous question. Sarah is still surprised at how intimate his father's new girlfriend is becoming. When Tess picks Sarah up after school, she tells the girl that they are going to buy a *junior bridesmaid's dress*. Sarah is surprised to hear the word, and she is clearly unaware that Tess is to become her father's *bride*.

Step Four: Predict the Answer

Remember how we rephrased the question:

Why does Sarah wonder at the word "Bride"?

As we saw in the reference window, Sarah is surprised that Tess is to become her father's bride, just as she is surprised at how quickly Tess is becoming a part of her family. We could answer this question this way: *Sarah didn't know Tess was going to be a "bride."*

Step Five: POE

Now here are the answer choices:

(A)   cannot hear Tess over the noisy car
(B)   is unaware of a planned future event
(C)   is acting as if she does not know any words
(D)   resists the idea of having Tess as a mother
(E)   refuses to pay attention when Tess talks to her

Although choice (B) sounds a little odd, it matches up best with our predicted answer. Choices (A) and (C) are silly and are not mentioned in the passage. Choice (E) indicates an extreme tone that isn't supported by the passage. Choice (D) is partially correct: Sarah is grappling with *the idea of having Tess as a mother*, but there's no indication that Sarah *resists* this idea.

Now, try the other one without the steps listed. Here's the relevant part of the passage and the question:

> 40   In the coming weeks, though, Sarah was not to be
> so involved again. She was usually asked to watch her
> brother as her daddy and Tess met with planners, caterers,
> and decorators. How many guests would they have? What
> was the color scheme of the place? What kind of music
> 45 should the band play? Sarah's father sat back admiringly
> and let Tess make most of the decisions. Sarah had never
> seen him so calm—he was usually such an over-planner,
> barking orders at all within his sight.

4. The questions in lines 43-45 ("How … play?") primarily serve to

(A) set up the scene in the next paragraph
(B) name specific topics of discussion
(C) demonstrate the depths of the disagreement
(D) suggest Sarah's continued exclusion
(E) create suspense in a reader who wants to know the answers

Rephrase the question first. Something like *Why are there so many questions in this paragraph?* would work. Now, when you read the paragraph, you'll see that all the questions are those that Tess and Sarah's father would ask the *planners, caterers, and decorators*. As we learn after the questions, the answers to these questions will mostly come down to Tess, who is making *most of the decisions*.

We started by asking, *Why are there so many questions in this paragraph?*

Now we can answer, *These are the questions that Tess and Sarah's father are asking the planners, caterers, and decorators.*

We can't comment on choice (A) because we don't have the next paragraph, but we can probably eliminate it, because the questions themselves are not that important. They're just there to show how much is going in to planning the wedding. Choices (C) and (D) are too extreme. There is no *disagreement* in this paragraph, and while Sarah is described as *not… involved*, there is no indication that she is being actively *excluded*. Choice (E) is just silly.

Our best answer here is choice (B). If this answer seems a little dull, that's okay! It's the only one that's supported in the passage.

A FINAL WORD: BIG QUESTIONS AND THE GOLDEN THREAD

As you pick good questions, the earliest ones should focus on the details of the story or passage you are reading. This will not only ensure you the easier points, it will also build your knowledge of the passage and will make the big questions that much easier to answer.

We've seen only three questions from this passage so far, but you've already probably noticed that some of these questions deal with similar topics. Questions #2 and #3 are both about Sarah's surprise. So if we get a question like this one, we can probably guess the answer.

> 5. In context, "shifting around some furniture" (line 6) is best characterized as an example of
>
>   (A) one of many possible improvements that a homeowner can make
>   (B) something typically done by someone who lives in the house containing the furniture
>   (C) one of Sarah's biggest problems with her father's new girlfriend
>   (D) an aspect of home decorating in which Sarah is particularly interested
>   (E) the reason Tess is invited so often to the house

We know that Sarah is surprised to see his father's girlfriend moving in so quickly. We've seen that Sarah doesn't know what to do with Tess's intimacy. Therefore, we can go with choice (B), which picks up on that theme.

And from these few questions, we can answer the whole-passage question with which we began.

> 6. The passage as a whole suggests that Sarah wishes that, in her family's life, she were
>
>   (A) somewhere else
>   (B) away at school
>   (C) more involved
>   (D) getting married
>   (E) her brother's age

The answer here must be choice (C). We haven't read much, but of all these answer choices, the only one that seems to have any relevance is choice (C), which addresses both Sarah's confusion and her wish to be more involved. Think of this like the half-right/half-wrong answer choices. If it's not true for a small part of the passage, it can't be true for the whole thing!

SO HOW EFFECTIVE IS THE BASIC APPROACH?

Let's revisit our list of challenges from the beginning of this chapter. We said the following things make SAT reading difficult:

- There's not enough time to read the passage and work the questions.
- Large parts of each passage don't seem to matter, so it's impossible to focus your reading.
- You end up reading a ton of stuff you don't need.
- The questions are written in a confusing way.
- It often seems like more than one answer can work.

The Basic Approach addresses all of these difficulties in the following ways:

- When we skip or skim the passage rather than reading it in its entirety, we save a tremendous amount of time.
- When we are guided by the questions, we read only what we need to answer those questions.
- When we are guided by the questions, we don't read the stuff we don't need.
- When we rewrite the questions, we make them clearer and more answerable.
- When we try to predict the answer, we are much less likely to pick distracting answers.

Chapter 14
Critical Reading
Exercises

PASSAGE I

Printmaking advanced the art world as well as the realm of communication. The following passage, written in 1985, discusses its history.

"Printmaker!" The connotation of this word, curiously absent from other languages, began to have some meaning only after World War II. Surely, before
Line the war, and often in the long, splendid history of prints,
5 there had been artists who created nothing but prints. However, in most cases, the artists drew a composition before going to the plate or block of stone, rather than working exclusively on these materials. Even this is not the entire distinction between earlier artists such
10 as Callot and Meryon and those followers of Hayter who could only be called "printmakers." Callot and Meryon made prints that, following the original object of working in a multiple medium, were meant to be printed in large numbers for wide distribution of the image.
15 Indeed, many painters made prints for this sole reason. But the printmakers of the second half of the twentieth century found creating in a print medium itself totally satisfying; they often did not care if no more than a few copies were made. Instead, the complex techniques of
20 printmaking itself were what entranced them. In the words of Sylvan Cole, former Director of Associated American Artists (AAA, the largest print gallery in America and publisher of over 1,500 prints since 1934), "The change that was taking place was the breakup with
25 the artist/painter (or abstract expressionist) who was not interested in printmaking, and out of this came a man called a printmaker, people like Karl Schrag, Peterdi, Lasansky, Misch Kohn—who built their reputations as printmakers."
30 Before the war, artists made considerable numbers of prints. This was their only work; no doubt it was often a matter of survival, not preference. Dozens of prints in a relatively new medium, silkscreen, were turned out for the adornment of schools and other government
35 buildings.
The G.I. Bill filled the colleges, universities, and art schools of post-war America during a period of prosperity that encouraged such institutions to enlarge their facilities or open new ones, particularly those
40 devoted to the arts. Many veterans who would never have had the opportunity to attend college if they had not been drafted had little direction—were "lost," so to speak—and found that the unrestrained atmosphere of post-war art schools and art departments represented just
45 the sort of freedom they needed after years of military conformity. (Many others, of course, had profited from the organized lifestyle of the military and sought it in more disciplined fields such as medicine, law, and business. The famous "Organization Man" could
50 hardly have had such success if this less independent group had not also made a major contribution to post-war society.) In the late 1940s, then, one could observe the beginnings of a phenomenal expansion of art education in institutions of higher learning, where art
55 departments attracted returning G.I.s who had completed their undergraduate work before the war, and in older, established art schools that were filled to capacity with those who had only finished high school. Students who fell under the spell of Lasansky during his first years
60 at the State University of Iowa went on to found print workshops in other universities. Soon students of these workshops pioneered others, so that in a very short time there were facilities for the study of printmaking in most universities in the United States.
65 The proliferation of places where printmaking was taught and the subsequent increase in the number of printmakers led to the birth of related institutions: the Brooklyn Museum's annual National Print Exhibition, an open exhibition, in contrast with the traditional
70 invitational showings of the Society of Etchers (note that these artists referred to themselves as etchers, not printmakers) or the other one-medium groups such as the National Serigraph Society; the International Group Arts Society, a membership-subscription organization
75 whose purpose was to publish and sell prints by new, less conservative artists than those of the AAA; and regional and international exhibitions devoted exclusively to prints, such as the Northwest Printmakers Society, the Philadelphia Print Club, and international biennials
80 of prints in Cincinnati, Ljubljana, and Tokyo. Thus, in the United States and elsewhere, the need to show and distribute the outpourings of the print workshops produced new organizations that in turn further encouraged the creation of prints.

Find the Window

Identify the lines you will read in order to answer each question. This will rarely be limited to the lines mentioned in the question! Complete answers and explanations can be found in Chapter 15.

13. In lines 10-14, the author asserts that Callot and Meryon

14. In lines 16-19, the author suggests that printmakers of the late twentieth century

15. The author quotes Sylvan Cole in lines 24-29 in order to

16. The purpose of the second paragraph (lines 30-35) in relation to the passage is to

17. The word "adornment" in line 34 most nearly means

18. The purpose of the G.I. Bill, mentioned in lines 36-40, was to

19. The word "lost" in line 42 most nearly means

20. The author suggests that an "Organization Man" (line 49) is

21. In lines 53-58, the author attributes the "phenomenal expansion of art education" primarily to

22. In the last paragraph, the author cites which of the following effects of the "proliferation of places where printmaking was taught" (lines 65-66) in the United States?

23. The author's description in the last paragraph of the new organizations indicates that

24. All of the following could be expected of a discipline of Lasansky EXCEPT

Predict the Answer

Now that you have found and read the window for each question, try to predict the answer for each of these questions. Complete answers and explanations can be found in Chapter 15.

13. In lines 10-14, the author asserts that Callot and Meryon

14. In lines 16-19, the author suggests that printmakers of the late twentieth century

15. The author quotes Sylvan Cole in lines 24-29 in order to

16. The purpose of the second paragraph (lines 30-35) in relation to the passage is to

17. The word "adornment" in line 34 most nearly means

18. The purpose of the G.I. Bill, mentioned in lines 36-40, was to

19. The word "lost" in line 42 most nearly means

20. The author suggests that an "Organization Man" (line 49) is

21. In lines 53-58, the author attributes the "phenomenal expansion of art education" primarily to

22. In the last paragraph, the author cites which of the following effects of the "proliferation of places where printmaking was taught" (lines 65-66) in the United States?

23. The author's description in the last paragraph of the new organizations indicates that

24. All of the following could be expected of a discipline of Lasansky EXCEPT

POE

Now that you have predicted the answers to these questions, use those predictions to eliminate bad answers. Complete answers and explanations can be found in Chapter 15.

13. In lines 10-14, the author asserts that Callot and Meryon

   (A) were early examples, with Hayter, of what have since been called "printmakers"

   (B) were more concerned with producing vast quantities of prints than Hayter's disciples had been

   (C) were painters who regarded printmaking as an inferior vocation

   (D) found complete satisfaction in the creation of art through a print medium

   (E) were difficult to distinguish from earlier artists, like Hayter

14. In lines 16-19, the author suggests that printmakers of the late twentieth century

   (A) were more concerned with the quantity of their prints than with the intricacy of their work

   (B) were often distracted from their primary intention by the complexity of printmaking

   (C) were fulfilled by the act of printmaking itself, while mass production was a secondary concern

   (D) faced a production quota of prints which became an insurmountable handicap for most artists

   (E) wanted to achieve international recognition for their groundbreaking work

15. The author quotes Sylvan Cole in lines 24-29 in order to

   (A) demonstrate how Cole changed the art of printmaking during the turn of the century

   (B) pay homage to a notable pioneer of the art of printmaking

   (C) introduce the term "Abstract Expressionist" and examine its place in the art movement

   (D) explain the relationship between printmaking and painting

   (E) provide support for his assertions about the new developments in printmaking

16. The purpose of the second paragraph (lines 30-35) in relation to the passage is to

   (A) provide support for the idea that modern printmaking emerged only after World War II

   (B) acquaint the reader with the long-established history of printmaking as a distinct art form

   (C) question the originality of such artists as Callot and Meryton who claimed to have invented modern printmaking

   (D) argue for the recognition of artists who were forced to create prints for the government

   (E) lament the deplorable situation of those artists who could find no other opportunity for expression than printmaking

17. The word "adornment" in line 34 most nearly means

   (A) distribution

   (B) inundation

   (C) decoration

   (D) enjoyment

   (E) construction

18. The purpose of the G.I. Bill, mentioned in lines 36-40, was to

   (A) allow veterans to bypass college in order to concentrate on artistic pursuits

   (B) allow veterans to attend colleges or specialized schools by offering assistance after the war

   (C) provide the "lost" veterans with a place to study

   (D) open new facilities or strengthen already established art institutions

   (E) discourage veterans uninterested in any type of artistic pursuit

19. The word "lost" in line 42 most nearly means

(A) unfound
(B) denied
(C) desperate
(D) aimless
(E) aberrant

20. The author suggests that an "Organization Man" (line 49) is

(A) one who resisted entering the military in order to focus on more structured pursuits
(B) one who benefited from the infusion of former soldiers into the workforce
(C) a college student who helped enlarge facilities such as art schools
(D) a failed attempt by an elected member to organize the artists into a more formal union
(E) a veteran who used his strict military training to succeed as part of the workforce

21. In lines 53-58, the author attributes the "phenomenal expansion of art education" primarily to

(A) increased membership in the military
(B) the appeal of art departments both to veterans who had graduated from college and to those who had not
(C) Lasansky's trickery in brainwashing students
(D) the State University of Iowa's groundbreaking work which accounted for the dynamic influx of art-school students
(E) the influence in the late 1940s of the famous "Organization Man"

22. In the last paragraph, the author cites which of the following effects of the "proliferation of places where printmaking was taught" (lines 65-66) in the United States?

(A) The increased desire to have prints from the workshops displayed encouraged the production of additional prints.
(B) The financial success of the AAA encouraged many businesses to establish their own institutions.
(C) Attempts to expose the public to works of less conservative artists produced a backlash against all printmakers.
(D) Printmakers desperate to entice more artists into printmaking neglected their own work.
(E) Increased publicity spurred a rise in public appreciation and financial support.

23. The author's description in the last paragraph of the new organizations indicates that

(A) while printmaking ceases to be an actively pursued art, many institutes still display old prints
(B) etchers are being neglected because of the extraordinary popularity of printmakers
(C) today, exhibitions of prints can be found around the world
(D) the demand for prints has grown beyond all expectations
(E) older organizations were reluctant to display prints because they didn't consider printmaking to be a true art form

24. All of the following could be expected of a discipline of Lasansky EXCEPT

(A) advocating that artists work in multiple medium formats
(B) establishing new programs in universities devoted to printmaking
(C) forgoing the composition stage in the creation of new art
(D) caring little for the mass production or distribution of new prints
(E) viewing the intricacies of print production as a vital part of their art

PASSAGE II

The following passage was taken from the autobiography of Helen Keller, who was stricken with an illness that left her deaf and blind as a young child.

I guessed vaguely from my mother's signs and from the hurrying to and fro in the house that something unusual was about to happen, so I went to the door
Line and waited on the steps. The afternoon sun penetrated
5 the mass of honeysuckle that covered the porch, and fell on my upturned face. My fingers lingered almost unconsciously on the familiar leaves and blossoms which had just come forth to greet the sweet southern spring. I did not know what the future held of marvel or surprise
10 for me. Anger and bitterness had preyed upon me continually for weeks and a deep languor had succeeded this passionate struggle.

Have you ever been at sea in a dense fog, when it seemed as if a tangible white darkness shut you in,
15 and the great ship, tense and anxious, groped her way toward the shore with plummet and sounding-line, and you waited with beating heart for something to happen? I was like that ship before my education began, only I was without compass or sounding-line, and had no way
20 of knowing how near the harbour was. "Light! Give me light!" was the wordless cry of my soul, and the light of love shone on me in that very hour.

I felt approaching footsteps, I stretched out my hand as I supposed to my mother. Someone took it, and I was
25 caught up and held close in the arms of her who had come to reveal all things to me, and, more than all things else, to love me.

The morning after my teacher came she led me into her room and gave me a doll. When I had played with it
30 a little while, Miss Sullivan slowly spelled into my hand the word "d-o-l-l." I was at once interested in this finger play and tried to imitate it. When I finally succeeded in making the letters correctly I was flushed with childish pleasure and pride. Running downstairs to my mother
35 I held up my hand and made the letters for doll. I did not know that I was spelling a word or even that words existed; I was simply making my fingers go in monkey-like imitation. But my teacher had been with me several weeks before I understood that everything has a name.
40 One day, while I was playing with my new doll, Miss Sullivan put my big rag doll into my lap also, spelled "d-o-l-l" and tried to make me understand that "d-o-l-l" applied to both. Earlier in the day we had a tussle over

the words "m-u-g" and "w-a-t-e-r." Miss Sullivan had
45 tried to impress it upon me that "m-u-g" is mug and that "w-a-t-e-r" is water, but I persisted in confounding the two. In despair she had dropped the subject for the time, only to renew it at the first opportunity. I became impatient at her repeated attempts and, seizing the new
50 doll, I dashed it upon the floor. I was keenly delighted when I felt the fragments of the broken doll at my feet. Neither sorrow nor regret followed my passionate outburst. I had not loved the doll. In the still, dark world in which I lived there was no strong sentiment or
55 tenderness.

We walked down the path to the well-house, attracted by the fragrance of the honeysuckle with which it was covered. Someone was pumping water and my teacher placed my hand under the spout. As the cool stream
60 gushed over one hand she spelled into the other the word water, first slowly, then rapidly. I stood still, my whole attention fixed upon the motions of her fingers. Suddenly I felt a misty consciousness as of something forgotten—a thrill of returning thought; and somehow
65 the mystery of language was revealed to me. I knew then that "w-a-t-e-r" meant the wonderful cool something that was flowing over my hand. That living word awakened my soul, gave it light, hope, joy, set it free! There were barriers still, it is true, but barriers that could in time be
70 swept away.

I left the well-house eager to learn. Everything had a name, and each name gave birth to a new thought. As we returned to the house every object which I touched seemed to quiver with life. That was because I saw
75 everything with the strange, new sight that had come to me. On entering the door I remembered the doll I had broken. I felt my way to the heart and picked up the pieces. I tried vainly to put them together. Then my eyes filled with tears; for I realized what I had done, and for
80 the first time I felt repentance and sorrow.

Find the Window

Identify the lines you will read in order to answer each question. This will rarely be limited to the lines mentioned in the question! Complete answers and explanations can be found in Chapter 15.

10. According to the passage, the narrator views language as

11. The word "succeeded" in line 11 most nearly means

12. The analogy to "being at sea in a dense fog" (lines 13-20) is used to show that the author felt

13. The author's reference to "finger play" in lines 31-32 emphasizes her

14. The narrator's attitude toward breaking the doll changes from

15. The author implies that, prior to the arrival of her teacher, she

16. The passage suggests that the author broke the doll in order to

17. It can be inferred from the passage that the author would most likely agree with which of the following statements?

18. The difference between the author's experience in lines 32-38 ("When I...imitation") and in line 65-70 ("I knew...away") can best be characterized as the difference between

Predict the Answer

Now that you have found and read the window for each question, try to predict the answer for each of these questions. Complete answers and explanations can be found in Chapter 15.

10. According to the passage, the narrator views language as

11. The word "succeeded" in line 11 most nearly means

12. The analogy to "being at sea in a dense fog" (lines 13-20) is used to show that the author felt

13. The author's reference to "finger play" in lines 31-32 emphasizes her

14. The narrator's attitude toward breaking the doll changes from

15. The author implies that, prior to the arrival of her teacher, she

16. The passage suggests that the author broke the doll in order to

17. It can be inferred from the passage that the author would most likely agree with which of the following statements?

18. The difference between the author's experience in lines 32-38 ("When I...imitation") and in line 65-70 ("I knew...away") can best be characterized as the difference between

POE

Now that you have predicted the answers to these questions, use those predictions to eliminate bad answers. Complete answers and explanations can be found in Chapter 15.

10. According to the passage, the narrator views language as

   (A) a necessary but impractical part of life
   (B) the key to her appreciation of the world around her
   (C) a phenomenon that remains mysterious
   (D) the only method she can use to express her feelings
   (E) a barrier to understanding her own thoughts

11. The word "succeeded" in line 11 most nearly means

   (A) accomplished
   (B) split
   (C) followed
   (D) broken
   (E) performed

12. The analogy to "being at sea in a dense fog" (lines 13-20) is used to show that the author felt

   (A) scared, because she felt like she was sinking in her dark, still life
   (B) angry, because she could not control her life
   (C) adventurous, because she knew that learning could be like a journey
   (D) lost, because she had difficulty communicating with the world
   (E) confused, because her new teacher was trying to accomplish too much

13. The author's reference to "finger play" in lines 31-32 emphasizes her

   (A) childish need to learn by playing games with dolls and toys
   (B) teacher's technique for teaching her grammar
   (C) initial inability to understand that she was spelling words with her hands
   (D) opinion that learning sign language was as easy as a child's game
   (E) mother's helplessness in teaching her to communicate with her teacher

14. The narrator's attitude toward breaking the doll changes from

   (A) sorrow to understanding
   (B) excitement to disgust
   (C) anger to joy
   (D) pleasure to regret
   (E) indifference to enjoyment

15. The author implies that, prior to the arrival of her teacher, she

   (A) experienced feelings of resentment, followed by a time of inactivity
   (B) had never felt loved before
   (C) did not expect anything good to happen in her future
   (D) was eager to learn about the world but lacked the means to
   (E) was not dominated by sentimentalism and tenderness

16. The passage suggests that the author broke the doll in order to

   (A) express her frustration at her inability to understand her teacher's lesson
   (B) lash out at her teacher for her teacher's failure to instruct her properly
   (C) reveal the extent to which she felt enraged by her situation
   (D) see if her teacher would become angry at her childish actions
   (E) compare her teacher's reaction to her behavior to her mother's reaction

17. It can be inferred from the passage that the author would most likely agree with which of the following statements?

    (A) Without language, humans are destined to feel anger and bitterness.

    (B) In order for people to overcome their flaws, they must open themselves up to new situations.

    (C) People often destroy treasured objects without fully realizing the consequences of their actions.

    (D) Learning can free a person from the barriers they construct around themselves.

    (E) Children need positive role models to help shape their lives.

18. The difference between the author's experience in lines 32-38 ("When I…imitation") and in line 65-70 ("I knew…away") can best be characterized as the difference between

    (A) pride and humility
    (B) physical sensation and mental capability
    (C) memorization and comprehension
    (D) truth and mystery
    (E) childishness and maturity

PASSAGE III

Discovering a previously unknown plant or animal is not an unusual occurrence in the scientific community. Biologists are constantly in the process of identifying and classifying new species. The following passage describes one recently discovered animal, Nanaloricus mysticus, *which lives in the sand on the ocean floor.*

In 1983, a previously unknown creature, *Nanaloricus mysticus*, which vaguely resembles an ambulatory pineapple, was described as a new species, new genus,
Line new family, new order, and new phylum of animals.
5 Barrel-shaped, a quarter of a millimeter long (one-hundredth of an inch), sheathed in neat rows of scales and spines, it possesses a snout up front and, when young, a pair of flippers like penguin wings at the rear. Almost nothing is known about its ecology or behavior,
10 but we can guess from its body shape and armament that it burrows like a mole in search of microscopic prey.

To place a species in its own phylum, the decision made in this case by the Danish zoologist Reinhardt Kristensen, is a bold step. He said—and other zoologists
15 agreed—that *Nanloricus mysticus* is anatomically distinct enough to deserve placement alongside major groups such as the phylum Mollusca, comprising all the snails and other mollusks, and phylum Chordata, consisting of all the vertebrates and their close relatives.
20 Kristensen named the new phylum Loricifera, from Latin *lorica* (corset) and *ferre* (to bear). The "corset" in this case is the cuticular sheath that encases most of the body.

The Loriciferans—now a larger group, since about thirty other species have been discovered in the past
25 decade—live among a host of other tiny, bizarre animals found in the spaces between grains of sand and gravel on the ocean bottom. This Lilliputian fauna is so poorly known that most of the species lack a scientific name. They are nevertheless cosmopolitan and extremely
30 abundant. And they are almost certainly vital to the healthy functioning of the ocean's environment.

The existence of Loriciferans and their submicroscopic associates is emblematic of how little we know of the living world, even that part necessary
35 for our existence. We dwell on a largely unexplored planet. Large numbers of new species continue to be discovered every year. And of those already discovered, more than 99 percent are known only by a scientific name, a handful of specimens in a museum, and a few
40 scraps of anatomical description in scientific journals. It is a myth that scientists break out champagne when a new species is discovered. Our museums are glutted with new species. We don't have time to describe more than a small fraction of those pouring in each year. How many
45 more unknown pieces of the ecological puzzle remain to be found? No one has the faintest idea; it is one of the great unsolved problems of science.

Find the Window

Identify the lines you will read in order to answer each question. This will rarely be limited to the lines mentioned in the question! Complete answers and explanations can be found in Chapter 15.

19. The passage serves primarily to

20. The passage suggests that new species are classified according to their

21. In describing the *Nanaloricus mysticus*, the author provides all of the following EXCEPT

22. The word "cosmopolitan" (line 30) most nearly means

23. It can be inferred that the author states "It is a myth… discovered" (line 41-42) because

24. The passage implies one consideration that goes into the placement of a new species into a phylum is

Predict the Answer

Now that you have found and read the window for each question, try to predict the answer for each of these questions. Complete answers and explanations can be found in Chapter 15.

19. The passage serves primarily to

20. The passage suggests that new species are classified according to their

21. In describing the *Nanaloricus mysticus*, the author provides all of the following EXCEPT

22. The word "cosmopolitan" (line 30) most nearly means

23. It can be inferred that the author states "It is a myth… discovered" (line 41-42) because

24. The passage implies one consideration that goes into the placement of a new species into a phylum is

POE

Now that you have predicted the answers to these questions, use those predictions to eliminate bad answers. Complete answers and explanations can be found in Chapter 15.

19. The passage serves primarily to

    (A) describe one of the ways in which scientists categorize formerly undiscovered species
    (B) encourage zoologists to be bolder when making classifications
    (C) reveal the extent of scientific ignorance concerning the life forms that inhabit the ocean floor
    (D) point out the abundance of undiscovered life forms through the discussion of a new phylum
    (E) express approval for the scientists who discovered *Nanaloricus mysticus*

20. The passage suggests that new species are classified according to their

    (A) position in the food chain
    (B) reproductive behavior
    (C) geographical location
    (D) relationships to other animals
    (E) physical characteristics

21. In describing the *Nanaloricus mysticus*, the author provides all of the following EXCEPT

    (A) precise measurements
    (B) an evolutionary description
    (C) a literal description
    (D) a physical comparison
    (E) speculations about function

22. The word "cosmopolitan" (line 30) most nearly means

    (A) worldly
    (B) widespread
    (C) wise
    (D) sophisticated
    (E) cultured

23. It can be inferred that the author states "It is a myth…discovered" (line 41-42) because

    (A) scientists no longer care about the discovery of new species
    (B) new species are evolving at a faster rate than that at which scientists can discover them
    (C) each new species represents discovered represents new knowledge about the world
    (D) it is true that scientists view the discovery of a new species as a significant event
    (E) the number of species that remain unstudied is staggering

24. The passage implies one consideration that goes into the placement of a new species into a phylum is

    (A) the relative abundance of the new species in the ecosystem
    (B) the structural characteristics of the newly discovered species
    (C) the importance of the new species to the ecosystem as a whole
    (D) the geographical distribution of the new species
    (E) the name given to the new species by its discoverer

POE EXERCISES

Choose the correct answer of the remaining two. Underneath the question, list the reason that the wrong answer was wrong: Extremes, Half-Right/Half-Wrong, or Out the Window. Complete answers and explanations can be found in Chapter 15.

Passage I

Although humans have hunted many species nearly to extinction, few imperiled animals have received as much international attention as have the whales. The International Whaling Commission was established by the world's fourteen major whaling countries in order to preserve sufficient stocks of whales. The Commission now boasts 51 members, including such landlocked and minor maritime powers as Switzerland, which joined the Commission in order to support its strong whaling industry. What was once viewed as a merely regulatory body for one industry is now perceived as an open forum for discussing a globally relevant issue.

1. In discussing Switzerland, the author uses irony in order to

   (A)
   (B) discredit the actions of certain members
   (C) explain the expansion of an organization's membership
   (D)
   (E)

Type of wrong answer _____

2. It can be most reasonably inferred from the passage that

   (A)
   (B) countries are not required to have a major whaling industry in order to join the International Whaling Commission
   (C)
   (D) the International Whaling Commission no longer regulates the whaling industry but merely serves as a forum for discussion
   (E)

Type of wrong answer _____

Passage II

In 1801 astronomer William Herschel posited that one hundred years of recording solar activity showed that periods with few sunspots coincided with the highest wheat prices. The connection was recently confirmed when a study of wheat prices in England between 1259 and 1702 showed that the price peaks occurred at the same intervals as low points in a typical cycle of sunspot activity. Additionally, chemical analysis of Greenland's ice cores shows that in the seventeenth century high levels of cosmic rays, which indicate low solar activity, peaked in the same cycles as wheat prices.

3. Which of the following statements, if true, does the most to strengthen the link between wheat price and sunspot activity?

   (A)

   (B)

   (C) Meticulous records have been kept for hundreds of years on the market price of corn.

   (D) Low sunspot activity causes cooler, rainy weather in England, resulting in lower crop yields.

   (E)

Type of wrong answer _____

4. According to information in the passage, all of the following methods have been used to determine the effects of sunspot activity EXCEPT

   (A)

   (B)

   (C) use of scientific equipment near the sun's atmosphere that measures cosmic rays

   (D)

   (E) a comparison of wheat prices to two methods of documenting sunspot activity

Type of wrong answer _____

Passage III

The transmission of most diseases was poorly understood prior to the twentieth century, and widespread panic was common whenever epidemics broke out. For example, frequent yellow fever epidemics killed thousands of people in the southern United States during the 1800s. Afraid that the disease might spread over long distances, Americans demanded that the postal service fumigate mail originating from affected areas. Fumigation consisted of perforating letters and then blowing sulfur or formaldehyde vapors into the envelope. Common wisdom held that noxious odors would kill whatever germs carried the deadly disease. Not until 1900 did people learn that mosquitoes, not letters, were the true carriers of yellow fever.

5. It can be most reasonably inferred from the passage that

   (A) the southern United States had a significant mosquito population in the 1800s
   (B)
   (C) yellow fever epidemics occurred only in the southern United States
   (D)
   (E)

Type of wrong answer _____

6. The last sentence serves primarily to

   (A)
   (B)
   (C) present the correct alternative to an erroneous idea
   (D)
   (E) emphasize the timeliness of a scientific discovery

Type of wrong answer _____

Passage IV

With just two pitches in his repertoire—a fastball and a curveball—Sandy Koufax has been hailed as the greatest left-handed pitcher in baseball. Biomechanical researchers recently analyzed his pitching motions and determined that he was kinetically perfect from the windup to the release of the ball. Batters who faced him several decades ago testified to his perfection by describing remarkable pitches that were virtually impossible to hit. For example, his four-seam fastball had a "rising" motion due to its underspin and implausibly appeared to rise as it approached the batter.

7. The primary purpose of the passage is to

   (A)

   (B)

   (C) discuss Koufax's title as baseball's best left-handed pitcher

   (D)

   (E) describe aspects of Koufax's superiority as a pitcher

Type of wrong answer _____

8. As described in the passage, Koufax's pitches

   (A) seemed to challenge the law of gravity

   (B)

   (C) were recreated by biomechanical researchers

   (D)

   (E)

Type of wrong answer _____

Passage V

An excess of carbon dioxide—a chemical produced in great quantities by automobiles, manufacturing, and human beings—is thought to cause global warming and a host of other environmental problems. To combat the effects of this compound, some scientists have suggested that the government simply plant more trees. Because trees and other green plants consume carbon dioxide and produce oxygen, a greater number of trees could reduce the amount of carbon dioxide in the air, thus decreasing the negative impact on the environment. Unfortunately, trees cannot lessen the concentration of other harmful pollutants such as carbon monoxide. Therefore, planting more trees is not by itself an effective solution to air pollution.

9. The author's tone can best be described as

    (A) derisive
    (B)
    (C)
    (D) objective
    (E)

Type of wrong answer _____

10. The third sentence ("Because trees … the environment") serves primarily to

    (A) provide an explanation for a proposed course of action
    (B)
    (C)
    (D) point out flaws in an opposing argument
    (E)

Type of wrong answer _____

POE EXERCISES WITH NO PASSAGE

Use what you know about SAT's wrong answers to select the correct answer from the remaining two. Complete answers and explanations can be found in Chapter 15.

11. It can be reasonably inferred that Gertrude Elion

    (A)
    (B) was instrumental to the success of the first organ transplants
    (C) is considered the greatest female scientist of the twentieth century
    (D)
    (E)

12. The main purpose of this passage is to

    (A) link Johnson's personality with his presidential performance
    (B)
    (C)
    (D)
    (E) document Johnson's dangerous mental instability

13. The author's attitude toward Johnson is one of

    (A)
    (B)
    (C) intense regret
    (D) measured sympathy
    (E)

14. The measures listed by the orator of Passage 2 in lines 38-46 serve to

    (A) suggest that rebellion is impossible in an armed society
    (B)
    (C)
    (D) alert the people of the city to Catiline's subversive actions
    (E)

15. Which of the following best describes the attitude toward be-bop music expressed by the author of Passage 1?

    (A)
    (B)
    (C) Although he came to understand the form, he found it uninteresting.
    (D)
    (E) He considered it an important and inevitable link in the evolution of jazz.

16. Which of the following best expresses the idea conveyed by Dizzy Gillespie in lines 36-37?

(A) Musicians must experiment with different instruments to perfect jazz.

(B)

(C)

(D) Music, including jazz, is in a constant state of evolution.

(E)

17. The authors of both passages would agree with which of the following?

(A)

(B)

(C)

(D) Change is essential for human progress.

(E) Men are more likely to discover new ideas when they are exercising.

18. In lines 15-19, the author contends that printmakers of the late twentieth century

(A)

(B)

(C) were fulfilled by the act of printmaking itself, while mass production was a secondary concern

(D) faced a production quota of prints which became an insurmountable handicap for most artists

(E)

19. The author of Paragraph 1 mentions the detail about the United States Patent and Trademark Office in the last sentence in order to

(A) condemn Whitney for his decision to seek a patent

(B)

(C)

(D)

(E) offer a possible reason why Whitney claimed sole authorship

20. The author implies that, prior to the arrival of her teacher, she

(A)

(B)

(C) did not expect anything good to happen in her future

(D) was eager to learn about the world but lacked the means to

(E)

PUT IT ALL TOGETHER

Racial profiling is a procedure by which law enforcement officials take a suspect's ethnicity into account when evaluating likely guilt or innocence. The following is an excerpt from a 1999 article written by a legal scholar on legal and ethical issues surrounding the practice of racial profiling. Complete answers and explanations can be found in Chapter 15.

Passage I

At the heart of the American judicial system lies the presumption of innocence until guilt is proven. Presumption of innocence is the foundation for the many
Line court-decreed rights of suspects, such as the right to a
5 public defender, guaranteed by the Supreme Court case *Gideon v. Wainright*, or the numerous rights guaranteed by the case *Miranda v. Arizona*. As few citizens ever require such protection from police, the Constitutional provision against unreasonable search and seizure and
10 the right to equal protection under the law are more relevant for most individuals. These are the rights that are most often at risk in the ever-increasing phenomenon of racial profiling.

Racial profiling is defined as the process by which
15 law enforcement officials make judgments about a given individual based solely or predominantly upon external racial traits. It would be foolish to say that all police do this for overtly racist motives. Indeed many have what they deem to be a compelling reason to racially
20 profile. Police defend the practice by asserting that statistically, minorities commit a disproportionately high percentage of crimes in the United States. The reason for this trend matters little to law enforcement officials, as their sworn duty is not to correct society's ills, but
25 rather to apprehend those who commit crimes against society and, if possible, to prevent those crimes. It is for this reason that police officials often use racial traits as proxies for criminal traits. The assumption that underlies this practice is the belief that racial traits can signify
30 an increased risk of criminality. Seen in this light, it is easy to understand, if not accept, why police officials are likely to use racial profiling as a tool to prevent crime.

Thus, if racial profiling is merely a tool, then the only relevant considerations in whether to use this tool relate
35 to its efficacy. If racial profiling truly does prevent crime and effectively apprehend criminals, then it is entirely justified, their logic continues. This is the commonly held belief among many law enforcement officials and defenders of racial profiling.
40 However, there is a dissenting opinion.

Critics of racial profiling reject the notion that it is only a useful tool. They oppose the notion that judging a potential criminal by his appearance is only a technique that should be evaluated solely on the basis of its
45 efficacy. To its detractors, racial profiling is offensive to both civil and human rights.

The so-called "technique" suspects guilt based not upon relevant traits such as past criminal record or suspicious behavior, but upon an assumption that
50 as minorities are more likely to commit crimes, this

particular minority probably committed a crime. At its heart, this type of assumption is at least prejudiced in that it makes judgments about individuals' characters without any primary evidence, and at most racist,
55 as it promotes negative treatment based upon those judgments. According to this line of thinking, racial profiling singles out individual groups and treats them with different standards than others; therefore, racial profiling violates individuals' rights to equal protection.
60 It is inevitable that while employing this "technique," innocent individuals will be harassed, detained, arrested and possibly even convicted. Supporters of racial profiling contend that these cases, while regrettable, are limited and outweighed by the number of guilty
65 individuals captured and put to justice. This response is not acceptable for believers of inalienable human rights. For those who value individual rights, any violation of those rights in pursuit of some greater good is unacceptable, especially when that good is as vague
70 a notion as security. One can not use people as a means to an end, however noble that end might be. Thus, critics of racial profiling find untenable the position that individuals' rights should be subservient to those of society.

1. The author's tone in the passage can best be described as

   (A) sarcastic
   (B) persuasive
   (C) dispassionate
   (D) apathetic
   (E) ubiquitous

2. It can be inferred from the passage that

   (A) racial profiling is an important issue
   (B) the author is a victim of racial profiling
   (C) racial profiling is illegal
   (D) racial profiling is based on assumption, not facts
   (E) racial profiling has resulted in a large number of erroneous convictions

3. All of the following could be examples of racial profiling EXCEPT

(A) a policeman asking a car to pull over merely because its driver was from a minority group

(B) a security guard asking a minority individual to step out of line for a search

(C) a district attorney's office assigning a minority lawyer to a case because the lawyer was the same race as the defendant

(D) a policeman calling for extra backup after seeing a criminal's race

(E) a policeman being more likely to fire his weapon if the person he was facing as a minority

4. The word "proxies" (line 28) in this context most nearly means

(A) guesses

(B) substitutions

(C) synonyms

(D) insults

(E) theories

5. The author inserts the word "technique" in quotation marks most likely to

(A) sarcastically introduce a new theme

(B) quote a previously mentioned source

(C) draw the reader's attention to an important term

(D) create an ironic juxtaposition

(E) express his doubt that the word applies to the situation

6. According to the author, primary evidence needed for profiling of criminals would consist of all of the following EXCEPT

(A) knowledge of a suspect's previous arrests

(B) the suspect's suspicious actions

(C) the suspect's being caught in the act of committing a crime

(D) knowledge that an area of town is especially crime-ridden

(E) having a complaining witness identify the suspect

7. The act of racial profiling is most analogous to

(A) thinking that one rotten apple spoils an entire bunch

(B) dangling a carrot in front of a horse

(C) being afraid of a dog that has bitten you

(D) ordering a dish you've had before

(E) judging a book by its cover

8. The author states that critics of racial profiling believe it is unfair because

(A) only innocent people get arrested

(B) only one minority is the target

(C) some racial groups receive unfair treatment

(D) it is judged only on its effectiveness

(E) it does not help the greater good

9. The structure of the passage can be best described as

(A) a polemic is stated, and several opinions are juxtaposed

(B) a history is given, and then the author explains how it relates to modern society

(C) a topic is introduced and its supporters are criticized

(D) a topic is introduced, and the supporters' arguments are countered by those of its detractors

(E) a history is given and several reasons for its origins are explained

Passage II

The following excerpt was taken from a 1995 book of essays that includes current scientific observations.

Whether in life or after death, Vincent van Gogh has never been a painter of moderation. He painted ferociously, drank great quantities of the potent liqueur absinthe, went for days without eating, slashed off
Line 5 his left earlobe, and took his own life at the age of thirty-seven. And since his suicide in 1890, the great post-impressionist has been the subject of no fewer than 152 medical diagnoses. Doctors pore over van Gogh's paintings and his extensive correspondence,
10 preposterously claiming that he suffered temporal lobe epilepsy, a brain tumor, glaucoma, cataracts, manic depression, schizophrenia, magnesium deficiency, and poisoning by digitalis—which once was given as a treatment for epilepsy and can cause yellow vision—thus
15 explaining, the story goes, van Gogh's penchant for brilliant yellows.

The latest entries in the van Gogh malaise-of-the-month club are part of a continuing exercise that certain aesthetically minded doctors engage in, either for
20 cerebral sport or for a better understanding of the natural history of diseases. The game is called "Diagnosing the Canvas." In one approach, physicians attempt to identify an artist's illness or to chart its progression by considering suggestive details in the artist's work, like
25 color choice, perspective, and subject matter. That sort of analysis has yielded the proposal that Claude Monet's near-blinding cataracts and eventual eye surgery deeply influenced the evolution of his water lily series.

In the second version of the pastime, doctors study
30 abnormal or deformed subjects portrayed in works of art and attempt to explain a figure's anomalous appearance by making a medical diagnosis. Noting the distinctively gnarled hand of the woman shown in Corot's painting *Girl with Mandolin*, two physicians and an art student
35 have suggested that the musician had rheumatoid arthritis, a crippling autoimmune condition relatively common among young women.

Most art-loving doctors say they engage in diagnosing canvases less for scientific reasons and more
40 because it is an irresistible diversion. They feel a kinship with artists, since a good diagnostician, like a good painter, observes the tiny, revealing details that ordinary eyes usually miss. So when doctors see artists paying attention to the same clues in their paintings, they can't
45 help but regard the canvas as a patient, silently awaiting their professional opinions.

For all the pleasure it affords, however, the temptation to pin a syndrome to an artist the doctor has never met, or to diagnose a painted figure unable to so
50 much as say where it hurts, has led to outlandish notions about art and artists. In 1913, Parisian doctors suggest that Spanish painter El Greco (1541-1614) painted his elongated figures because he may have had astigmatism,

a vision problem in which the eyeball is shaped more like
55 a football than a sphere. In some types of astigmatism that have been corrected with glasses, objects may appear slightly elongated in one direction and squashed in the other.

But as ophthalmologists and others have repeatedly
60 argued in the intervening years, the theory about El Greco is nonsense. To begin with, an astigmatic whose vision is not corrected with glasses doesn't see objects as elongated, but merely as blurs, and there were no corrective lenses for astigmatism in El Greco's day. In
65 any case, X-ray images taken of El Greco's painting show that beneath the painted figures are drawings of a more naturalistic composition, indicating that the artist consciously chose to stretch out his images when he applied paint, very likely to lend them an ethereal
70 quality.

10. As it is used in line 8, "pore over" most nearly means

(A) imagine
(B) contrast
(C) discuss
(D) critique
(E) scrutinize

11. The passage suggests that some believe that "van Gogh's penchant for brilliant yellows" (lines 15-16) was caused by

(A) magnesium deficiency
(B) cataracts
(C) large quantities of absinthe
(D) digitalis
(E) epilepsy

12. The phrase "malaise-of-the-month club" (lines 17-18) conveys the

(A) author's ironic attitude toward the number of outlandish theories about van Gogh put forth by modern doctors

(B) extensive research done by the author chronicling each theory of van Gogh's medical condition

(C) author's admiration for the skill that doctors seem to have for diagnosing disease from artwork

(D) purely frivolous nature of the "game" doctors play when evaluating a canvas for clues to an artist's health

(E) author's attempt to add humor to an otherwise disturbing account of physical and mental illness

13. Which example most accurately illustrates what is being described in lines 29-32?

(A) A doctor recommends that a contemporary painter be examined for an eye disease which may be causing ripples in the painter's field of vision.

(B) Observing the bulging eye on a Mayan sculpture, a doctor suggests that the subject had retinoblastoma, a tumorous eye cancer.

(C) Using existing photos, scientists hypothesize that Abraham Lincoln had Marfan's syndrome, which results in excessively elongated bones.

(D) A psychiatrist theorizes that the painter Chagall may have suffered from a condition that causes its victims to be unable to distinguish dreams from reality.

(E) From a study of Picasso's paintings, a sociologist suggests that Picasso distorted the features of his model, Gabrielle, in order to make a statement about women in society.

14. The author believes that the doctors mentioned in lines 38-40 ("Most art-loving…diversion.")

(A) regard artworks as patients awaiting diagnosis

(B) feel that diagnosing artwork is the only way they can understand it

(C) feel a connection to the art, not the artist

(D) view artists as amateur physicians

(E) view themselves as modern-day artists

15. In the discussion of El Greco, the author implies which of the following?

(A) Corrective lenses for astigmatism were in existence in Paris in 1913.

(B) Astigmatism was not yet discovered in El Greco's day.

(C) El Greco's figures are visible only on X-ray images of his paintings.

(D) An astigmatic with uncorrected vision sees objects as squashed.

(E) Parisian doctors in El Greco's day misunderstood the painter's ailment.

Passage III

In the 1940s, a musical form called "bop" or "be-bop" evolved out of traditional jazz music. Some of its great proponents were Dizzy Gillespie, Charlie Parker, and Thelonious Monk. The first passage was written in 1987 by a contemporary of Dizzy Gillespie's, and the second is an analysis of be-bop written in 1991.

Passage 1

In Philadelphia in 1940 or 1941—just before I got drafted, anyway—I had a concert going on in the Academy of Music. I don't remember who was playing,
Line but it must have been an authentic New Orleans jazz
5 band, with maybe a Chicagoan or two thrown in. I'm sure Joe Sullivan was on piano. A local entrepreneur named Nat Segal, who owned a club called the Downbeat in South Philadelphia, asked me if I would, as a favor to him, permit a young trumpet player and a girl singer
10 to participate. In those days there weren't any major music controversies going on in the business. We were still saying, in our sublime ignorance, "It's all jazz." So I agreed to have Nat's people on stage briefly, to give them an opportunity to be exposed to a concert audience.
15 The skinny little girl singer, whom I judged to be about sixteen, told me her name was Sarah Vaughan. And the trumpeter, whom I had met before in Minton's in New York, where he had seemed to be only fooling around with the other musicians on the stand, Thelonious Monk
20 and Charlie Parker and, I think, Slim Gaillard (it's hard to remember for sure—after all, it was more than forty years ago), was Dizzy Gillespie.

So, anyway, he played in one or two sets at the Academy, and he still seemed to be just fooling around. I
25 talked to him for a while backstage, and it struck me that he was far more personable and intelligent than most of the musicians I had been associated with the in the world of authentic jazz. On reflection, I admitted to myself that most of these younger musicians playing that strange
30 music they were calling "be-bop" were superior folks, generally better educated, more civilized. Their manners were better, they were more polite, more considerate of each other. I found what they were playing to be very boring, and the more I heard it and understood it, the
35 less I liked it. I said all that to young Dizzy, and he said, "Everything moves along, man. It's not a question of whether it's better or worse, it just keeps movin'. There's no reason musicians, especially young ones, shouldn't experiment with the instruments—find out how far they
40 can go."

Passage 2

In the early 1940s, an alternative direction in jazz was congealing in the styles of altoist Charlie "Bird" Parker and trumpeter John "Dizzy" Gillespie with more than a little assistance from pianist/composer/arranger
45 Thelonious Monk. Parker, an alumnus of the Kansas City-styled big band of Jay McShann, had been "goofing around" with upper harmonics—ninths, elevenths, and thirteenths—since about 1939. At a Harlem club called Minton's Playhouse, Gillespie and Monk were also
50 looking for something. When they all came together in 1944 and 1945, be-bop was born.

Put as simply as possible, be-bop was swing music turned inside out. If a swing drummer played beats one and three, the bop drummer would emphasize two and
55 four—or any beats that took his fancy, if that's what he felt like. Since swing drummers laid heavy emphasis on the bass drummer and tom-toms, the bop drummer played mostly high up, on the snares and cymbals. Because swing bands usually played reeds versus
60 brass, the bop bands mixed sections. Solos tended to be more frantic, with plenty of sixteenth and thirty-second notes, exploring variations on the harmony rather than the melody. At such high speeds they also altered the concept of rhythm, moving away from uneven
65 ("swinging") pairs of notes to even ("bopping") figures. And last, the boppers tried to reject or at least alter the regular Tin Pan Alley tunes that swing musicians played. Their compositions, though based on early swing songs, had more unusual chording, and melodies that were in
70 themselves authentic jazz compositions (for instance, Dizzy Gillespie's "Groovin' High" as an improvisation on the chord pattern of the old song "Whispering"). I am not altogether convinced that bop was a better or more creative way of playing jazz—it was simply
75 different, more harmonically advanced, and inevitably more difficult to do well. This is one reason that the great interpreters of bop during the period from 1945 to 1955 amount to fewer than two dozen, whereas there were scores of excellent jazz musicians working in older
80 idioms.

In 1945, a small label called Musicraft became the first to record and issue the "new music" commercially. Gillespie's quintet made "Groovin' High," included on *Jazz Vol. 11*, and others that first confused and then
85 influenced many other musicians. The first Gillespie group wasn't all bop; the band had a somewhat mixed style. Nevertheless, the 1945 Musicrafts are the first bop records.

After this initial stage of togetherness, however, the
90 bop pioneers went essentially different ways. Gillespie formed the first bop big band, one that enjoyed unusual popular success for so experimental a group (possibly due to a general public interest in "new" things, as well as the pioneering of Kenton). Despite the fact that Monk
95 was an arranger for a time, both he and Parker tended to prefer the intimacy of small groups.

16. It can be most reasonably inferred from the author's reference to "music controversies" (line 11) that

(A) the jazz industry would not always remain free of controversy
(B) jazz had been divided by fierce disagreements amongst musicians since its inception
(C) the narrator is ignorant of the vast popularity of be-bop
(D) rock-and-roll musicians often sparked controversies in the media
(E) music was undergoing a radical change in the early 1940s

17. In Passage 1, the author uses the expression "It's all jazz" (line 12) to indicate that

(A) different types of jazz were musically identical where non-musicians were concerned
(B) the jazz music business was crippled by controversy
(C) all music was derived from a form of jazz
(D) there were not sub-genres within the broader category of jazz
(E) the jazz community was ignorant of other musical styles

18. According to the author of Passage 1, bop musicians tended to differ from other jazz musicians in that

(A) they were better educated and more polite
(B) they were less concerned with making their music popular
(C) their music was more refined
(D) they were strongly influenced by swing music
(E) they had a better understanding of different types of music

19. Which of the following best describes the attitude toward be-bop music expressed by the author of Passage 1?

(A) He considered it an inferior imitation of traditional jazz forms.
(B) He found it intriguing but extremely difficult to understand.
(C) Although he came to understand the form, he found it uninteresting.
(D) He disliked it initially but grew to appreciate it.
(E) He considered it an important and inevitable link in the evolution of jazz.

20. Which of the following best expresses the idea conveyed by Dizzy Gillespie in lines 36-40 ("Everything....go")?

(A) Musicians must experiment with different instruments to perfect jazz.
(B) Musicians most easily achieve fame by developing new types of music.
(C) The evolution of musical forms inevitably leads to richer, more complex musical styles.
(D) Music, including jazz, is in a constant state of evolution.
(E) The future of jazz lies in the hands of young musicians.

21. In Passage 2, the phrase "be-bop was swing music turned inside out" (lines 52-53) serves to

(A) highlight the interchangeable roles of pianist, composer, and arranger
(B) bestow greater respect upon bop musicians than upon swing musicians
(C) contrast the rhythmic, instrumental, and harmonic elements of swing and bop
(D) compare the work of Charlie "Bird" Parker to that of Jay McShann
(E) contrast the uses of upper and lower harmonic scales

22. Which of the following is NOT given in Passage 2 as a style element of be-bop music?

(A) De-emphasis of the first and third beats
(B) Increased use of snares and cymbals
(C) Riffs based on variations of the harmony
(D) Solos composed of more sixteenth and thirty-second notes
(E) Heavy dependence on Tin Pan Alley tunes

23. The author of Passage 2 uses "Groovin' High" as an example of which of the following?

(A) A swing piece upon which bop musicians improvised
(B) One of Dizzy Gillespie's early solo works
(C) A Tin Pan Alley piece rejected by bop musicians
(D) A swing piece written by a musician who later became involved in bop
(E) A bop piece based in part upon an earlier swing piece

24. In line 77, the word "interpreters" is closest in meaning to

(A) composers
(B) performers
(C) translators
(D) critics
(E) inventors

25. According to lines 73-76, which of the following is true of bop music?

(A) It is a more creative form than swing music.
(B) It emphasizes uneven note pairing.
(C) It was first recorded by Jay McShann's big band.
(D) It was a more harmonically sophisticated form of jazz music than swing was.
(E) It was the earliest form of jazz music.

26. The author of Passage 2 states that "there were scores of excellent jazz musicians working in older idioms" (lines 78-80) to emphasize that

(A) the public did not come to appreciate and support bop music until the 1950s
(B) fewer performers were able to master the demanding form of bop
(C) traditional forms could be appreciated by a larger group
(D) most jazz musicians preferred the greater discipline and complexity of traditional forms
(E) bop was a style that major record labels were initially reluctant to carry.

27. In discussing Dizzy Gillespie, both the author of Passage 1 and the author of Passage 2

(A) express personal affection for him
(B) state that he was the most influential bop musician
(C) explore the significance of his compositions
(D) argue for his importance to the evolution of jazz
(E) refer to his music in a discussion of be-bop

28. Which of the following best summarizes the difference in perspective between the two passages?

(A) Passage 1 considers the origins of a musical form, while Passage 2 is concerned with the future of the form.
(B) Passage 1 expresses ambivalence, while Passage 2 expresses a strong opinion.
(C) Passage 1 presents a specific incident, while Passage 2 offers a historical overview.
(D) Passage 1 discusses the evolution of jazz, while Passage 2 focuses on musical theory.
(E) Passage 1 presents an emotional argument, while Passage 2 is primarily factual.

Chapter 15
Reading Drills:
Answers and
Explanations

CHAPTER 12—SENTENCE COMPLETIONS

Roots Drill

1. Acrimonious—Bitter or angry in tone or manner. (Relevant root: *ac/acr-*, "sharp"). The tone, in this case, is "sharp," or hard-edged. The *–ous* comes from Latin and usually means "abounding in."

2. Ambidextrous—Able to use both hands. (Relevant roots: *ambi-*, "both"; *dext-*, "ability"). The roots literally form the word in this case. The *–ous* comes from Latin and usually means "abounding in."

3. Androgynous—Uniting the physical characteristics of both sexes. (Relevant roots: *andr-*, "male"; *gyn-*, "female"). This word combines the male and female roots to create its larger meaning. The *–ous* comes from Latin and usually means "abounding in."

4. Anteroom—A room before, or forming an entrance to, another. (Relevant root: *ante-*, "before"). Literally a *before*-room.

5. Arboreal—Pertaining to, or of the nature of, trees. (Relevant root: *arbo-*, "tree"). Literally relating to trees.

6. Embrace—The act of folding in the arms, hugging. (Relevant roots: *em-*, "into"; *bra-*, "arm"). The act of taking someone *into* your *arms*.

7. Circumscribe—To draw a circle around; to encompass with a bounding line. (Relevant roots: *circu-*, "around"; *scrib-*, "write"). The word is built from the roots: to *write around*.

8. Exculpate—To free from blame; to declare free from guilt. (Relevant roots: *ex-*, "out"; *culp-*, "guilt"). To take one *out* of *guilt*.

9. Dermatology—The branch of the sciences that studies skin. (Relevant roots: *derm-*, "skin"; *ology-*, "study of"). Literally the study of the skin.

10. Dormant—Sleeping or lying asleep. (Relevant root: *dorm-*, "sleep"). The word is just an extended form of the root. Typically *–ant* words come from Old French, in which the –ant operates the same way –ing does in English.

11. Fraternize—To cultivate friendly relations. (Relevant root: *frat-*, "brother"). So to treat someone like a brother.

12. Herbivorous—Eating only plants or leaves of plants. (Relevant roots: *herb-*, "plant"; *vor-* "eat"). Literally plant-eating. The *–ous* comes from Latin and usually means "abounding in."

13. Homophone—Applied to words having the same sound. (Relevant roots: *homo-*, "same"; *phon-*, "sound"). The word is built from its roots.

14. Ingratiate—To bring into favor. (Relevant roots: *in-*, "in"; *grat-*, "grateful"). This word, too, is built from its roots.

15. Hypothermia—The condition of having a body temperature substantially below normal. (Relevant roots: *hypo-*, "under, insufficient"; *therm-*, "heat, temperature"). Literally having *insufficient heat*.

16. Lavish—Unrestrained, impetuous. (Relevant root: *lav-*, "wash"). Essentially to *wash over* something, as with words or money. The *-ish* comes from Old English, and means "of or belonging to a person or thing."

17. Loquacious—Talkative. (Relevant root: *loqui-*, "speak"). The *-ous* comes from Latin and usually means "abounding in." So this word means *abounding in speech*.

18. Matrilineal—Of, or relating to the mother or the female line of a family. (Relevant roots: *matri-*, "mother"; *linea-*, "line"). Literally from the *mother's line*.

19. Misogynist—A person who hates or is prejudiced against women. (Relevant roots: *mis-*, "bad"; *gyn-*, "female"). Literally one who has a *bad* idea of *females*. The suffix *-ist* comes from Greek and usually designates a person who practices some particular idea or method.

20. Olfaction—The action of smelling. (Relevant root: *olfac-*, "smell"). Just the noun form of the verb "to smell." The *-ion* is from Old French, where it is used to form nouns from verbs.

21. Paragraph—A distinct passage or section of text, usually composed of a few sentences, dealing with a particular point or idea. (Relevant roots: *para-*, "beyond"; *graph-*, "write"). Literally, the unit beyond or above basic writing.

22. Potentate—A monarch, prince, or ruler. (Relevant root: *poten-*, "power"). Literally the holder of power.

23. Proximity—Closeness. (Relevant root: *prox-*, "near"). Literally the state of nearness.

24. Pseudonym—A false or fictitious name. (Relevant roots: *pseudo-*, "false"; *nym-*, "name"). This word is built exclusively from its roots.

25. Schism—A disunion or cleft. (Relevant root: *schi-*, "split"). The original Greek word was also occasionally written as "schism" (but in Greek!) depending on its position within a sentence.

26. Trepidation—Confused hurry or alarm. Tremor. (Relevant root: *trep-*, "fear"). There was an earlier word, *trepid*, which is no longer used, though its opposite, *intrepid*, still is.

27. Verdure—The fresh green color of flourishing vegetation. (Relevant root: *verd-*, "green"). Literally *greenness*.

28. Veteran—One who has had long service in a particular practice. (Relevant root: *vete-*, "experienced"). Literally, one of long experience.

29. Vociferous—Uttering loud cries or shouts; noisy. (Relevant root: *voc-*, "call, talk"). The *–ous* comes from Latin and usually means "abounding in." So this word means literally *abounding in voice*.

30. Voracious—Eating with greediness; devouring food in large quantities. (Relevant root: *vor-*, "eat, consume"). The *–ous* comes from Latin and usually means "abounding in." So this word means literally *abounding in eating*.

These explanations feature the correct answer, the clue, the trigger, and the definition of the word in the correct answer. Make sure to look up any other words you don't know!

Try It Drill 1

1. **D** Clue: *study complex texts and ideas endlessly*

   Trigger: *like*

   Definition: *erudite*—having or showing great knowledge or learning

2. **B** Clue: *couldn't see it*; *could feel it as if it were a physical presence*

   Triggers: *colon (:)*; *although*

   Definition: *palpable*—able to be touched or felt

3. **B** Clue: *if you don't have it, you're often treated like a heretic*

   Trigger: *colon (:)*

   Definition: *sacrosanct*—regarded as too important or valuable to be interfered with

4. **B** **Note!** This sentence tests the relationship between the two blanks because the clues are contained in the blanks themselves. In this case, the relationship between the meanings of the words in the blanks will have to be one of similarity (either *love…attract* or *hate…anger*).

   Definitions: *antipathy*—a deep-seated feeling of dislike or aversion

   Alienate—to cause someone to feel isolated or estranged

5. **E** Clue: (first blank) *overstatement*; (second blank) *subtle*

   Trigger: (first blank) *and*; (second blank) *Although*

   Definition: *hyperbole*—the use of exaggeration for effect

   Nuances—subtle differences in meaning, expression, or sound

6.   **E**   Clue: *allowing him to take what he wanted in hopes that he would not start war*

Trigger: none

Definition: *appeasement*—to bring to a state of peace, or to yield or concede to belligerent demands in hopes of preserving peace

7.   **E**   Clue: *no product… should be any better or worse than the others*

Trigger: *colon (:)*

Definition: *uniformity*—overall sameness or homogeneity

8.   **E**   Clue: *argument… only evidence was his intuition*

Trigger: *colon (:)*

Definition: *substantiate*—to provide evidence to support or prove the truth of

9.   **B**   Clue: *bright orange summer dress*

Trigger: *Although*

Definitions: *gaudy*—flashy or showy

Flair—stylishness or originality

10.   **D**   Clue: (first blank) *the idea to his readers*; (second blank) *real master*

Trigger: *rather*

Definitions: *promulgated*—promoted or made widely known

Virtuoso—a person who possesses outstanding technical ability in a particular field

Try It Drill 2

1.   **A**   Clue: *get a little more attention*

Trigger: *Tired of living*

Definition: *recondite*—little known; abstruse

2.   **D**   Clue: *after such a cold week*

Trigger: *lack… after*

Definition: *balmy*—pleasantly warm

Veracity—truthfulness

3.　E　Clue: *in addition to writing… he also writes, directs, and stars…*

　　　　Trigger: *colon (:)*

　　　　Definition: *indefatigably*—in a tirelessly persistent way

4.　A　Clue: *no longer so dangerous*

　　　　Trigger: *but … no longer*

　　　　Definition: *precarious*—dangerously likely to fall or collapse

5.　A　Clue: *gridlock… get things done*

　　　　Trigger: none

　　　　Definition: *transcend*—to rise above

6.　B　Clue: *praise… almost to the point of excess*

　　　　Trigger: *unlike… less likely*

　　　　Definition: *fulsome*—praising excessively or flattering

7.　E　Clue: (first blank) *common interests and laid-back attitudes… as among friends*; (second blank) *conflicts… quickly and maturely*

　　　　Trigger: *led to… meaning*

　　　　Definitions: *collegiality*—the cooperative relationship of colleagues

　　　　Resolved—settled or solved

8.　A　Clue: (first blank) *learning another language, speakers*; (second blank) *insulting*

　　　　Trigger: *colon (:)*

　　　　Definition: *employing*—using

　　　　Pejorative—expressing contempt or disapproval

9.　C　Clue: *nearly shutting its doors for good… influx of cash*

　　　　Trigger: *when*

　　　　Definition: *providential*—occurring at a favorable time; opportune

10.　C　Clue: *showed up on time… acted in a professional way*

　　　　Trigger: none

　　　　Definition: *punctilious*—showing great attention to detail or correct behavior

Try It Drill 3

1. **C** Clue: (first blank) *never be able to tame… wildness*; (second blank) *wildness of any wild animal*

   Trigger: *because*

   Definitions: *intransigent*—uncompromising, stubborn

   Inherent—inborn or natural

2. **A** Clue: *present an extreme version… in order to shake people out*

   Trigger: *colon (:)*

   Definition: *polemical*—involving strongly critical, controversial, or disputatious writing or speech

3. **B** Clue: *making things up on the spot*

   Trigger: *colon (:)*

   Definition: *improvisational*—being and creating without pre-planning

4. **E** Clue: *religious and spiritual topics*

   Trigger: none

   Definition: *metaphysical*—of or relating to things that are thought to exist but cannot be seen

5. **D** Clue: *carousing partiers, fears….had come true*

   Trigger: *and*

   Definition: *debauchery*—excessive indulgence in sensual pleasures

6. **A** Clue: *fortune teller… totally misguided… things have turned out*

   Trigger: *but*

   Definition: *prescient*—having or showing knowledge of events before they take place

7. **D** Clue: *so incredibly steep… nauseous*

   Trigger: none

   Definition: *vertiginous*—causing vertigo, especially by being extremely high or steep

8. **D** Clue: *satirist, sharp criticisms*

   Trigger: *colon (:)*

   Definition: *acerbic*—sharp and forthright

9. **E** Clue: *bitterly cold temperatures, heavy snowfall*

   Trigger: *and*

   Definition: *inhospitable*—harsh and difficult to live in

   Frigid—extremely cold

10. **B** Clue: *low productivity, frequent procrastination*

    Trigger: *While, and*

    Definitions: *assiduousness*—attentive and persistent effort

    Belie—to give a misleading impression of

CHAPTER 14—CRITICAL READING EXERCISES

Passage I

Find the Window

13.   Callot and Meryon are mentioned in the previous sentence, but that one starts with a *this*. Best to start a sentence earlier, so the window goes roughly from, *However, in most cases…* to *Indeed, many painters made prints for this sole reason*

14.   This window begins where the window from #13 ends. Go from *But the printmakers…* to *Instead, complex techniques of printmaking itself were what entranced them.*

15.   The quote appears in the lines given in the question, but it is best to read at least the full sentence. Start from *In the words of Sylvan Cole…* and read to the end of the paragraph.

16.   For this question, the window should be the second paragraph and the first line of the third. From *Before the war…* to *…particularly those devoted to the arts.*

17.   Read the entire second paragraph to make sure you can zoom in on the meaning of this word.

18. Although the G.I. Bill is mentioned only on the first lines, it is safer to read up to the parentheses to make sure you've got a full sense of what the Bill is.

19. Read the entire sentence in which the word appears. *Many veterans who would never have had the opportunity…*

20. The long parenthetical remark in the third paragraph discusses the "Organization Man." Read that long parenthetical.

21. The quotation is taken from a very long sentence, so read that one and the next one.

22. Read the last paragraph. You'll notice many lists in this paragraph, so pay particular attentions to the sections of text that introduce those lists.

23. You've already read the last paragraph for question #22!

24. "Lasansky" appears in the third paragraph. Read the two sentences that discuss him directly: *Students who fell under the spell…* and *Soon students of…*

Predict the Answer

13. Callot and Meryon made prints that were based on other works, and they were early examples of printmakers.

14. Late twentieth-century printmakers like the medium of printmaking on its own, not merely copying the work from some other medium.

15. Sylvan Cole's quote is meant to support the author's assertion about the transition from printmaking as a side-medium to printmaking as its own medium.

16. This paragraph talks about the origins of silk-screening and suggests that it might lead to some more established form of printmaking after the war.

17. Decoration or interior design

18. The G.I. Bill gave veterans the opportunity to go to college without having to pay tuition.

19. Use the clue *had little direction* from the passage! Something like *having little direction* or *aimless* would work.

20. The "Organization Man" is someone who uses military strictness in his non-military life, someone who works in a field like law, medicine, or business.

21. The popularity of the G.I. Bill

22. The author is interested in showing that all kinds of organizations and shows devoted to printmaking were created in the United States and around the world.

23. This "proliferation" of printmaking organizations shows that the medium of printmaking is continuing to grow.

24. We can't know what these students *won't* do, but some of the few things that they *would* typically do were as follows: found workshops in other universities, promote the study of printmaking, and practice printmaking.

POE

13. A
14. C
15. E
16. C
17. C
18. B
19. D
20. E
21. A
22. E
23. C
24. C

Passage II

Find the Window

10. Language is discussed throughout the passage, so this is probably a question that would best be saved for later. Once you do get to this question, use the word "language" as a lead word. It appears in the sixth paragraph.

11. The word appears in the first paragraph, and because the first paragraph is often useful for setting up the rest of the passage, use the whole thing as your window.

12. The quotation appears in the first sentence of the second paragraph. Read that sentence and the next one for context.

13. Read one sentence above and one sentence below for context; therefore go from, *When I had played with it a little while...* to *When I finally succeeded...*

14. This is another more general question. Use "breaking the doll" as your lead word. The initial breaking of the doll appears in the middle of the fifth paragraph, and the reassessment occurs at the end of the passage.

15. The first mention of the teacher appears in the third paragraph. Read a few lines in the second paragraph and a few into the third to get a sense of what change this teacher brings.

16. Use "break the doll" as a lead word. This event occurs in the middle of the fifth paragraph, so use this as your window.

17. This is a general statement that should be left for the end. The window cannot be determined from the question itself.

18. Read the lines indicated in the question, with special emphasis on the second half of the sixth paragraph because you have not yet read it.

Predict the Answer

10. Initially, she views it as meaningless, but then it shows her a new side of the world.

11. Came after, followed

12. She felt like she didn't understand anything before her education began.

13. "Finger play" emphasizes her confusion at what the teacher is doing.

14. Initially, she feels nothing after breaking the doll, but after learning what a "doll" is, she feels great remorse.

15. Prior to the arrival of her teacher, the author lives in a fog and doesn't understand the world around her.

16. She breaks the doll because she is so frustrated with her spelling lessons.

17. **Note:** There's no possible way to predict this answer. Use POE!

18. Initially, she was excited about her ability to play a game, but later, she understood the true significance of what she had learned.

POE

10. B
11. C
12. D
13. C
14. D
15. D
16. A
17. D
18. E

Passage III

Find the Window

19.   The window for this question is the whole passage! Save the question for the end.

20.   The discussion of classifications is in the second paragraph. Use this paragraph as your window.

21.   The discussion of *Nanaloricus mysticus* occurs primarily in the second paragraph, so use this as your primary window, though the discussion continues throughout the passage.

22.   Read one line above and one below. The window should run from *This Lilliputian fauna…* to the end of the paragraph.

23.   Read from line 41 to the end of the passage.

24.   Use the word "phylum" as a lead word. The discussion of these various phyla occurs in the second paragraph, which can act as your window.

Predict the Answer

19.   This answer can't be predicted. Save it for the end, and use POE!

20.   These species seem to be classified by their physical characteristics and similarities to other species.

21.   This answer can't be predicted. Save it for the end, and use POE!

22.   Found all over the place

23.   The discovery of new species is so common as to be mundane.

24.   As in question #20, new species are placed into a phylum based on their physical characteristics.

POE

19.   D
20.   E
21.   B
22.   B
23.   E
24.   B

POE Exercises

1. **C**   Choice (B) is extreme
2. **B**   Choice (D) is half-right, half-wrong
3. **D**   Choice (C) is outside the window.
4. **C**   Choice (E) is correct! (note the EXCEPT: choice (C) is outside the window)
5. **A**   Choice (C) is extreme
6. **C**   Choice (E) is half-right (it mentions a year), half-wrong
7. **E**   Choice (C) is extreme
8. **A**   Choice (C) is half-right, half-wrong
9. **D**   Choice (A) is extreme
10. **A**   Choice (D) is outside the window

POE Exercises With No Passage

11. **B**	16. **A**
12. **A**	17. **D**
13. **D**	18. **C**
14. **D**	19. **E**
15. **C**	20. **D**

Put It All Together

Passage I

1. C
2. A
3. C
4. B
5. C
6. D
7. E
8. C
9. D

Passage II

10. E
11. D
12. A
13. B
14. E
15. A

Passage III

16. A
17. D
18. A
19. C
20. E
21. C
22. E
23. E
24. B
25. D
26. B
27. E
28. C

Chapter 16
Reading Test 1:
Sentence Completion

Directions: For each question in this section, select the best answer from among the choices given and fill in the corresponding circle on the answer sheet.

Each sentence below has one or two blanks, each blank indicating that something has been omitted. Beneath the sentence are five words or sets of words labeled A through E. Choose the word or set of words that, when inserted in the sentence, <u>best</u> fits the meaning of the sentence as a whole.

Example:

Desiring to ------- his taunting friends, Mitch gave them taffy in hopes it would keep their mouths shut.

(A) eliminate (B) satisfy (C) overcome
  (D) ridicule (E) silence

ⒶⒷⒸⒹ●

---

1. The number of customers in the store always seemed to go from one extreme to the other: it was either ------- or -------.

   (A) scarcity . . lack
   (B) plenty . . riches
   (C) commerce . . trade
   (D) summation . . subtraction
   (E) dearth . . surfeit

2. The author openly stated that his story was -------, that it had a moral, but he refused to be ------- about what that moral was.

   (A) fictional . . honest
   (B) novel . . secretive
   (C) composed . . forthright
   (D) didactic . . candid
   (E) ethical . . non-committal

3. Customer service departments are rarely ------- in answering customer complaints: there's really no reason for them to be quick.

   (A) politic (B) expedient (C) unsettling
     (D) decorous (E) uncouth

4. James Franco's body of work is truly -------: he has published a novel and some stories in addition to starring in a number of films.

   (A) divested (B) literary (C) eclectic
     (D) focused (E) confounding

5. The lawyer feared that the evidence against his client was -------, but when the not-guilty verdict came in, the lawyer felt ------- that he had let a guilty man go free.

   (A) convincing . . triumphant
   (B) incontrovertible . . ambivalent
   (C) coherent . . amorphous
   (D) inconclusive . . euphoric
   (E) cogent . . pacified

6. Already considered one of the great forward thinkers of his age, the philosopher further ------- his readers with his ------- take on the issue.

   (A) shocked . . surprising
   (B) alienated . . charming
   (C) pleased . . mysterious
   (D) educated . . scholarly
   (E) impressed . . novel

7. Covered with trees, vegetation, and lush, green grass, the park was a ------- paradise.

   (A) beautiful (B) savage (C) verdant
     (D) civilized (E) thrilling

8. The public was confused by the author's ------- lifestyle: she gave few interviews and made even fewer public appearances.

   (A) fictional (B) bombastic (C) humble
     (D) reticent (E) artistic

9. Maybe a music critic could find the modern composer's dissonant sounds -------, but as far as I'm concerned, the music is pure -------.

   (A) mellifluous . . laudability
   (B) harsh . . noxiousness
   (C) sonorous . . cacophony
   (D) atonal . . noise
   (E) melodious . . sweetness

10. Unlike my math teacher's focused and direct lectures, those of my economics professor tend to be more -------.

   (A) insightful (B) tangential (C) financial
     (D) abstract (E) pragmatic

11. In the early days, new parents are often -------: they have to navigate the troubling challenges of parenting with very little practical -------.

    (A) childish . . experience
    (B) anxious . . adolescence
    (C) rewarding . . pedagogy
    (D) retrospective . . future
    (E) solicitous . . guidance

12. Some early populations lived ------- lifestyles, moving from place to place with many of the difficulties that accompany such a ------- existence.

    (A) transitive . . flighty
    (B) challenging . . primitive
    (C) anxious . . stationary
    (D) transient . . nomadic
    (E) itinerant . . staid

13. Always -------, Erica had a tendency to keep her thoughts and feelings to herself.

    (A) reserved (B) gregarious (C) amicable
    (D) condescending (E) warming

14. Even though the film was characterized by its ------- tone, I could not help but sense a different undercurrent, one that was much more about ------- than levity.

    (A) comical . . amusement
    (B) risible . . debauchery
    (C) whimsical . . gravity
    (D) somber . . profundity
    (E) free-spirited . . liberty

15. While the playwright's long plays are well-liked, his ------- are universally acknowledged to be the place where his ideas are presented in the most succinct, ------- way.

    (A) vignettes . . economical
    (B) writings . . loquacious
    (C) scribblings . . terse
    (D) one-acts . . expansive
    (E) excerpts . . dramatic

16. The congressman's decision to promote the unpopular law through secret meetings and negotiations was derided by his constituents as -------.

    (A) politicking (B) equivocation (C) hoarding
    (D) democratic (E) subterfuge

17. Doubting the ------- of her boyfriend's claims, Seema eventually had all the evidence she needed to show that Lars was -------.

    (A) honesty . . forthright
    (B) thoroughness . . exhaustive
    (C) coherence . . pellucid
    (D) veracity . . mendacious
    (E) speciousness . . irreverent

18. Unlike RC Cola, which can be found only in certain markets, Coca-Cola is internationally -------.

    (A) adored (B) contractual (C) cloying
    (D) ubiquitous (E) obfuscated

19. The other congressman accused him of lobbying for -------, money that would enrich his home district but would have little benefit for others.

    (A) pork (B) enactment (C) redistricting
    (D) filibusters (E) partisanship

20. The chair's supports were becoming more ------- with age, so we called the carpenter to come and ------- them.

    (A) tenuous . . reinforce
    (B) sonorous . . lubricate
    (C) knotty . . plane
    (D) stained . . redouble
    (E) flexible . . bolster

21. Because Megan could foresee events almost as precisely as if they had already happened, there was little to distinguish her ------- from her -------.

    (A) quiescence . . hindsight
    (B) clairvoyance . . predication
    (C) prescience . . retrospection
    (D) thoughtfulness . . reflection
    (E) foresight . . consideration

22. Although the principal made every effort to ------- it, the whoopee-cushion fad spread like wildfire throughout the school.

    (A) burgeon (B) castigate (C) squelch
    (D) disobey (E) bolster

23. The nation's all-powerful ------- was despised for his enactment of laws that were considered too harsh, or -------, without any consultation with the people or other branches of government.

    (A) monarch . . clement
    (B) president . . obscure
    (C) tyrant . . forgiving
    (D) oligarch . . sanctimonious
    (E) potentate . . draconian

24. Richard always felt a little bit guilty for eating cookies, as if he were committing some misdemeanor, so when he ate an entire chocolate sundae, he had a feeling of downright -------.

    (A) ecstasy (B) voracity (C) turpitude
    D) atonement (E) ablution

25. The new student-council president was truly -------: he foolishly believed he could change the entirety of the student experience in just one semester.

    (A) prescient (B) equivocal (C) bombastic
    (D) surreptitious (E) quixotic

Chapter 17
Reading Test 2:
Sentence Completion

Directions: For each question in this section, select the best answer from among the choices given and fill in the corresponding circle on the answer sheet.

Each sentence below has one or two blanks, each blank indicating that something has been omitted. Beneath the sentence are five words or sets of words labeled A through E. Choose the word or set of words that, when inserted in the sentence, best fits the meaning of the sentence as a whole.

Example:

Desiring to ------- his taunting friends, Mitch gave them taffy in hopes it would keep their mouths shut.

(A) eliminate (B) satisfy (C) overcome
  (D) ridicule (E) silence

Ⓐ Ⓑ Ⓒ Ⓓ ●

---

1. John's boss was always moving his employees to think more about -------, pushing them to work together in ways that complemented one another and contributed to the greater good of the company.

   (A) productivity (B) equity (C) synergy
     (D) economy (E) fastidiousness

2. Unlike the population of her high school, which Cassandra considered homogeneous and uniform, the population of her college was ------- and -------.

   (A) sundry . . close
   (B) sweltering . . varied
   (C) diverse . . multifarious
   (D) heterogeneous . . magnanimous
   (E) similar . . different

3. The child could already read at a higher level than his much older brothers and sisters, so all of his teachers acknowledged him as a ------- scholar.

   (A) precocious (B) prodigious (C) portentous
     (D) perspicacious (E) pedantic

4. The orchestra blended so harmoniously that listeners were hard-pressed to find ------- element in the performance.

   (A) a sonorous (B) a symphonic (C) a disparate
     (D) an incongruous (E) an operatic

5. The columnist did little to hide his -------, presenting only the facts that supported his -------.

   (A) bias . . equanimity
   (B) partisanship . . prejudices
   (C) composure . . leanings
   (D) ambivalence . . indifference
   (E) discrimination . . egalitarianism

6. The poet's verses were characterized by awkward rhyme schemes, childish meter, and immature diction, leading many critics to label them as -------.

   (A) doggerel (B) dramatic (C) prosaic
     (D) satirical (E) specious

7. To ------- his opponent's reputation, the candidate ------- the other man's past actions and stances.

   (A) mar . . decried
   (B) bolster . . cited
   (C) smear . . lauded
   (D) applaud . . chafed
   (E) impugn . . admired

8. The editor's comments on the article were -------: they showed that the editor had engaged closely with the article and caught things that most others wouldn't see.

   (A) perfunctory (B) glib (C) perspectival
     (D) syntactical (E) perspicacious

9. After a recent camping trip, John swore he would ------- all the mosquitoes in the world, so they'd never be able to bite him again.

   (A) castigate (B) eradicate (C) appropriate
     (D) cultivate (E) populate

10. The fraternity's pranks were impressively -------: no one was able to trace the pranks back to any of its members.

    (A) elaborate (B) clairvoyant (C) clandestine
      (D) ephemeral (E) expedient

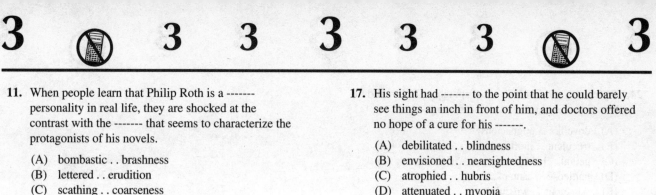

11. When people learn that Philip Roth is a -------
personality in real life, they are shocked at the
contrast with the ------- that seems to characterize the
protagonists of his novels.

   (A) bombastic . . brashness
   (B) lettered . . erudition
   (C) scathing . . coarseness
   (D) jocular . . elation
   (E) retiring . . effrontery

12. Samantha's guidance counselor provided appropriately
------- advice, which helped her to assess the risks in
choosing her major.

   (A) pedantic (B) arcane (C) deleterious
      (D) cynical (E) circumspect

13. Mariah's style of dress was certainly -------: she loved
to wear vintage clothes, such as skirts from the 1950s
and hats from an even earlier era.

   (A) chic (B) informed (C) regressive
      (D) motley (E) anachronistic

14. Cheryl lived an affluent lifestyle with all of the most
luxurious amenities, but when she lost her job, she had
to live a more ------- lifestyle with more ------- goods.

   (A) spartan . . extravagant
   (B) auspicious . . shoddy
   (C) fortuitous . . elegant
   (D) austere . . modest
   (E) exorbitant . . common

15. The team's presentation was a true ------- of its
interests: the diversity of each person's talents was on
full display.

   (A) conflation (B) concession (C) extrication
      (D) effusion (E) amalgam

16. The hockey team's confidence had begun to -------:
the players were no longer certain they could win the
game.

   (A) bloom (B) concretize (C) unite
      (D) despair (E) flag

17. His sight had ------- to the point that he could barely
see things an inch in front of him, and doctors offered
no hope of a cure for his -------.

   (A) debilitated . . blindness
   (B) envisioned . . nearsightedness
   (C) atrophied . . hubris
   (D) attenuated . . myopia
   (E) perpetuated . . illiteracy

18. The new brand of brownie mix was -------: the
brownies it made were so sweet that they made my
teeth hurt.

   (A) innovative (B) delectable (C) pasteurized
      (D) pulverized (E) cloying

19. While the ------- made to the previously abused group
have been a step in the right direction, they have not
been enough to ------- those who still bear the guilt of
the atrocities.

   (A) amends . . lionize
   (B) advances . . impugn
   (C) aspersions . . decry
   (D) gaffes . . pillory
   (E) reparations . . exculpate

20. Although the play had some ------- elements, overall it
was not as ------- as many high-school productions.

   (A) sophomoric . . jejune
   (B) disparate . . amateurish
   (C) melodramatic . . understated
   (D) histrionic . . emotional
   (E) immature . . sophisticated

21. Many misinterpreted Kyle's ------- as egotism: since he
was so often loud and boastful, they assumed that he
was -------.

   (A) bravado . . narcissistic
   (B) hubris . . immaterial
   (C) detachment . . confident
   (D) knavery . . misanthropic
   (E) prodigality . . phlegmatic

22. The invading army found itself in a ------- with no
sense of how it could win the battle or retreat safely.

   (A) belligerence (B) stalemate (C) trench
      (D) revolution (E) quagmire

23. The fashion designer's new line received many -------
for its combination of economy and modishness.

   (A) explications (B) outpourings (C) effacements
      (D) plaudits (E) retractions

24. Trying to get rid of his ------- reputation, Bobby did his best to present himself as amicable and -------.

    (A) dovelike . . pugnacious
    (B) truculent . . inoffensive
    (C) genial . . belligerent
    (D) bellicose . . cantankerous
    (E) voracious . . wistful

25. We all suspected that Erica's British accent was -------: as far as we knew, she had never been to England in her life, and she thought the accent made her sound smarter.

    (A) an aberration (B) a dalliance
      (C) a conundrum (D) an encumbrance
        (E) an affectation

Chapter 18
Reading Test 3:
Passage-Based

Directions: Each passage below is followed by questions based on its content. Answer the questions on the basis of what is <u>stated</u> or <u>implied</u> in each passage and in any introductory material that may be provided.

Questions 1–2 are based on the following passage.

You can tell Jack Molinaro whatever you like, but what you say may fall on deaf ears. The chances of becoming an NFL football player are so low as to be nearly non-
Line existent; a player's level of size and skill must be like
5 those of a Greek god. Hard work might not get the average player even close to the big leagues as it would in any other industry, and a huge number of the biggest and best are neither big enough nor good enough. Going pro is like being born into a royal family: the chances of it happening
10 are almost nil, and it has to happen at the right time. Still, Jack has taken his 6′8″ frame, his feet as quick as birds' wings, and his hands as soft as cotton all the way to NFL Draft Day, where he's expected to be picked within the first ten.

1. The passage characterizes "becoming an NFL football player" (lines 2-3) as predominantly

   (A) fierce and dangerous
   (B) alluring and godlike
   (C) difficult and exclusive
   (D) quixotic and insulting
   (E) regal and lucrative

2. The passage is notable for its repeated use of which literary technique?

   (A) Dramatic irony
   (B) Soliloquy
   (C) Simile
   (D) Paradox
   (E) Personification

Questions 3–4 are based on the following passage.

Economics is a social science that studies how nations, organizations, and families manage their resources. Unlike other social sciences, economics is blessed with
Line precisely these resources, whether they be money, goods,
5 or natural resources, because they are tangible and can be counted. As a result, economics can be applied on the macro- or the micro- levels, offering explanations for everything from global finance to how to balance a personal checking account. In the classical era, when
10 Aristotle was analyzing things on a much smaller scale, he used the word *oikonomia*, or "management of a household." In today's world, though, although we still use Aristotle's term, our understanding of economics has either extended well beyond the household, or we are left with the quaint
15 thought that the global family of humans is living in a house together.

3. According to the passage, economics is "blessed with precisely these resources" (lines 3-4) because those resources are

   (A) plentiful
   (B) countable
   (C) universal
   (D) manageable
   (E) lucrative

4. The passage suggests that the Greek word *oikonomia* (line 11) is

   (A) a more accurate descriptor of contemporary practices in economics
   (B) the first printed use of the word "economics" in history
   (C) no longer applicable to the work of most economists
   (D) the basis for a contemporary study though that study has changed
   (E) initially coined to describe living expenses in Ancient Greece

Questions 5–9 are based on the following passage.

In this passage from a 2012 article about music, the author analyzes the relationship between music and individual identity.

No one would ever question that music is a pleasant thing, for atmosphere as much as for pleasure; when the quality of that music comes up in conversation, though,
Line the debates begin, and one of those debates surrounds
5 necessity. Who cares what kind of music it is if we like it? What's wrong, after all, with music created not to advance the complexity of the form, but composed by teams of producers or attached to the spectacle of a reality-TV show? There are still forty songs to fill the Top 40 every
10 week, so if people are still listening, where's the problem? What could be the difference if that music is familiar or unfamiliar, easy or challenging, authentic or inauthentic?

Music's continuing importance to the human experience is present in its initial role within Western culture: in the
15 religious ceremonies for which early choral and chamber music was written, the music was there, like the grand cathedrals themselves, to raise the worshipers higher, to make them feel the glory of the intangible spirit they were there to worship, to make those worshipers, almost literally,
20 holy men and women themselves.

Religion does not play the role in modern life that it did in the middle of the last millennium, and now, in our relentlessly secular world, we may also have lost that ability to rise so powerfully above ourselves as well. We
25 rely on the visual stimuli of television, the Internet, and advertising for our feelings of transcendence, but these stimuli are never fully adequate. Music surrounds us all the time, whether in our headphones, our car stereos, or on the soundtracks to television shows and movies. Increasingly,
30 music is there to enhance our experience of the visual, not to stand on its own as an equally important sensory experience.

We have some nagging sense, though, that music has a special kind of power. We might listen to a song with our
35 eyes closed, but it would be almost inconceivable to watch a movie or show with no soundtrack or score. Music can hold our attention even though it draws upon one of our most devalued senses. We get something from music that we can't get anywhere else. In fact, the music we listen to
40 says what kind of people we are—and like the purest forms of painting or poetry—music can help us to find ourselves, can shield us from the onslaught of the visual, and can be more private than just about anything else in a world where very little is still private.

45 As a result, the term "soundtracks of our lives" holds more potency than we may realize. Just as our memories help us to keep a sturdy sense of who we are, so too can the music of our past give us some touchstones for who we were and who we can become. The soundtracks of our
50 lives can include the songs that get us through difficult times, those we heard when special things happened to us, or those that showed us a new part of the world for the first time. Our soundtracks are not always voluntarily chosen, but the better our soundtracks are, the more likely we may
55 be to unlock and revisit those old parts of ourselves.

The importance of the "soundtrack," then, should remind us that while the world is more and more a visual one, our sense of ourselves is just as auditory as ever. Just as we would not want to fill a life with disposable,
60 derivative experiences, neither should we want to fill it with the ethereal churnings of the culture industry. We need important music for the same reason that we need important memories: to help us live the lives we were meant to live. We need important music for the same reason
65 that churchgoers in the Middle Ages needed it: to help us commune with something bigger than our daily existence, even if that "something bigger" is our own lost selves.

5. The primary purpose of the passage is to

(A) solve a mystery
(B) describe a paradox
(C) analyze a religion
(D) argue for alternatives
(E) posit a connection

6. In line 8, the author's use of the phrase "the spectacle of" serves to

(A) emphasize the importance of sight in many products of contemporary media
(B) disparage those who watch a certain type of television show or movie
(C) concede that many television shows offer an exceptional sensory experience
(D) indicate that the television-watching public is likely to ignore soundtracks
(E) argue that the music in spectacle-oriented shows should be more complex

7. The passage as a whole suggests that "music's continuing importance to the human experience" (line 13) is

(A) acknowledged though misunderstood
(B) appreciated though impractical
(C) persistent though devalued
(D) misguided though promising
(E) foresighted though underfunded

8. As it is used in line 33, the word "nagging" most nearly means

(A) unrelenting
(B) irritating
(C) sensitive
(D) musical
(E) irksome

9. As it is used in line 59, the word "disposable" most nearly means

(A) trashy
(B) torn
(C) impermanent
(D) unused
(E) inclined

Questions 10–22 are based on the following passage.

This passage is adapted from the 2009 autobiography of a Mexican-restaurant owner. In discussing his family, the author mentions Marta, his niece, and Jorge, his best friend.

About twenty years ago, I moved to the city, and I went vegetarian. Where my parents lived, in rural Mexico, you didn't have to be a farmer to have a few pigs and chickens
Line and, if you were lucky, a cow. The life expectancy there
5 wasn't high, and the food supplies were always limited. On a recent trip back, I wanted to share with them all the benefits of this healthier lifestyle. In short, I wanted to go back to an all-meat little town and show them what I had learned.

10 I don't cook as well as my mother, but when I had been home for a few days, I asked her to let me cook dinner for the family. I made the rice and beans (without bacon fat) and a clever mix of green-chile cheese enchiladas, and at the center of the table, I set a steaming stir-fried mix
15 of mushroom fajitas. Proud of my creation, I dug in right away, scooping the chunks of marinated mushroom into my corn tortillas. I ate with a relish that was part pride, part encouragement for the family of skeptics around me. As I finished my first plate, I saw my sister and my father
20 pushing their rice and beans listlessly back and forth as the steam from the fajitas fizzled out. I soon realized that they were waiting for the main dish, and before I could apologize, my mother had fired up the comal to dash off some breaded chicken breasts for the rest.

25 Marta looked up at my sister to announce, innocently, "I can't wait to eat." My father ruffled her hair, consciously avoiding my gaze just as I was consciously avoiding the loud rumbles in his stomach, "Me too, mija." I smiled at both of them and nodded, though I'm not quite sure what I
30 was nodding at.

When my father, out of a sense of decorum, returned his hand to his own place setting, he told me, ever so casually, "You should've seen what Javier's boy brought back last weekend: a real lamb! And we only just stopped
35 eating the leftovers from it before you got here." My mother saved me from responding, as she ushered in the plate of chicken as if it were something they had all been waiting for for years.

To say that I "understood" the role of vegetables in my
40 town's diet isn't quite true. Whenever someone said *comer*, to eat, or referred to *comida*, he or she was always referring to some meat dish. We had a number of fruits, vegetables, and grains growing in the town, but people only "ate" what they got from the butcher or from the animals that many kept
45 in their backyards. By the time I was ten years old, I could slaughter a chicken to be eaten that evening, and I watched in awe as the butcher showed me all the different cuts of a cow. When we bought our first freezer, it was more or less understood that it was there for us to store whatever excess
50 we might have when we butchered our own animals. When I learned these techniques, I felt that I had learned some great secret and that I would never go hungry again.

Even in my adopted homeland in the United States, meat has always been a symbol of plenty. Living "off the
55 fat of the land" or "high on the hog" are just two of many old sayings for living well. So what would it mean for me to introduce my parents to a diet in which meat was not so central? It would mean a revolution in their way of life, nothing less.

60 I called home in despair, giving Jorge all the ugly details of the failed fajitas. He tried to comfort me: "It wasn't your food, man. Don't you think it was the fact that you tried to change a culture that predated you by hundreds of years? Sure, it was food, but it wasn't comida."

65 The names for meat have an authority in Spanish that another staple of the diet, the pepper, does not. While names like carne, its diminutive *carnitas, pollo,* and *puerco* subcategorize the different varieties of meat, the name chile is applied to any of the countless varieties of pepper. The
70 meat is always the centerpiece of the dish in Spanish and Mexican culture, and even if some vegetarian substitute, like seitan or tofu, looks well enough like meat, it can't bestow that comfortable sense of completeness on a meal. Frijoles pintos, pinto beans, may be part of most meals as
75 well, but they are an essential side, and no meal can stand on the strength of the frijol alone.

American carnivores condescend to salads and other greens as "rabbit food," something unfit for the higher species of human. There is a similar attitude in my
80 hometown, where the animals are fed an all-vegetarian diet, and perhaps it is the close proximity of those animals that makes us feel that we need to differentiate ourselves, reaffirm our superiority on the food chain. I must admit that I suffered from this same prejudice for a long time: I
85 didn't even tell my family about my switch to vegetarianism for many years. For a long time, I didn't feel like I was "going home" if I didn't go back and share in the typical diet. But if I could reap the benefits of a change in diet, couldn't I convince them of its benefits also?

90 The old and the new in a single dish: I've seen it at the restaurant a number of times, as younger people bring their parents to eat. The daughter has her menu closed, or the son is waving to the waiter to place his order, but mom and dad are still scouring the menu, wondering if they've missed
95 the meat dishes. "I'm just not sure what to get," dad says. What he really means is, where's the beef?

The son or daughter answers, "It's a vegetarian place. Just try something that sounds good."

"Hmm," grumbles the parent, trying to find a new set of
100 buzzwords, like "sweet" or "fried."

When the waiter brings the meal, mom and dad look at the plates incredulously, but after the necessity of their hunger compels them, they take their tremulous first bites. A moment of "sweet" and "fried" epiphany follows, and
105 while mom and dad may not finish first, they finish.

These little tableaux give me hope for my next trip home. I've watched enough of them to know how I'll approach my next visit, how I'll try to make that carnivorous culture back home just a little more omnivorous.

110   It will happen, maybe just in time. In many parts of Europe and the United States, it took a food supply of extreme plenty and the diminishment of manual and farm labor to make the vegetarian diet seem viable. Perhaps I think that bringing this diet home will bring with it some
115   of the new prosperity I've known in my new home. But whether they realize it or not, my parents live amid a culinary paradise. If I can get them to see that the things hanging from the trees or growing from the ground can be just as nourishing and delicious as the cows they buy from
120   livestock auctions, they might come to know a new kind of satisfaction.

10. The passage is primarily concerned with

(A) praising those who uphold traditional ways of eating
(B) unearthing the basis for a particular cultural practice
(C) contrasting the eating styles of two different countries
(D) outlining the relationship between two approaches to food
(E) narrating a crucial event in the author's own life

11. In lines 17-18 ("I…me"), the author's actions are intended to convey mainly that his vegetarian meal is

(A) delectable
(B) innovative
(C) subpar
(D) chic
(E) fresh

12. The author portrays his attitude toward the situation described in lines 25-30 ("Marta … at") as one of

(A) joviality
(B) ignorance
(C) uneasiness
(D) anger
(E) hopefulness

13. The father's statement in lines 33-35 ("You … here") serves mainly to

(A) explain a disgust
(B) suggest a willingness
(C) imply a preference
(D) cite a precedent
(E) question a motive

14. The shift between the discussion in lines 1-38 and the discussion in lines 39-121 is best characterized as a transition from

(A) personal experience to cultural analysis
(B) minute aspects to grander schemes
(C) conscious memory to unconscious inheritance
(D) serious discussion to satirical commentary
(E) substantiated claim to unsubstantiated speculation

15. The childhood memories related in lines 45-52 ("By … again") contribute to the overall development of the passage by

(A) narrating the history of meat-eating in Mexico
(B) justifying narrator's decision to eat a vegetarian diet
(C) describing the horror of animal cruelty and slaughter
(D) underlining the importance of all childhood experiences
(E) depicting the role of meat in the narrator's family

16. In line 54, "plenty" most nearly means

(A) prosperity
(B) excess
(C) lucre
(D) obesity
(E) diversity

17. The questions posed in lines 56-58 ("So … central?") and lines 88-89 ("But … also?") serve to

(A) seek answers from other characters
(B) interrogate a historical dilemma
(C) solve the author's central predicament
(D) outline detailed solutions
(E) emphasize the author's problem

18. In lines 61-64 ("It … comida"), Jorge's statements serve to

(A) share in the narrator's confusion
(B) develop a plan for success
(C) disparage the author's condescension
(D) present an alternate way of understanding
(E) doubt the narrator's central claims

19. In lines 65-76 ("The … alone"), the author does all of the following EXCEPT

(A) explain an exception
(B) offer a cultural explanation
(C) describe a difference
(D) define foreign words
(E) contradict his central thesis

20. In line 90, "the old and the new" refers to

(A) parents and children trying new foods
(B) differing attitudes toward food
(C) contrasting styles of food preparation
(D) arguments over the quality of meat
(E) American food and Mexican food

21. The author implies that the "'sweet' and 'fried' epiphany" described in line 104 represents an example of a

(A) sickened admission
(B) vengeful action
(C) pleasant experiment
(D) concession to difference
(E) refusal to compromise

22. The author's tone in the last paragraph is best described as

(A) despairing
(B) euphoric
(C) ashamed
(D) apprehensive
(E) hopeful

Chapter 19
Reading Test 4:
Passage-Based

Directions: Each passage below is followed by questions based on its content. Answer the questions on the basis of what is <u>stated</u> or <u>implied</u> in each passage and in any introductory material that may be provided.

Questions 1–4 are based on the following passage.

Passage 1

The classical tradition has it that the creative writer works under "inspiration," some force outside of him- or herself that infuses the writer. No great writer's personal
Line experience is adequate to the greatness of his or her craft,
5 so there must be some extra-worldly influence, some muse, whether that muse is Erato, the Greek Muse of lyric poetry, or Dante's Beatrice, the poet's real-life love, to inspire that craft. With this inspiration, the author has that extra something, that spirit that enables the production of great
10 work.

Passage 2

Author Henry Miller once issued the dictum, "When you can't be creative, you can always work." One can't, this idea seems to imply, simply wait for inspiration to strike: writing is, at its very root, labor. As writers like Miller
15 became increasingly secular in the twentieth-century, more and more of them believed that their writings were "inspired" primarily by the earthly things that shaped them, whether those things were life experiences or lifetimes of reading. While this idea may make writers
20 seem less lofty than they once did, it also increases the authority of authors, whose works are now entirely the product of their own genius.

1. The "classical tradition" (line 1, Passage 1) would most likely consider Miller's "dictum" (line 11, Passage 2) to be

   (A) correct, because the belief in Greek gods is no longer common
   (B) mundane, since the inspiration for art comes from a much more inexplicable place
   (C) controversial, because no writer can be expected to pen a great work unassisted
   (D) exacting, since it requires that the writer be willing to labor intensively
   (E) refreshing, because it presents a new idea about how books are written

2. Passage 2 suggests that those who share Miller's ideas view "the extra-worldly influence" (line 5, Passage 1) as

   (A) an overstated component of a writer's work
   (B) essential to the composition of great literature
   (C) a necessary aspect of the labor of writing
   (D) a secular version of a religious idea
   (E) an underappreciated form of creativity

3. Passage 2 suggests that Miller's attitude toward a "great writer's personal experience" in lines 3-4, Passage 1, would most likely be one of

   (A) unabashed endorsement
   (B) virulent criticism
   (C) polite disregard
   (D) qualified acknowledgment
   (E) doubtful belief

4. Those holding the view presented in Passage 1 would most likely maintain that the "authority of the author" referred to in lines 19-22, Passage 2, is

   (A) a fallacy based on the idea of divine inspiration
   (B) inadequate to describe the source of creativity
   (C) achieved primarily through labor
   (D) similar in output to work inspired by a Muse
   (E) an impediment to the production of truly great work

Questions 5–13 are based on the following passage.

In this passage, excerpted from a 2004 article, a deer biologist describes her first encounter with a Key deer in its natural habitat.

Though my family and I have been going to Florida for twenty years, I had never seen the mysterious Key deer in its home on the Florida Keys until a recent trip. We were
Line staying in Fort Lauderdale, about an hour and a half north
5 of the Keys, when I decided that I would take the car for a day and go to see the fabled creature. My target was the Big Pine Key, a place whose pines may have been huge but whose population was tiny, only about 5,000 people. Once I parked, I carried my notepad and binoculars into the thick,
10 balmy thrush of the Refuge and, once I was sure that no one was looking, slipped past the marked trails, where the footprints were only those of wild animals. I walked softly, listening for the patter of animal feet, and I understood, as I hadn't in the northern cities, why the Spanish might
15 have named this place *Florida* after its many and beautiful *flores*, or flowers. As I got further and further from my car, expectation gripped me. Would I finally see one of these little mysteries?

I had my share of trepidation. I knew these uncharted
20 parts of the Key were not free of animal dangers; while I didn't see any alligators (though I suspect they took note of me), I did see one or two green iguanas, whose tongues flicked in and out as their eyes seemed to communicate a certain sense of "go-on-ahead-but-don't-say-we-didn't-
25 warn-you." I think I may have also seen a lower Keys marsh rabbit, one of the Key deer's endangered cohabitants, speeding home anxiously along the undergrowth at the Refuge. However, I was getting tired, and the oppressive Florida heat seemed to foretell a vicious thunderstorm. In
30 another hour, the sun would be going down, and I'd have to get out of the Refuge before they locked the front gates. Just as I took my first disappointed steps toward the entrance though, I heard a quick scurrying of steps outpacing mine: two or three four-legged creatures who must have sensed
35 the storm before I did. I turned completely around, looking for the tell-tale rustling of leaves or indentations of pine needles on the ground. And then I saw them—like a family of feral dogs, but with white spots and bushy white tails. They were surprisingly small, as if I was seeing them
40 through the wrong end of a telescope, but they rustled for food just as the deer I had seen in the north. For some reason, I had imagined that this first sighting would be different. I thought I would be with my kids, and I could begin to reveal to them the work that I did in studying deer.
45 But here I was, all alone, not much inclined to say anything, looking at these little deer, moved with the same awe that had led me to study the species in the first place.

Why do I still think so much about this chance encounter with the Key deer? How are these animals any
50 different than the deer whose migratory patterns I've been studying for decades? Perhaps it has something to do with their rarity, for as their name suggests, the Key deer appear

only on these remote and mysterious Keys in Florida, almost as if the Key deer is to Florida what the yeti is to
55 Tibet. Or is it something about their size, their miniaturized forms set against the backdrop of this chain of tiny islands? It's hard to imagine the north, after all, without its deer: deer there are so common that they are more a nuisance than a source of wonder. Though the Key deer behave in
60 many of the same ways as do deer of the north, their rarity communicated something special to me that day. The quest had reminded me of the knightly romances I had read as a boy, and this discovery of a world in miniature seemed to confirm the firmest tenet of my boyhood, that this is
65 a world for small children, one that does not need the watchful and spying eye of grown-ups to continue on.

5. The discussion in lines 12-16 ("I … flowers") emphasizes which characteristic of the area?

(A) Its humidity
(B) Its biodiversity
(C) Its darkness
(D) Its natural beauty
(E) Its mystery

6. The author's attitude in lines 16-18 ("As…mysteries?") is best characterized as one of

(A) placidity
(B) joyfulness
(C) anticipation
(D) indifference
(E) concern

7. Lines 19-28 ("I…Refuge") are distinctive primarily for their use of

(A) empirical description
(B) suspenseful foreboding
(C) humorous overstatement
(D) suggestive personification
(E) speculative hypothesizing

8. In lines 41-44 ("For…deer"), the author indicates that

(A) he was disappointed at his first sighting
(B) his projection was ultimately inaccurate
(C) his car trip had not been worthwhile
(D) it was not worth spending time away from his family
(E) his sighting was more important than he knew

9. The author's reaction in lines 45-47 ("But…place"), is best described as

(A) loneliness
(B) shyness
(C) shock
(D) befuddlement
(E) fascination

10. By posing the questions in lines 48-51 and lines 55-56, the author does which of the following?

(A) Reassesses his career as an analyst of deer's migratory patterns
(B) Wonders if his sighting of the key deer will change his research
(C) Looks to explain his powerful reaction to Key deer
(D) Preempts the negative comments his family will make when he returns
(E) Plans a new study that will explain the habits of Key deer

11. Which characteristic of Key deer is emphasized in line 56 ("the…islands")?

(A) Their fear of humans
(B) Their family intimacy
(C) Their camouflaging ability
(D) Their surprising movements
(E) Their integration with the environment

12. The author suggests that in comparison with the north's deer (lines 60-62), Key deer are

(A) behaviorally similar but less known
(B) smaller in size but equally bothersome
(C) genetically identical but regionally rare
(D) more likely to be considered a nuisance
(E) more mysterious but also more immature

13. Which best describes the author's remarks in lines 61-66 ("The…on")?

(A) Confessing a secret
(B) Describing an impression
(C) Conceding an error
(D) Preempting a critique
(E) Disregarding a disagreement

Questions 14–25 are based on the following passage.

"Film studies" is a discipline concerned with the history and aesthetics of film. These passages are adapted from a collection published in 2012.

Passage 1

Nationalist film historians in the United States situate the origin and development of film in an American context from the 1890s onward. These nationalist scholars
Line generally see the foundations of film in Thomas Edison's
5 early film experiments, silent shorts only a few seconds in length. These scholars credit Edison with the invention and then early American filmmakers, such as Edwin S. Porter, with the popularization of the medium. These scholars credit early American film with the introduction
10 of narrative and the growth of film's widespread popularity throughout the nation and eventually the world. Such dissemination was possible in "the Gilded Age," that period of the late nineteenth and early twentieth centuries, when the U.S. had arrived as an industrial and technological
15 superpower. The United States, this theory goes, embraced a spirit of newness and innovation after the cruel and lasting divisions of the Civil War, and the nation's forward-thinking version of market capitalism put in place the infrastructure by which companies could become national
20 and multi-national relatively quickly. In other countries, the other arts, particularly the theater, held a place of such prominence in the cultural imagination that in its early days, film was considered an idle technological curiosity. It was not until the late 1910s that other countries began
25 producing worthy feature-length films, and many of these were inspired by D.W. Griffith's 1915 controversial American classic *The Birth of a Nation*.

One has to take only a quick look at marquees around the globe to see that the American film industry is the
30 gold standard on the international film market. Hollywood blockbusters dominate the film listings in many countries outside the United States. This prominence, the nationalists add, has led to California's shocking position as the eighth largest economy in the world: its GDP is larger
35 than those of Russia, Canada, and many other prosperous nations. This otherworldly popularity has helped to grow the medium internationally and gives all the evidence nationalist historians need to argue that American film speaks the closest thing the world has to a universal
40 language. Since the 1890s, the increasing popularization of the medium of film has waxed and waned in direct correlation with that of American film itself. Even the medium of film studies itself, particularly the version of it that was popularized in film journals in the 1960s
45 in France, was largely concerned with the analysis of American films and with lionizing directors such as Orson Welles, Howard Hawks, and Buster Keaton.

Nationalists thus maintain that the history of American film is in many ways the history of film itself, and that
50 just as the United States became *the* global superpower in the twentieth century, so too did its Hollywood output

inspire filmmakers from all over the world to create their own national twists on the original American models. According to film professor Mariah Eppes, "The twentieth
55 century was both the 'American century' and film's finest hour. There's no question that the two phenomena were related."

Passage 2

In the global world that had begun to emerge at the end of the nineteenth century, claiming national origins
60 for some things became nearly impossible—there was simply too much exchange in this era, both of people and ideas, and the big events, such as the two World Wars of the early twentieth century, cannot be said to have a single national heritage. The globalist contingent of film criticism
65 that has become the norm in contemporary film-studies departments was born out of its critique of the American nationalist critics. This school argues that film is and has always been a global medium and to set one nation, even one as powerful as the United States, as either the origin
70 of or the engine for growth is hopelessly short-sighted. National histories intersect in film, and the medium would not be what it is today without contributions from all over the globe. Although Edison did create an early version of film, the Lumière brothers in France were showing their
75 work to audiences as early as 1894, and the first film school appeared in Moscow in 1919, whereas the first in the U.S., at the University of Southern California, did not appear until a decade later. American contributions were notable, the globalists insist, but they were only a small portion of
80 the development that was taking place all over the world.

So why was Hollywood able to achieve the prominence that it had in the 1940s and 1950s? A large factor, the globalists argue, was the new class of émigré directors, such as Billy Wilder, Douglas Sirk, and Jacques Tourneur,
85 who were fleeing horrendous conditions in their home continent. Even the creator of some of the greatest "American" films, Alfred Hitchcock, had studied in Germany and made many films in his native England before moving to the United States in 1941. The real
90 popularization of film studies in the United States came in the 1960s, when writers such as Pauline Kael took inspiration from French critics and began to understand cinema as a world phenomenon. While even Kael's range seems small now compared with those of the new globalist
95 critics, her writings pointed art-conscious filmgoers not to Hollywood productions but to the exciting new work coming out of Italy, France, India, and Japan. Kael was merely one among many who considered the national origin of film almost irrelevant, as the medium became a
100 universal language that was not affected by the linguistic and cultural borders of music or literature. In the 1970s, directors from "the new Hollywood" such as Martin Scorsese were pushing this idea further, openly citing world-cinema directors as their primary influences.
105 Film writers in the 1960s helped to expand the cinema beyond its national borders. The globalist contingent of

critics has sought to think beyond "nationality" altogether. Such critics see film as the true global medium, its visual language more universally intelligible than any spoken dialogue. Globalist criticism is now the norm in film studies, regardless of the criticism from the few remaining nationalists that the globalists put blinders on to American influence and overstate the contributions of countries that have contributed far less.

14. Both passages are chiefly concerned with

(A) the influence of 1960s film criticism
(B) the places in which film originated
(C) the power of the Hollywood film industry
(D) American influence on international films
(E) famous directors and film critics

15. The first sentence of Passage 1 (lines 1-3) and the final sentence of Passage 2 (lines 110-114) are similar in that both focus primarily on the

(A) substance of the disagreement between nationalist and globalist film historians
(B) imbalance between American and international contributions to film history
(C) historical conditions in the United States during the invention of film
(D) globalist perspective on the central disagreement within film studies
(E) predominant critical perspectives on the role of nation in film history

16. In line 14, "arrived" most nearly means

(A) attended
(B) entered
(C) drove
(D) succeeded
(E) spent

17. In lines 15-20 ("The…quickly"), the author of Passage 1 discusses the Civil War in order to

(A) suggest that a discovery was made earlier than is believed
(B) concede a major exception to the nationalist argument
(C) develop an extended metaphor for cultural trends
(D) provide historical context for a cultural belief
(E) disparage the overstatements of those who disagree

18. According to Passage 1, nationalist film critics view the "marquees" mentioned in line 28 as evidence that American film is

(A) misunderstood
(B) multiethnic
(C) lucrative
(D) collaborative
(E) prevalent

19. The description of film studies in lines 42-47, Passage 1 ("Even…Keaton"), would most likely have struck members of the "contingent" (line 64, Passage 2) as

(A) subtle
(B) hostile
(C) misguided
(D) bewildering
(E) convincing

20. In line 62, "big" most nearly means

(A) oversized
(B) inflated
(C) frequent
(D) notable
(E) beloved

21. In Passage 2, the reference to "the new class of émigré directors" (line 83) most directly serves to

(A) suggest a possible cause
(B) narrow the focus of an argument
(C) discard an old understanding
(D) retell a well-known anecdote
(E) name some famous personages

22. Passage 2 suggests that compared with globalist critic Kael, "the new globalist critics" (lines 94-95) consider the history of film to be

(A) less cooperative
(B) less determined by country of origin
(C) less concerned with origins
(D) more indebted to American film
(E) more European than American

23. According to Kael, the "national origin of film" (lines 98-99) was

(A) the result of historical conditions
(B) a simultaneous occurrence in Europe and Asia
(C) a crucial moment in the history of film
(D) not a fundamentally important issue
(E) more important in some countries than in others

24. The nationalists discussed in Passage 1 would most likely have responded to Scorsese's discussion of his own influence (lines 101-104, Passage 2) by asserting that

  (A) Pauline Kael's more cautious approach was more representative

  (B) the discussion was overstated given American cinema's position in the world

  (C) film had already become so global that Scorsese's point was obvious

  (D) the influence of world cinema on Scorsese's films is clearly present

  (E) Pauline Kael was more of an authority on film history than was Scorsese

25. Film historians who are part of the "contingent" mention in line 106, Passage 2, would most likely respond to the position summarized in lines 8-11, Passage 1 ("These…world"), by asserting that

  (A) the United States has been important to the history of film but has not been the only important place

  (B) films produced in countries other than the United States have had more influence than those produced within it

  (C) the popularity of D.W. Griffith's *The Birth of a Nation* gives conclusive proof of the United States's importance within film history

  (D) international filmmakers were inspired to make films after reading the works of Pauline Kael

  (E) nationalist historians overlook the true importance of Edison's early discoveries

Chapter 20
Reading Tests:
Answers and
Explanations

READING TEST 1

1. **E** The clue in this sentence is *one extreme or the other*, and the trigger is the colon. While we don't know what order the words will be in, we know that the words will need to be opposites. Choices (A), (B), and (C) give pairs of similar words, and there is no relationship between the words in choice (D). Only choice (E) works, with *dearth*, scarcity or lack, and *surfeit*, excess.

2. **D** Start with the first blank, which has the more obvious clue, *it had a moral*. Only choices (D) and (E) could work with this blank, eliminating choices (A), (B), and (C). Then, the second blank has as its clues *openly stated* and *refused* with the trigger *but*. With this complex syntax, the word in the blank must mean something like *openly stated*, which only choice (D) does, with *didactic*, having a moral and meant to teach, and *candid*, honest or forthright.

3. **B** The clue in this sentence is *to be quick*, and the trigger is the colon. Although your experiences with customer-service departments may have been *politic, unsettling, decorous,* or *uncouth,* go with the word that fits the clue! Only choice (B) works, with *expedient*, speedy or efficient.

4. **C** The clue is implied in everything that comes after the trigger, the colon. We need some word that means large and varied, which only choice (C), *eclectic,* does. Choice (D), *focused*, suggests the opposite, and choice (B), *literary*, is only partially correct.

5. **B** The second blank has the more obvious clue, *he had let a guilty man go free*, which presents a contradiction, or something that would produce *ambivalent*, both positive and negative, feelings. Only choice (B) can work in this context, which is fortunate, because choices (A), (B), and (E) could work in the first blank: the lawyer *feared that the evidence against his client* would be conclusive.

6. **E** The second blank has the more obvious clue, *forward thinkers*, so the second blank must mean something like *forward* or *prescient*, which choices (A) and (E) do. There is no reason, however, to think that his readers were *shocked*, when he is *already considered* a *great forward thinker*, so only the more neutral *impressed* can work. Choice (E) is correct, with *impressed* and *novel*, new or innovative.

7. **C** The clue is *trees, vegetation, and lush, green grass*, which supports choice (C), *verdant*, meaning "green with grass or other rich vegetation." While choices (A) and (B) may sound good in the context, only choice (C) works with the clue.

8. **D** The clue is *gave few interviews and made even fewer public appearances*, and the trigger is the colon. Only choice (D) can work with this clue. We do not know if the author is *humble*, as in choice (C), only that she is private, or *reticent*.

9. **C** The clue for both blanks is *dissonant*, but the trigger, *but*, means that the words will have opposite meanings. Choices (D) and (E) present pairs of synonyms, so these cannot work. Only choice (C) can work, with *sonorous*, sweet sounding, and *cacophony*, harsh noise.

10.   **B**   The clue is *focused and direct*, and the trigger is *unlike*. Therefore, the blank must mean the opposite of *focused and direct*, which only choice (B) does, with *tangential*, digressive or straying from the topic. While this professor's lectures may be *insightful*, *abstract*, or *pragmatic*, these words do not agree with the clue, thus eliminating choices (A), (D), and (E).

11.   **E**   The clue for the first blank is *troubling challenges*, which means that the early days are often *anxious*, or *solicitous*, eliminating choices (A), (C), and (D). Then, the second blank must mean something like "advice" or *guidance*, making choice (E) the best answer.

12.   **D**   The clue for both blanks is *moving from place to place*. For the first blank, choices (A), (B), and (C) cannot work. (Note: *transitive* has nothing to do with transit.) For the second blank, choice (E) can be eliminated because *staid* means "respectable" or "unadventurous." Only choice (D) works, with *transient*, moving from place to place, and *nomadic*, which also means moving from place to place.

13.   **A**   The clue for this blank is *to keep her thoughts and feelings to herself*, which works with choice (A), *reserved*. The other words either mean the opposite, as in choices (B) and (E), or are unrelated, as in choices (C) and (D).

14.   **C**   The clue for the first blank is *levity*, or comical lightness, which works with choices (A), (B), and (C). The trigger *even though* and the clue *different undercurrent*, mean that the second blank will mean the opposite of *levity*, which works with choice (C). *Whimsical* means "playfully quaint or fanciful," and *gravity* means "seriousness."

15.   **A**   The clue for the first blank is *long plays*, and the opposite-direction trigger is *while*. Therefore, the first blank must be something like *short plays*, which works with choices (A), (D), and (E). The clue for the second blank is *succinct*, or concise, which works with choice (A), with *vignettes*, short pieces, and *economical*, giving good value in relation to the amount of effort spent.

16.   **E**   The clue in this sentence is *secret meetings and negotiations*, which works with choice (E), *subterfuge*, or deceit used to in order to achieve one's goal. While politicians may be accused of *politicking* or *equivocation*, these do not work with the clue.

17.   **D**   The two blanks in this sentence will have opposite meanings, as cued by the clue *doubting* and the trigger *eventually*. Choices (A) and (B) are pairs of synonyms, which cannot work, and choices (C) and (E) are not relevant to the context. Only choice (D) can work, with *veracity*, truthfulness, and *mendacious*, dishonest.

18.   **D**   The clue in this sentence is *can only be found in certain markets*, and the trigger, *unlike*, suggests that the word in the blank will mean the opposite of the clue. Only choice (D), *ubiquitous*, meaning "present everywhere," can work in this context. While Coke may be *adored* by some and *cloying* ("overly sweet") to others, these words do not work in the context, eliminating choices (A) and (C).

19.   A   The SAT will occasionally use jargon words like this one. "Pork barrel spending," often shortened to "pork," refers to government spending on localized projects that benefits one particular district. Words such as *bicameral* (both parties), *gerrymandering* (redistricting for political gain), and *filibustering* (extending debate to delay or prevent a vote on a given proposal) may also appear.

20.   A   The clue for the first blank is *with age*, which suggests some kind of wear or disrepair. Only choice (A) can work in this context. The *carpenter* will likely be called in to fix, or *reinforce*, the chair's supports. Choice (C) gives some woodworking terms, but these do not work with the clues.

21.   C   The clue for the first blank is *foresee events*, which works with choices (B), (C), and (E). Then, the clue for the second blank is *as if they had already happened*, which works with choices (A) and (C). The only choice in which both blanks match is (C), with *prescience*, or foresight, and *retrospection*, looking back.

22.   C   The clue in this sentence is *spread like wildfire*, and the trigger is the opposite-direction word *although*. The principal is attempting to stop this spread, or to *squelch* it, as choice (C) suggests. Choices (A), *burgeon*, means "to spread rapidly," which describes the fad, but not what the principal is trying to do. The principal may be *castigating*, or punishing, certain people, but she is attempting to *squelch* the fad itself.

23.   E   The second blank has the more obvious clue, *too harsh*, which works only with choice (E), *draconian*, or excessively harsh and severe. The clues for the first blank are *all-powerful* and *without any consultation with the people or other branches of government*. These words refer to a single dictator or *potentate*, though choices (A) and (C) could also work in this context.

24.   C   The clue here is *a little bit guilty*, and the word in the blank must be an intensified sense of this guilt. Choice (A) means the opposite. Choice (B) simply refers to how much he has eaten. Choice (D) refers to making amends for one's guilt, and choice (E) is a religious term referring to washing oneself of guilt. Only choice (C), *turpitude*, or moral depravity, can work in this context as an intensification of Richard's guilty feeling.

25.   E   The clue in this sentence is *foolishly believed he could change the entirety of the student experience in just one semester*. The key word here is *foolishly*, which suggests that there is no possible way the president can do this, though he believes he can, which eliminates choices (A), (B), (C), and (D). Choice (E), *quixotic*, means unrealistic and impractical.

READING TEST 2

1. **C** The clue in this sentence is *to work together in ways that complemented one another and improved the greater good of the company*. While *productivity, economy,* and *fastidiousness* may be expected of employees, these do not work with the clue, so choices (A), (D), and (E) can be eliminated. Only choice (C) works: *synergy* is the interaction of multiple elements in a system to produce an effect different from or greater than the sum of their individual effects.

2. **C** The clue in this sentence is *homogeneous and uniform*, and the trigger is *unlike*. Therefore, the blanks will both need to be opposites of the synonyms *homogeneous* and *uniform*. Choice (E) presents a pair of antonyms, so this can be eliminated. Choices (A), (B), and (D) contain pairs of words that are not so directly related. Only choice (C) can work with *diverse* and *multifarious*, consisting of many different types.

3. **A** The clue in this sentence is *could already read at a higher level than his much older brothers and sisters*, and the trigger is the same-direction trigger *so*. The correct answer is therefore choice (A), *precocious*, which means "having developed certain abilities at an earlier age than usual." The other answers sound similar, but none of them have the correct meaning.

4. **D** The clue in this sentence is *blended so harmoniously*, and the word *hard-pressed* suggests that the word in the blank will refer to something outside of this blending. Choices (A), (B), and (E) refer to types of music, but do not work with the clue. Choice (C), *disparate*, means dispersed or different, but choice (D) works the best. *Incongruous* means "not harmonious."

5. **B** The clues in this sentence are contained in the blanks themselves, so look for two words that complement each other. Choices (A) and (E) give pairs of rough opposites, so they can be eliminated. Choices (C) and (D) contain words that are unrelated to one another. (Note: *ambivalence* refers to mixed feelings, while *indifference* refers to no strong feelings at all. These words are commonly misunderstood to be synonyms!) Only choice (B) works, with *partisanship*, or obvious favoring of a particular side, and *prejudices*.

6. **A** The clue in this sentence is *awkward rhyme schemes, childish meter, and immature diction*. Choices (B) and (C) do not work with this clue. Choice (D) might be tempting, but we have to read literally, and if there is no indication that this author is doing something *satirical*, we can't pick this answer. Only choice (A) can work because *doggerel* refers to a low, or trivial, form of verse, loosely constructed and unsophisticated.

7. **A** The subtle clue here is in the word *opponent*, which suggests competition or some negative treatment. As a result, although choice (B) might seem to make sense, it does not work with the word *opponent*. Only choice (A) can work, with the synonyms *mar*, to damage, and *decried*, denounced publicly.

8.   **E**   The clue in this sentence is *had engaged closely…and caught things that most others wouldn't see*. In other words, the editor paid close attention and was sharp enough to find some subtle mistakes. Choices (C) and (D) are not relevant. Choices (A) and (B) mean essentially the same thing, *perfunctory* and *glib* both mean hasty or offhand. If the words mean basically the same thing, you can eliminate both! Only choice (E) can work because *perspicacious* means shrewd and having a ready understanding of things.

9.   **B**   The clue in this sentence is *so they'd never be able to bite him again*. John is therefore planning to destroy or get rid of all the mosquitoes in the world, which makes choice (B) *eradicate*, the correct answer. While choice (A), *castigate*, is a negative word, this means to punish or chide, so it cannot work in this sentence.

10.   **C**   The clue in this sentence is *no one was able to trace the pranks back*, meaning that the fraternity is *secretive* or *sneaky*. Choice (C), *clandestine*, works in this context, because the word means "kept secret or done secretively." While the words in choices (A), (D), and (E) can describe *pranks*, those words do not work with the clue in this sentence.

11.   **E**   There is no clue in this sentence, so pay close attention to the trigger words: *shocked at the contrast*. Therefore, the words in the blanks must be opposites, which only the words in choice (E) are. *Retiring* means reserved or quiet, and *effrontery* means boldness or brashness.

12.   **E**   The clues in this sentence are *appropriately* and *helped her to assess the risks*. The advice is not negative, which eliminates choices (C) and (D). Only choice (E) can work, because *circumspect* means appropriately cautious and aware of risks.

13.   **E**   The clue in this sentence is *vintage clothes, skirts from the 1950s, hats from an even earlier era*. This clue emphasizes that her clothes are from the past, which eliminates choices (A), (B), and (D), which have nothing to do with time. While choice (C), *regressive*, may sound right, it doesn't work: *regressive* means "becoming less advanced." Only choice (E), *anachronistic*, can work: this word means "seeming to belong to the past and not to fit in the present."

14.   **D**   The clue for the first blank is *affluent*. The clue for the second is *luxurious*. The trigger for both words is *but*, which means that the words in the blank will have meanings that contrast with those of their clues. Choices (A) and (D) offer appropriate words for the first blank, and choices (B), (D), and (E) work for the second blank. Therefore, the best answer is choice (D), with *austere*, simple or plain, and *modest*.

15.   **E**   The clue here is *the diversity of each person's talents was on full display*. Therefore, the word in the blank must indicate some kind of mixture, which eliminates choices (B), and (C), and (D). Choice (A) cannot work because a *conflation* is a combination based on confusion or without respect for differences. We need a word with a neutral or positive tone, as in choice (E), *amalgam*, which means a combination or mixture of different things.

16.   **E**   The clue here is *were no longer certain they could win the game.* The team's confidence is therefore fading, though a word like *despair,* in choice (D), is too strong. Choice (A) suggests an opposite meaning. Choices (B) and (C) are not relevant to the clue. Only choice (E) can work, with its secondary meaning of the word *flag,* to waver.

17.   **D**   The clue for both blanks is *he could barely see things an inch in front of him.* The first blank must mean something like "weakened," which works with choices (A), (C), and (D). The second blank must refer to his nearsightedness, which choices (B) and (D) do. Choice (A), *blindness,* is too extreme. Only choice (D) can work, with *attenuated,* weakened, and *myopia,* nearsightedness.

18.   **E**   The clue in this sentence is *so sweet that they made my teeth hurt.* The word in the blank must mean something like "extremely sweet." Only choice (E) can work, with *cloying,* overly sweet. While sweet brownies may be *delectable,* or delicious, there's nothing in the clue to suggest that the writer found them so, which eliminates choice (B).

19.   **E**   The clues for the first blank are *previously abused group* and *step in the right direction.* The clue for the second blank is *those who still bear the guilt,* and the trigger *while* indicates that the results of the actions have been different for each group. Choices (A), (B), and (E) could work in the first blank. While choices (B), (C), and (D) all contain negative words, only choice (E) can work. *Exculpate* means "to free from blame," and this matches with the clue, *bear the guilt. Reparations* are things that are done or given as a way of correcting a mistake or atoning for a bad situation.

20.   **A**   This sentence does not contain any specific clues, but the blanks must have similar meanings to one another. Choices (B) and (E) contain pairs of opposites. Choice (D) contains words that are mainly unrelated: *histrionic* means artificially theatrical, so it doesn't have anything to do with being *emotional.* Only choice (A) can work, with *sophomoric,* or immature, and *jejune,* which means the same.

21.   **A**   The clue for the first blank is *loud and boastful,* and the clue for the second blank is *egotism.* Choices (A) and (B) could work with the first blank, and choices (A) and (C) work with the second blank. Therefore, only choice (A) works for both, with *bravado,* confident or brave talk or behavior that is intended to impress other people, and *narcissism,* extreme self-centeredness.

22.   **E**   The clue in this sentence is *with no sense of how it could win the battle or retreat safely.* Choice (B), *stalemate,* may be tempting, but it does not account for the army's inability to *retreat safely.* Only choice (E) can work because *quagmire* refers to a complex or hazardous situation.

23.   **D**   The clue in this sentence is *its combination of economy and modishness,* or style. These are objects of praise, so the word in the blank must mean something like accolades or *plaudits,* as in choice (D). While *outpourings,* choice (B), can often be positive, they can just as well be negative, so this word is not specific enough.

24.   **B**   The clue for both blanks is *amicable,* or friendly and congenial, though the first blank must mean the opposite (he is trying to *get rid* of this), and the second blank must mean the same. Choices

(B) and (D) work in the first blank, but only choice (B) works in the second. Therefore, the correct answer is choice (B), with *truculent*, aggressive or prone to fight, and *inoffensive*, kind or harmless.

25. E The clue in this sentence is *thought the accent made her sound smarter*, which is given as a contrast with *never been to England in her life*. Therefore, the accent is artificial in a way that makes Erica seem to be from England, when in fact she is not. Choice (C) may be tempting, but the writer of this sentence understands *why* Erica does this, so it cannot be described as a *conundrum*. Only choice (E) works because an *affectation* is something, usually a behavior, speech or type of writing, that is artificial and designed to impress.

READING TEST 3

1. C According to the second sentence, *The chances of becoming an NFL football player are so small as to be nearly non-existent*, and *a huge number of the biggest and best are neither big enough nor good enough*. In other words, becoming an NFLer is extremely difficult, and those who do are part of a very exclusive group; the experience is *like being born into a royal family*. These sentences agree with choice (C). Choice (B) reads the remark about *a Greek god* too literally. Choice (E) may be true, but there is no indication in this passage that being an NFL player is *lucrative*, or profitable.

2. C There are four similes in this short passage: *like those of a Greek god, like being born into a royal family, as quick as birds' wings, as soft as cotton*. Choice (C) is therefore the best fit. Choice (E) cannot work because a person cannot be personified. Choices (A), (B), and (D) are irrelevant to this short, relatively straightforward passage.

3. B The full sentence reads as follows: *Unlike other social sciences, economics is blessed with precisely these resources, whether they be money, goods, or natural resources, because they are tangible and can be counted.* In other words, the resources themselves *can be counted*, or are *countable*, as choice (B) suggests. Be careful with choices (A), (D), and (E). Each of these may describe some aspect of economics, but this particular sentence narrows the focus to one aspect of *these resources*.

4. D The full idea reads as follows: *In the classical era, when Aristotle was analyzing things on a much smaller scale, he used the word* oikonomia, *or "management of a household."* In today's world, though, *although we still use Aristotle's term, our understanding of economics has either extended well beyond the household, or we are left with the quaint thought that the global family of humans is living in a house together.* In other words, Aristotle's term is the basis, but it is no longer fully applicable to the contemporary study of economics. Choice (D) is the correct answer. Choice (C) may be tempting, but the passage does suggest that economists still draw on the basic ideas of *oikonomia*. Choice (A) may also be tempting, but the passage does not suggest that the Greek word is a fully accurate descriptor of contemporary practices.

5. **E** This question can actually be answered with the blurb, which states that *the author analyzes the relationship between music and individual identity*. Every paragraph contains some reference to this connection. The questions in the first paragraph point back to it. The first sentence of the second paragraph mentions *music's continuing importance to the human experience*, and so on. Although there are a few mentions of religion, analysis of religion is not the primary purpose of the passage, eliminating choice (C), neither are there any "mysteries" or "paradoxes" under scrutiny. Finally, while the author believes that the state of music is somewhat perilous, he does not use this passage to *argue for alternatives* to the current state; he only points out some of its shortcomings.

6. **A** The full sentence reads as follows: *What's wrong, after all, with music created not to advance the complexity of the form, but composed by teams of producers or attached to the spectacle of a reality-TV show?* The idea is more explicitly stated in the third paragraph: *Increasingly, music is there to enhance our experience of the visual, not to stand on its own as an equally important sensory experience.* In this sense, *the spectacle of* is used to emphasize the visual nature of reality-TV shows, as choice (A) indicates. The remainder of the answer choices might be inferred with a bit of extra work, but only choice (A) is supported by textual evidence. Don't assume you know what the author is thinking! Work with what he or she says.

7. **C** The phrase is initially given in the second paragraph: *Music's continuing importance to the human experience is present in its initial role within Western culture.* The word *continuing* suggests that music's importance is *persistent*, though as the remainder of the passage suggests, music's importance is increasingly *devalued*. The third paragraph contains specific evidence of this: *Increasingly, music is there to enhance our experience of the visual, not to stand on its own as an equally important sensory experience.* Parts of all the remaining answer choices work, but none of these answer choices work in their entirety.

8. **A** Note the transition from the third paragraph to the fourth:

   Increasingly, music is there to enhance our experience of the visual, not to stand on its own as an equally important sensory experience.

   We have some nagging sense, though, that music has a special kind of power.

   In other words, music is no longer *equal* to the visual in importance, but the sense *persists* or *lingers* that music has its own special importance. Choice (A), *unrelenting*, works well in this context. Choices (B), (C), and (E) all contain synonyms for the word *nagging*, but they do not work in this context.

9. **C** The word appears in this context: *Just as we would not want to fill a life with disposable, derivative experiences, neither should we want to fill it with the ethereal churnings of the culture industry. We need important music for the same reason that we need important memories: to help us live the lives we were meant to live.* The second sentence provides the clue, *important*, so the word *disposable* must mean something like *unimportant*, as choice (C) does. Choices (A), (B), and (D) may work as synonyms for *disposable* in some contexts, but not in this one.

10.   **D**   The passage is largely concerned with the narrator's discussion of vegetarianism versus meat eating. While there is some indication that he learned his vegetarianism in the United States, he also says that Americans are largely carnivorous, which eliminates choice (C). While he is concerned with the basis for his hometown's sense of food, that is not the primary purpose of the passage, eliminating choice (B). Only choice (D) is adequately general to describe the whole passage.

11.   **A**   The full sentence reads as follows: *I ate with a relish that was part pride, part encouragement for the family of skeptics around me.* He eats this way to convince his family that the food he has made is delicious. Read the question carefully; it's not asking how he was feeling but what his actions are *intended to convey.* Ultimately, the narrator is trying to convince his family that the food is delicious and that they should eat it. While choices (B), (D), and (E) may be true, only choice (A) is supported in the text.

12.   **C**   The full paragraph reads as follows: *Marta looked up at my sister to announce, innocently, "I can't wait to eat." My father ruffled her hair, consciously avoiding my gaze just as I was consciously avoiding the loud rumbles in his stomach, "Me too, mija." I smiled at both of them and nodded, though I'm not quite sure what I was nodding at.* The narrator refers to the fact that he is *consciously avoiding* the rumblings in his father's stomach and then that he is nodding uncomfortably along with his family. The narrator is thus *uneasy,* as choice (C) suggests. He is neither happy nor hopeful in this moment, eliminating choices (A) and (E), nor is he particularly angry, eliminating choice (D).

13.   **C**   The narrator's father says the following: *"You should've seen what Javier's boy brought back last weekend: a real lamb! And we only just stopped eating the leftovers from it before you got here."* The father is excited by the prospect of lamb, and his comments suggest the rest of the family enjoyed eating the lamb as well. With this statement, the father implies his preference for meat over the narrator's vegetarian offerings, as choice (C) suggests. The father is not "disgusted" by his son's meal, eliminating choice (A), nor is he especially willing to try his son's meal, eliminating choice (B).

14.   **A**   The first part of the passage describes the narrator's visit home, and while some aspects of his personal narrative persist, the remainder of the passage gives the narrator's analysis of cultural practices of meat eating in Mexico and the United States. This shift is best captured in choice (A). While aspects of all the remaining answer choices can work, none is correct in its entirety.

15.   **E**   The narrator's childhood memories read as follows: *By the time I was ten years old, I could slaughter a chicken to be eaten that evening, and I watched in awe as the butcher showed me all the different cuts of a cow. When we bought our first freezer, it was more or less understood that it was there for us to store whatever excess we might have when we butchered our own animals. When I learned these techniques, I felt that I had learned some great secret and that I would never go hungry again.* In these memories, meat plays an important role in the narrator's family, and his ability to work with animals (and slaughter them) makes him feel that he has learned *some great secret.* Choice (E) adequately captures this sentiment. Choice (D) is too extreme. Choice (A) is too general, and choices (B) and (C) run contrary to the pleasant tone of these memories.

16. **A** The context for the word in question is as follows: *Even in my adopted homeland in the United States, meat has always been a symbol of plenty. Living "off the fat of the land" or "high on the hog" are just two of many old sayings for living well.* The clue appears at the end of the second sentence, *living well.* Choice (A) agrees with the idea of living well. Choices (B) and (C) might be relative synonyms of *plenty*, but they do not work in this context. Choices (D) and (E) are not relevant in this context.

17. **E** The full questions read as follows: *So what would it mean for me to introduce my parents to a diet in which meat was not so central?* And, *But if I could reap the benefits of a change in diet, couldn't I convince them of its benefits also?* When we place these questions side by side, it becomes clearer that each is concerned with something similar: How is he going to convince his parents that vegetarianism is the way to go? This is the narrator's central problem, as choice (E) suggests. Choice (C) would work if not for the word *solve*, which overstates the narrator's success.

18. **D** Jorge's full statement reads as follows: *It wasn't your food, man. Don't you think it was the fact that you tried to change a culture that predated you by hundreds of years? Sure, it was food, but it wasn't comida.* In these lines, Jorge tries to explain to the narrator why the narrator's family reacted the way they did to the narrator's vegetarian meal. The narrator calls home *in despair*, and Jorge comforts him with this alternate explanation, as choice (D) suggests. Choice (A) cannot work because Jorge is providing an alternative. Choice (B) cannot work because Jorge does not offer any concrete solutions. Choices (C) and (E) cannot work because Jorge does not criticize the narrator.

19. **E** The narrator explains the exception of *frijoles pintos*, calling them essential but as a side dish rather than as a central part of a meal. The narrator offers a cultural explanation in discussing how *meat is always the centerpiece of the dish in Spanish and Mexican culture.* The narrator describes a difference in the ways that peppers and meats are referred to. The narrator defines foreign words such as *frijoles pintos, carne,* and *carnitas.* The narrator does NOT, however, contradict his central thesis, that vegetarianism will be a tough sell in his hometown because of the strong preference for meat. In other words, the narrator does all of the things described in the answer choices EXCEPT the action in choice (E).

20. **B** The narrator refers to *The old and the new in a single dish.* He then offers a general example of people who come to his restaurant expecting meat dishes but are then surprised to find a happy medium with his vegetarian dishes. *The old and the new* do not refer to the people themselves, eliminating choice (A). For the narrator, *the old and the new* refer to the old prominence of meat-centered dishes and the new idea of vegetable-centered dishes, as in choice (B). Choices (C) and (E) may be tempting, but neither can work. Choice (C) is about *styles of preparation*, where the narrator is more concerned with ingredients. Choice (E) contrasts nationalities of food, but the narrator does not give any evidence in support of such a contrast.

21.   **D**   The words *"sweet"* and *"fried"* show up twice in the following paragraphs:

> *"Hmm," grumbles the parent, trying to find a new set of buzzwords, like "sweet" or "fried."*

> *When the waiter brings the meal, mom and dad look at the plates incredulously, but after the necessity of their hunger compels them, they take their tremulous first bites. A moment of "sweet" and "fried" epiphany follows, and while mom and dad may not finish first, they finish.*

In this case, the parent initially looks for familiar terms in an unfamiliar situation, but then *mom and dad... finish*, conceding that the food that they have been forced to eat is okay, as choice (D) suggests. This is not an overly negative experience, eliminating choices (A), (B), and (E), nor is it an especially pleasurable one, eliminating choice (C).

22.   **E**   The last paragraph is filled with hopeful remarks that contribute to its hopeful tone, as choice (E) suggests: *It will happen... bringing this diet home will bring with it some of the new prosperity... they might come to know a new kind of satisfaction.* The author's tone is generally positive, thus eliminating choices (A), (C), and (D). He has not achieved his goals yet, though, so his tone is also a bit reserved, not fully *euphoric*, eliminating choice (B).

READING TEST 4

1.   **B**   Miller's dictum reads as follows: *When you can't be creative you can always work.* The classical tradition has it instead that *the creative writer works under "inspiration," some force outside of him- or herself that infuses the writer.* Where Miller's quotation suggests that writing is essentially work or labor, the classical tradition holds that the inspiration for writing comes from a much loftier place. The classical tradition would disagree with Miller, eliminating choices (A), (D), and (E). Only choice (B) can work, in suggesting that creative writing does not come from this lofty place.

2.   **A**   As Passage 2 states, *One can't... simply wait for inspiration to strike: writing is, at its very root, labor.* With this statement, those who agree with Miller would call the *extra-worldly influence* a romantic and overstated idea, as choice (A) suggests. While choice (D) may use some terminology from Passage 2, the author does not state this idea. Choices (B), (C), and (E) all agree with Passage 1, but they do not agree with Passage 2.

3.   **D**   As Passage 2 states, *As writers like Miller became increasingly secular in the twentieth-century, more and more of them believed that their writings were "inspired" primarily by the earthly things that shaped them, whether those things be life experiences or lifetimes of reading.* The writer's "personal experience," then is one part of the production of great work, though not the only part, as choice (D) suggests. Choice (A), *unabashed endorsement*, is too extreme. Choices (B), (C), and (E) all work more with the ideas in Passage 1 than with the ideas in Passage 2.

4. **B** Passage 2 concludes by mentioning *the authority of authors, whose works are now entirely the product of their own genius.* Passage 1 states that *the creative writer works under "inspiration," some force outside of him- or herself that infuses the writer.* Passage 1 represents a view in which a writer's *own genius* is inadequate to explain the creative process, as choice (B) suggests. Choices (A) and (C) agree with Passage 2, but not with Passage 1. Choice (D) uses words from the passage but is not supported by any part of it, and choice (E) mentions an *impediment*, which is not discussed in the passage at all.

5. **D** The full sentence reads as follows: *I walked softly, listening for the patter of animal feet, and I understood, as I hadn't in the northern cities, why the Spanish might have named this place* Florida *after its many and beautiful* flores, *or flowers.* In other words, the author is struck by the natural beauty of the place and its vegetation. While all the other choices may appear at various points throughout the passage, only choice (D) can work in this question relating to the author's discussion of the Spanish name *Florida*.

6. **C** The full sentence reads as follows: *As I got further and further from my car, expectation gripped me. Would I finally see one of these little mysteries?* The words *expectation* and *finally* emphasize the author's excitement and anticipation, as in choice (C). He may be *joyful* or *concerned*, but nothing in the passage indicates this, eliminating choices (B) and (E). His reaction is not *indifferent*, eliminating choice (D), and his *expectation* prevents him from being *placid*, eliminating choice (A).

7. **D** The lines in question read as follows: *I knew these uncharted parts of the Key were not free of animal dangers; while I didn't see any alligators (though I suspect they took note of me), I did see one or two green iguanas, whose tongues flicked in and out as their eyes seemed to communicate a certain sense of "go-on-ahead-but-don't-say-we-didn't-warn-you." I think I may have also seen a lower Keys marsh rabbit, one of the Key deer's endangered cohabitants, speeding home anxiously along the undergrowth at the Refuge.* Alligators *took note*, green iguanas communicate verbally, and lower Keys marsh *rabbits* speed home *anxiously*: all three of these animals are personified, as choice (D) suggests. While these may be *humorous*, they are not especially *overstated*, eliminating choice (C). The author mentions his *trepidation*, but *suspenseful foreboding*, as in choice (B), is too extreme to be substantiated by the passage. Choices (A) and (E) suggest a scientist's tone that the author does not use in this passage.

8. **B** The full sentence reads as follows: *For some reason, I had imagined that this first sighting would be different. I thought I would be with my kids, and I could begin to reveal to them the work that I did in studying deer.* In other words, the author's first encounter with the Key deer was *different* and not what he *thought*, as choice (B) suggests. While the sighting was different from what he imagined, there is no indication that he was *disappointed*, eliminating choice (A), or that he misunderstood the sighting's importance, eliminating choice (E). Choices (C) and (D) infer too much from the passage and cannot be supported.

9. **E** The full sentence reads as follows: *But here I was, all alone, not much inclined to say anything, looking at these little deer, moved with the same awe that had led me to study the species in the first place.* The word *awe*, in particular, communicates the author's *fascination*, as in choice (E). While the encounter is not what the author expected that it would be, his reaction is mainly calm and positive, eliminating choices (A), (B), (C), and (D).

10. **C** The questions are as follows: *Why do I still think so much about this chance encounter with the Key deer? How are these animals any different than the deer whose migratory patterns I've been studying for decades?... Or is it something about their size, their miniaturized forms set against the backdrop of this chain of tiny islands?* The main question is the first, in which the author seeks to understand the strong impression that the Key deer produced on him, as choice (C) suggests. The other choices may be plausible, but none has support in the passage.

11. **E** The full sentence reads as follows: *Or was it something about their size, their miniaturized forms set against the backdrop of this chain of tiny islands?* The essential part here is *forms set against the backdrop*, which refers to the deer's integration with the environment, as choice (E) suggests. Choices (A), (B), and (D) are not mentioned, and choice (C) gives an extreme and too-literal reading of the author's lines.

12. **A** The full sentences read as follows: *It's hard to imagine the north, after all, without its deer: deer there are so common that they are more a nuisance than a source of wonder. Though the Key deer behave in many of the same ways as do deer of the north, their rarity communicated something special to me that day.* In other words, Key deer are similar to deer of the north in some ways, but they are much rarer, as choice (A) suggests. Choice (C) cannot work because *identical* is too extreme. Choice (B) may be true, but the second part of it, *equally bothersome*, is not supported in the text. Choice (E) can be eliminated because the deer are not *more immature*, just smaller.

13. **B** The final line of the passage reads as follows: *The quest had reminded me of the knightly romances I had read as a boy, and this discovery of a world in miniature seemed to confirm the firmest tenet of my boyhood, that this is a world for small children, one that does not need the watchful and spying eye of grown-ups to continue on.* This is the author's attempt to explain his powerful reaction to the Key deer, which he does by tying this impression to some nostalgic feelings for his childhood. Choice (B) best encapsulates the author's musings. Choice (A) cannot work because the author does not speak of a *secret*, and choices (C), (D), and (E) cannot work because they each imply some negative aspect that the passage does not contain.

14. **B** Each passage takes a different attitude toward film history: Passage 1 is concerned with nationalist critics, who set film history in an American context, and Passage 2 is concerned with globalists, who set film history in an international context. Both passages, therefore, are concerned with *the places in which film originated*, as choice (B) suggests. While both address aspects of the other answer choices, neither is "chiefly" concerned with any of these.

15. **E** The first sentence of Passage 1 reads as follows: *Nationalist film historians in the United States situate the origin and development of film in an American context from the 1890s onward.* The final sentence of Passage 2 reads as follows: *Globalist criticism is now the norm in film studies, regardless of the criticism from the few remaining nationalists that the globalists put blinders on to American influence and overstate the contributions of countries that have contributed far less.* Both are interested in outlining critical perspectives on the history of film, as choice (E) suggests. Because the selection from Passage 1 does not address globalist criticism, choices (A), (B), (C), (D) can be eliminated.

16. **D** The full sentence reads as follows: *Such dissemination was possible in "the Gilded Age," that period of the late nineteenth and early twentieth centuries, when the U.S. had arrived as an industrial and technological superpower.* This sentence is referring to the moment that the U.S. *became* or *succeeded* as an international superpower, as choice (D) suggests. Choices (A), (B), and (C) are partial synonyms for *arrived*, but they do not work in this context.

17. **D** The full sentence reads as follows: *The United States, this theory goes, embraced a spirit of newness and innovation after the cruel and lasting divisions of the Civil War, and the nation's forward-thinking version of market capitalism put in place the infrastructure by which companies could become national and multi-national relatively quickly.* After the Civil War, in other words, the United States was interested in moving forward into *newness and innovation.* In this sense, the Civil War provides a historical context for this belief in newness, as choice (D) suggests. There is no indication that the Civil War is used to address a disagreement, eliminating choices (B) and (E), nor is there an indication that film was discovered during the Civil War, eliminating choice (A). Choice (C) can be eliminated because the Civil War is not being used metaphorically.

18. **E** The word *marquees* appears in the following context: *One has to take only a quick look at marquees around the globe to see that the American film industry is the gold standard on the international film market. Hollywood blockbusters dominate the film listings in many countries outside the United States.* The *marquees* are used here as evidence that Hollywood films appear all over the world and are thus *prevalent,* as choice (E) suggests. While choices (C) and (D) may be true, they are not supported in the passage and can be eliminated. Choices (A) and (B) can also be eliminated because they reflect the views of the globalist critics in Passage 2.

19. **C** The claim from Passage 1 reads as follows: *Even the medium of film studies itself, particularly the version of it that was popularized in film journals in the 1960s in France, was largely concerned with the analysis of American films and with lionizing directors such as Orson Welles, Howard Hawks, and Buster Keaton.* The *contingent* of globalist critics from Passage 2 take a much more international approach, even citing these film journals as the influence for the American film criticism of Pauline Kael. The *contingent* would therefore find the nationalist critics' assessment as unrepresentative or *misguided,* as in choice (C). The globalist critics disagree with the nationalist critics, eliminating choices (A) and (E), but choices (B) and (D) give too extreme a version of that disagreement.

20.　**D**　The relevant section of this sentence reads as follows: *there was simply too much exchange in this era, both of people and ideas, and the big events, such as the two World Wars of the early twentieth century, cannot be said to have a single national heritage.* The events referred to as *big* are the World Wars, suggesting that *big*, in this context, means something like *important* or *notable*, as in choice (D). Choices (A), (B), and (E) all represent other synonyms for the word *big*, but they do not work in this context. Choice (C) can be eliminated because while the *exchange of ideas* might have been frequent, the important events like World Wars were not.

21.　**A**　The reference appears in the following context: *So why was Hollywood able to achieve the prominence that it had in the 1940s and 1950s? A large factor, the globalists argue, was the new class of émigré directors, such as Billy Wilder, Douglas Sirk, and Jacques Tourneur, who were fleeing horrendous conditions in their home continent.* These *émigré directors*, in other words, made American films even though they were not Americans themselves, contributing to the idea that film is international. They suggest a *cause* for the phenomenon named at the beginning of the paragraph, as choice (A) indicates. While this perspective may effectively *discard an old understanding*, namely that of the nationalists, this is not the intention in this passage, eliminating choice (C). The focus is not narrowed but explained by this argument, eliminating choice (B). The passage does not indicate that this is an *anecdote*, nor that it is *well-known*, eliminating choice (D), and the names are here as examples of the *new class of émigré directors*, not merely as a last of famous people, eliminating choice (E).

22.　**B**　The comparison of Kael and later film historians is given as follows: *Kael was merely one among many who considered the national origin of film almost irrelevant, as the medium became a universal language that was not affected by the linguistic and cultural borders of music or literature. In the 1970s, directors from "the new Hollywood" such as Martin Scorsese were pushing this idea further, openly citing world-cinema directors as their primary influences.* In other words, Kael presented the idea but later critics pushed the idea further away from the idea of national origins altogether, as choice (B) suggests. While choice (C) may be tempting, there is no indication that the globalist critics are uninterested in *origins*, only in *national origins*. Choice (D) would work if the question were asking about nationalist critics, but it is not. Choices (A) and (E) take words from the passage, but they do not apply to the comparison between Kael and the new global critics.

23.　**D**　The discussion of Kael appears in the following sentences: *While even Kael's range seems small now compared with those of the new globalist critics, her writings pointed art-conscious filmgoers not to Hollywood productions but to the exciting new work coming out of Italy, France, India, and Japan. Kael was merely one among many who considered the national origin of film almost irrelevant.* In other words, *national origins* for Kael were not of particular concern, as choice (D) suggests. While she may have believed the things listed in choices (A), (B), and (E), these are not addressed in the passage and can be eliminated. While choice (C) may be true, it is not discussed *according to Kael*, as the question asks.

24. **B** The mention of Scorsese appears at the end of the second paragraph: *In the 1970s, directors from "the new Hollywood" such as Martin Scorsese were pushing this idea further, openly citing world-cinema directors as their primary influences.* Because the nationalist critics believed that all film was derived from American sources, they would likely disagree with Scorsese's assessment, arguing that American influence is so broad that it cannot be escaped, as suggested in choice (B). Choices (C) and (D) might be the positions of globalist critics, not those of nationalist critics. Choices (A) and (E) cannot be substantiated because there is no real indication that either Scorsese or Kael share any tenets of the nationalist perspective.

25. **A** The lines from Passage 1 read as follows: *These nationalist scholars generally see the foundations of film in Thomas Edison's early film experiments, silent shorts only a few seconds in length. These scholars credit Edison with the invention and then early American filmmakers, such as Edwin S. Porter, with the popularization of the medium.* The globalist contingent would find this perspective far too narrow, as choice (A) would suggest. Choices (C), (D), and (E) would seem to align more with the nationalist perspective than the globalist one, and choice (B) cannot be supported by information from the passage.

Part IV
Writing

Chapter 21
Introduction to
SAT Writing

WHAT DOES THE SAT WRITING SECTION REALLY TEST?

Like the other sections of the SAT, the Writing section really just tests how well you can perform on a standardized writing test; your scores don't necessarily reflect how strong you are as a writer or what kinds of grades you'll receive in your college English classes. Instead, your scores demonstrate your ability to crank out an essay that conforms to ETS's idea of a "good" essay in a short period of time and your ability to pick out the best of five answers to a grammar question. In fact, if many of the essays written by eminent writers such as Ernest Hemingway, William Shakespeare, and e.e. cummings were graded according to SAT standards, those essays would receive substandard scores!

What Does This Mean For You?

Fortunately, once you know what SAT essay graders are looking for, you'll discover that crafting an essay that meets their standards is fairly straightforward. You may find that writing an SAT essay doesn't exactly show off just how creative you can be, but you'll also find that you don't need to write the latest, greatest English novel in order to receive a strong score. You just need to write an essay that makes it easy for your graders to see that your essay meets their specific criteria for a top-notch essay. Even if you're already receiving high scores, understanding exactly what your graders want from you can provide you with that extra edge that changes an essay with a score of 9 or 10 into an essay with a score of 11 or 12.

Additionally, the grammar portion of the Writing test covers only a handful of specific rules, so you don't have to memorize an entire grammar textbook in order to score well on this section of the test. Once you know these rules and understand how to apply them, you'll discover that acing the grammar section of the test is significantly easier.

What Will You See in The Writing Section?

The first section of each SAT is the Essay section. ETS will present you with a quote on a particular topic, usually from a notable individual, and then ask you to present an opinion on a question related to the topic. You'll have 25 minutes to write your essay.

The writing section also contains two scored grammar sections: one 25-minute, 35-question section, and one 10 minute, 14-question section (always the last section of each test). In the first grammar section, you'll see three types of questions:

- **Improving sentences questions.** These types of questions will present you with a sentence, part or all of which will be underlined. You will have five answer choices, each of which contains a different version of the underlined portion of the sentence. Your job will be to pick out the best version. The first eleven questions in the first grammar section will be improving sentences questions, and the questions will get progressively harder through the section.

- **Error ID questions.** Each of these questions will contain a single sentence, four parts of which are underlined. Your job is to pick out the part that contains an error, or to choose the answer that indicates that there is no error in the sentence. Questions 12 through 29 in the first grammar section will be error ID questions, and the questions will get progressively harder as you move through the section.

- **Improving paragraphs.** When you work these questions, you'll first be presented with a poorly written paragraph. The questions that accompany this paragraph will ask you to fix grammatical and organizational errors in the paragraph. Questions 30 through 35 in the first grammar section will be improving paragraphs questions, and the questions will not be arranged in any particular order of difficulty, although you'll find that most of these questions are of either easy or medium level difficulty.

In the second grammar question, that is, in the last section of the test, you will see only 14 improving sentences questions. Note that if one of your grammar sections is an experimental section, you will have two 25-minute grammar sections.

ETS calculates your final writing score on the 200–800 point scale by combining your essay and grammar scores. You'll learn more about how ETS scores these individual sections in later chapters.

ACING THE WRITING PORTION OF THE SAT

Whether you're preparing to take the SAT for the first time, or you're a veteran test taker who's already scoring well but just needs a bit of a boost to reach that perfect score, you will find taking the following actions helpful:

- Review and learn the rules of grammar, SAT-style.
- Know the appropriate plan of attack for each type of question.
- Understand what the essay graders want from you.

Chapter 22
The Essay

If you're going to write a high-scoring SAT essay, then you first need to know something about how graders assign scores and what they want to see.

SCORING

Each essay has two graders, each of which provides a score between 0 and 6. ETS then adds the two scores together, so that you receive a total score between 0 and 12. The scoring guidelines that each grader receives are shown below.

Score of 6	Score of 5	Score of 4
An essay in this category is **outstanding**, demonstrating **clear and consistent mastery**, although it may have a few minor errors. A typical essay • effectively and insightfully develops a point of view on the issue and demonstrates outstanding critical thinking, using **clearly appropriate** examples, reasons, and other evidence to support its position • is **well organized and clearly focused**, demonstrating **clear coherence** and a smooth progression of ideas • exhibits **skillful use of language**, using a varied, accurate, and apt vocabulary • demonstrates **meaningful variety** in sentence structure • is free of most errors in grammar, usage, and mechanics	An essay in this category is **effective**, demonstrating **reasonably consistent mastery**, although it will have occasional errors or lapses in quality. A typical essay • effectively develops a point of view on the issue and demonstrates strong critical thinking, **generally using appropriate examples**, reasons, and other evidence to support its position • is **well organized and focused**, demonstrating **coherence** and progression of ideas • exhibits **facility in the use of language**, appropriate vocabulary • demonstrates **variety** in sentence structure • is generally free of most errors in grammar, usage, and mechanics	An essay in this category is **competent**, demonstrating **adequate mastery**, although it will have lapses in quality. A typical essay • develops a point of view on the issue and demonstrates competent critical thinking, using **adequate examples**, reasons, and other evidence to support its position • is **generally organized and focused**, demonstrating some coherence and progression of ideas • exhibits **adequate but inconsistent facility in the use of language**, using generally appropriate vocabulary • demonstrates **some variety** in sentence structure • has some errors in grammar, usage, and mechanics
Score of 3	Score of 2	Score of 1
An essay in this category is **inadequate**, but demonstrates **developing mastery**, and is marked by one or more of the following weaknesses: • develops a point of view on the issue, demonstrating some critical thinking, but may do so inconsistently or use **inadequate examples**, reasons, or other evidence to support its position • is **limited in its organization or focus**, but may demonstrate some lapses in coherence or progression of ideas • displays **developing facility in the use of language**, but sometimes uses weak vocabulary or inappropriate word choice • **lacks variety** or demonstrates problems in sentence structure • contains an accumulation of errors in grammar, usage, and mechanics	An essay in this category is **seriously limited**, demonstrating little mastery, and is flawed by one or more of the following weaknesses: • develops a point of view on the issue that is **vague or seriously limited**, demonstrating weak critical thinking, providing inappropriate or insufficient examples, reasons, or other evidence to support its position • is **poorly organized and/or focused**, or demonstrates serious problems with coherence or progression of ideas • displays **very little facility in the use of language**, using very limited vocabulary or incorrect word choice • demonstrates **frequent problems** in sentence structure • contains errors in grammar, usage, and mechanics so serious that meaning is somewhat obscured	An essay in this category is **fundamentally lacking**, demonstrating very little or no mastery, and is severely flawed by one or more of the following weaknesses: • develops **no viable point of view** on the issue, or provides little or **no evidence** to support its position • is **disorganized or unfocused**, resulting in a disjointed or incoherent essay • displays fundamental **errors in vocabulary** • demonstrates **severe flaws** in sentence structure • contains pervasive errors in grammar, usage, or mechanics that persistently interfere with meaning
Score of 0		
Essays not written on the essay assignment will receive a score of zero.		

What do these guidelines really mean? Note that in the chart above, the essays that score between 4 and 6 are defined by what they do well; ETS uses phrases such as *clearly appropriate examples*, *exhibits facility in the use of language*, and *generally organized and focused* to describe these essays. On the other hand, essays that score between 1 and 3 are often defined by the things that they are missing; ETS uses phrases such as *inadequate examples*, *very little facility in the use of language*, and *no viable point of view* to describe these essays. Therefore, when graders look at your essay, they first put it into one of two categories: either the 1–3 scoring range or the 4–6 scoring range. If your essay is generally well written and organized, presents a clear point of view, and supports that point of view with examples, then your essay should receive a score between 4 and 6, inclusive. However, if it does not meet these criteria, then it may receive a score of 3 or less.

Note that scores of 0 are highly unusual. If you leave the page blank, if you only write, "this essay is stupid," or if you write your essay in a language other than English—Latin, for instance—then you will receive a score of 0. However, if you write anything at all related to the topic, even just a single sentence, you should receive a score of at least 1.

Make Your Graders Happy

So what can you do to convince your essay graders to give you the scores you want? There are a few things that can help you to make a great first impression:

- **Length:** Writing a long essay will not, by itself, necessarily guarantee you a good score. However, you are writing to make an argument, and it's very difficult to make a cogent argument in only one or two short paragraphs. For that reason, longer essays tend to receive higher scores than shorter ones. Try to fill up the full two pages that ETS provides.
- **Legibility:** Graders will not specifically grade you on your handwriting, but if they can't read your handwriting, they cannot accurately grade what you have written. Additionally, they're less likely to be generous if they have to struggle to read your writing. Make your graders happy and write neatly! If your cursive script is indecipherable, don't be afraid to print.
- **An organized appearance:** An essay that has clearly separated paragraphs, indented topic sentences, relatively few strikeouts or erasures, and no writing outside the lines looks like an essay that was written by someone who knows what he or she was doing. If your essay appears well organized, then your grader is more likely to assume that the content will be well organized also.

The Big Three

The criteria mentioned above will help you to make a good first impression, but what is inside your essay will be even more important. Ultimately, SAT graders have three main requirements:

1. *You must have a clear point of view.* Your graders should never have to guess which side of the question posed in the prompt you are supporting. Pick a side and stick to it. Be sure to have a clear thesis statement.
2. *Support your position.* It's not enough simply to state your argument; you must also back up that argument with relevant examples.
3. *Have a logical structure.* Your essay should have an obvious introduction, separate body paragraphs, and a conclusion.

In addition to the requirements listed above, the quality of your writing will also factor into your score. While one or two grammar or spelling mistakes may not really make a difference in your grade, dozens of them will. Diction and sentence variety also contribute to your grade.

In the end, you will labor for 25 minutes to craft an essay that meets all of the criteria above. If that seems overwhelming, keep in mind that your graders will spend an average of only two and a half minutes reading your essay! Essay graders grade holistically, which means that rather than picking apart every detail of your essay, they will look at your essay as a whole to determine whether you have effectively completed the assigned task.

Sample Essays

So what does an essay that receives a score of 6 from one grader look like? What's the difference between an essay that scores a 5 and an essay that scores a 6? Examine the essays that follow to discover just exactly what SAT essay graders want to see.

The essay that follows was written in response to the following assignment:

Is it better to be consistent, and maintain the same ideas, opinions, and practices, or to embrace change? Plan and write an essay in which you develop your point of view on this issue. Support your position with reasoning and examples taken from your reading, studies, experience, or observations.

Despite Robert Cialdini's assertion that change is a sign of weakness, true growth will always be dependent on exactly that. It is understood by all mature people that consistency and reliability are hallmarks of a responsible person's life, yet openness to change is an even greater necessity.

Proof of this is found in many examples, most notably in two places—in the current scandal involving steroids in baseball and in Huckleberry Finn written by Mark Twain.

In headlines every day, we now read reports of the terrible problems facing Major League Baseball. Clearly, many players have been illegally abusing banned substances to improve their playing ability. Denials to the allegations are no longer taken seriously. Most fans and reporters can now see that too much of the joy surrounding the excitement of homeruns was the result of an unnatural substance and not increased skill.

Now everyone—players, fans, and baseball players—must address this problem head on or else it will destroy the very game that they all revere. Here, change must happen. It's not an option. It's crucial to the hope that baseball will retain any semblance of its innocent past. To maintain the past course of stalling and pointless "investigation" would be harmful for the very reason that it doesn't move forward. Contrary to Robert Cialdini's idea, here is an example of where not changing is a greater danger than true, revolutionary change. If baseball's leaders and players were to continue to keep the same approach, that would not show integrity or strength. It would be a poor choice. In this case, it is not inconsistency, it is growth that will save the game. A new approach will lead to change and growth.

The example of Huck Finn shows the evolution of the main character through many changes. Initially, Huck's personality is shown to be consistent, but not in a good way. He continually acts in a self-interested manner. But this does not show stability in any way. Repeatedly, he finds himself in trouble through his actions and decisions remain the same. What Huck needs is a great deal of change—internal change.

What does this essay do well?

Notice that this essay is well-structured; it has a clear, beginning, middle, and end. The writer also uses the relevant, specific examples of a scandal in baseball and *Huckleberry Finn*, and includes relevant details about the book such as the author's name. The essay writer also takes a clear stand on the issue, stating, *It is understood by all mature people that consistency and reliability are hallmarks of a responsible person's life, yet openness to change is an even greater necessity*. Finally, the essay is well-written; it uses varied sentences structure, strong vocabulary—note the use of words such as *hallmark*—and does not contain glaring grammatical flaws or multiple misspellings. This essay may not be a work of art, but it contains everything that an SAT essay grader wants to see!

So how does an essay scoring a 5 differ from an essay scoring a 6? Check out the essay below, and see if you can identify the reasons that this essay did not receive a perfect score. This essay was written in response to the following assignment:

Are those who pay attention to details, rather than the focusing on the bigger picture at a disadvantage? Plan and write an essay in which you develop your point of view on this issue. Support your position with reasoning and examples taken from your reading, studies, experience, or observations.

No, it is not a disadvantage to pay attention to details because the success of individual parts leads to the ultimate success of the bigger picture. Paying attention to details allows for critical thinking and quality assessment of protocols, and it also allows for more accurate conjectures to maximize the probability for success. The lack of attention to the minute aspects can often lead one astray from the task at hand, and disastrous consequences could result from ignoring the behind-the-scenes work that ensures success. Mark Zuckerberg of Facebook and the Super Bowl champion Baltimore Ravens exemplify the levels of success that can be enjoyed when attention is paid to details.

Mark Zuckerberg began Facebook as a small, personal project from his college dorm room. As user access to his website exponentially increased, so too did the complexities within which he could satisfy user demand while still working within the framework of his evolving vision for what would ultimate become what is now known today as Facebook. As Facebook grew, Zuckerberg had to carefully manage the software aspects of designing Facebook, hardware aspects of attaining the requisite server space to facilitate the deluge of online traffic, business aspects to take his burgeoning idea to investors to secure the funds he needed to expand his product, and marketing aspects to get a pulse of what the business market and user market wanted from Facebook. The conglomeration of details could easily overwhelm an individual, but Zuckerberg was able to pay the necessary attention to all these details to become the billionaire that he is today.

Similar to the wild success of Facebook, the Super Bowl champion Baltimore Ravens also had to pay careful attention to details if they were to win the Super Bowl. Designing an offensive game plan to attack one of the top defenses in the NFL and meticulous game-planning in the video rooms and classrooms. The Ravens had to identify the weaker points of a fundamentally sound 49ers defense and attempt to cleanly execute the right plays that would expose the defense. The 49ers defensive backfield were not strong tacklers, so the Ravens devised a game plan to air out the ball to their bigger and stronger receivers to physically dominate the 49ers defensive backs. If this critical element were not identified, the Baltimore Ravens may not have won the Super Bowl. This attention to detail on the part of Baltimore was a clear strategy to ensure success.

It is clearly not a disadvantage to pay attention to details. The success of an organization rests in the success of the many intricate, moving parts of an organization. Only by paying attention to such detail can the group as a whole enjoy the sweet taste of success and victory.

Why did this essay not receive a score of 6?

_____

_____

_____

_____

Note that there are many things that this essay writer does well. The essay has an introduction, body paragraphs, and conclusion. The examples that the writer uses are relevant, and contain many details. The writer also takes a strong stand on the issue, stating, *No, it is not a disadvantage to "pay attention to details."*

So what is this essay missing that the previous one was not? Often, the differences between essays that score a 5 and those that score a 6 are quite small. In this case, note the differences between the thesis statements. The writer of the essay scoring a 6 rephrased the language in the assignment, rather than simply quoting from the assignment. In other words, rather than writing, *it is better to embrace change than to be consistent, and maintain the same ideas, opinions and practices,* the writer instead created a stronger thesis statement by using his or her own language.

On the other hand, the writer of the essay scoring a 5 quotes the assignment almost word-for-word in his or her thesis statement, and repeats this language in the conclusion.

Additionally, notice that the essay scoring a 6 does a slightly more thorough job of tying each example back to the thesis statement. For example, at the end of the first example, the essay says, *A new approach will lead to change and growth.* This statement relates, not only to the example of the baseball scandal, but also to the essay's thesis. However, the essay scoring a 5 concludes its first example by stating, *Zuckerberg was able to pay the necessary attention to all these details to become the billionaire that he is today.* This conclusion to the body paragraph leaves the grader to fill missing thought: *thus we can see that paying attention to detail can ensure, rather than detract, from success.* While stating this thought may seem redundant, graders prefer to have writers present each link in the logical chain, even if such links appear obvious.

How does an essay scoring a 4 differ from an essay scoring 5? Consider the essay below, which was written in response to the following assignment:

Is striving to be a hero a reasonable goal in today's world? Plan and write an essay in which you develop your point of view on this issue. Support your position with reasoning and examples taken from your reading, studies, experience, or observations.

Yes, it is possible to be a hero in the modern world because there are those select individuals in today's society who demonstrate extraordinary vision or perseverance in any circumstance—with no regard to themselves—to lead others into the future. The manifestation of such attributes is what emboldens us to regard them, correctly, as heroes for their works are atypical and memorable and serve as reminders of the good in humanity. Mark Zuckerberg, the founder of Facebook, and Martin Luther King, Jr. are a mere two representatives of how heroes can evolved into society-changing personas.

Mark Zuckerberg founded Facebook in college with extraordinary skills and vision. While his social life was apparently nothing memorable, at best, he used troubling episodes in his social life to fuel his intellectual genius that parlayed into what can now be termed as "social networking" through a medium (the Internet) that has been around for a couple decades. The evolution of what was first known as "The Facebook"—starting as a fun project among college guys into the multi-billion dollar empire that it is today—serves as a hero of every entrepreneur as his rise to fame and fortune is envied by many and serves as a benchmark for those seeking to impact society as much as Mark has. For his efforts and abilities, Mark can be perceived as a hero for society as a model to young entrepreneurs.

Similar to Zuckerberg, Dr. Martin Luther King, Jr. was a powerful figure during the Civil Rights movement in which he spoke to masses of people about the unfairness of segregation and power of equal rights for all Americans, regardless of color. His non-violent protests sparked hopes and dreams for many who were defeated and accepted segregation for what it was. His persistence and energy that emanated from his passion speaks loudly even today, so that all can be reminded of the wrongness of racial discrimination. It is hope that makes Dr. King a hero for all times.

In conclusion, Zuckerberg and King were preeminent in their respective fields that cast them, thus, as heroes. Without them, our world would be remarkably different probably for much worse, both socially and technologically, which would thus make them heroes.

Why did this essay receive a score of 4?

_____

_____

_____

_____

Note that this essay still contains all of the basic elements for which graders look: a thesis statement, specific examples, and clear organization. However, in this case, each of those components is in very basic form. The writer has accomplished the essential tasks, but nothing more. For instance, compare the level of detail in the Mark Zuckerberg example in the essay scoring a 5 with the level of detail in the Mark Zuckerberg example in the essay scoring a 4. You can see from the differences in the lengths of the paragraphs alone that the essay scoring a 5 includes much more detail. Ultimately, you prove your point in an SAT essay through your examples, so outlining those examples as thoroughly as possible, and showing just how those examples relate to your thesis statement, is critical.

CRAFTING YOUR ESSAY

So now that you know what a great essay looks like, how can you write your own masterpiece? Before you begin to write, you must brainstorm. Sometimes, you may be tempted simply to dive right into your essay and begin writing. However, such an approach may result in an unfocused and illogical essay. Before you begin to write, therefore, it's critical to spend a few minutes planning.

Brainstorming

First, you need to decide which side of the argument that you will support. When making this choice, there is one big question that you should consider: Which side can you actually support with examples? Like a lawyer, you need to argue for not just what you believe, but what you can prove. That means that your first brainstorming step is to come up with a list of relevant examples.

For most students, finding good examples is the most challenging part of writing the essay. Fortunately, while you don't know what prompt you'll see on test day, you can nevertheless prepare examples in advance. How is that possible? Some examples tend to lend themselves to multiple prompts. For instance, Shakespeare's *Romeo and Juliet* tends to apply to many SAT assignments. So, if you have a good list of such examples, chances are that you're less likely to be stumped on test day.

What kinds of examples should you choose? The instructions that accompany each essay state that you should choose examples that come *from reasoning and examples taken from your reading, studies, experience, or observations*. More specifically however, great examples tend to come from the following categories:

- **Literature.** This category may include books that you've read in school, such as The *Catcher in the Rye* or *The Great Gatsby*. However, the books don't have to be classics; if you feel that your prompt is especially suited to *The Hunger Games*, you may be able to write a great essay that uses that example. The most important feature of the book that you choose is how well it relates to the prompt. If you choose to use a book as one of your examples, be sure that it is a work with which you're familiar. You should be able to cite the author, the protagonist's name, the general plot, and other details.

  List two to three books that you have read that you think might apply to multiple SAT prompts.

  _____

  _____

  _____

- **History.** If you choose to use a historical example, be sure to make that example as specific as possible. For instance, *World War II* is a very broad example; that war covered the entire globe and lasted for several years. Using *the discrimination faced by Japanese Americans living on the Pacific Coast during 1942* would be much less vague. If you choose to use an example from history, be sure that you can discuss the names of people involved, the dates when the event occurred, and other specifics of the event.

  List two to three historical examples that you are familiar with that you think might apply to multiple SAT prompts.

  _____

  _____

  _____

- **Current events.** The same rules that apply to historical examples also apply to current events examples. Be sure to include specifics! Use names, dates, and other details.

  List two to three historical examples that you are familiar with that you think might apply to multiple SAT prompts.

  _____

  _____

  _____

- **Famous people.** This category may include prominent business people, scientists, artists, political leaders, and other individuals with influence. If you use a person as an example, make sure that you can discuss specific events in that person's life.

  List two to three people with whom you are familiar and whom you think might apply to multiple SAT prompts.

  _____

  _____

  _____

- **Pop culture.** Surprised? While you may think that television shows, movies, and the lives of celebrities are off limits on the SAT essay, the truth is that such examples can be effective. If you suddenly realize that an episode of *Keeping up with the Kardashians* or *Sherlock* perfectly relates to your essay assignment, don't be afraid to use that example.

  List two to three pop culture examples that you think might apply to multiple SAT prompts.

  _____

  _____

  _____

- **Personal examples.** If you've got a great personal anecdote that you think applies to your essay assignment, go for it! A word of caution about personal examples though: you can absolutely use a personal example and get a top score. However, be sure that your example is profound and relevant. If you wouldn't write about the experience in your college application essay, then you probably don't want to write about it in your SAT essay. For example, you might not want to discuss your last breakup, but talking about the time that you spent volunteering at the local homeless shelter might be entirely appropriate.

  List two to three personal examples that you think might apply to multiple SAT prompts.

  _____

  _____

  _____

Now that you have a list of potential examples, check out the essay prompt below:

Think carefully about the issue presented in the following excerpt and the assignment below.

Society may limit our actions, but it cannot limit our thoughts. Even if society disapproves of our opinions, we are ultimately free to decide whatever we want. Those decisions may, of course, have consequences, but they are still ours to make.

Assignment: Do society's rules limit our decisions such that our choices are not freely made? Plan and write an essay in which you develop your point of view on this issue. Support your position with reasoning and examples taken from your reading, studies, experience, or observations.

Using the examples you listed above, could you write an essay on this topic? What about on the topic below?

Think carefully about the issue presented in the following excerpt and the assignment below.

Making decisions is something we all struggle with. We worry that we need more time to think things through, or that we need more information, or that we will simply make the wrong decision regardless. But inaction gets you nowhere. Even a bad decision can teach us something valuable.

Adapted from Alicia Smith

Assignment: Is making a bad decision better than making no decision at all? Plan and write an essay in which you develop your point of view on this issue. Support your position with reasoning and examples taken from your reading, studies, experience, or observations.

If you found that you could in fact use your examples, then you likely have a pretty good list. Memorize your examples so that you can use them on test day! While having a list may not absolutely guarantee that you will have examples that fit the prompt, it can prove valuable.

Writing

Once you've finished brainstorming, then you need to begin the actual task of writing. How should you organize that writing? Start by considering the elements of a strong introduction.

The Introduction

Your essay introduction really needs to have only three components:

1. *A clear thesis statement.* Be sure your graders know exactly which side of the prompt you support. Remember to respond specifically to the *assignment*, rather than to the quote or information provided in the box above the assignment.
2. *Elaboration.* Include a sentence or two in which you explain *why* you support the side that you do.
3. *Preview your examples.* Tell the graders in advance which examples you will use to support your point of view. This requires that you brainstorm examples *before* you begin writing.

That's it! However, as you have already seen, it's possible to include all of these elements in an introduction, but still score only an 8, rather than a 10 or a 12. So, how do you take an introduction that scores an 8, and turn it into one that scores a 12? Examine the introduction below from an essay that scored a 9—meaning one grader gave it a 4, and another gave it 5. The essay was written in response to the following prompt:

Is it possible, through progress, to reduce the number of problems in the world, or will making progress simply replace one set of problems with another? Plan and write an essay in which you develop your point of view on this issue. Support your position with reasoning and examples taken from your reading, studies, experience, or observations.

Progress does not reduce the number of problems in the world, because the advancement of technology and accumulation of new knowledge often ends up being detrimental to society. The utilization of such technological devices and advancement of social tolerance spawns new—and often more dangerous—issues that require an inordinate amount of effort to resolve than did the original problem. The construction and the use of the atomic bomb and the advent of gene therapy are examples in which the resolution of the original problem or issue resulted in a graver, more serious situation.

Overall, this introduction is well written, and includes all of the essential elements. However, note that the thesis statement parrots the language of the assignment, using almost exactly the same wording. Try to rewrite the thesis statement in your own words, using different language than that used in the assignment.

_____

_____

_____

_____

Now examine the following introduction from an essay that scored an 8. The essay was written in response to the following prompt:

Which is preferable: to be innovative, or to make use of the conceptions and works of others? Plan and write an essay in which you develop your point of view on this issue. Support your position with reasoning and examples taken from your reading, studies, experience, or observations.

Some of the greatest minds of all time have built on the ideas of others. Their work, while astonishingly creative, was nevertheless built upon the remains of the work of someone else, and thus in some form was an imitation of another's achievement. Thus, to state in absolute terms that originality is always the better course would be to err in judgment, failing to recognize the full complexity of the issue at hand. A glimpse into the works of some well-known figures of the past can only serve to strengthen this argument.

Note that this essay takes a clear stand on the issue discussed in the prompt and provides explanation for that stand. However, the introduction does not mention the specific examples of Albert Einstein and Thomas Jefferson that will be discussed in the essay. See if you can rewrite this introduction to include some mention of the examples that will follow.

_____

_____

_____

_____

What if you already include an original thesis, explanation, and preview of your examples in each of your introductions? There are a few other things that you may wish to include.

Begin with a rhetorical question

Using a question is a great way to get your reader's attention. For instance, consider the introduction above that discussed the merits of progress. You might rewrite that introduction as follows:

Does progress truly improve the world? While many would argue that it does, the truth is that advancements in technology and the accumulation of new knowledge often create as many issues as they eradicate. Technological devices may solve some dilemmas, but they also spawn new—and often more dangerous—dilemmas that require an inordinate amount of effort to resolve and are perhaps more complex than the original problems. The construction and the use of the atomic bomb and the advent of gene therapy are examples in which the resolution of the original problem or issue resulted in a graver, more serious situation.

Now try to rewrite the introduction below so that it too includes a rhetorical question:

Some of the greatest minds of all time have built on the ideas of others. Their work, while astonishingly creative, was nevertheless built upon the remains of the work of someone else, and thus in some form was an imitation of another's achievement. Thus, to state in absolute terms that originality is always the better course would be to err in judgment, failing to recognize the full complexity of the issue at hand. A glimpse into the works of some well-known figures of the past can only serve to strengthen this argument.

_____

_____

_____

_____

Attack the Opposing Point of View

Arguing that your own point of view is the correct view is one way to prove your point, but an alternative way is to show that the opposing side is wrong. This approach can also demonstrate that you have an appreciation for the complexity of the issue. Just make sure it's absolutely clear which side of the argument you support.

The introduction below is from an essay that scored a 6. Note how it begins by acknowledging the opposing side of the argument, but then goes on to argue the author's point of view.

Warren Johnson states that "community or group cannot function effectively unless people are willing to set aside their personal interests." Most people would agree with this statement. However, Johnson's claim that "success of a community is limited unless personal interests are set aside" is false. In fact, there have been countless examples throughout history that show that personal interests and community interests are often the same thing. Many times they influence each other. The examples of flight 93 and the story of the 2004 Red Sox demonstrate the truth of this statement.

Read the introduction that follows and see if you can rewrite it to include an attack on the opposing side of the argument

Those whom we idolize reveal a great deal about us, and often, we choose to focus too much on the wrong individuals. There is a big difference between idolizing your parents and idolizing the most popular sports or singing stars. When we choose certain people to follow, we are making a choice about our values. So, we need to choose people who have strong characters. The examples of Rudy Giuliani and today's major sports stars demonstrate why this is true.

_____

_____

_____

_____

Paint a Suggestive Picture

An alternative way to grab your reader's attention is to paint a picture using a hypothetical example. While such examples are not appropriate for your body paragraphs, when used in an introduction, they can serve to get your grader excited about reading your essay. Check out the example below.

A small child toddles towards the kitchen, attracted by the aroma of fresh baked cookies. Eager to taste as well as smell the chocolaty goodness, he reaches up and grabs a treat, only to howl as his finger briefly comes in contact with the still-piping-hot stove. The child has learned a valuable, albeit painful lesson: touching the hot stove is dangerous! Like that child, we too learn from experiences that may seem painful at the time. While suffering is, by definition, a terrible thing, if we take to heart the lessons that those bad experiences teach us, we may in the end benefit. The examples of Jean Valjean from Les Miserables and Thomas Edison illustrate this principle.

Now read the introduction that follows and see if you can rewrite it so that it paints a suggestive picture.

Throughout history, successful people have repeatedly shown that achieving goals is usually done despite the opinions of others. Positive opinion may support a successful person, but often the most vocal opinions are those that come from those who disagree. Therefore, it is crucial to push on toward worthwhile goals, especially when faced with resistance. Two strong examples of this are Gandhi and Spud Webb.

_____

_____

_____

_____

The Body Paragraphs

Once you've completed your introduction, then it's time to tackle your body paragraph. You need to accomplish four things in your first body paragraph:

1. *Introduce your example.* You might use a simple transition phrase such as, *one example*, or *for example*. On the other hand, you may prefer to use a command, such as *consider the example.*

2. *Provide a brief summary of your example.* Even if you're discussing an example so well known that you think that everyone in the world is familiar with it, try to imagine that you are explaining the example to someone who has never heard of it. For instance, rather than saying, *When Leonardo da Vinci painted the Mona Lisa* you might say, *When Italian Renaissance artist Leonardo da Vinci completed his most famous painting, the Mona Lisa*…That way, even a grader who was previously unfamiliar with your example will understand its context.

3. *Show how the example supports your point of view.* Remember, the only reason that you're discussing your examples is to demonstrate how they support your argument. Therefore, it's vital that you make the link between each example and your argument. Don't make the grader fill in the blanks, even if you believe that you're simply restating the obvious.

4. *Restate your position.* Again, don't worry about being redundant. Restating your position demonstrates that the point that you prove through your example applies, not just to that example, but to the broader argument that you make in your thesis.

What if you're already receiving scores of 8, but want to bring your score up to a 10 or 12? Examine the paragraph below from an essay that you read earlier in the chapter. This paragraph was from an essay that scored an 8, but with a few minor tweaks, this paragraph might be more representative of a higher-scoring essay.

Mark Zuckerberg founded Facebook in college with extraordinary skills and vision. While his social life was apparently nothing memorable, at best, he used troubling episodes in his social life to fuel his intellectual genius, that parlayed into what can now be termed as "social networking," through a medium (the internet) that has been around for a couple of decades. The evolution of what was first known as "The Facebook"—starting as a two-day project among college guys into the billion-dollar empire that it is today—serves as a hero for every entrepreneur as his rise to fame and fortune is envied by many, and serves as a benchmark for those seeking to impact society as much as Mark has. For his efforts and abilities, Mark can be perceived as a hero to society as a model for young entrepreneurs.

Note that this body paragraph does not contain an introduction. Even a simple phrase such as, *for example* may serve as an introduction. How could you rewrite the beginning of this paragraph so that it includes an introduction?

_____

_____

_____

_____

Additionally, while this paragraph does include details about Zuckerberg's rise to fame, it does not begin by explaining who Mark Zuckerberg is; the writer essentially assumes that everyone already knows about Zuckerberg, rather than explaining that he was a Harvard University student who was known as a programming prodigy. How could you rewrite the first sentence of the paragraph so that it provides a bit more information about Zuckerberg's identity? (If you're not familiar with Mark Zuckerberg, you may do a quick internet search.)

_____

_____

_____

_____

The assignment in this case asks whether striving to be a hero is reasonable in today's world. The final sentence does relate the example back to the prompt, saying *For his efforts and abilities, Mark can be perceived as a hero to society as a model for young entrepreneurs.* However, since the paragraph ends there, this paragraph does not restate the author's position. How could you rewrite the end of the paragraph so that it does so?

_____

_____

_____

_____

Finally, writing skills really do matter. Diction, grammar, and sentence variety all contribute to your score. Consider the following sentence from the paragraph above:

The evolution of what was first known as "The Facebook"—starting as a two-day project among college guys into the billion-dollar empire that it is today—serves as a hero for every entrepreneur as his rise to fame and fortune is envied by many, and serves as a benchmark for those seeking to impact society as much as Mark has.

While you should include a mixture of long and short sentences in your essay, you don't want your sentences to be *too* long. In fact, if you make them too lengthy, you may inadvertently slip in a few grammatical errors. Note that if you remove the part of the sentence set off by dashes, you're left with the following *The evolution of what was first known as "The Facebook" serves as a hero for every entrepreneur as his rise to fame and fortune is envied by many….*

As it's currently written, the sentence seems to suggest that *the evolution* serves as a hero, rather than *Zuckerberg*. The sentence also refers to *his rise*, but since Zuckerberg's name is not actually mentioned in the sentence, the word *his* does not refer to any specific person.

Finally, this writer falls into another common trap; he or she uses the passive voice. What's the passive voice?

Consider the following sentence:

> *Daniel ran a mile.*

The subject of the sentence is *Daniel*, and the verb is *ran*. Daniel is both the subject of the sentence and the person performing the action, so this sentence is in the active voice.

Now consider this sentence:

> *A mile was run by Daniel.*

This sentence has basically the same meaning as the one before it, but it changes a few things. The subject of this sentence is *A mile*, and the verb is *was run*. However, the person performing the action is still *Daniel*. Since the person performing the action is not the subject of the sentence, this sentence is in the passive voice.

Therefore, the phrase *his rise to fame and fortune is envied by many* is passive. The subject is *his rise*, and the verb is *is envied*. The people who are doing the actual envying are not the subject of the sentence.

While one or two such errors may not affect your score, multiple errors will. Strive to write in the active voice!

Now see if you can rewrite the sentence to fix the errors. You may wish to break it up into more than one sentence.

The evolution of what was first known as "The Facebook"—starting as a two-day project among college guys into the billion-dollar empire that it is today—serves as a hero for every entrepreneur as his rise to fame and fortune is envied by many, and serves as a benchmark for those seeking to impact society as much as Mark has.

_____

_____

_____

_____

Finally, don't forget about diction. If you're studying for the SAT, then you're likely learning a lot of great vocabulary words. Don't be afraid to use a few of them in your essay. While you don't want to sound as if you've swallowed a dictionary, you should try to include one or two advanced vocabulary words in your essay. For example, note that the writer of the paragraph above used *parlayed*—a great vocab word. Of course, if you're going to use three-syllable terms, be sure that you can both use and spell them correctly.

Can you think of any other words in the paragraph above that you might be able to replace with more sophisticated words?

Transitions

You'll want to write two body paragraphs. Often, when students attempt to write three body paragraphs, they end up with very short paragraphs lacking in sufficient detail. In contrast, students who use only one example generally do not have enough support for their arguments. Therefore, if you attempt two body paragraphs, you should have just the right number—neither too many nor too few.

How should the second body paragraph differ from the first? The only difference between the requirements for the two paragraphs lies in the introductory sentence. You'll want to introduce your second body paragraph with a transition that provides a bridge between your first example and your second. Here are a few sample transition sentences:

Like the Russian revolution, the protest in Tiananmen Square, China is an example of a popular uprising that quickly became bloody.

Just as the events of 9/11 demonstrate that we do not appreciate the things that we possess until we lose them, so too the novel Huckleberry Finn by Mark Twain proves this point.

Using effective transitions is one way to transform an essay that otherwise might score an 8 into an essay that scores a 10 or 12!

Examine the excerpt below, which shows the conclusion of one paragraph and the beginning of another:

...Michelangelo completed the rest of the Sistine Chapel ceiling in only three months, thus demonstrating that great artists are, in fact, often more productive when under pressure.

The engineers working on NASA's Apollo 13 moon landing mission in the early 1960's experienced significant pressure when a technical issue nearly killed the Apollo spacecraft crew...

How could you rewrite the beginning of the second paragraph so that it contains a transition that connects the two examples?

_____

_____

_____

_____

Conclusion

Once you've completed your body paragraphs, then it's time to write your conclusion. You should do the following in your conclusion:

1. *Restate your position, and say why.*
2. *Recap your examples.* It's fine to vary the order of steps 1 and 2.
3. *Give a concluding thought that comments on the topic.* This is where you get to be philosophical. You might discuss how the issue in question affects the world at large, and what the broader consequences are.

Consider the example below:

As the examples of Isaac Newton and Leonardo da Vinci show, originality alone can't be used as a barometer of greatness. In fact, most scientific progress is made by brilliant developers working with the ideas of true innovators: a beautiful compromise. Only if we learn to find the balance between borrowing from the ideas of others and relying on our own ingenuity can we achieve true greatness.

Such a conclusion is well-written and effectively wraps up the essay. However, if you have time, you may wish to add a few flourishes to your conclusion. You may consider the following:

- **Use an analogy.** Using a comparison can help to make your conclusion more thought provoking.
- **Give a shout out to the other side.** You may wish to point out that while you support one side of the issue, the problem is actually quite complex. This approach can demonstrate that you're thinking deeply about the question in the asssignment, but be sure that you don't give the impression that you're undecided or confused about the issue.

The most important part about your conclusion though is that it must be present. You *must* have a conclusion. If you find that you're running out of time and have only one or two minutes left, stop, skip down a couple of lines, and write a quick conclusion, even if it's nothing more than, *In conclusion, it's better to embrace change than to always resist it.* You'll be penalized a lot less for having a short conclusion than for having none at all.

That's it! Are you ready to write your own essay? Check out the sample prompts on the pages that follow.

Think carefully about the issue presented in the following excerpt and the assignment below.

Communication is a continual balancing act, juggling the conflicting needs for intimacy and independence. To survive in the world, we have to act in concert with others, but to survive as ourselves, rather than simply as cogs in a wheel, we have to act alone.
—Deborah Tannen

Assignment: Is more important to be independent, or to rely on a community for support? Plan and write an essay in which you develop your point of view on this issue. Support your position with reasoning and examples taken from your reading, studies, experience, or observations.

Think carefully about the issue presented in the following excerpt and the assignment below.

The ultimate end of education is happiness or a good human life, a life enriched by the possession of every kind of good, by the enjoyment of every type of satisfaction.
—Mortimer Adler

Assignment: Does education promote happiness? Plan and write an essay in which you develop your point of view on this issue. Support your position with reasoning and examples taken from your reading, studies, experience, or observations.

Chapter 23
Basic SAT
Grammar

You may not have officially studied grammar in quite some time. However, if that is the case, take heart! The good news is that the SAT does not test an unlimited number of grammar rules. Instead, it tests the same few rules over and over in every exam. Once you know and understand those rules and understand how to approach each question type, you'll find that the grammar section of the SAT isn't as intimidating as you once may have thought.

GRAMMAR TRAPS

When you tackle a grammar problem, it may be tempting to think about how the sentence *sounds*. However, the problem is that most of us abuse grammar on a daily basis. What you hear around you in school, in the movies, and on television may not be proper grammar, even if it *sounds* fine. Unfortunately, SAT question writers know that rather than consulting the grammar rules, most students use their ears when they answer grammar problems. Therefore, the question writers often create sentences that may sound odd, but are grammatically correct, and sentences that sound okay, but are grammatically incorrect. What's the moral of the story? On the SAT, focusing on whether a sentence sounds fine will not necessarily lead you to the correct answer. You need to know the rules.

THE BASIC APPROACH

In this chapter, we'll focus on two types of grammar questions: Improving Sentences and Error ID.

Improving Sentences

Improving Sentences questions contain a single sentence, part of which is underlined. You will have five answer choices, each of which contains a different version of the underlined portion of the sentence. Your job is to pick out the best version. Here are a few important facts that you should know about these questions:

- **Answer choice (A) always repeats the original version of the sentence.** Therefore, you never need to read answer choice (A).
- **You shouldn't be afraid to choose answer choice (A); it's not a trap answer.** The sentence in question may actually be correct as written. In fact, about one-fifth of the Improving Sentences questions in the test will have choice (A) as the correct answer.
- **The non-underlined portion of the test is always correct.** You can compare this part of the sentence to the underlined portion to help you spot errors.

- **Avoid trying to fix the sentences in your head.** The chance that your revised version will be one of the answer choices is small, because there may be other, equally correct ways to rewrite the sentence. Instead, focus on whether each answer choice breaks any grammar rules.
- **Questions become progressively harder throughout the section.** Question 1 will be much easier than question 11.

How should you approach these questions? Here are the steps that you should take.

1. **Ask yourself whether you spot a grammatical error.** Make sure that the error breaks a rule that you can identify. You should be able to say "this sentence contains a subject-verb agreement error" or "this sentence contains a parallelism error," for instance.
2. **If you do spot a grammatical error, eliminate any answer that repeats that error.** For instance, if you notice that the original sentence uses *is*, which is a present tense verb, but that the rest of the sentence calls for the past tense verb *was*, then you can eliminate any answer choice that contains *is*. Often, this will allow you to eliminate two or three answer choices immediately.
3. **If you don't spot a grammatical error, or if you have eliminated all of the answers that repeat the original error in the sentence, compare your remaining answer choices.** Do the answer choices alternate between *is* and *are*? If so, the question is testing the difference between singular and plural verbs. Once you figure out which type of verb that you need, you can likely eliminate a few answers. If looking at all of the answers at once is overwhelming, focus on just two at a time.
4. **Use Process of Elimination.** As you compare your answers, eliminate those that break known rules.

The flowchart below outlines this process in visual form:

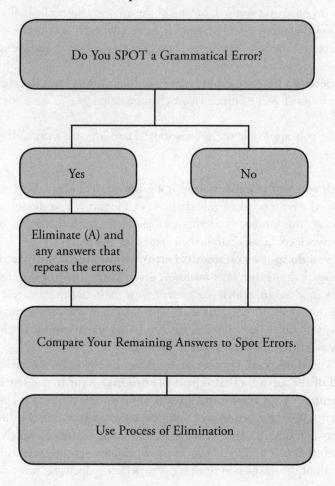

A few final Improving Sentences hints:

- Eliminate any answer that changes the intended meaning of the sentences.
- If you're down to two answers that are grammatically similar—they do not contain verbs of different tenses, for instance—go with the shorter answers. The SAT favors more concise answers over long, wordy ones.
- If you're stuck between choice (A) and another answer choice, don't eliminate choice (A) just because it repeats the original sentence. Sometimes the sentence really is correct as written, so you should have a grammatical reason for eliminating choice (A).

Error ID

Error ID questions consist of single sentences, parts of which are underlined. Your job is to find the underlined portion that contains an error, or to select choice (E), no error, if the sentence does not contain an error. Here are a few important facts that you should know about these questions:

- **Error ID questions have, at most, only one error per question.** If you have identified an error in the underlined portion of the sentence and can name the rule associated with that error, then you've found the answer.
- **It's important to focus on what must be wrong rather than on what could be wrong.** It may be tempting to read an Error ID question and think, "I would rewrite the sentence this way. Therefore, the way that the sentence is currently written is incorrect." Your alternative way of writing the sentence may be absolutely acceptable. However, what's important is not whether there may be another way of writing the sentence, but whether there's anything grammatically wrong with the sentence as it's currently written. If it's not grammatically wrong, it's not your error.
- **You should eliminate any answer choice that contains parts of the sentence that are error-free.** If you know an answer choice is grammatically correct, cross it off the page.
- **Approximately one-fifth of the Error ID questions on the test will not contain an error.** Choice (E) isn't a trap answer in this case; sometimes the sentence really doesn't contain an error.
- **Error ID questions get progressively harder throughout the section**. You'll have only one scored section that contains Error ID questions; the first Error ID question in that section will be number 12, and the last will be number 29. Therefore, number 12 should be much easier than number 29.

How should you approach these questions? Follow the steps below:

1. **Ask yourself whether you spot a grammatical error.** Avoid thinking about how the sentence *sounds;* instead focus on examining whether it breaks any known rules.
2. **If you do spot an error, make sure that you can name that error.** You should be able to say "this sentence contains a subject-verb agreement error" or "this sentence contains a parallelism error," for instance. Check the other choices just to be safe.
3. **If you don't spot an error, use the Process of Elimination to get rid of answer choices that don't break any rules.** For each word in each answer choice, ask yourself these questions: What part of speech is this word? What rules apply to this part of speech? Does using this word in its current form break any of those rules?
4. **Select the answer containing the error OR select (E) if the sentence does not contain an error.** Again, remember: Sometimes the answer really is choice (E)!

The chart below outlines these steps in visual form.

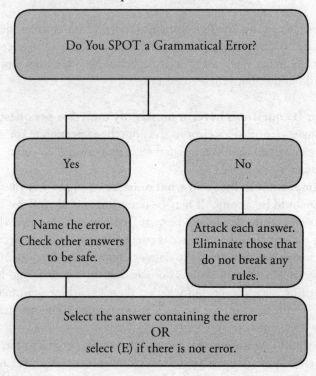

Now that you know *how* to approach grammar questions, we'll review some of the basic grammar rules that the SAT tests, and show you just exactly to apply those rules.

What if you already have a strong grasp of grammar? Complete the quiz below. If you score 100% on this quiz, then you are ready to move on to the next chapter! On the other hand, if you miss a few questions, then you may benefit from the review that follows in the rest of this chapter.

GRAMMAR DRILL

Let's try a drill. Answers and explanations can be found in Chapter 26.

1. When employers place pressure upon their employees,

   production quality <u>may be affected</u> because high stress
   A

   levels <u>can cause</u> employees to work too quickly and <u>thus</u>
   BC

   make more mistakes than <u>low stress levels.</u> <u>No error</u>
   DE

2. Most archaeologists believe that the number of dinosaur
   species that were larger than humans <u>have been greatly
   exaggerated</u>, perhaps due to misconceptions that resulted
   from the fact that large, sturdy bones are more likely to
   survive as fossils than are small bones, and are therefore
   more likely to be discovered.

   (A) have been greatly exaggerated
   (B) as having been greatly exaggerated
   (C) to have greatly been exaggerated
   (D) has been greatly exaggerated
   (E) was being greatly exaggerated

3. The narwhal, a medium-sized, toothed whale, uses sound

   to hunt: clicks and whistles <u>allow them</u> <u>to find food</u>
   ABC

   through echolocation, <u>while</u> banging sounds disorient
   D

   prey. <u>No error.</u>
   E

4. After he wrote his famous *April Theses,* Vladimir Lenin
   led the Russian October <u>Revolution, which resulted in his
   becoming</u> leader of the new Bolshevik Party in 1917.

   (A) Revolution, which resulted in his becoming
   (B) Revolution, this is the reason he became
   (C) Revolution; as a result, becoming
   (D) Revolution and consequently became
   (E) Revolution, he therefore became

5. In this class, the students frequently use their phone to
   A   B   C
   text and play games during class and fail to pay attention
                                        D
   to the professor. No error.
                      E

6. Australia's Great Barrier Reef is home to more than
                                   A   B
   1,500 species of fish, each amazing in their beautiful
                               C   D
   colors and remarkable abilities. No error.
                                    E

7. This week the museum has a new impressionism exhibit
   and a new cubism exhibit, neither appear interesting to
   me.

   (A) appear
   (B) of which appears
   (C) have appeared
   (D) were appearing
   (E) is appearing

8. What least pleased my family and I about the resort
   A   B
   was that the cleaning was so indifferently done that we
                              C
   initially thought that our room had not been cleaned at all
                                    D
   before our arrival. No error.
                       E

9. While located on the outskirts of the city, the restaurant's
   famous seafood dishes attract customers from all over the
   country.

   (A) restaurant's famous seafood dishes attract
   (B) restaurant famous seafood dishes attracting
   (C) restaurant is famous for its seafood dishes and
       attracts
   (D) famous seafood dishes of the restaurant
       attracts
   (E) famous seafood dishes of the restaurant attract

10. Discovering creative ways to explain new concepts
    A   B
    both clearly and entertainingly are among the
                                    C
    biggest challenges facing high school teachers. No error.
    D   E

Subject-Verb Agreement

Subject-verb agreement is one of the most commonly tested errors on the SAT grammar section. The following rule applies to subjects and verbs:

> Singular nouns must be paired with singular verbs, and plural verbs must be paired with plural verbs.

For example, consider the sentence below:

> *The boy plays.*

The subject of the sentences is *boy*, which is singular. The verb in the sentence is *plays,* which is also singular.

Now examine this sentence:

> *The boys play.*

What changed? Now the subject is *boys*, which is plural. The verb in the sentence is *play*, which is also plural.

The fact that the verb *plays* is singular, while *play* is plural may seem odd, especially because nouns and verbs seem opposite in this respect. If you add an *s* to a noun, you generally make that noun plural, and if you remove the *s*, you generally make that noun singular. However, if you add an *s* to a verb, you generally make that verb singular, and if you remove the *s*, you generally make the noun plural. Verbs are backwards from nouns!

Now, if the SAT only gave you sentences as such as *the boys plays*, you might easily be able to pick out any errors. Unfortunately, however, you'll see longer, more complicated sentences on the SAT, ones in which you may not be able to identify the errors as easily. Check out the sentence below and see whether you can identify the subject and the verb.

> *The rules of the game states that the first person who scores 500 points wins the game.*

What is the subject of this sentence? Is the subject singular or plural?

What is the main verb in this sentence? Is the main verb singular or plural?

If you answered that the subject is *rules*, which is plural, and that the main verb is *states*, which is singular, you found the correct subject and verb. Notice that since the subject is plural and the verb is singular, this sentence contains a subject-verb agreement error.

Try this next sentence:

> *George's love of apple tarts entice him to go to the bakery every day.*

What is the subject of this sentence? Is the subject singular or plural?

What is the main verb in this sentence? Is the main verb singular or plural?

If you answered that the subject is *love*, which is singular, and that the main verb is *entice,* which is plural, you found the correct subject and verb. Since the subject of this sentence is singular while the verb is plural, this sentence contains a subject-verb agreement error.

Notice that in these last two sentences, the subjects and verbs were not placed next to each other. In fact, the noun that appears right before the singular verb *states* in the first sentence is the noun *game,* which is also singular. It might be tempting to assume that the subject is *game,* and therefore decide that the subject and the verb match in that sentence. However, *game* is not the subject of the sentence. Similarly, the word that appears right before the plural verb *entice* in the second sentence is the plural noun *tarts*. You might therefore have been tempted to assume that the subject of the sentence was *tarts*, and that the subject and verb in that sentence agree. One of ETS's favorite tricks on subject-verb agreement questions is to place other words between the subject and the verb in a given sentence, thus making agreement errors harder to identify.

How can you spot subject-verb agreement errors then? One convenient way to spot such errors is to "trim the fat." Identify extra words that separate the subject and verb in a sentence, and cross those words out. Often, ETS separates subjects and verbs using *prepositional phrases*.

What is a prepositional phrase? It's a phrase that begins with a preposition. What's a preposition? Prepositions tell you about *where* things are in relation to other things. For example, you could think of a preposition as any word that describes where a squirrel could be in relation to a tree. You could have *the squirrel of the tree, the squirrel for the tree, the squirrel below the tree, the squirrel above the tree, the squirrel beside the tree, the squirrel in the tree,* or *the squirrel running up the tree.* All of these words—*of, for, below, above, beside, in,* and *up*—are prepositions. They are not the only prepositions, but should give you a good idea as to what a preposition is. Look for prepositional phrases in SAT grammar questions, and cross out those phrases.

SUBJECT-VERB AGREEMENT DRILL

Let's try a drill. Answers and explanations can be found in Chapter 26.

Now test your skills by trying the subject-verb agreement drill below. Circle the answer that corresponds to the correct subject or verb in each case.

1. The customers in the store (*is/are*) in a hurry.

2. Robin's determination to gain better working hours and better pay for herself and her fellow employees (*was/were*) impressive.

3. Emile's sense of ethics and fair play (*prevent/prevents*) him from cheating at croquet.

4. The number of puffins remaining in Iceland (*have/has*) increased during the last two years.

5. Discovering alternatives to using fossil fuels to power automobiles (*is/are*) an important step toward creating a healthy environment.

Now that you've identified a few subject-verb agreement errors, try the SAT question below. Use process of elimination and cross off answers that you know are incorrect. Circle the correct answer.

1. The biggest motivations cited by the volunteer crew for helping the disaster victims <u>is that they love helping others and have a desire to use their talents productively</u>.

   (A) is that they love helping others and have a desire to use their talents productively
   (B) is love of helping others and they have a desire to use their talents productively
   (C) are that they have a love of helping others and that they have desire to use their talents productively
   (D) is having a love of helping others and having a desire to use their talents productively
   (E) are a love of helping others and a desire to use their talents productively

The correct answer to the question above is choice (E). Note that in the original sentence, the subject is *motivations*, which is plural, while the verb is *is*, which is singular. Since the subject and verb do not agree, this choice contains a subject-verb agreement error. Eliminate choice (A). Choices (B) and (D) also use the verb *is*, and thus repeat the original error, so you can eliminate both of these choices. Only choices (C) and (E) remain. Choice (C) uses the plural pronoun *they* to refer to *the volunteer crew*, which is singular, so choice (C) is incorrect. The correct answer is choice (E).

Parallelism

Items in a list must be parallel. The following rule applies:

> All items in a list must be in the same form, and must be the same part of speech. A list may consist of only two items, or may consist of more items.

For example, consider the sentence below:

Every Sunday morning Xavier goes running, swimming, and plays tennis.

What is the problem with this sentence? It lists three actions—*running, swimming,* and *plays*—but notice that these verbs aren't all in the same form. This sentence should read *Xavier runs, swims, and plays tennis.* Anytime you have items in a list, you want those items to be in the same form.

Consider the sentence below:

The critics praised the artist because of his bold use of color and he placed his subjects in surreal, beautiful surroundings.

Note that in the sentence above, the critics praised the artist for two reasons: *his use of color* (a thing), and where *he placed his subjects* (an action). In this case, the sentence contains a parallelism error because the first item in the list is a noun phrase, while the second item in the list is a verb phrase. Items in a list should all be the same part of speech. Correctly rewritten, this sentence might read something like *The critics praised the artist because he used color boldly and placed his subjects in surreal, beautiful surroundings.*

PARALLELISM DRILL

Let's try a drill. Answers and explanations can be found in Chapter 26. In each of the sentences below, circle the parts of the sentence that are not parallel.

1. The monkey grabbed the banana, peeled it, and he ate it quickly.

2. The Taj Mahal is famous both for its remarkable beauty and because it has a romantic history.

3. Hong Kong is a city of breathtaking views, great food, and has many shopping boutiques.

4. Since she moved out of the city, Jessica has gotten more exercise by hiking daily, has gone on picnics at least once per week, and learned how to snowshoe.

5. Vipers are poisonous snakes with long hollow fangs, short tails, and have powerful jaws.

Now that you know what parallelism errors look like, check out the SAT question below, and see if you can pick out the correct answer.

2. Last week, after she went on a whale watching tour,
            A   B

   Karen decided that she wanted to become a marine
                                    C

   biologist and will begin applying for an internship at
                      D

   local aquariums. No error
                      E

The sentence above lists two things that Karen does: she *decided* and she *will begin applying*. Notice that while both items in the list are verbs, the verbs are not in the same form. In order for the list to be parallel, the verbs should be *decided* and *applied*. Therefore, choice (D) is the correct answer.

Pronoun Agreement

The SAT also tests pronouns. What's a pronoun? It's a noun that replaces another noun within a sentence. For example, *he, she, it, they, we, him, her, them,* and *us* are all pronouns. The first rule that you need to know regarding pronouns is this one:

> Pronouns must agree with the nouns that they replace. Singular pronouns must replace singular nouns, and plural pronouns must replace plural nouns.

For example, check out the sentence below:

> *The golden retriever is a great companion because they are loyal, gentle, and obedient.*

The pronoun in the sentence above is *they*, which is plural. However, the noun that the pronoun replaces is *retriever*, which is singular. Therefore, this sentence contains a pronoun agreement error. Anytime you see a pronoun in a sentence, be sure to check to see what noun it replaces, and that the noun and pronoun agree.

Consider this sentence:

> *Today the physics club met to plan the trip to the planetarium, where they will go next Wednesday.*

In the sentence above, the subject is *club*, which is singular, but the pronoun is *they*, which is plural. Therefore, the sentence above has a pronoun agreement error.

Pronoun Agreement Drill

Try out the drill below, and see if you can identify the correct pronoun in each case. Answers and explanations can be found in Chapter 26.

1. The restaurant made (*their/its*) spaghetti sauce from scratch.

2. One should not complain about what is served for dinner if (*one/they*) does not cook.

3. When you ski down the mountain, (*one/you*) should be careful not to collide with other skiers.

4. When the team came up with the idea for the club, (*they/it*) had no idea that it would be such a huge financial success.

5. The band performed better last night than (*it/they*) did the previous night.

Now try the SAT question that follows:

8. <u>While some fondly refer to them as</u> "the king of fruits," others claim that durian emits an aroma reminiscent of raw sewage and is therefore inedible.

    (A) While some fondly refer to them as
    (B) Despite the fact that some fondly referring to it as
    (C) Despite their being fondly referred to by some as
    (D) While some fondly refer to it as
    (E) In spite that some fondly refer to them as

The pronoun in the underlined portion is *them*, which is plural. However, the noun that the pronoun replaces is *durian*, which is singular. Thus, this sentence contains a pronoun agreement error. You need a singular pronoun rather than the plural pronoun *them*, so eliminate choice (A). Choices (C) and (E) repeat the original error by also using plural pronouns, so you can also eliminate both of those choices. Only choices (B) and (E) remain. Choice (B) uses *referring*, which is the wrong verb form, so the correct answer is choice (D).

Pronoun Ambiguity

Pronouns must not only agree with the nouns that they replace, but they must also clearly replace one specific noun. The following rule applies.

> There should be no confusion about which noun a pronoun replaces. If you can't determine which noun a pronoun replaces, then you have discovered a pronoun ambiguity error.

Consider the following sentence:

> *Rebekah and Julie went to the movies, but when they arrived she realized that she had forgotten her wallet.*

In the sentence above, the pronoun *she* doesn't clearly refer to any one specific person. Julia may have forgotten her wallet, but alternatively Rebekah may have forgotten her wallet. Thus, this sentence contains a pronoun ambiguity error.

Now examine the sentence below:

> *I asked my parents for permission to buy the train tickets and go to the concert in Philadelphia, but they said that this was too much for me to do alone.*

Notice that this sentence uses the pronoun *this*. However, *this* does not clearly refer to any one noun. The writer seems to be using *this* to replace the actions of buying train tickets and going to the concert, but you cannot use pronouns to replace verbs. Even though you may be able to understand the intent of the writer's sentence, the sentence nevertheless contains a pronoun ambiguity error, because you can't point to a specific word in the sentence that the pronoun is replacing. You should always be able to underline the noun in the sentence that a pronoun replaces.

PRONOUN AMBIGUITY DRILL

Test your skills in the drill below! Circle the ambiguous pronouns in each sentence. Answers and explanations can be found in Chapter 26.

1. Thibault went rock climbing with Ludovic, and he soon mastered the skills necessary to reach the top of the mountain.

2. Some in the local transportation department argued that raising subway fees would allow the city to keep subway stations cleaner and provide better security for those traveling at night, but their opponents argued that this was not necessary.

3. The quarterback from the visiting team met the quarterback from the home team in the hall, and he looked ready for a fight.

4. The sky turned dark, a large cloud hovered overhead, and I thought that it looked threatening.

5. After Jonas left town that night, he was horrified to realize that he had forgotten to pack both his sweatshirt and his laptop because he would need it on the trip.

Chapter 24
Advanced
Grammar

TACKLING THE TOUGH QUESTIONS

Now that you have an approach for the grammar questions, it's time to learn some of the rules that the SAT tests, and how it tests them. Even if you have a solid grasp of grammar basics, you may be surprised to discover some of the unusual ways that SAT question writers manage to test your knowledge. In this chapter, we'll cover some of the trickier grammar rules that you'll see on the exam, and give you an opportunity to work through some sample problems on these concepts.

Subject-Verb Agreement with Conjunctions

The rule is, singular verbs go with singular subjects, and plural verbs go with plural subjects. Seems simple enough, right? However, on the SAT, you may discover that even this rule can be a bit tricky to apply. Why? Well, the exam writers like to test this rule by using sentences in which it may be difficult to discern whether the subject is singular or plural. Specifically, they like to use subjects that involve conjunctions. There are two rules that you need to know that govern subjects that contain conjunctions. The first is this:

> Two singular nouns joined by *and* make a plural subject.

For example, check out the sentence below:

> *Havalah and Abigail is going to visit New York City during Fashion Week.*

In this sentence, the subject is *Havalah and Abigail*. Even though each of the nouns is singular, when joined together these two nouns create a plural subject. Therefore, the singular verb *is* does not agree with the subject of the sentence, and is incorrect.

There's one other rule that relates to conjunctions within sentences:

> If two or more nouns are joined by "or" or "nor," the verb must agree with the last element in the list.

Consider this sentence:

> *Neither Luke nor his next door neighbor enjoy being woken early on a Saturday morning by the sound of jackhammers.*

The sentence above lists two nouns: *Luke* and *his neighbor*. The two nouns are joined by the conjunction *nor*, so the verb in the sentence must agree in number with the last element in the list: *neighbor*. Since *neighbor* is singular, the verb should also be singular. However, *enjoy* is plural, so this sentence contains a subject-verb agreement error. Note, however, that if the sentence read, *Neither Luke nor his next door neighbors*, then in that case the verb would need to agree with *neighbors*, which is plural, and *enjoy* would be the correct verb.

Now try the SAT questions below.

1. The most experienced employees in the company, Francine and Aurelian <u>serves as executive assistant</u> to the CEO.

   (A) serves as executive assistant
   (B) serving as the executive assistants
   (C) has served as the executive assistant
   (D) serve as executive assistants
   (E) serve as executive assistant

Here's How to Crack It

The correct answer is choice (D). In the original sentence, *Francine and Aurelian* form a plural subject, but the verb *serves* is singular. Thus, this sentence contains a subject-verb agreement error. Eliminate choice (A). Choice (C) uses the singular verb *has served*, and repeats the error in the original sentence. Choice (B) inappropriately changes the verb to *serving*, thus making the sentence incomplete, so choice (B) is incorrect. Choices (D) and (E) differ only in that choice (D) uses the plural noun *assistants*, while choice (E) uses the singular noun *assistant*. Since Francine and Aurelian are two different assistants, you need the plural noun, so choice (D) is correct.

25. Neither the flowers in the garden nor the dogwood

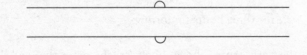

   tree in the front yard <u>have received</u> enough water <u>this</u>
                  B   C

   summer, and unfortunately the current drought

   <u>is likely to continue</u> for the next few months. <u>No error</u>
           D   E

Here's How to Crack It

The correct answer to this question is choice (B). This sentence connects two nouns—*flowers* and *tree*—using *nor*. The verb must agree with the last noun in the list, which in this case is the singular noun *tree*. Therefore, the plural verb *have received* does not agree with the subject, and the sentence contains a subject-verb agreement error. Choice (B) should read *has received*.

Verb Tense

The rule below applies to verb tenses.

> Tenses should remain consistent throughout a sentence unless the meaning of the sentence requires a change.

So what are the verb tenses that the SAT is likely to test? First, there are the three basic verb tenses below.

Past

I *skated* for three hours yesterday.

Present

I *skate* for three hours each day.

Future

I *will skate* for three hours tomorrow.

In addition to the basic tenses above, however, there are three additional tenses that the SAT may test.

Present Perfect

The present perfect tense involves the use of either *has* or *have*, depending upon whether the verb is singular or plural. Use the present perfect for one of the following two reasons:

1. To describe an event that happened at some unspecified time in the past.

    *Jana **has seen** the movie <u>Despicable Me</u> twenty times.*

    *The kitten **has caught** five mice.*

    *The apartment **has been** completely **remodeled.***

2. To describe an event that started in the past and continues to the present.

    *Macy **has held** the same job for five years.*

    *I **have gone** to the same coffee shop every day for the past month.*

    *They **have been dating** since August.*

Past Perfect

The past perfect involves the use of the auxiliary verb *had*. Use the past perfect to discuss an event that occurred before some other event that also occurred in the past. For example, consider the sentence below:

> *Before she attended the geography class, Vanessa had thought that Mongolia was a town in central Europe.*

A timeline of the events in the sentence above might appear similar to this:

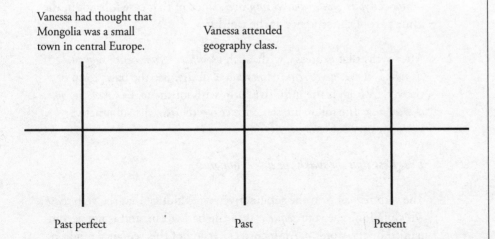

In the past, Vanessa attended geography class, but *before* that, she had thought that Mongolia was a small town in central Europe. Thus, this sentence requires the past perfect verb *had thought*.

Here are a few more examples involving the use of the past perfect tense:

*Julian **had been waiting** in the doctor's office for three hours when the nurse finally called his name.*

*When study hall period ended, I **had written** four pages of my book report.*

*Aisha **had planned** to attend the concert before she discovered that the tickets cost three hundred dollars each.*

Subjunctive

Use the subjunctive voice to express a wish or a command, or to discuss a hypothetical situation. There are two rules that you'll need to know regarding the subjunctive voice.

1. Do not use the word *would* in a clause that begins with the word *if.* Instead, use either a past tense verb or *were* in the part of the sentence containing the *if.* For example, the following sentence correctly uses the subjunctive voice:

    ***If** you **were** to attend class every day, then your grades would likely improve.*

    In the sentence above, notice that the verb *were* follows the word *if.* An incorrect version of this sentence might begin, *if you would attend class every day.* This version of the sentence would break the rule regarding the subjunctive voice, and would thus contain an error. Notice that the word *would* can appear in the second half of the sentence (*your grades would improve*), since in that case it is not in the same part of the sentence as the word *if.*

2. After verbs that express a wish, such as *insist, recommend, suggest, demand, desire, urge, require, mandate,* or *ask,* use the basic form of the verb, which is the infinitive form without the *to,* i.e., *run, be, go, dance, sing.* The following sentence correctly uses the subjunctive voice:

    *I **request** that she **wash** the dishes tonight.*

    The verb *request* is in the subjunctive voice. Notice that the verb *wash,* which follows the verb *request,* is in the basic form, and is not accompanied by the word *to.* An incorrect version of this sentence might be something like *I request Maria to wash the dishes tonight.* Using the word *to* in front of the verb would introduce a subjunctive voice error.

Now that you know the verb tenses that the SAT tests, try out the problems below.

---

16. In 1986 Richard Feynman and other members of the

Rogers committee demonstrated <u>that</u> the *Challenger*
                                    A

space shuttle disaster, which <u>horrifies</u> the world, could
                                     B

be <u>attributed</u> to faulty O-rings that cracked <u>in</u> cold
    C   D

temperatures. <u>No error</u>
                 E

Here's How to Crack It

The correct answer is choice (B). Notice that all the other verbs in the sentence—*demonstrated, attributed,* and *cracked*—are in the past tense, while the verb *horrifies* is in the present tense. Nothing in the sentence calls for a change in tense, so choice (B) should say *horrified* instead.

---

1. Steven <u>has been wanting to visit</u> Thailand, but after discovering that he would have to fly for twenty hours to get there, he decided that he wanted to visit Greece instead.

  (A) has been wanting to visit
  (B) had wanted to visit
  (C) would have wanted to visit
  (D) was to have wanted to visit
  (E) has been wanting to go visiting

Here's How to Crack It

The correct answer to the question above is choice (B). Notice that this sentence lists two things that Steven has done: he *has been wanting to visit Thailand* and he *decided that he wanted to visit Greece*. Both actions occur in the past, but because the first action—wanting to visit Thailand—occurred before the second action—deciding to that he wanted to visit Greece—the first action requires the past perfect verb. Only choice (B) uses the past perfect verb *had wanted*, so choice (B) is the correct answer.

---

2. Perhaps Anne <u>would be more likely to get a job if she would not</u> bring her Great Dane to each job interview.

(A) would be more likely to get a job if she would not
(B) were more likely to get a job if she would not
(C) will be more likely to get a job if she would not
(D) would be more likely to get a job if she was to not
(E) would be more likely to get a job if she did not

Here's How to Crack It

The correct answer is choice (E). The original sentence contains the phrase, *if she would not*. Since this phrase uses the word *would* right after the word *if*, the sentence contains a subjunctive voice error. Eliminate choice (A) and all other answers that use *would* right after *if*. Choices (B) and (C) both repeat the original error and are therefore incorrect. Choice (D) uses the phrase *if she was to not bring*. The rules regarding the subjunctive voice state that after word *if* you should use the base form of the verb without the word *to*. Thus, this choice contains a subjunctive voice error, since it uses the word *to* before the verb *bring*. The correct answer is choice (E).

TRICKY PRONOUN AGREEMENT QUESTIONS

Even if you know that singular pronouns must replace singular nouns, and plural pronouns must replace plural nouns, pronoun agreement questions can be tricky. Why? There are some pronouns that most of us use incorrectly on a daily basis, so if you focus on how these pronouns "sound" rather than on the rules that determine whether they are singular or plural, you may miss certain questions. Consider the sentence below:

> *Everyone who wants to go to Knott's Berry Farm with me should buy their tickets online tonight.*

This sentence may "sound" fine. However, notice that the possessive pronoun *their* refers to the pronoun *everyone*. Since *their* is plural, and *everyone* is singular, this sentence actually contains a pronoun agreement error. Correctly written, this sentence would read *everyone who wants to go to Knott's Berry Farm with me should buy his or her tickets online tonight*. This version of the sentence may seem odd, but it's the grammatically correct version!

Here's another example:

Each of the turtles laid their eggs in the sand.

In the above sentence, the plural possessive pronoun *their* refers to the singular pronoun *each*. Therefore, this sentence also contains a pronoun agreement error. This sentence should read, *each of the turtles laid its eggs in the sand.* To spot tricky pronoun agreement errors, remember the rules below.

The following pronouns are SINGULAR.

anybody	everybody	no one	neither
everyone	someone	either	anyone
something	nothing	nobody	everything
much	somebody	anything	each

The following pronouns are PLURAL.

few	many	both	several

The following pronouns can be singular OR plural, depending on the context.

all	most	some	none	more	any	less

Try out this challenging pronoun agreement question:

8. The gallery displays more than 500 works of art, each <u>unique in their</u> subject and use of color.

   (A) unique in their
   (B) is unique in its
   (C) unique in its
   (D) of them having uniqueness in their
   (E) of them being unique in their

The correct answer to this question is choice (C). The original question uses *their*, which is a plural possessive pronoun, to refer to *each*, which is singular. Thus, the original sentence contains a pronoun agreement error. Eliminate choice (A). Choices (D) and (E) repeat the error in the original sentence, and are also incorrect. Choice (B) introduces the verb *is*, and therefore turns the second half of the sentence—*each is unique in its subject and use of color*—into a complete thought. Since the first half of the sentence also contains a complete thought, and the two halves of the sentence are joined only by a comma, choice (B) creates a comma splice error. Thus, the correct answer is choice (C).

Pronoun Case

When you see a pronoun in the underlined portion of a grammar question, you should not only check for agreement and ambiguity errors, but you should also check for case errors. Pronoun case refers to the differences between pronouns such as *I* and *me*, *he* and *him*, *she* and *her*, and *they* and *them*. How can you determine which case to use? One method is to use the drop test. To see how the drop test works, check out the sentence below.

> *Dan let Sheila and I borrow his car.*

This sentence uses the pronoun *I*. To determine whether *I* is the correct pronoun, or whether you should use *me* instead, drop the other person with whom the pronoun is paired from the sentence. In this case, eliminate the words *Sheila and* from the sentence. If you do this, then you are left with *Dan let I borrow his car*. Now it's much easier to see that you need *me*, rather than *I*, in this particular sentence.

One way in which the SAT particularly likes to test pronoun case is in sentences such as the following:

> *Between you and I, I think that the gym teacher is wearing a wig.*

The correct phrase is always *between you and me*, so this sentence contains a pronoun case error. The grammatical reason for this is that *I* is a subject pronoun, meaning that serves as the subject of a verb, whereas *me* is an object pronoun, meaning that it is always the object of a verb or a preposition (such as *between*).

Knowing the difference between subject and object pronouns is especially helpful when you're trying to decide whether to use *who* or *whom*. Consider this sentence:

> *My neighbors, whom are moving this week, threw a large, loud party last night.*

Determining whether the pronoun *whom* is appropriate in this case may seem a bit tricky. However, knowing the difference between subject and object pronouns can help. Check out the lists of pronouns below.

Subject Pronouns		Object Pronouns
I		me
we		them
he		him
she	went to the movies with	her
they		them
who		whom

In the example above, note the phrase *went to the movies with*, which appears between the two columns. You could place any of the subject pronouns on the left-hand of the phrase. For example, you could say any of the following:

I went to the movies with him.
They went to the movies with him.
She went to the movies with him.
Who went to the movies with him?

All of the above are grammatically correct. Alternatively, however, you could place any of the object pronouns on the right-hand side of the sentence. For example, you could say any of the following:

She went to the movies with them.
She went to the movies with him.
She went to the movies with me.
She went to the movies with whom?

All of the above are also grammatically correct. Most of the time, determining whether you need *he* or *him*, or *they* or *them* may not be terribly difficult; it's determining whether you need *who* or *whom* that proves challenging. Therefore, you can use the above chart to help; if you could replace the *who* or *whom* in a sentence with *he, she,* or *they* (all subject pronouns), then you should use *who*. On the other hand, if you could replace the *who* or *whom* in a sentence with *him, her,* or *them* (all object pronouns), then you should use *whom*.

Try out this approach with the sentence that you read earlier:

My neighbors, whom are moving this week, threw a large, loud party last night.

Would you say *they are moving this week*, or would you say *them are moving this week*? Since the correct version would be *they are moving this week*, you need a subject, rather than an object pronoun. Thus, *who*, rather than *whom* is the correct pronoun.

29. What <u>least</u> pleased my father <u>and I</u> when we went to the
　　　　 A　　　　　　　　　　　　 B

car dealership was the salesman, <u>who</u> was <u>so pushy</u> that
　　　　　　　　　　　　　　　　　　　 C　　　　 D

we almost left without even taking any of the cars for a

test drive. <u>No error</u>
　　　　　　　　 E

Here's How to Crack It

The correct answer to this question is choice (B). If you use the drop test and eliminate the words *my father and* from the sentence, you are left with, *what least pleased I.* The pronoun *I* is in the wrong case, and should be replaced with *me.*

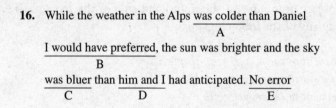

16. While the weather in the Alps <u>was colder</u> than Daniel
　　　　　　　　　　　　　　　　　　　　 A

<u>I would have preferred</u>, the sun was brighter and the sky
　　　　 B

<u>was bluer</u> than <u>him</u> and <u>I had anticipated</u>. <u>No error</u>
　　 C　　　　　 D　　　　　　　　　　　　 E

Here's How to Crack It

The correct answer is choice (D). If you eliminate the words *and I* from that part of the sentence, you are left with *him had anticipated. Him* is an object pronoun and cannot form the subject of a verb, and therefore is in the wrong case. Correctly written, this sentence would either read *than he and I had anticipated,* or simply *than we had anticipated.*

Collective Nouns

Collective nouns are nouns that refer to a group of things as if they were one. For example, *staff, faculty,* and *flock* are all collective nouns. While a staff may be composed of many people, there is only one staff, so the noun is singular.

Collective nouns are singular, and should be paired with singular verbs and replaced by singular pronouns.

Consider this sentence:

> *Every morning the herd of sheep slowly cross the road, blocking traffic for miles and making me late for work.*

In the sentence above, the subject of the sentence is *herd*, which is a collective noun and is therefore singular. The verb in the sentence is *cross*, which is plural, so this sentence contains a subject-verb agreement error.

Now see if you can spot the error in the following sentence:

> *The committee of planners spend more and more time in the conference room as the big event approaches.*

In this sentence, *the committee* is the subject of the sentence. However, *the committee* is a collective noun, and is therefore singular, while the verb *spend* is plural.

Check out the SAT question below and see if you can identify the error.

————————————⌒————————————

22. The jury <u>hearing evidence</u> in the case <u>against</u> the thieves
           A   B

   <u>want</u> to see the surveillance footage <u>once more</u>.
    C   D

   <u>No error</u>
    E

Here's How to Crack It

The correct answer is choice (C). The subject of the sentence is *jury*, which in this case is a singular collective noun. The verb in the sentence is *want*, which is plural. Therefore, the sentence contains a subject-verb agreement error.

————————————⌒————————————

Now try this question.

9. The audience, which immediately rose in unison and applauded loudly at the end of the performance, <u>were composed</u> mostly of friends and family members of the play's cast.

(A) were composed
(B) were being composed
(C) having been composed
(D) was composed
(E) has been composed

Here's How to Crack It

The correct answer is choice (D). The subject of the sentence, *audience*, is a singular collective noun. However, the verb *were* is plural. Eliminate choice (A). Choices (B) and (C) both have plural nouns and are also incorrect. Choice (D) fixes the error without introducing any new errors, so choice (D) is the correct answer. Choice (E) changes the tense, and therefore the meaning of the sentence, so choice (E) is incorrect.

FAULTY COMPARISONS

Faulty comparisons are very easy to miss! What is a faulty comparison? Examine the sentence below:

> *My apartment, like James, is decorated in soft blue and green tones and is very sunny.*

Notice that this sentence uses the comparison word *like*. Anytime you see comparison words, such as *like, unlike, similar to, different than, more than,* or *less than,* consider what two things the sentence is comparing. In this case, the sentence compares *my apartment* (a place) to *James* (a person). However, it is unlikely that James himself is decorated in blue and green colors and is very sunny. More likely, the author is trying to state that *James's apartment* is decorated in blue and green and is very sunny. However, since the sentence does not actually reference James's apartment, the sentence contains a comparison error.

Anytime you see a comparison word in a sentence, check to see what two things the sentence is comparing. You must compare similar things: apples to apples and oranges to oranges.

See if you can spot the error in this sentence:

> *While the Egyptian pyramids are more famous than the Mayans, the largest pyramid in the world is actually the Great Pyramid of Cholula, which is of Mayan origin.*

This sentence uses the comparison phrase *more famous than*, which should serve as a clue that the sentence may contain a comparison error. Here, the sentence compares *the Egyptian pyramids* to *the Mayans*. However, in order to form a correct comparison, the sentence should compare *the Egyptian pyramids* to *the Mayan pyramids* or *those of the Mayans*.

Try out the following SAT questions:

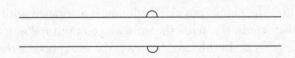

26. Statisticians <u>have determined</u>, based on the most recent
                      A
    U.S. census poll, <u>that</u> <u>there is a larger number of</u>
                        B   C
    American citizens aged 65 and over today <u>than last year.</u>
                                              D
    <u>No error</u>
    E

Here's How to Crack It

The correct answer is choice (D). This sentence uses the words *larger...than* to make a comparison. Here, the sentence compares the *number of American citizens aged 65 years and over today* to *last year*. However, you cannot compare a number of citizens to a year. Correctly written, choice (D) might read *than there were*.

28. Greenhouse gases <u>emitted by</u> burning fossil fuels
                      A
    <u>have increased</u> the present <u>concentration of carbon</u>
         B   C
    dioxide in the earth's atmosphere to 392 parts per
    million, which is 40% greater <u>than the beginning of the</u>
                                    D
    Industrial Revolution. <u>No error</u>
                            E

Here's How to Crack It

The correct answer is choice (D). This sentence uses the comparison words *greater than*, and compares *the present concentration of carbon dioxide in the earth's atmosphere* to *the beginning of the Industrial Revolution*. However, since you cannot compare a concentration to an event, this sentence contains a comparison error. Correctly written, choice (D) might read, *than the concentration present in the earth's atmosphere at*.

IDIOMS

The SAT tests idioms, although they are not technically grammar. Idioms essentially are composed of words that just simply must go together. For example, you would say *I am going to the cinema*. You would not say *I am going at the cinema*. Why? You need to use *to* simply because the verb *going* requires the preposition *to*, rather than the preposition *at*. Unfortunately, there isn't a simple rule that you can apply to find the correct idiom in a given sentence in the same way that you might be able to find the correct verb tense in a sentence. The only solution is really just to memorize your idioms.

> Memorize your idioms!

Fortunately, the SAT does not test an unlimited number of idioms; it tests only a handful of commonly accepted ones. Consider the following example:

> *Jonathan is just as eager to go to the picnic than I am.*

This sentence uses the phrase *just as*. The idiom is associated with this phrase is *as…as…*. In other words, if you use the word *as*, you must follow it up later in the sentence with another *as*. In this case, however, the sentence uses *than*, rather than *as*, and therefore contains an idiom error.

Check out this sentence:

> *Laura has doctorates in both criminology and psychology, and therefore can easily distinguish individuals who are lying and individuals who are simply nervous.*

This sentence uses the word *distinguish*, which must be used in one of the following two ways. You can either use *distinguish....from,* or *distinguish between... and .....* As it is currently written, the sentence above uses *distinguish...and*, but is missing the word *between*. Correctly written, the sentence could read in either of ways listed below.

> *Laura has doctorates in both criminology and psychology, and therefore can easily distinguish between individuals who are lying and individuals who are simply nervous.*

or

> *Laura has doctorates in both criminology and psychology, and therefore can easily distinguish individuals who are lying from individuals who are simply nervous.*

Make sure that you know your idioms! Here is the list of idioms commonly tested on the SAT.

About

Worry...about

If you **worry** too much **about** the SAT, you'll develop an ulcer.

As

Define...as

Some people **define** insanity **as** repeating the same action but expecting a different outcome.

Regard...as

Art historians **regard** the *Mona Lisa* **as** one of the greatest works of art.

Not so...as

He is **not so** much smart **as** cunning.

So...as to be

She is **so** beautiful **as to be** exquisite.

Think of...as

Think of it more **as** a promise than a threat.

See...as

Many people **see** euthanasia **as** an escape from pain.

The same...as

Mom and Dad gave **the same** punishment to me **as** to you.

As...as

Memorizing idioms is not **as** fun **as** playing bingo.

At

Target…at

The commercials were obviously **targeted at** teenage boys.

For

Responsible for

You are **responsible for** the child.

From

Prohibit…from

He was **prohibited from** entering the public library after he accidentally set the dictionary on fire with a magnifying glass.

Different…from

Democrats are not so **different from** Republicans in the United States.

Over

Dispute over

The men had a **dispute over** money.

That

So…that

He was **so** late **that** he missed the main course.

Hypothesis…that

The **hypothesis that** aspartame causes brain tumors has not been proven yet.

To be

Believe…to be

His friends do not **believe** the ring he bought at the auction **to be** Jackie O's; they all think he was tricked.

Estimate…to be

The time he has spent impersonating Elvis is **estimated to be** longer than the time Elvis himself spent performing.

To

Forbid…to

I **forbid** you **to** call me before noon.

Ability...to

If you take the test enough times, you might develop the **ability to** choose the credited responses without reading the questions.

Attribute...to

Many amusing quips are **attributed to** Dorothy Parker.

Require...to

Before you enter the house you are **required to** take off your hat.

Responsibility...to

You have a **responsibility to** take care of the child.

Permit...to

I don't **permit** my children **to** play with knives in the living room.

Superior...to

My pasta sauce is far **superior to** my mother-in-law's.

Try...to

Try to stay awake during the essay section of the test.

With

Credit...with

Many people **credit** Christopher Columbus **with** the discovery of America, but Native Americans were here first.

Associate...with

Most politicians prefer not to be **associated with** the Mafia.

Contrast...with

My father likes to **contrast** my grades **with** my brother's.

No preposition

Consider...(nothing)

Art historians **consider** the *Mona Lisa* one of the greatest works of art.

More than one preposition

Distinguish...from

I can't **distinguish** day **from** night.

Distinguish between...and

I can **distinguish between** black **and** white.

Native (noun)... of

Russell Crowe is a **native of** Australia.

Native (adjective)…to
The kangaroo is **native to** Australia.

Comparisons and Links

Not only…but also
She is **not only** beautiful, **but also** smart.

Not…but
The review was **not** mean-spirited **but** merely flippant.

Either…or
I must have **either** chocolate ice cream **or** carrot cake to complete a great meal.

Neither…nor
Because Jenny was grounded, she could **neither** leave the house **nor** use the telephone.

Both…and
When given the choice, I choose **both** ice cream **and** cake.

More…than; Less…than
The chimpanzee is much **more** intelligent **than** the orangutan.

As vs. like
As is used to compare actions.

Like is used to compare nouns.

He did not vote for the Libertarian Party, **as** I did.

Her coat is just **like** mine.

Like vs. such as
Like means *similar to*.

Such as means *for example*.

The mule, **like** the donkey, is a close relative of the horse.

Many of my favorite ice cream flavors, **such as** chocolate chip and strawberry, are also available as frozen yogurt.

The more…the -er
The more you ignore me, the **closer** I get.

From…to
Scores on the SAT range **from** 200 **to** 800.

Just as...so too
Just as I crossed over to the dark side, **so too** will you, my son.

Miscellaneous

Each vs. all or both

Use *each* when you want to emphasize the separateness of the items.

Use *both* (for two things) or *all* (for more than two things) when you want to emphasize the togetherness of the items.

Each of the doctors had his own specialty.

Both of the women went to Bryn Mawr for their undergraduate degrees.

All of the letters received before January 15 went into the drawing for the $10 million prize.

Whether vs. if

Use *whether* when there are *two possibilities*.

Use *if* in *conditional statements*.

Eduardo wasn't sure **whether** he could make it to the party.

If Eduardo comes to the party, he will bring a bag of chips.

Refer to the idiom list above to answer the questions that follow.

———————◯———————

9. Before the film finally arrived in theaters, anticipation for its release was created not only by intense, visually stunning trailers <u>and by rumors that</u> the lead actor would likely win an Academy Award for his remarkable performance.

   (A) and by rumors that
   (B) and rumors by which
   (C) but rumors that
   (D) but also the rumors that
   (E) but also by rumors that

Here's How to Crack It

The correct answer is choice (E). This sentence uses the phrase *not only*, which, according to the idiom list above, must be followed by the words *but also*. Choices (A), (B), and (C) do not contain the words *but also*, and are therefore incorrect. Choice (D) does use the correct idiom, but notice that this sentence states that anticipation was created through two things, which, according to choice (D), are *by intense, visually stunning trailers* and *the rumors*. However, these two items are not parallel, since the first item in the list begins with *by*, but the second begins with *the*. Choice (E) makes the two items parallel, so that you have *by intense, visually stunning trailers* and *but also by rumors*. Thus, choice (E) is the correct answer.

The *not only…but also* idiom is one of the most commonly tested idioms. Make sure that you know this idiom!

---

22. Deep Blue, an IBM designed, chess-playing computer,

   defeated world chess champion Gary Kasparov by
   A

   means of its ability of calculating 200 million positions
   B   C

   per second. No error
   D   E

Here's How to Crack It
The correct answer is choice (C), because the correct idiom is *ability to*, rather than *ability of*. Therefore, choice (C) should read, *ability to calculate*.

DICTION ERRORS
A diction error is another type of error that doesn't necessarily fall under the heading of a grammar mistake, but that you may nevertheless see on the SAT. A diction error involves simply using the wrong word. Consider the following example:

> *The auditions for perspective cast members are not going well, because all of the applicants we have seen so far sound like dying ducks.*

The sentence above contains a diction error because it uses *perspective*, which refers to a view or outlook, rather than *prospective*, which means *potential*.

Consider this second example:

> *The red in Mathilde's lipstick compliments the colors in her skirt and shoes and brings her whole outfit together.*

This sentence incorrectly uses the word *compliments*, which means *says something good about a person or thing*, rather than *complements*, which means *to complete something or make it better*. Thus, this sentence also contains a diction error.

The words in the list below are commonly confused. See if you can identify the differences in meanings in each pair of words. Be sure to look up any words with which you are not familiar!

_____allusion vs. illusion_____

_____implicate vs. imply_____

_____perspective vs. prospective_____

_____describe vs. ascribe_____

_____deduce vs. induce_____

_____consciousness vs. conscience_____

_____compliment vs. complement_____

_____elude vs. allude_____

_____desirous vs. desirable_____

_____principal vs. principle_____

_____accept vs. except_____

_____indict vs. induct_____

_____declined vs. descended_____

_____precede vs. proceed_____

_____affect vs. effect_____

Take a look at the practice question below.

29. The Senate's vote was <u>proceeded</u> by lengthy debates
                          A

<u>in which</u> the healthcare bill's strengths and shortcomings
B

<u>were outlined</u> <u>in detail.</u> <u>No error</u>
C   D   E

The correct answer is choice (A). This sentence incorrectly uses *proceeded*, which means *began a course of action*, in place of *preceded*, which means *came before*. Therefore, choice (A) contains an error.

You're not likely to see many diction error questions on the SAT; most tests do not contain more than one or two of these errors in total. However, if you're looking at a grammar question and can't identify an error, do a quick check for diction errors!

MISPLACED MODIFIERS

Modifying phrases describe a person or thing. When misplaced, they can cause all sorts of havoc with the meanings of sentences. For example, consider the sentence below.

> *While riding a bicycle down the street, a dog ran in front of me.*

The phrase *riding a bicycle down the street* is a modifying phrase. It describes something or someone who is riding a bicycle, but if you read that part of the sentence alone, you would not know who was riding the bicycle; you must read the rest of the sentence in order to discover whom the phrase describes. However, modifying phrases modify whatever nouns are closest to them. In a sentence such as this one, the phrase must modify whatever word appears after the comma.

What does that mean here? Since *a dog* appears right after the comma, this sentence, as it is currently written, implies that a dog was riding a bicycle down the street. Now, that is clearly not what the author intended, so this sentence contains a misplaced modifier.

There are two ways to fix misplaced modifier errors. One is to place the correct person or thing after the comma. For example, you might rewrite the sentence above as, *while riding a bicycle down the street, I saw a dog run in front of me.*

Alternatively, you might correct a sentence such as this one by placing the subject within the modifying phrase, so that the resulting sentence might be something such as *while I was riding a bicycle down the street, a dog ran in front of me.*

Both of the versions shown above fix the error in the sentence. In an Improving Sentences question, the method the SAT uses to correct a misplaced modifier error will depend upon which part of the sentence is underlined; if the modifying phrase is underlined, then the correct answer will place the subject within the phrase. If the part of the sentence following the modifying phrase is underlined, then the correct answer will place the appropriate noun immediately before or after the modifying phrase.

Try to spot the modifier error in the sentence below:

> *Wild and extremely vicious, Kira was able to tame the dog only after months of obedience training.*

The modifying phrase in this sentence is *wild and extremely vicious*, and *Kira* comes right after the comma. However, it is presumably the dog, and not Kira, that is wild and vicious. Therefore, this sentence contains a misplaced modifier.

What about this sentence?

> *The planner rented a hall for Jean's wedding with a glowing disco ball.*

This one may be a bit trickier because it doesn't have the usual *phrase* then *comma* structure. However, note that the phrase *with a glowing disco ball* is a modifying phrase; that is, it describes something with a glowing disco ball. Here, *Jean's wedding*, rather than *a hall* is the noun closest to the phrase. Presumably, however, it is the hall, rather than the wedding, that has the disco ball.

Now try a few practice questions that test modifying phrases.

---

13. When the columnist researched her article on the scandal she talked to the <u>eyewitness, whom she interviewed on the steps of city hall in a dark suit.</u>

    (A) eyewitness, whom she interviewed on the steps of city hall in a dark suit.
    (B) eyewitness in a dark suit, she interviewed him on the steps of city hall.
    (C) eyewitness, a man in a dark suit whom she interviewed on the steps of city hall.
    (D) eyewitness, it was this man whom she had planned to interview on the steps of city hall in a dark suit.
    (E) eyewitness, who, having planned to interview him on the steps of city hall in a dark suit.

Here's How to Crack It

The correct answer is choice (C). The original sentence contains the modifying phrase *in a dark suit*, which is closest to *city hall*, but city hall is clearly not wearing a dark suit. Presumably either the eyewitness or the columnist is wearing the dark suit, but nothing in the sentence indicates which of the two is wearing the suit. Therefore, this sentence contains a misplaced modifier error. Eliminate choice (A). Choices (D) and (E) repeat the original error and are also incorrect. Only choices (B) and (C) remain. Choice (B) contains two complete thoughts: *when the columnist researched her article on the scandal she talked to the eyewitness in a dark suit*, and *she interviewed him on the steps of city hall*. Choice (B) also links these two complete ideas with only a comma, and therefore contains a comma splice error. Thus, choice (B) is incorrect. Choice (C) makes it clear that the eyewitness is wearing the suit, and does not contain any comma splice errors, so choice (C) is correct.

4. Arguably the most popular vacation destination in Europe, <u>tourists have flocked to Paris for centuries, and so admire its architecture, food, and culture</u>.

   (A) tourists have flocked to Paris for centuries, and so admire its architecture, food, and culture
   (B) Paris has for centuries attracted flocks of tourists, who admire its architecture, food, and culture
   (C) Paris, which has for centuries attracted flocks of tourists who admire its architecture, food, and culture
   (D) the admiration of Paris' architecture, food, and culture has attracted flocks of tourists for centuries
   (E) tourists, having flocked to Paris for centuries to admire its architecture, food, and culture

Here's How to Crack It

The correct answer is choice (B). The phrase *arguably the most popular vacation destination in Europe* is a modifying phrase. However, as the sentence is currently written, the word *tourists* appears right after the comma. Since *Paris*, not *tourists* is the most popular vacation destination in Europe, this sentence contains a misplaced modifier. Eliminate choice (A). Choice (E) repeats the original error and is incorrect. Note that choice (D) also contains a modifier error, since *the admiration*, rather than *Paris*, comes right after the comma in choice (D). Choice (B) fixes the error and does not introduce any new errors, so choice (B) is the correct answer. Choice (C) does place *Paris* immediately after the comma, but because this choice uses the word *which,* the sentence is incomplete. Therefore, choice (C) is incorrect.

CONJUNCTIONS

Consider the sentence that follows:

The sandy beach is beautiful, but the water is a very striking shade of turquoise.

The sentence above joins two thoughts with the conjunction *but*. The first thought in the sentence—*the sandy beach is beautiful*—discusses a positive aspect of the beach. The second thought in the sentence—*the water is a very striking shade of turquoise*—also discusses a positive aspect of the beach. Therefore, using a change-of-direction conjunction such as *but* does not work in this sentence. The correct conjunction is *and*.

Conjunction errors do not appear frequently on the SAT, but you may see one or two such errors. If you see a conjunction underlined, makes sure that the conjunction goes on the direction required by the meaning of the sentence!

Check out this sentence:

The author's new novel had a gripping plot, and it was poorly written.

This sentence lists two things about the novel: it *had a gripping plot* (a good thing), and *it was poorly written* (a bad thing). Since one of the things listed is positive, and the other is negative, this sentence calls for a change-of-direction conjunction such as *but*, rather than for a same-direction conjunction such as *and*.

Try the following question:

---

3. Known for its immense size and colorful landscape, Arizona's Grand Canyon is home to both 34 species of mammals or 1,700 varieties of plant life.

   (A) is home to both 34 species of mammals or
   (B) is home to both 34 species of mammals and
   (C) is home to 34 species of mammals but
   (D) being home to 34 species of mammals yet
   (E) being home to 34 species of mammals, and also

Here's How to Crack It

The correct answer is choice (B). The original sentence uses *both*, which idiomatically must be paired with the conjunction *and*. Eliminate choice (A). Choices (C) and (D) both use change-of-direction conjunctions. However, since the Grand Canyon is home to both types of life—mammals and plants—a same direction conjunction is appropriate here. Thus, choices (C) and (D) are incorrect. Choices (B) and (E) both use the same-direction conjunction *and*, but choice (E) also uses the word *being*, which makes the sentence incomplete. Therefore, the correct answer is choice (B).

Chapter 25
Improving
Paragraphs

In addition to the Improving Sentences and Error ID questions, five Improving Paragraphs questions will appear on your SAT. These will be based on a short passage, which will resemble the first draft of a student essay. For each question, your job will be to choose the answer choices that improve the essay. Here are a few key points you should know about these questions:

- Improving Paragraphs questions are almost always easy or medium questions. Sometimes, you may be better off skipping the last few difficult Error ID questions, and tackling the Improving Paragraphs questions instead.
- The passages in these sections contain multiple errors, but you will not be asked about every error. Therefore, don't try to edit as you read.
- Improving Paragraphs questions are unlike the Error ID and Improving Paragraphs questions, in which one-fifth of the sentences are correct as written.

THE BASIC APPROACH

How should you tackle these questions? Here's the basic approach:
1. Skim the passage for the following:
   - the main idea of the passage as a whole
   - the main idea of each paragraph
2. Read the question, and refer back to the passage for context when necessary.
3. Use Process of Elimination to get rid of incorrect answers. For some questions, you may find it helpful to compare answers using the same approach that you use in Improving Sentences questions.
4. Repeat steps 2 and 3 until you only have one answer.

IMPROVING PARAGRAPHS QUESTION TYPES

Improving Paragraphs questions come in three flavors:
- **Revision questions.** These questions resemble Improving Sentences questions: They'll present you with a sentence from the passage, and ask you to choose the best version of the underlined portion from among the answer choices. Your approach to these questions should also be similar to your approach to Improving Sentences questions. If you spot the error in the sentence right away, eliminate any choices that repeat the original error, and then compare your remaining answers to spot additional errors. Note that choice (A) may not always repeat the original sentence. If you get down to two answers that both seem grammatically correct, examine the passage and choose the answer that best fits the context.

- **Combination questions.** These questions are similar to revision questions, but require you to work with two sentences rather than just one.
- **Weird questions.** There's really no better way to describe these questions! These questions are among the more challenging of the Improving Paragraphs questions, and they relate to the flow of the passage. They may ask you to add or delete sentences, or to change the location of sentences already in the passage. Here are a few guidelines to keep in mind when working these questions:
  - Focus on the order of ideas. What comes before the sentence in question? What comes after? Where do ideas flow in an illogical order?
  - Stick as closely to the passage as you can. A sentence that will precede the passage should relate to the first sentence of the passage. A sentence that will follow the passage should relate to the final sentence of the passage.
  - Choose answers that maintain the focus of the main idea of the passage.

Try the Basic Approach! Read the paragraphs below and answer the questions that follow.

(1) I grew up in the country, and have always preferred rural life to urban life. (2) This is true for a couple of reasons. (3) First, city traffic can be very noisy, whereas the countryside is very peaceful and quiet. (4) The biggest reason on the other hand, is that in the country I am not surrounded by crowds. (5) In the city, I feel as if I am always bumping into others. (6) There are people everywhere, packed into supermarkets, subway cars, and coffee shops, and I have no personal space. (7) It's only in the country that I can enjoy true solitude and tranquility.

What is the main idea of this paragraph?

This paragraph focuses on the differences between the city and the country, and the reasons that the author prefers the country. The main idea of this paragraph is that the author prefers the country to the city, because the country is quieter and less crowded.

(**8**) But last week I changed my mind. (**9**) A friend has asked me to visit her in New York City for the weekend. (**10**) While we walked down Fifth Avenue my friend happily sang the praises of the city she loved, but I could not share her enthusiasm. (**11**) Looking farther down the street, I spotted a large stone building with imposing columns. (**12**) "Do you want to visit the Metropolitan Museum of Art today?" my friend asked, pointing to the building. (**13**) Actually I did not want to visit the museum, and it was reluctantly that I gave my agreement to go. (**14**) My dislike of everything in the city faded. (**15**) I discovered a whole new world inside the museum. (**16**) I was fascinated by the Egyptian temple, the arms and armor section, and the Byzantine art. (**17**) We spent the next three hours wandering through the museum and exploring history. (**18**) I enjoyed the visit so much that I found myself reconsidering my opinion; perhaps there were good things about the city after all. (**19**) I may even want to visit the city for a longer period of time on my next visit.

What is the main idea of this paragraph?

This paragraph focuses on a positive experience that the narrator has while visiting the city and the ways in which the experience changed her point of view regarding the city. The main idea of this paragraph is therefore that the narrator's opinion of the city changed when she visited the Metropolitan Museum of Art.

What is the main idea of the passage as a whole?

Consider the main idea of each paragraph. If you combine the main ideas of the two paragraphs, then you can see that the main idea of the passage as a whole must be that, while the narrator initially disliked the city, her recent visit to the Metropolitan Museum of Art changed that opinion somewhat.

Now that you understand the passage as a whole, it's time to tackle the questions!

Revision Questions

Revision questions often resemble Improving Sentences questions, and will test some of the same concepts. Try the revision question below.

---

30. In context, which of the following is the best revision of the fourth sentence in the passage (shown below)?

The biggest reason <u>on the other hand</u> is that in the country I am not surrounded by crowds.

(A) (as it is now)
(B) thus
(C) though
(D) for example
(E) likewise

Here's How to Crack It

Note that each of the answer choices in this question contains transition words. Therefore, you must find the appropriate transition from the first half of the sentence to the second half of the sentence. As it is now, the sentence uses the word *consequently* as a transition. However, the word *consequently* implies that one thing is an outcome or an effect of another, which is not what this sentence is attempting to convey. Therefore, you can eliminate choice (A). The word *thus* similarly implies that one thing is an outcome or an effect of another, so choice (B) is also incorrect. The word *though* indicates a contrast between two things. Since the preceding sentences discusses other reasons that the narrator dislikes the city, and the sentence in question discusses the biggest reason that the narrator dislikes the city, this sentence introduces a contrast between this reason and the other reason: unlike the other reason, this is *the biggest reason*. Therefore, choice (C) is the correct answer. Since the sentence does not introduce an example of any kind, choice (D) is incorrect. Finally, since the sentence does not indicate a similarity between any two things, you can eliminate choice (E).

Now that you've worked the first question, try the second revision question!

32. Based on the context, which of the following is the best revision of the underlined portion of sentence 9 (shown below)?

A friend has asked me to visit her in New York City for the weekend.

(A) (as it is now)
(B) are asking
(C) will have asked
(D) would ask
(E) had asked

Here's How to Crack It

Did you spot an error in the underlined portion? Note that the underlined verb *has asked* is in the present perfect tense, which you use to indicate that an action began in the past and continues into the present. However, the sentence immediately preceding sentence 9 states, *But last week I changed my mind.* This sentence is in the past tense, and sentence 9 is discussing an event that occurred before this past event, so you can eliminate any choice that indicates that the action is still occurring in the present. Eliminate choices (A) and (B). Choice (C) uses the future tense, which is also inappropriate. Choice (D) uses *would ask*, which implies a hypothetical situation that has not actually occurred. Since the friend actually asked the narrator to visit, choice (D) is also incorrect. Choice (E) appropriately uses the past perfect verb *had asked*, which indicates that the friend asked the narrator to visit before the author changed her mind. Therefore, the correct answer is choice (E).

Some Revision questions simply require you to use Process of Elimination to get rid of answers that do not improve the sentence in question. Check out question 33 below.

33. Which of the following is the best way to edit sentence 13 (reproduced below)?

Actually I did not want to visit the museum, and it was reluctantly that I gave my agreement to go.

(A) Change "did not want to visit" to "disliked the idea of visiting"
(B) Insert "only" immediately before "reluctantly"
(C) Change "gave my agreement" to "agreed"
(D) Change "Actually" to "Essentially"
(E) Change "gave" to "had given"

Here's How to Crack It

Note that choice (A) just makes the sentence longer without fixing an error within the sentence. Therefore, choice (A) is not the correct answer. While adding *only* immediately before *reluctantly* does not introduce any errors into the sentence, it also does not fix any problems with the sentence, so you can eliminate choice (B). Choice (C) turns the unnecessarily wordy phrase *gave my agreement* into the simple verb *agreed*. Since choice (C) makes the sentence more concise without introducing any new errors, choice (C) is the correct answer. Choice (D) does not fix any errors within the sentence, and changes the transition word *Actually*, which is appropriate to the meaning of the sentence, to *Essentially*, which is not quite as appropriate. Therefore, you can eliminate choice (D). The verb *gave* is in the past tense, whereas *had given* is in the past perfect tense. You use the past perfect to indicate that one past action or event occurred before another action or event. However, in this case, the narrator does not give her agreement before some other past event, so you do not want the past perfect tense.

Combination Questions

These questions will simply ask you to combine two sentences. Pay attention to the direction. For instance, are you joining two similar ideas? If so, you may need to use a same-direction conjunction such as *and*. On the other hand, if you're joining two opposing ideas, you may need a transition word such as *although* or *though*.

You'll also want to think about the completeness of the two ideas, as shown in the answer choices. Since you cannot join two complete ideas using a comma—otherwise you have a sentence that contains a comma splice error—you'll need to either make one of the ideas incomplete by beginning it with a word such as *although*, or you'll need to join the two ideas with something other than a comma alone, such as a comma coupled with a conjunction.

Try the combination question shown below.

---

34. Which of the following is the best way to revise the underlined portion of sentences 14 and 15 (shown below) so as to combine the two sentences?

My dislike of everything in the city faded. I discovered a whole new world inside the museum.

(A) My dislike of everything in the city faded though, when I

(B) My dislike of everything in the city faded, and I

(C) My dislike of everything in the city faded when I therefore

(D) When my dislike of everything in the city faded, I had

(E) Although my dislike of everything in the city faded, I

Here's How to Crack It

Choice (A) links the two ideas using the words *though, when*. Sentence 13 discusses the fact that the narrator did not want to visit the museum, and sentences 14 and 15 discuss the fact that the narrator's dislike faded and she discovered a whole new world inside the museum. Since sentences 14 and 15 change the direction of the paragraph, a change-of-direction transition word such as *though* is appropriate. Choice (A) is therefore the correct answer. You need a change-of-direction transition word, so choice (B), which uses *and* to link the two sentences, and choice (C), which uses *therefore*, are incorrect. Choice (D) begins the sentence with the word *when*, and changes the intended meaning of the sentence, so choice (D) is incorrect. Choice (E) does use the change-of-direction transition word *although*. However, the placement of the word *although* in this choice suggests that the two thoughts within sentences 14 and 15 contrast each other, rather than suggesting that sentences 14 and 15 contrast with the sentence that precedes sentence 14. Sentences 14 and 15 both discuss the fact that the author began to enjoy the museum, and therefore do not contain thoughts that contrast with each other. Eliminate choice (E).

Weird Questions

These questions tend to be among the most challenging of the Improving Paragraphs questions, and they require you to pay attention to the flow of the passage. For each of the questions below, consider what comes before, what comes after, and what information is contained in the statement in question.

---

31. Based on context, which of the following could most appropriately be placed immediately before the phrase *in the country* in sentence 7 (shown below)?

    It's only in the country that I can enjoy true solitude and tranquility.

    (A) spending time
    (B) with personal space
    (C) peacefully
    (D) here
    (E) with people around me

Here's How to Crack It

Choice (A), *spending time*, does not add anything to the meaning of the sentence, since if one is in the country, one is already spending time in the country. Since the sentences immediately before sentence 7 already imply that there is more personal space in the country than in the city, adding the phrase *with personal space* would be redundant. Similarly, the rest of the sentence already indicates that the country is tranquil, so adding the word *peacefully* would be redundant. The word *here* fixes the narrator's current location in the country, and therefore clarifies the meaning of the sentence, so choice (D) is the correct answer. The narrator indicates that one reason that she enjoys the country is that there are fewer people around her, so adding the phrase *with people around me* would make this sentence disagree with one of the main ideas of the paragraph. Thus you can eliminate choice (E).

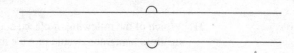

35. Where would the sentence below be best placed within the passage?

Then, remarkably, my feelings changed.

(A) Immediately before sentence 7
(B) Immediately before sentence 9
(C) Immediately before sentence 11
(D) Immediately before sentence 14
(E) Immediately before sentence 18

Here's How to Crack It

For each choice, consider what comes immediately before the sentence in question, and what the sentence itself discusses. Sentence 6 discusses the fact that cities are crowded, and sentence 7 discusses the fact that the narrator finds the countryside more tranquil. Since there is no change in the author's feelings introduced in either sentence 6 or 7, you would not want to insert the new sentence in between these two. Sentence 8 does discuss the fact that the narrator's opinion changed, but since sentence 9 does not begin a discussion of this change, you would not want to introduce the new sentence before sentence 9. Sentence 10 discusses the fact that the narrator and her friend are walking down the street, and sentence 11 describes the outside of the museum. Neither sentence discusses a change in the narrator's attitude, so eliminate choice (C). In sentence 13, the narrator mentions that she did not want to visit the museum, but sentence 14 discusses the fact that her dislike faded. Since these two sentences do discuss a change in the narrator's attitude, adding the sentence in question into this part of the paragraph is logical. Thus, choice (D) is the correct answer. Sentence 17 says that the narrator and her friend wandered through the museum for a long time, and sentence 18 states that the narrator enjoyed her visit. Since this is not the first time in the paragraph that the narrator has stated that she found the visit surprisingly enjoyable, you would not want to place the sentence in question immediately before sentence 18.

Improving Paragraphs Drill

Complete answers and explanations can be found in Chapter 26.

Drill 1

(1) The number of proposed locations for Plato's fictional city Atlantis is well over a dozen. (2) Additionally, they believe it to be very likely that the city was supposed to be situated in or near the Mediterranean Sea. (3) Those who study the remains of ancient cities are called archaeologists.

(4) Of course, there is no proof that Plato based Atlantis on an actual city or had a real location in mind when he wrote his tale; no such location has been definitely found yet. (5) Nevertheless, there are some scholars who have discovered the remains of what they believe to be cities that served as the inspiration for Atlantis. (6) Others fix the location in Marismas de Hinojos, just north of the city of Cádiz, arguing that satellite imagery supports this hypothesis. (7) For instance, some suppose that remains found in Tartessos fix the location of Atlantis at that point.

(8) Some claim that the origins of the remains discovered in Tartessos are well documented, and dismiss speculation regarding them as fanciful. (9) Equally skeptical are those who argue that satellite imagery alone cannot provide information to determine the location of Atlantis.

(10) Such scoffers will likely never be persuaded that Atlantis was inspired by a real city without undeniable proof. (11) Believers however, should feel reassured by growing evidence that supports the hypothesis. (12) Perhaps the most encouraging recent development was the discovery in 2011 of the remains of a city destroyed by a tsunami in the marshlands of southwestern Andalusia.

30. Based on the context, which of the following is the best way to alter sentence 3 (shown below)?

    Those who study the remains of ancient cities are called archaeologists.

    (A) Delete the sentence.
    (B) Move it to the beginning of the passage.
    (C) Insert "classical" immediately before "ancient."
    (D) Change "called" to "referred to as."
    (E) Insert "only" before "archaeologists.

31. Which of the following, if placed at the beginning of the third paragraph, would provide the best transition between the second and third paragraphs?

    (A) Of course, some historians argue that Plato may have used several cities as his inspiration for Atlantis.
    (B) But there are those who believe that the satellite images were forged.
    (C) Of course, there are many other equally viable potential locations for Atlantis.
    (D) Many scholars question whether the findings either in Tartessos or Marismas de Hinojos have any relation to Atlantis, however.
    (E) This evidence is widely accepted as proof that Atlantis was based on a real city.

32. Which of the following statements would best serve to clarify a sentence in the last paragraph of the passage?

    (A) The word "scoffer" derives from the Middle English "scoff," which likely came from the Danish word "skof," which meant "jest."
    (B) Professor Richard Freund from the University of Hartford led the team that discovered the remains in Andalusia.
    (C) Andalusia is in the southern part of the Iberian peninsula, and is composed of eight separate provinces.
    (D) Other proposed locations for Atlantis include the submerged island of Spartel, the Canary Islands, and Doggerland.
    (E) Atlantis is supposed to have been wiped out by a tsunami.

33. Which of the following is the best place for the sentence below?

    Scholars hypothesize that while Atlantis was imaginary, it was inspired by a real city.

    (A) Immediately before sentence 2
    (B) Immediately before sentence 5
    (C) Immediately before sentence 6
    (D) Immediately before sentence 8
    (E) Immediately before sentence 11

34. Based on the context, which of the following could most appropriately be placed immediately before "information to determine" in sentence 9 (shown below)?

Equally skeptical are those who argue that satellite imagery alone cannot provide information to determine the location of Atlantis.

(A) thought-provoking
(B) enough
(C) imaginative
(D) a normal amount of
(E) easily accessible

35. Swapping the placement of which of following pairs of sentences would best improve the organization of the essay?

(A) Sentences 4 and 5
(B) Sentences 5 and 6
(C) Sentences 6 and 7
(D) Sentences 8 and 9
(E) Sentences 11 and 12

Chapter 26
Writing Drills:
Answers and
Explanations

CHAPTER 23—BASIC SAT GRAMMAR

Grammar Drill

1. **D** This sentence compares the number of mistakes that employees make when they have high stress levels, and low stress levels. However, anytime you make a comparison, you need to compare similar things—apples to apples and oranges to oranges. Therefore, this sentence should compare the number of mistakes that employees make when they have high stress levels to the number of mistakes that employees make when they have low stress levels. Thus, the correct answer is choice (D).

2. **D** The subject of the sentence is *number*, which is singular, but the verb is *have been...exaggerated*, which is plural. Therefore, this sentence contains a subject-verb agreement error. Choices (A), (B), and (C) all have plural verbs and therefore repeat the original error. Choice (D) fixes the error by changing the verb to *has been...exaggerated*, which is singular. Choice (D) also does not introduce any new errors, and is therefore the correct answer. Choice (E) changes the tense of the verb and therefore changes the meaning of the sentence, so choice (E) is incorrect.

3. **B** The subject of the sentence is *narwhal*, which is singular. However, the pronoun *them* is plural, and therefore cannot replace the noun *narwhal*. Therefore, choice (B) contains an error and is the correct answer.

4. **D** This sentence lists two things that Lenin did: he *led the October Revolution* and *his becoming leader of the new Bolshevik Party*. Notice, however, that the verbs *led* and *becoming* are not parallel, even though they form part of a list. Therefore you can eliminate choice (A). Choice (C) also repeats this error and is also incorrect. Now examine choice (B). The phrase *After he wrote his famous* April Theses, *Vladimir Lenin led the October revolution* is a complete thought. The phrase *this is the reason he became leader of the new Bolshevik Party in 1917* is also a complete phrase. Choice (B) connects these two complete thoughts with a comma, and therefore contains a comma splice error. Eliminate choice (B). Choice (E) also repeats this error, since choice (E) would turn the second half of the sentence into a complete thought. Only choice (D) remains. Choice (D) corrects the original error in the sentence, since the verbs *led* and *become* are parallel, and does not introduce any new errors, so choice (D) is therefore the correct answer.

5. **C** In this case, the noun *students* is plural, but the noun *phone* is singular. Since all of the students do not have the same phone, the noun *students* should agree with the noun *phone*, so this sentence contains a noun agreement error. The correct answer is choice (C).

6. **D** The pronoun *each* is singular, but the pronoun *their* is plural. Therefore, you cannot use *their* to refer to *each* species of fish. The correct answer choice is thus choice (D).

7. **B**   The phrase *This week the museum has a new impressionism exhibit and a new cubism exhibit* is a complete thought. The phrase *neither appear interesting to me, however,* is also a complete thought. This sentence joins these two complete thoughts with a comma, so this sentence contains a comma splice error. Since the first part of the sentence is not underlined, the correct answer choice must change the second half of the sentence so that it no longer contains a complete thought. Choices (A), (C), (D), and (E) all repeat the original error and are incorrect. Choice (B) fixes the original error by adding *of which*, thus making the second half of the sentence incomplete. Since choice (B) does not introduce any additional errors, choice (B) is the correct answer.

8. **B**   Use the drop test; if you eliminate *my family and* from the sentence, you're left with *What least pleased I about the resort....* When you use the drop test, it becomes easier to see that the *I* is misplaced. Since the pronoun is not the subject of the sentence, the pronoun should be *me* instead. Therefore, choice (B) is the correct answer.

9. **C**   The phrase *While located on the outskirts of the city* must describe something specific. A modifying phrase such as this one describes whatever appears immediately after the comma. However, in this case *the restaurant's famous seafood dishes* appears immediately after the comma. Since presumably the restaurant itself, and not its seafood dishes, is located on the outskirts of the city, this sentence contains a misplaced modifier error. *The restaurant* must appear immediately after the comma. Choices (A), (B), (D), and (E) repeat the original error and are therefore incorrect. Only choice (C) remains, so choice (C) is the correct answer.

10. **C**   The subject of this sentence is *Discovering*, which is singular. However, the verb is *are*, which is plural. Therefore this sentence contains a subject-verb agreement error, and choice (C) is the correct answer.

Subject-Verb Agreement Drill

1. *Are.* The subject is *customers*, which is plural, so the verb should also be plural. The verb *are* is plural, and is therefore correct.

2. *Was.* The subject of the sentence is *determination*, which is singular, so the verb should also be singular. The verb *was* is singular, and is therefore correct.

3. *Prevents.* The subject of the sentence is *sense*, which is singular. (Don't forget to cross out the prepositional phrase *of ethics and fair play*!) Therefore, the verb should also be singular. *Prevents* is a singular verb, and is therefore the correct answer.

4. *Has.* The subject of the sentence is *number*, which is singular, so the verb should be singular also. The verb *has* is singular, and is therefore correct.

5. *Is.* The subject of the sentence is *discovering*, which is singular, so the verb should be singular also. The verb *is* is singular, and is therefore correct.

Parallelism Drill

1. This sentence includes a list of three things that the monkey did: he *grabbed, peeled, and he ate it quickly*. Notice that the last item in the list is not parallel; it should simply read *and ate it quickly*.

2. This sentence cites two reasons that the Taj Mahal is famous: *its remarkable beauty* (a thing) and *it has a romantic history* (an action). The first phrase is a noun phrase, but the second phrase is a verb phrase. One way to rewrite the sentence might be *The Taj Mahal is famous both for its remarkable beauty and its romantic history*. Alternatively, you could rewrite the sentence to say *The Taj Mahal is famous both because it is remarkably beautiful and because it has a romantic history*. Either alternative would make the two parts of the sentence parallel.

3. This sentence lists three facts about Hong Kong: it *is a city of breathtaking views, great food, and has many shopping boutiques*. Notice that the third item in the list is not parallel. The third item in the list should simply be "*many shopping boutiques*." The word *has* creates a parallelism error.

4. This sentence lists three things that Jessica has done: she *has gotten more exercise, has gone on picnics...and learned how to snowshoe*. The first two verbs in the list begin with *has*, but the last one does not. One way to fix this sentence is to simply place the word *has* before *learned*. Alternatively, you could simply remove the *has* that appears before *gone*. In that case the list of verbs would be *has gotten, gone, and learned*, in which case the first *has* would apply to all of the verbs in the list. Either alternative is acceptable; you just can't mix and match.

5. This sentence lists three facts about vipers: they are snakes with *long hollow fangs, short tails, and have powerful jaws*. Notice that the last item in the list begins with the verb *have*, while the other items contain only nouns and adjectives. Therefore, the last item in the list is not parallel. Eliminate the word *have*, and the sentence becomes parallel.

Pronoun Agreement Drill

1. *Its*. The *restaurant* is singular, so you need a singular pronoun. Since *its* is singular, it is therefore the correct pronoun.

2. *One* is singular, so you need a singular pronoun. *One* is singular, and is the correct answer.

3. *You*. In this case, the sentence begins with *you*. Replace *you* with *you*, rather than with another pronoun.

4. *It*. The subject of the sentence is *team*, which is singular. *It* is a singular pronoun, and is therefore the correct answer.

5. *It*. The subject of the sentence is *band*, which is singular. Therefore, you need to replace the subject with a singular pronoun. *It* is singular, and is therefore the correct choice.

Pronoun Ambiguity Drill

1. The ambiguous pronoun is *he*. The sentence could mean that *Thibault soon mastered the skills* or that *Ludovic soon mastered the skills*. Since nothing in the sentence indicates to whom the pronoun refers, the pronoun is ambiguous.

2. The ambiguous pronoun is *this*. The opponents may be arguing that *raising subway fees* is unnecessary, or they could be arguing that *keeping subway stations cleaner* is unnecessary, or finally that *providing better security* is unnecessary. Therefore, this sentence contains an ambiguous pronoun.

3. The ambiguous pronoun is *he*. You don't know whether the quarterback from the home team looked ready for a fight or the quarterback from the visiting team looked ready for a fight.

4. The ambiguous pronoun is *it*. You don't know whether the sky or the cloud appeared threatening, or whether the author is referencing the weather as a whole.

5. The ambiguous pronoun is *it*. You don't know whether the pronoun refers to the *sweatshirt* or to the *laptop*.

CHAPTER 25—IMPROVING PARAGRAPHS

Drill 1

30. **A** The first two sentences of the first paragraph focus on the location of the fictional city of Atlantis. However, the last sentence defines the term for those who study ancient cities. Since the final sentence is unrelated to the rest of the paragraph, deleting the sentence in question makes sense. Therefore, choice (A) is the correct answer. Since the first sentence of the passage also discusses the location of Atlantis, rather than the people who study ancient cities, moving the sentence to the beginning of the passage would not be appropriate. Therefore, choice (B) is incorrect. Inserting the word *classical* immediately before *ancient* would not add necessary meaning to the sentence, so you can eliminate choice (C). *Called* and *referred to* are synonymous, so making the change suggested in choice (D) would not improve the sentence. Finally, whether archaeologists have another name is irrelevant, so inserting *only* before *archaeologists* would not add necessary meaning to the sentence.

31. **D** The second paragraph discusses possible locations for Atlantis, while the third paragraph discusses those who are skeptical of the proposed locations for Atlantis. You need a transition thought that will tie these two ideas together. Choice (A) simply discusses the idea that Plato may have used more than one city for inspiration. Since neither paragraph expands on this idea, choice (A) is

incorrect. Choice (B) incorrectly begins the sentence with *but*, and discusses the idea that satellite images may have been forged, an idea neither paragraph discusses. Thus, you can eliminate choice (B). Choice (C) introduces the idea that there are other locations, not mentioned in paragraph two, which may have been the site of Atlantis. However, since neither paragraph discusses other possible locations, choice (C) is incorrect. Choice (D) mentions the findings in Tartessos and Marismas de Hinojos, both of which were discussed in paragraph two, and also introduces the idea that some doubt these findings, which is the topic of paragraph three. Thus, choice (D) is the correct answer. Choice (E) mentions that the evidence found in Tartessos or Marismas de Hinojos is widely accepted. Since paragraph three focuses on those who do not accept that evidence, choice (E) does not appropriately link the two paragraphs.

32. **E** Since you don't need to know the origins of the word *scoff* in order to understand the sentence, choice (A) does not clarify any statements in the paragraph. Choice (B) provides more information regarding the remains discovered in Andalusia, but since the information that it adds does not provide information that clears up any confusion, choice (B) is not the credited answer. Since knowing the location of Andalusia is not critical to understanding the paragraph, you can eliminate choice (C). Nothing in the final paragraph discusses other proposed locations for Atlantis, so choice (D) does not relate to any information in the paragraph. Finally choice (E) explains that Atlantis is supposed to have been wiped out by a tsunami. The paragraph states that the city discovered in Andalusia had been wiped out by a tsunami, so choice (E) explains why the findings in Andalusia are important. Therefore, choice (E) is the correct answer.

33. **A** Sentence 1 mentions that Atlantis was imaginary, while sentence 2 discusses possible locations of Atlantis. Thus, inserting the sentence in question immediately before sentence 2 would link the two sentences. Choice (A) is therefore the correct answer. Sentences 4 and 5 do discuss the fact that Atlantis may have been inspired by a real city. However, the two sentences are already appropriately linked by the word *nevertheless*, and do not need a new sentence to create a transition between them. Adding the sentence in question would actually interrupt the flow of the paragraph, so choice (B) is incorrect. Both sentences 5 and 6 discuss possible locations for Atlantis. Neither discusses the idea that Atlantis was imaginary, so choice (C) is incorrect. Since the sentence in question focuses on the idea that Plato may have been inspired by a real city, but paragraph 3 focuses on those who doubt that the proposed locations for Atlantis are legitimate, the sentence in question would be a poor topic sentence for the paragraph. Eliminate choice (D). Sentence 10 focuses on scoffers who do not believe that Atlantis was inspired by a real city, thus suggesting that some do accept this belief. Since the idea that Atlantis may have been inspired by a real city has been clearly introduced prior to sentence 11, choice (E) is incorrect.

34. **B** Since the question is not whether the evidence is thought-provoking, but rather whether it constitutes sufficient proof, adding *thought-provoking* would not improve the sentence. On the other hand, adding *enough* would add the necessary meaning to the sentence. Thus, choice (B) is the correct answer. Imaginative evidence would be unlikely to be convincing, so adding the word

imaginative immediately before *information* would not improve the sentence. Eliminate choice (C). There is nothing in the paragraph to indicate what could be considered *a normal amount of* evidence, so adding the phrase in choice (D) would not relate to anything in the rest of the paragraph or sentence. The question is not whether the information in question is easily accessible, but rather whether it is convincing, so you can eliminate choice (E).

35.   C   Sentence 5 discusses those who have discovered what they believe to be the remains of cities that served as the inspiration for Atlantis. Since the rest of the paragraph continues this discussion, whereas sentence 4 discusses the idea that there is no proof that Plato had a particular city in mind when he wrote the tale of Atlantis, switching the two sentences would interrupt the flow of the paragraph. Thus, you can eliminate choice (A). Sentence 5 uses the word *nevertheless* to transition from the ideas in sentence 4 into the ideas in sentence 5. Since the two sentences contain contrasting ideas, this transition word is appropriate. Switching the locations of sentences 5 and 6 would thus interrupt the flow of the paragraph. Choice (B) is therefore incorrect. Sentence 6 begins with *others*, suggesting that another type of people was mentioned in the previous sentence. However, since, while sentence 5 does mention *scholars*, it does not discuss any people who claim to have found the remains of Atlantis in a location other than Marismas de Hinojos, sentence 6 is out of place. On the other hand, sentence 7 mentions that *some suppose that the remains discovered in Tartessos fix the location* there. Thus, switching the order of the two sentences would clarify the reference to *others* in sentence 6. Choice (C) is therefore the correct answer. Sentence nine begins with *Equally skeptical are those*. Switching the locations of sentences 8 and 9 would cause the third paragraph to begin with sentence 9. However, the word *equally* would no other, equally skeptical people would have been discussed at that point. Choice (D) is incorrect. Sentence 12 discusses developments that believers in Atlantis may find encouraging, but sentence 10 discusses those who are unlikely to ever believe that Atlantis was inspired by a real city. Switching the order of sentences 11 and 12 would mean that sentence 12 would immediately follow sentence 10. These two ideas contain opposite ideas, but nothing in either sentence serves as a transition between these two opposite ideas. Since sentence 12 should therefore not follow sentence 10, you can eliminate choice (E).

Chapter 27
Grammar Test 1

Directions: For each question in this section, select the best answer from among the choices given and fill in the corresponding circle on the answer sheet.

The following sentences test correctness and effectiveness of expression. Part of each sentence or the entire sentence is underlined; beneath each sentence are five ways of phrasing the underlined material. Choice A repeats the original phrasing; the other four choices are different. If you think the original phrasing produces a better sentence than any of the alternatives, select choice A; if not, select one of the other choices.

In making your selection, follow the requirements of standard written English; that is, pay attention to grammar, choice of words, sentence construction, and punctuation. Your selection should result in the most effective sentence—clear and precise, without awkwardness or ambiguity.

EXAMPLE:

Bobby Flay baked his first cake <u>and he was thirteen years old then</u>.
(A) and he was thirteen years old then
(B) when he was thirteen
(C) at age thirteen years old
(D) upon the reaching of thirteen years
(E) at the time when he was thirteen

1. Lavender is useful not only as a culinary herb <u>and also</u> as an ornamental plant.

   (A) and also
   (B) and
   (C) but also
   (D) being additionally
   (E) but also existing

2. Anticipating the arrival of more than one million attendees at the 2014 winter Olympic games in Sochi, Russia, <u>organizers deciding to pave</u> more than 220 miles of new road.

   (A) organizers deciding to pave
   (B) the decision of organizers is for paving
   (C) what the organizers decided is to pave
   (D) organizers decided to pave
   (E) organizers decided on paving

3. William Shakespeare is best known as a poet and a playwright, <u>but acting was also done by him</u>.

   (A) but acting was also done by him
   (B) there was also acting by him
   (C) but having also acted
   (D) he also was an actor
   (E) although he was also an actor

4. <u>In a 1912 discussion about the value of abstract painting, poet Guillaume Apollinaire stated that they</u> display new structures that have not been borrowed from anywhere else, but have been created entirely by the artist.

   (A) In a 1912 discussion about the value of abstract painting, poet Guillaume Apollinaire stated that they
   (B) On the subject of the value of abstract painting, poet Guillaume Apollinaire, who stated in a discussion that abstract paintings
   (C) In a 1912 discussion about the value of abstract painting, poet Guillaume Apollinaire stated that abstract paintings
   (D) Poet Guillaume Apollinaire's 1912 discussion about the value of abstract art, which stated that it
   (E) In a 1912 discussion, poet Guillaume Apollinaire stated about the value of abstract painting that they

5. The retail corporation's executive officer approved a plan <u>to improve profits by offering</u> more frequent sales, but the strategy failed because of a lack of interest from board members.

   (A) to improve profits by offering
   (B) to improve profits, offers
   (C) for profit improvement and they offer
   (D) for the improvement of profits, this offered
   (E) on improving profits, it offers

6. After the artist finished hanging her paintings in the gallery, she searched for the <u>art director with whom she had planned to eat lunch carrying a red carnation</u>.

  (A) art director with whom she had planned to eat lunch carrying a red carnation

  (B) art director carrying a red carnation with whom she had planned to eat lunch

  (C) art director carrying a red carnation, she had planned to eat lunch with him

  (D) art director, it was he with whom she had planned to eat lunch with a red carnation

  (E) art director who, having planned to eat lunch with a red carnation

7. <u>When microwaves, cellular phones, and laptop computers were originally</u> designed to be luxury items, they are now considered necessities in many parts of the world.

  (A) When microwaves, cellular phones, and laptop computers were originally

  (B) Being that microwaves, cellular phones, and laptop computers were original

  (C) Microwaves, cellular phones, and laptop computers had originally been

  (D) Despite microwaves, cellular phones, and laptop computers being originally

  (E) Although microwaves, cellular phones, and laptop computers were originally

8. One of the main objectives that NASA has had in developing the Mars rover <u>program has been met</u> in 2003, when the rover *Exploration* successfully landed on the planet.

  (A) program has been met

  (B) program, which was met

  (C) program, it was met

  (D) program was met

  (E) program meeting

9. The only comet visible to the naked eye from Earth, <u>the materials from which Halley's Comet is composed include ice and carbon dioxide</u>.

  (A) the materials from which Halley's Comet is composed include ice and carbon dioxide

  (B) Haley's Comet is composed of materials that include ice and carbon dioxide

  (C) what Haley's Comet is composed of includes ice and carbon dioxide

  (D) included in the materials from which Haley's Comet is composed are ice and carbon dioxide

  (E) ice and carbon dioxide are included in the materials of which Haley's Comet is composed

10. Leon Trotsky was initially a member of the Russian Social Democratic Labor Party, but later joined the Bolsheviks and soon <u>began managing foreign affairs and to serve</u> as leader for the party.

  (A) began managing foreign affairs and to serve

  (B) beginning to manage foreign affairs, serving

  (C) began to manage foreign affairs and serve

  (D) began to manage foreign affairs and serving

  (E) begins management of foreign affairs, he served

11. One hundred and twelve feet tall and situated on the island of Lantau in Hong Kong, <u>monks at the Po Lin monastery built Tian Tan Buddha statue in 1993, and so it became a major tourist attraction</u>.

  (A) monks at the Po Lin monastery built the Tian Tan Buddha statue in 1993, and so it became a major tourist attraction.

  (B) the building by the monks of the Po Lin monastery of the Tian Tan Buddha statue in 1993 was what turned it into a major tourist attraction

  (C) monks at the Po Lin monastery, having built the Tian Tan Buddha statue in 1993, turned it into a major tourist attraction.

  (D) the Tian Tan Buddha was built in 1993 by the monks of the Po Lin monastery and is now a major tourist attraction

  (E) the Tian Tan Buddha, which was built by the monks of the Po Lin monastery in 1993 and became a major tourist attraction

The following sentences test your ability to recognize grammar and usage errors. Each sentence contains either a single error or no error at all. No sentence contains more than one error. The error, if there is one, is underlined and lettered. If the sentence contains an error, select the one underlined part that must be changed to make the sentence correct. If the sentence is correct, select choice E. In choosing answers, follow the requirements of standard written English.

EXAMPLE:

The other players and her significantly improved
A   B   C

the game plan created by the coaches. No error
D   E

Ⓐ●ⒸⒹⒺ

12. Although Mount Everest has the most greatest height
A

above sea level of any mountain in the world, Mauna
B

Kea actually has a base-to-height measurement that
C

is nearly twice that of Mount Everest. No error
D   E

13. The rise of violent crime in small suburban towns,

like the rise in petty theft in such places, revealing
A   B

an alarming trend of which law enforcement officials
C

should take note. No error
D   E

14. The foremost priority of most students in the district

is not education, as implicated by the high
A   B

percentage of students who leave school without
C   D

graduating. No error
E

15. Long hours of labor without breaks were common
A

during the Industrial Revolution, as was dangerous
B   C

working conditions that often resulted in sickness,
D

maiming, and even death among workers. No error
E

16. Last year, following the unemployment crisis in our
A

town, a large percentage of the local population moved
B

to a neighboring city and will start searching for jobs
C   D

there. No error
E

17. The Edinburgh Phrenological Society,

the first and foremost phrenological society in Great
A

Britain during the 1820's, promoted the idea that
B

certain areas of the brain controlled specific emotions
C

and that it could change size if personality traits
D

changed. No error
E

18. Before the ratification of an antismoking ban
A

in 1574, no existing regulations forbade individuals
B   C

to smoke in churches in Mexico. No error
D   E

19. While the pie shop was the more famous of the thirty-
A   B

five pie shops in the city, it did not have seating for
C   D

more than ten people at a time. No error
E

20. Tina <u>once believed</u> that physics courses and the algebra
        A

courses were equally challenging, but experience

<u>has taught</u> her that physics courses are much more
  B

difficult than <u>that</u> of algebra courses. <u>No error</u>
        C   D   E

21. Thomas Jefferson's <u>most enduring</u> contribution
               A

to history <u>is perhaps</u> his draft of the United States
         B

constitution, <u>in which</u> he announced the intention of
         C

the thirteen American colonies <u>to be</u> independent of
                       D

British rule. <u>No error</u>
         E

22. Prior to <u>accepting</u> an employment offer, a candidate
        A

<u>should consider</u> the working hours of the job in
  B

addition to <u>their</u> pay <u>and benefits</u>. <u>No error</u>
        C   D   E

23. The <u>earliest types</u> of lizards appeared <u>during</u> the
        A   B

Jurassic period, <u>there was</u> an increase in the number of
             C

species on Earth because the climate shifted

to include more lush rainforests. <u>No error</u>
    D   E

24. Some dog types, <u>such as</u> the Chihuahua, <u>is</u> very high
           A   B

strung, while <u>other types</u>, such as the Golden Retriever,
         C

are more <u>laid back</u>. <u>No error</u>
        D   E

25. The ingredients in some skin medications

<u>proscribed by</u> dermatologists <u>do clear up</u> acne,
  A   B

but also unfortunately <u>affect</u> mood. <u>No error</u>
  C   D   E

26. The Spanish Armada was a fleet <u>composed of</u> 130
                       A

ships that <u>they used to</u> <u>attempt to</u> overthrow Queen
        B   C

Elizabeth I <u>in</u> 1588. <u>No error</u>
        D   E

27. During the weeks that led to her demise, Marie

Antoinette was accused of multiple crimes <u>such as</u>
                          A

plotting to kill the Duke of Orléans, a charge that had

<u>no validity</u> <u>despite</u> her well-publicized <u>dislike</u> of the
  B   C   D

duke. <u>No error</u>
    E

28. The lunisolar calendar <u>created by</u> the ancient Greeks
                A

<u>allowed for</u> twelve months of alternating lengths of 29
  B

and 30 days per year, and <u>was</u> less complex
               C

<u>than the ancient Mayans</u>. <u>No error</u>
    D   E

29. Making time <u>to learn</u> both the local language and
        A

customs <u>are</u> among the <u>biggest</u> priorities for those who
      B   C

<u>move to</u> foreign countries. <u>No error</u>
    D   E

Directions: The following passage is an early draft of an essay. Some parts of the passage need to be rewritten.

Read the passage and select the best answers for the questions that follow. Some questions are about particular sentences or parts of sentences and ask you to improve sentence structure or word choice. Other questions ask you to consider organization and development. In choosing answers, follow the requirements of standard written English.

Questions 30–35 are based on the following passage.

(**1**) From the 15th century onward, choreographers and dancers have told stories through dance. (**2**) Some works are written particularly for ballet, and use elaborate costumes and staging. (**3**) *The Nutcracker*, for example. (**4**) It has been performed in theaters around the world since December 18, 1892. (**5**) Among these productions, perhaps the most famous is George Balanchine's, as performed by the New York City Ballet in 1954.

(**6**) The process of writing a full-length story and then choreographing a ballet to tell that story through a two or three hour dance is actually quite formidable. (**7**) Since ballet does not involve speech, writers and choreographers must find ways to communicate a narrative through movement, music, and scenery alone. (**8**) To address such difficulties, the American Ballet Theater hired award-winning dancer and choreographer Twyla Tharp to choreograph its original production of *Push Comes to Shove*, featuring dance phenomenon Mikhail Baryshnikov. (**9**) She used music from Joseph Lamb's *Bohemia Rag 1919* and Joseph Haydn's *Symphony 82 in C Major* to create the score, creating an ingenious and witty ballet. (**10**) This proved advantageous: *Push Comes to Shove* is now regarded as one of the most successful examples of crossover ballet in the history of dance.

(**11**) Audiences are often unhappy with adaptations of otherwise popular ballets, especially if the choreography is poor. (**12**) When the classical ballet *Swan Lake* was first performed, it was not a critical success because Julian Reinsinger's choreography was considered subpar. (**13**) Nevertheless, even well-choreographed ballets have been known to fail. (**14**) Having its roots in the ballet originally staged by world-renowned choreographer Alexander Gorsky, Ross Stretton's production of *Don Quixote* was extremely unsuccessful. (**15**) Stretton resigned as artistic director of London's Royal Ballet after only 13 months.

30. Which of the following is the best revision of the underlined sections of sentences 3 and 4 (shown below)?

    The Nutcracker, *for example. It has been performed in theaters all around the world* since December 18, 1892.

    (A) (no change)
    (B) *The Nutcracker,* for example, which has been performed in theaters all around the world
    (C) *The Nutcracker,* for example. In theaters all around the world it has been performed
    (D) *The Nutcracker,* for example, has been performed in theaters all around the world
    (E) For instance, performances of *The Nutcracker* have been taken place all around the world

31. Based on the context, which of the following would best be placed at the beginning of sentence 6 (shown below)?

    The process of writing a full-length story and then choreographing a ballet to tell that story through a two or three hour dance is actually quite formidable.

    (A) Because there is such focus on perfecting the musical score,
    (B) But whatever the tale that the dance seeks to tell,
    (C) While choreographers such as Balanchine make the job appear easy,
    (D) Dancers require years in order to learn their craft, but
    (E) Although the first ballet was choreographed in the 15th century,

32. Based on the information in the passage, which of the following is the best revision of the underlined section of sentence 10 (shown below)?

    This proved advantageous: Push Comes to Shove *is now regarded as one of the most successful examples of crossover ballet in the history of dance.*

    (A) (As it is currently written)
    (B) Using his music
    (C) Creating a ballet with a large cast
    (D) Hiring Tharp
    (E) That has eventually

33. Which of the following, if placed immediately before sentence 11, would best introduce the third paragraph?

(A) There are many reasons that this is true.
(B) Not all ballets have achieved such acclaim, however.
(C) You may not realize how much work goes into creating a successful ballet.
(D) Many classical ballets have been converted into crossover ballets.
(E) Most classical dance fans have a favorite ballet.

34. Based on the context, which of the following is the best way to rewrite the underlined part of sentence 14 (shown below)?

Having its roots in the ballet originally staged by world-renowned choreographer Alexander Gorsky, *Ross Stretton's production of* Don Quixote *was extremely unsuccessful.*

(A) (As it is currently written)
(B) Following the vain attempt to perform the
(C) Because it was a version of the
(D) As a box office hit like the
(E) While it closely resembled the

35. Which of the following would form the most appropriate subject for a paragraph immediately preceding this passage?

(A) A discussion of the purpose of dance prior to the 15th century.
(B) The role that types of dance other than ballet have played in storytelling.
(C) The methods by which other art forms, such as opera, tell stories.
(D) The part that dancers play in making a ballet successful.
(E) The level of education that choreographers must receive in order to be competent.

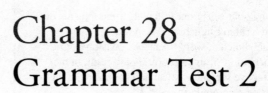

Chapter 28
Grammar Test 2

Directions: For each question in this section, select the best answer from among the choices given and fill in the corresponding circle on the answer sheet.

The following sentences test correctness and effectiveness of expression. Part of each sentence or the entire sentence is underlined; beneath each sentence are five ways of phrasing the underlined material. Choice A repeats the original phrasing; the other four choices are different. If you think the original phrasing produces a better sentence than any of the alternatives, select choice A; if not, select one of the other choices.

In making your selection, follow the requirements of standard written English; that is, pay attention to grammar, choice of words, sentence construction, and punctuation. Your selection should result in the most effective sentence—clear and precise, without awkwardness or ambiguity.

EXAMPLE:

Bobby Flay baked his first cake and he was thirteen years old then.
(A) and he was thirteen years old then
(B) when he was thirteen
(C) at age thirteen years old
(D) upon the reaching of thirteen years
(E) at the time when he was thirteen

1. The line "Belgians in the Congo" from Billy Joel's song *We Didn't Start the Fire* alludes to the authority Belgium wielded there, it annexed the Congo as a colony.

   (A) there, it annexed
   (B) there, which, having annexed
   (C) there, whose annexing of
   (D) there to have been annexing
   (E) there after it annexed

2. After his biking accident, Jeff tended to take the train rather than riding his bike to work because he was nervous that he would get into another accident.

   (A) tended to take the train rather than riding
   (B) tends to taking the train rather than riding
   (C) tended to take the train rather than ride
   (D) tends to take the train rather as take
   (E) tending to take the train rather than riding

3. Widely thought to be the least efficient employees in the company, Amy and Giselle serve as a receptionist at the front desk.

   (A) serve as a receptionist
   (B) serving as receptionists
   (C) has served as a receptionist
   (D) serve as receptionists
   (E) serves as a receptionist

4. Symbolically, the four-leaf clover, a rare variation on the common three-leaf clover, it represents luck, and if discovered accidentally is supposed to bring good fortune to its finder.

   (A) it represents
   (B) representing
   (C) which represents
   (D) represents
   (E) it represented

5. At most newspapers, the editor-in-chief works closely with the journalists, which are responsible for writing news stories.

   (A) which are responsible for writing
   (B) who are responsible for writing
   (C) who are responsible to write
   (D) whose responsibility is to write
   (E) which are responsible to write

6. Some individuals who are interested in globe-trotting are nevertheless hesitant to travel by plane, they erroneously think that automobile travel is safer than air travel.

   (A) are nevertheless hesitant to travel by plane, they erroneously think
   (B) and are nevertheless hesitant to travel by plane in that they erroneously think
   (C) were nevertheless hesitant to travel by air with the erroneous thought
   (D) had been nevertheless hesitant to travel by plane because of erroneously thinking
   (E) are nevertheless hesitant to travel by plane because they erroneously think

7. Once considered purely mythical, <u>the French gunboat *Alecton* captured a giant squid in 1861, after which its</u> existence was accepted by the scientific community at large.

   (A) the French gunboat *Alecton* captured a giant squid in 1861, after which its
   (B) a giant squid was captured by the French gunboat *Alecton* in 1861, after that its
   (C) a giant squid was captured by the French gunboat *Alecton* in 1861, after which its
   (D) but a giant squid was captured by the French gunboat *Alecton* in 1861, and their
   (E) the French gunboat *Alecton* captured a giant squid in 1861, after which their

8. Counter to prevailing beliefs, many elderly individuals continue caring for themselves well into their 80's, <u>and even support</u> spouses and other family members.

   (A) and even support
   (B) which they even support
   (C) but even supporting
   (D) even as well as supporting
   (E) but who also support

9. After the deplorable conditions in the country were publicized, relief efforts were initiated not only by what charity organizations did <u>but also what they encouraged others to do</u>.

   (A) but also what they encouraged others to do
   (B) and what was encouraged of others by them
   (C) and what they encouraged others to do
   (D) but also what encouragement they gave others
   (E) but also by what they encouraged others to do

10. In this neighborhood, burglary is on the rise, <u>which occurs</u> almost daily now.

    (A) which occurs
    (B) occurring
    (C) occurs
    (D) where it occurs
    (E) it occurs

11. Doctors at the hospital think that each of the patients in the ward <u>have become</u> infected and may be contagious.

    (A) have become
    (B) were
    (C) to become
    (D) has become
    (E) having become

The following sentences test your ability to recognize grammar and usage errors. Each sentence contains either a single error or no error at all. No sentence contains more than one error. The error, if there is one, is underlined and lettered. If the sentence contains an error, select the one underlined part that must be changed to make the sentence correct. If the sentence is correct, select choice E. In choosing answers, follow the requirements of standard written English.

EXAMPLE:

The other players and her significantly improved
   A   B   C

the game plan created by the coaches. No error
              D   E

Ⓐ ● Ⓒ Ⓓ Ⓔ

12. Although the two nurses had watched surgeons
                          A

perform the operation multiple times, and

had even assisted with the procedure themselves once
         B   C

or twice, neither Linda and Josie could remember how
                    D

to administer the anesthesia. No error
                     E

13. While touring Hong Kong, one can ride a bus to the
                          A

top of the mountain known as The Peak, view the
                           B

entire city from its height, and you can return down the
                       C

mountain on a funicular railroad. No error
        D   E

14. In the early 1900s, Marcel Duchamp, an eccentric
                          A

French-American sculptor and painter, helped to
                      B

revolutionize modern art by defining revolutionary
                   C

developments in the plastic arts. No error
    D   E

15. Alerting the citizens that the levee had finally broken,
    A

the suddenly rushing of water soon caused the city
     B   C   D

streets to flood. No error
         E

16. While more people attended the party than Zach and I
                A

would have invited had we been the planners, the party
      B   C

was still more enjoyable than him and I expected.
                   D

No error
 E

17. Parents who allow their children to cross the street
        A

when not having looked both ways first
        B

have not fulfilled their responsibility to teach their
        C   D

children basic safety precautions. No error
              E

18. Before each game, the members of the still-undefeated

soccer team enthusiastically sing "We Are the
         A

Champions," rallying their spirits before they finally
                   B

march onto the field, where they inevitably crush their
    C   D

opponents. No error
      E

19. With the exception of my dog, my friend Ahmed's dog
    A

is the only dog in the neighborhood that does not bark
 B

when someone enters their yard during the day.
             C   D

No error
 E

20. Historians remain divided as to <u>whether</u> the motives
⠀⠀⠀⠀⠀⠀⠀⠀⠀⠀⠀⠀⠀⠀⠀⠀⠀⠀⠀A

that led Lee Harvey Oswald to shoot John F. Kennedy

were <u>solely</u> the result of his own instability <u>or were</u>
⠀⠀⠀⠀B⠀⠀⠀⠀⠀⠀⠀⠀⠀⠀⠀⠀⠀⠀⠀⠀⠀⠀⠀⠀C

actually <u>inspired</u> by an organization that used Oswald
⠀⠀⠀⠀⠀⠀⠀⠀D

as its tool. <u>No error</u>
⠀⠀⠀⠀⠀⠀⠀⠀E

21. <u>Despite its location</u> in a much sought-after
⠀⠀⠀⠀A

neighborhood, Aurélien's new apartment is

<u>the less expensive</u> of the four apartments he
⠀⠀⠀⠀⠀⠀B

has rented in the city <u>over</u> the last ten years. <u>No error</u>
⠀⠀C⠀⠀⠀⠀⠀⠀⠀⠀⠀D⠀⠀⠀⠀⠀⠀⠀⠀⠀⠀⠀⠀E

22. The electrical telegraph, a device <u>invented by</u> Francis
⠀⠀⠀⠀⠀⠀⠀⠀⠀⠀⠀⠀⠀⠀⠀⠀⠀⠀⠀⠀A

Ronalds in 1823 as a way to transmit messages quickly

over long distances, <u>have become</u> obsolete <u>since</u> the
⠀⠀⠀⠀⠀⠀⠀⠀⠀⠀B⠀⠀⠀⠀⠀⠀⠀⠀⠀⠀C

<u>invention</u> of the internet. <u>No error</u>
⠀⠀D⠀⠀⠀⠀⠀⠀⠀⠀⠀⠀E

23. For the poetess, the <u>most disheartening</u> moment of the
⠀⠀⠀⠀A⠀⠀⠀⠀⠀⠀⠀⠀B

day occurred when <u>she</u> <u>opened</u> her mailbox and found
⠀⠀⠀⠀⠀⠀⠀⠀⠀⠀C⠀⠀D

four rejection letters inside. <u>No error</u>
⠀⠀⠀⠀⠀⠀⠀⠀⠀⠀⠀⠀E

24. Since the explosion <u>of</u> a nuclear plant on a nearby
⠀⠀⠀⠀⠀⠀⠀⠀⠀A

island that was <u>hit by</u> a tsunami, the region's number of
⠀⠀⠀⠀⠀⠀⠀⠀B

annual tourists <u>have decreased</u> <u>drastically.</u>
⠀⠀⠀⠀⠀⠀⠀C⠀⠀⠀⠀⠀⠀D

<u>No error</u>
⠀E

25. When companies allow employees <u>to work</u> remotely,
⠀⠀⠀⠀⠀⠀⠀⠀⠀⠀⠀⠀⠀⠀⠀⠀⠀A

overall company productivity <u>can increase</u> because
⠀⠀⠀⠀⠀⠀⠀⠀⠀⠀⠀⠀⠀⠀B

at home employees <u>are often</u> less distracted and are
⠀⠀⠀⠀⠀⠀⠀⠀C

therefore more focused than <u>the office.</u> <u>No error</u>
⠀⠀⠀⠀⠀⠀⠀⠀⠀⠀⠀⠀⠀D⠀⠀⠀⠀⠀⠀⠀E

26. In the 1970s, the <u>talented</u> swimmer <u>who won</u> his ninth
⠀⠀⠀⠀⠀⠀⠀⠀A⠀⠀⠀⠀⠀⠀⠀B

Olympic gold medal, a medal he <u>earned in</u> the freestyle
⠀⠀⠀⠀⠀⠀⠀⠀⠀⠀⠀⠀⠀⠀⠀⠀⠀C

competition, <u>which he won</u> by only half a stroke.
⠀⠀⠀⠀⠀⠀⠀⠀D

<u>No error</u>
⠀E

27. The golf cart, a vehicle originally <u>designed merely</u>
⠀⠀⠀⠀⠀⠀⠀⠀⠀⠀⠀⠀⠀⠀⠀⠀A

to transport golfers, is highly versatile; seats that are

open to the elements <u>make them</u> ideal for touring large
⠀⠀⠀⠀⠀⠀⠀⠀⠀B

outdoor attractions, <u>while</u> a relatively low top speed
⠀⠀⠀⠀⠀⠀⠀⠀⠀⠀C

almost <u>guarantees</u> safe travel. <u>No error</u>
⠀⠀⠀⠀D⠀⠀⠀⠀⠀⠀⠀⠀E

28. <u>While</u> <u>building it</u> over the course of many centuries,
⠀⠀⠀A⠀⠀B

the palace <u>collapsed</u> in a single day when it
⠀⠀⠀⠀⠀⠀⠀⠀C

<u>was stormed</u> by protestors and set on fire. <u>No error</u>
⠀⠀D⠀⠀⠀⠀⠀⠀⠀⠀⠀⠀⠀⠀⠀⠀⠀E

29. The <u>mood</u> of the crowd <u>was</u> negatively <u>effected</u> by the
⠀⠀⠀⠀A⠀⠀⠀⠀⠀⠀⠀B⠀⠀⠀⠀⠀⠀C

fact that the candidate's speech was held <u>outdoors</u> and
⠀⠀⠀⠀⠀⠀⠀⠀⠀⠀⠀⠀⠀⠀⠀⠀D

the weather was cold and damp. <u>No error</u>
⠀⠀⠀⠀⠀⠀⠀⠀⠀⠀⠀⠀⠀E

Directions: The following passage is an early draft of an essay. Some parts of the passage need to be rewritten.

Read the passage and select the best answers for the questions that follow. Some questions are about particular sentences or parts of sentences and ask you to improve sentence structure or word choice. Other questions ask you to consider organization and development. In choosing answers, follow the requirements of standard written English.

Questions 30–35 are based on the following passage.

(**1**) The number of species existing on planet Earth is currently estimated at approximately 8.7 million. (**2**) Given this incredible variety, they know that only 1.9 million of these species have been described to date, so in fact creatures often dismissed as mythical, such as Bigfoot, may still exist, but may simply not have been discovered. (**3**) Those who study biodiversity include wildlife scientists, climatologists, and biologists.

(**4**) Admittedly, no compelling evidence has come to light to prove the existence of Bigfoot, otherwise known as Sasquatch; no official sightings have yet been made. (**5**) Nevertheless, there are those who claim that unofficial sightings of Bigfoot suggest that the creature may in fact be real. (**6**) For instance, it was often claimed that a 1924 report from five miners who declared that they were attacked by "apemen" supports the idea that Bigfoot exists. (**7**) Some also point to a 2007 photo taken by hunter Rick Jacobs of a large, hairy, and odd-looking creature, arguing that the creature's size and appearance is consistent with that proposed for Bigfoot, and that the photo strongly supports the idea that Bigfoot may be real.

(**8**) Some contend that the 1924 attack was merely the work of pranksters who wore costumes and planted fake giant footprints. (**9**) Similarly skeptical are those who respond that the 2007 photo is merely of a large bear suffering from a severe case of mange.

(**10**) Those who question the existence of Bigfoot to such an extent are unlikely to ever become believers unless they see a large, hairy Sasquatch with their own eyes. (**11**) Those of us with more open minds may find the long list of Bigfoot sightings of the past, along with continued current sightings, fairly compelling. (**12**) In fact, one of the most powerfully convincing events was the killing, in September of 2012, of a creature that undeniably resembles Bigfoot, and on which Richard Dyer, the man who shot the creature, claims to have done DNA tests which conclusively prove that the creature really is a Sasquatch.

---

30. Based on the passage, which of the choices below is the best revision of the underlined portion of sentence 2 (shown below)?

    Given this incredible variety, they know that only 1.9 million of these species have been described to date, so in fact creatures often dismissed as mythical, such as Bigfoot, may still exist, but may simply not have been discovered.

    (A) (no change)
    (B) Although it is admitted that
    (C) Recognizing this astonishing diversity, they understand that
    (D) Moreover, only
    (E) According to this information, they believe that

31. Based on the context in which it appears, which of the following is the best way to edit sentence 3 (shown below)?

    Those who study biodiversity include wildlife scientists, climatologists, and biologists.

    (A) Place it at the beginning of paragraph two.
    (B) Insert the word "Additionally" at the beginning of the sentence.
    (C) Insert the words "on this planet" immediately after "biodiversity".
    (D) Change "include" to "are".
    (E) Remove the sentence from the passage.

32. Based on the information in the passage, which of the following is the best revision of the underlined part of sentence 6 (shown below)?

    For instance, it was often claimed that a 1924 report from five miners who declared that they were attacked by "apemen" supports the idea that Bigfoot exists.

    (A) (No change)
    (B) many believe
    (C) they speculate
    (D) it has been frequently supposed
    (E) you might think

33. Which of the following, if placed at the beginning of the second paragraph, would provide the most appropriate transition between the second and third paragraphs?

(A) However, there are those who suspect that this photo might be a hoax.
(B) This belief has since become generally accepted.
(C) Undoubtedly, creatures such as Bigfoot may also attack species other than humans.
(D) A lawyer might argue that there is a difference between modern reports backed up by scientific evidence, and historical reports backed up only by hearsay.
(E) Not everyone accepts such evidence, however.

34. Based on the passage, which of the choices below is the most appropriate revision of the underlined part of sentence 11 (shown below)?

Those of us with more open minds may find the long list of Bigfoot sightings of the past, along with continued current sightings, fairly compelling.

(A) Similarly, those of us
(B) Therefore, those of us
(C) Also, those of us
(D) However, those of us
(E) Ultimately, those of us

35. Which of the statements below would best serve to clarify a thought from the final paragraph of the passage?

(A) Richard Dyer's experience occurred just outside of San Antonio, Texas.
(B) The term "Sasquatch" originated in Southwest British Columbia, and created by speakers of the language Halkomelem.
(C) Richard Dyer nicknamed his Bigfoot corpse "Hank" and has promised to take it on tour throughout the United States in 2014.
(D) Between 1973 and 2009, primatologists conducted four formal studies to determine whether Bigfoot was real.
(E) DNA tests are widely accepted to be highly accurate and cannot be faked.

Chapter 29
Grammar Tests:
Answers and
Explanations

GRAMMAR TEST 1

1. **C** The correct idiom is *not only...but also*. Since this sentence instead uses *not only....and also*, this sentence contains an idiom error. Eliminate choices (A), (B), and (D), since they do not contain the word *but*. Choice (C) is more concise than choice (E), and maintains parallelism with the phrase *as a culinary herb*. Thus, the correct answer is choice (C).

2. **D** The phrase *organizers deciding to pave more than 220 miles of new road* is not a complete thought. Since the first half of the sentence is also an incomplete thought, this sentence does not contain a complete thought. Since using *deciding* instead of *decided* makes the second half of the sentence incomplete, you can eliminate the answer choices that contain *deciding*. Eliminate choices (A) and (E). The correct idiom is *decision to*, rather than *decision for*, so choice (B) contains an idiom error. That leaves only choices (C) and (D), but choice (D) is more concise than choice (C). Thus, the correct answer is choice (D).

3. **E** The phrase *acting was also done by him* is passive, and is not parallel with the first half of the sentence, which states that *William Shakespeare is best known as a poet and a playwright*. Thus, you can eliminate choice (A). Choice (B) repeats the error in the original answer choice, and is therefore incorrect. Choice (C) does not contain a complete thought, and is incorrect. In choice (D), the phrase *William Shakespeare is best known as a poet and a playwright* is a complete thought, and the phrase *he was also an actor* is also a complete thought. Since choice (D) connects these two ideas with only a comma, choice (D) contains a comma splice error. Choice (E) fixes the error in the original sentence and does not introduce any new errors, so choice (E) is the correct answer.

4. **C** The original sentence uses the plural pronoun *they*, which does not replace any plural nouns that appear earlier in the sentence. It appears to replace *art*, which is singular, but since *they* is plural, the sentence contains a pronoun agreement error. Eliminate choice (A). Choice (E) repeats the error in the original sentence and is therefore incorrect. Choice (B) does not contain a complete thought, and is thus not the correct answer. Choice (C) fixes the error in the original sentence and does not introduce any new errors, so choice (C) is the correct choice. Eliminate choice (D), because it does not contain a complete thought.

5. **A** The original sentence does not contain an error, so the correct answer is choice (A). Choice (B) turns the sentence into a fragment, and is therefore incorrect. Choice (C) uses the plural pronoun *they*, which in this case does not refer to any particular noun and is thus ambiguous. Choices (D) and (E) each connect two complete thoughts with a comma, and therefore each contains a comma splice error and is incorrect.

6. **B** In the original sentence, the phrase *carrying a red carnation* is a misplaced modifier because you cannot determine whether the artist or the art director was the one carrying a red carnation. Eliminate choice (A). Choices (D) and (E) repeat the error in choice (A) and are therefore incorrect. Choice (B) fixes the error in the original sentence and does not introduce any new errors, so choice (B) is the correct answer. In choice (C), the phrase *After the artist finished hanging her paintings in*

the gallery, she searched for the art director carrying a red carnation is a complete thought. The phrase *she had planned to eat lunch with him* is also a complete thought. Since choice (C) connects two complete thoughts using only a comma, choice (C) contains a comma splice error.

7. **E** The meaning of the sentence calls for a contrast between the time that *microwaves, cellular phones, and laptop computers were original designed* and *now*. However, the word *when* does not provide a contrast, so *when* is the wrong word. Eliminate choice (A). Neither choice (B) nor choice (C) uses a contrast word, so both are incorrect. Note that choice (C) also contains a comma splice error, since both the first half of the sentence and the last half of the sentence contain complete thoughts, and the two halves of the sentence are merely joined by a comma. Choice (D) is idiomatically incorrect, since *Despite* would need to be followed by a phrase such as *the fact that*. Choice (E) fixes the error in the original sentence by using the contrast word *Although*, and does not introduce any new errors. Thus choice (E) is the correct answer.

8. **D** The original sentence uses the present perfect verb *has met*, which suggests that the sentence is discussing an event that began in the past but continues into the present. Since the sentence is actually discussing an event that occurred in the past and is now completed—since the goal was met in 2003—the sentence currently contains a verb tense error. Eliminate choice (A). Choice (B) does not contain a complete thought and therefore turns the sentence into a fragment, so choice (B) is incorrect. Choice (E) repeats this error and is also incorrect. Choice (C) inappropriately uses the word *it*, which is ambiguous. Choice (D) corrects the error in the original sentence and does not introduce any new errors, so choice (D) is the correct answer.

9. **B** The modifying phrase *The only comet visible to the naked eye from Earth* must describe a comet. However, the phrase that appears immediately after the comma is *the materials*. Since the phrase should describe Halley's Comet, not the materials, this sentence contains a misplaced modifier error. Eliminate any choices in which *Halley's Comet* is not the thing that appears immediately after the comma. Choices (A), (C), (D), and (E) are all incorrect. Only choice (B) corrects the misplaced modifier error, so choice (B) is the correct answer.

10. **C** This sentence uses two verbs in a list: *managing* and *to serve*. Since the two verbs are not in the same form, this sentence contains a parallelism error. Eliminate choice (A). Choices (D) and (E) also contain parallelism errors and are incorrect. Choice (B) does use *beginning* and *serving*, both of which are in the same form, but it also turns the sentence into an incomplete thought. Thus, choice (B) is also incorrect. Choice (C) uses *to manage* and *serve*. Since the word *to*, when placed at the beginning of the list, applies to both verbs, this choice maintains parallelism. Choice (C) is the correct answer.

11. **D** The modifying phrase *One hundred and twelve feet tall and situated on the island of Lantau in Hong Kong* must describe whatever appears immediately after the comma. Since, as the sentence is currently written, the word *monks* appears immediately after the comma, the sentence currently suggests that the monks are one hundred and twelve feet tall and on the island of Lantau. However, the modifying phrase should presumably describe the statue, rather than the monks.

Eliminate choice (A). Choice (C) repeats the error in the original sentence and is also incorrect. Choice (B) places *the building*, rather than *the Tian Tan Buddha statue* immediately after the modifying phrase, and thus also contains a misplaced modifier error. Choice (D) fixes the error in the original sentence and does not introduce any new errors, so choice (D) is the correct answer. Choice (E) correctly places *the Tian Tan Buddha statue* immediately after the comma, but it also turns the sentence into an incomplete thought, and is therefore incorrect.

12. **A** The word *most* is redundant; the word *greatest* already implies that no other mountain has a greater height above sea level than Mount Everest. Thus, the correct answer is choice (A).

13. **B** This sentence uses *revealing*, rather than *reveals*, and thus does not contain a complete thought. Since choice (B) uses the wrong verb form, choice (B) is the correct answer.

14. **B** The word *implicated* means *suspected or involved*. However, the word that the sentence needs to use in order to create the correct meaning is a word such as *implied* or *demonstrated*. Hence, choice (B) contains a diction error and is the correct answer.

15. **C** The verb *was* is singular, but the subject of that verb is *conditions*, which is plural. Thus, choice (C) contains a subject-verb agreement error, and is the correct answer.

16. **C** The verb *will start* is in the future tense. However, the phrase *last year*, and the fact that the verb *moved* is in the past tense both indicate that the events described in the sentence occurred at some point in the past. Thus, choice (C) should be in the past tense and should say *started*, rather than *will start*. Choice (C) is the correct answer.

17. **D** The pronoun *it* is singular and should refer to a specific singular noun. However, since the sentence implies that *areas of the brain*, rather the brain itself, changes size, and *areas* is a plural noun, choice (D) contains a pronoun agreement error and should say *they*. Thus, the correct answer is choice (D).

18. **E** In choice (A), the word *ratification* is a singular noun. Since the noun is not the subject of a verb, and it does not disagree with any other nouns in the sentence, choice (A) does not contain an error. In choice (B), *in* is idiomatically the correct preposition, and the phrase *in 1574* correctly modifies *the ratification of an antismoking ban*. Thus, choice (B) does not contain an error. The adjective *existing* correctly modifies the noun *regulations*, and the plural noun *regulations* agrees with the *forbade* (which is past tense and therefore neither singular nor plural). Thus, choice (C) does not contain an error. The correct idiom is *forbid...to*, so the word *to* is correct in choice (D). The verb *smoke* has no agreement or tense errors in this sentence either, so choice (D) does not contain an error. Thus, the correct answer is choice (E).

19. **B** Use *more* to compare two things, but use *most* to compare three or more things. In this case, the sentence compares one pie shop and *the thirty-five pie shops in the city*. Since this sentence compares more than two things, the sentence should use *most* rather than *more*. Thus choice (B) contains an error.

20. **C** The phrase *that of* does not refer to any particular facet of algebra courses, and is therefore ambiguous. Thus, the correct answer is choice (C).

21. **E** Choice (A) begins with the word *most*. The sentence considers one of the many contributions that Thomas Jefferson made to history, and since he made more than two contributions, *most*, rather than *more*, is the appropriate word. The adjective *enduring* correctly describes the noun *contribution*, so choice (A) does not contain an error. In choice (B), the singular verb *is* agrees with the singular subject *history*, and is in the correct tense and form. The adverb *perhaps* appropriately modifies the verb *is*, so choice (B) does not contain an error. The phrase *in which* is not ambiguous, since it refers to Jefferson's draft of the Constitution. Additionally, the phrase correctly refers to a thing, rather than a person, place, or time, so choice (C) does not contain an error. The correct idiom is *intention to*, so choice (D) uses the correct preposition. The verb *be* does not introduce any tense, parallelism, or agreement errors, so choice (D) does not contain an error. Thus, the correct answer is choice (E).

22. **C** The pronoun *there* is plural, but refers to *job*, which is singular. Thus, choice (C) contains an error and is the correct answer.

23. **C** The phrase *the earliest types of lizards appeared during the Jurassic period* is a complete thought. The phrase *there was an increase in the number of species on Earth because the climate shifted to include more lush rainforests* is also a complete thought. Since this sentence joins two complete thoughts using only a comma, this sentence contains a comma splice error. Since you cannot change the punctuation in the sentence, you must turn one of the phrases into an incomplete thought. You can turn the second half of the sentence into an incomplete thought by changing the words that appear immediately after the comma. For instance, changing the words in choice (C) to *a time when there was* would correct the issue. Thus, choice (C) is the correct choice.

24. **B** The verb *is* is singular, but the subject *types* is plural, so choice (B) contains a subject-verb agreement error, and should say *are* instead.

25. **A** The word *proscribed* means *forbidden*, but the word *prescribed* means *to give directions for treatment*. Since the meaning of the sentence requires *prescribe*, rather than *proscribe*, choice (A) contains a diction error, and is the correct answer.

26. **B** The pronoun *they* is plural, but does not clearly replace any plural pronoun that appears elsewhere in the sentence. Thus, the pronoun *they* is ambiguous, and choice (B) contains an error. Choice (B) is therefore the correct answer.

27. **E** Use *such as* to introduce an example. Since this sentence uses the phrase *such as* to introduce an example of one crime of which Marie Antoinette was accused, this sentence correctly uses the phrase. Eliminate choice (A). The singular noun *validity* does not disagree with any other nouns or verbs in the sentence and does not introduce any diction or redundancy errors, so choice (B) does not

contain an error. The preposition *despite* is correctly used and does not introduce any idiom errors into the sentence, so choice (C) does not contain an error. The noun *dislike* is singular and does not disagree with any other nouns or verbs in the sentence, so you can eliminate choice (D). The correct answer is choice (E).

28.　**D**　This sentence says that the *calendar created by the ancient Greeks…was less complex than the ancient Mayans.* Since you cannot compare calendars to Mayans, this sentence contains a comparison error. Correctly written, choice (D) would read *than that of the ancient Mayans.* Thus, choice (D) contains an error and is the correct answer.

29.　**B**　The verb *are* is plural, but the subject of the sentence is *making time*, which is singular. Thus, choice (B) contains a subject-verb agreement error, and is the correct answer.

30.　**D**　As it is currently written, sentence 3 reads *The Nutcracker, for example.* This sentence does not contain a verb and is thus an incomplete thought. Eliminate choices (A) and (C), which repeat this error. Choice (B) merges sentences 2 and 3, but by using the word *which* turns the combination of the two sentences into an incomplete thought. Eliminate choice (B). Choices (D) and (E) both fix the error in the original version of the sentences, but choice (D) is more concise. Thus, the correct answer is choice (D).

31.　**C**　This question asks which answer contains the best phrase with which to open the second paragraph. Look for a phrase that connects what appears at the end of the first paragraph with what appears at the beginning of the second paragraph. The end of the first paragraph mentions George Balanchine's successful ballet, and the beginning of the second paragraph discusses the difficulties that choreographers face in creating ballets, so you need a phrase that transitions between these two thoughts. Choice (A) introduces a discussion of the musical score. Since neither the first paragraph nor the second paragraph focuses on the musical score, eliminate choice (A). Choice (B) inappropriately begins the sentence with a conjunction, and does not link the ideas in the two paragraphs, so choice (B) is not the correct answer. Choice (C) refers back to Balanchine, who is mentioned at the end of paragraph one, saying that he makes the job of choreographer appear easy. It also begins with the contrast word *while*, thus suggesting that the rest of the sentence will discuss cases in which choreography is not easy. Thus, choice (C) forms the best introduction to sentence 6, and is the correct answer. Choice (D) opens by discussing the challenges that dancers face. However, these challenges are not discussed elsewhere in the passage, so choice (D) introduces irrelevant information and is therefore incorrect. Choice (E) similarly introduces irrelevant information by discussing the time at which the first ballet was choreographed. Eliminate choice (E).

32.　**D**　As the sentence is currently written, the pronoun *this* is ambiguous; it's not clear whether it refers to the fact that the theater hired Tharp, the fact that the ballet featured Baryshnikov, or the fact that Tharp used Lamb's and Haydn's music. Thus, you can eliminate choice (A). In choice (B), the pronoun *his* is ambiguous, since it's not clear whether it refers to Lamb or Haydn, so choice (B) is incorrect. Nothing in the rest of the paragraph discusses the size of the cast, so choice (C) introduces new information that is irrelevant to the topic. Choice (D) clarifies the meaning of the sentence, indicating that hiring Tharp was the thing that was advantageous. Thus, choice (D) is the correct answer. Choice (E) uses the pronoun *that*, which is ambiguous since it does not clearly refer to any one thing, and also introduces a tense error by using the present perfect verb *has*, which would indicate that the sentence refers to an action that began in the past but continues into the present. Since the actions discussed in the passage all occurred entirely in the past, *has* is in the wrong tense.

33.   **B**   Sentence 10 discusses the fact that *Push Comes to Shove* is now regarded as one of the most successful examples of crossover ballet in history. Choice (A) says *There are many reasons that this is true*. In this sentence, the word *this* would have to refer to the fact that *Push Comes to Shove* was successful. Since nothing in the third paragraph discusses the reasons for this success, choice (A) introduces information irrelevant to the rest of the paragraph, and is incorrect. Since paragraph three discusses ballets that were unsuccessful, choice (B) effectively introduces paragraph three, and is the correct answer. Paragraph two, rather than paragraph three, discusses the difficulties in choreographing a ballet, so choice (C) does not form an effective introduction for paragraph three. Paragraph three does not discuss crossover ballets, so choice (D) introduces irrelevant information. The third paragraph discusses failed ballets, rather than favorite ballets, so choice (E) also introduces irrelevant information and is incorrect.

34.   **E**   As it is currently written, the sentence implies an association between the fact that the ballet was originally staged by a well-known choreographer and the fact that a later version of the ballet was unsuccessful. Since the fact that the ballet was originally choreographed by someone who was successful would indicate that the opposite would be true; that later versions of the ballet would be successful. Thus, you can eliminate choice (A). Choice (C) repeats this error and is also incorrect. Choice (B) suggests that there was more than one unsuccessful attempt to produce *Don Quixote*, a fact that is not supported anywhere else in the passage. Eliminate choice (B). Since Ross Stratton's version of *Don Quixote* was not a box office success, but rather the opposite, you can eliminate choice (D). Choice (E) uses the word *while* to appropriately introduce a contrast between the original version of the ballet, and the unsuccessful version that Ross Stratton produced. Thus, choice (E) is the correct answer.

35.   **A**   Examine the topic sentence of the passage. Since the correct answer should include information that could appropriately be discussed immediately before this topic sentence, the correct answer choice should contain information that relates to sentence 1. Sentence 1 introduces a discussion of the purpose of dance from the 15th century onward, so a paragraph preceding this sentence might logically discuss dance before the 15th century. Thus, choice (A) is the correct answer. Nothing in sentence 1 or in the rest of the passage discusses types of dance other than ballet, so choice (B) is incorrect. Similarly, nothing in the rest of the passage discusses opera or any art form other than ballet, so choice (C) is also incorrect. Sentence 1 discusses dancers, but does not discuss how they assist in making a ballet successful, so you can eliminate choice (D). Nothing in the passage discusses the kind of education that choreographers must receive, so choice (E) is incorrect.

GRAMMAR TEST 2

1. **E**   In the original sentence, the phrase *The line "Belgians in the Congo" from Billy Joel's song <u>We Didn't</u> <u>Start the Fire</u> alludes to the authority Belgium wielded there* is a complete thought. The phrase *it annexed the Congo as a colony* is also a complete thought. Since this sentence joins two complete thoughts using just a comma, this sentence contains a comma splice error. Eliminate choice (A). Choice (B) uses *having annexed* and turns the sentence into an incomplete thought, so choice (B) is incorrect. Choice (C) is similarly incomplete. Choice (D) is longer than choice (E) and changes the meaning of the sentence by implying that the reason that Belgium wielded power was so that it could annex the Congo, rather than implying that that Belgium wielded power because it had already annexed the Congo. Thus, choice (E) is the correct answer.

2. **C**   This sentence contains two verbs in a list: *to take* and *riding*. Since the verbs are not in the same form, this sentence contains a parallelism error. Eliminate choice (A). Choice (E) repeats this error, since *take* and *riding* need to be parallel, not *tending* and *riding*. Thus, you can also eliminate choice (E). The correct idiom is *tends to take*, rather than *tends to taking*. Thus, choice (B) is also incorrect. Choice (C) fixes the error in the original sentence and does not introduce any new errors, so the correct answer is choice (C). Since the correct idiom is *rather than*, not *rather as*, choice (D) contains an idiom error and is incorrect.

3. **D**   In this sentence, *a receptionist*, which is singular, refers back to *Amy and Giselle,* or plural people. Thus, this sentence contains a noun agreement error. Choices (C) and (E) repeat this error and are also incorrect. Choice (B) fixes the agreement error but uses *serving* rather than *serve*, and thus turns the sentence into an incomplete thought. Choice (D) fixes the error in the original and does not introduce any new errors, so the correct answer is choice (D).

4. **D**   In the original sentence, the word *it* is redundant, and turns the first half of the sentence into a fragment. Thus, choice (A) contains an error. Choice (E) repeats the error in the original sentence and is also incorrect. Choice (B) uses *representing*, which is the wrong verb form and does not agree with the verb *is supposed* which occurs later in the sentence. Thus, choice (B) is not the correct answer. In choice (C), using *which represents* would turn the entire sentence into an incomplete thought, so you can eliminate choice (C). Only choice (D) remains. Choice (D) fixes the error in the original sentence and does not introduce any new errors, so the correct answer is choice (D).

5. **B**   This sentence uses *which*, a word that should refer to things, to refer to *journalists*, who are people. You must use *who,* rather than which to refer to people, so choice (A) contains an error and is incorrect. Choice (E) repeats this error and is also incorrect. Choice (B) fixes the error in the original sentence and does not introduce any new errors, so choice (B) is the correct answer. The correct idiom is *responsible for*, rather than *responsible to*, so choice (C) contains an idiom error, as does choice (D).

6. **E**   In the original sentence, the phrase *Some individuals who are interested in globe-trotting are nevertheless hesitant to travel by plane* is a complete thought. The phrase *they erroneously think that automobile travel is safer than air travel* is also a complete thought. Since this sentence joins two complete thoughts using only a comma, this sentence contains a comma splice error. Eliminate choice (A). Choice (B) uses *in that* as a conjunction, but *in that* is not a conjunction. Thus, choice (B) is also incorrect. Choices (C) and (D) change the tense of the sentence by using either *were* or *had been*. Since the rest of the sentence is in the present tense, rather than the past tense, both choices (C) and (D) are incorrect. Choice (E) fixes the error in the original sentence and does not introduce any new errors, so choice (E) is the correct choice.

7. **C**   In the original sentence, the phrase *Once considered purely mythical* is a modifying phrase, and must modify whatever appears after the comma. Since *the French gunboat* appears after the comma, this sentence suggests that the French gunboat was once considered purely mythical. However, the sentence presumably is trying to state that the giant squid, not the gunboat, was once considered mythical. Thus, this sentence contains a misplaced modifier. Eliminate choice (A). Choice (E) repeats the error in the original sentence and is also incorrect. In choice (B), the clause *Once considered purely mythical, a giant squid was captured by the French gunboat* Alecton *in 1861* is a complete thought. The clause *after that its existence was accepted by the scientific community at large* is also a complete thought. This choice connects two complete thoughts using only a comma, and thus contains a comma splice error. Choice (C) fixes the error in the original sentence and does not introduce any new errors, so the correct answer is choice (C). Choice (D) uses the plural possessive pronoun *their* to refer to the singular *giant squid*, so choice (D) contains a pronoun agreement error and is therefore incorrect.

8. **A**   The same-direction conjunction *and* is appropriate here, the word *even* provides appropriate emphasis, and the verb *support* is parallel to the verb *continue*, so the original sentence does not contain an error. Thus, the correct answer is choice (A). In choice (B) the word *which* would have to refer to *their 80's*. However, since this changes and muddles the intended meaning of the sentence, choice (B) is incorrect. Choice (C) uses *supporting*, rather than *support*, which is not parallel with *continue* and which in context turns the sentence into a fragment. Thus, choice (C) is incorrect. Choice (D) is longer than choice (A), and is thus incorrect. Choice (E) inappropriately uses the change-of-direction conjunction *but*, rather than *and*, and by using the pronoun *who* also turns the sentence into a fragment. Thus, you can eliminate choice (E).

9. **E**   Phrases linked by the *not only…but also* construction should be in parallel form. In this case, the first phrase is *not only by what charity organizations did*, and the second phrase is *but also what they encouraged others to do*. Note that the first phrase uses *by what*, whereas the second does not. Thus, these two phrases are not parallel. Eliminate choice (A). Choice (D) repeats this error by omitting the word *by*, and is also incorrect. Choices (B) and (C) use *and* rather than *but also*. However, the correct idiom is *not only…but also*, rather than *not only…and*. Thus, these two choices contain idiom errors and are incorrect. Choice (E) fixes the error in the original sentence and does not introduce any new errors, so choice (E) is the correct answer.

10. **B** The word *which* must refer to whatever occurs immediately before the comma. However, since it is *burglary*, not *the rise*, that occurs almost daily, the word *which* in this case modifies the wrong thing. Eliminate choice (A). Choice (B) fixes the error in the original sentence and does not introduce any new errors, so choice (B) is the correct answer. Choice (E) turns the sentence into a fragment and is thus also incorrect. Choice (D) uses *where*. If the phrase *where it occurs almost daily now* were placed immediately after the word *neighborhood*, then this choice would be correct, since *where* can appropriately describe a neighborhood. However, in this case, the modifying phrase is placed too far away from the word it would need to modify. Thus, choice (D) is incorrect. In choice (C), the phrase *In this neighborhood, burglary is on the rise* is a complete thought. The phrase *it occurs almost daily now* is also a complete thought. Since this choice joins two complete thoughts using only a comma, this choice contains a comma splice error. Eliminate choice (C).

11. **D** The subject of the verb *have become* is *each*, which is singular. However, since *have become* is plural, this sentence contains a subject-verb agreement error. Eliminate choice (A). Choices (B) and (E) also contain plural verbs and thus repeat the error in choice (A). Choice (C) changes the tense of the verb from the past perfect, which implies that an action began in the past and continues into the present, to the present. Since the meaning of the sentence calls for the past perfect tense, choice (C) is also incorrect. Choice (D) fixes the error in the original sentence and does not introduce any new errors, so the correct answer is choice (D).

12. **D** The correct idiom is *neither….nor*. Since this sentence uses *neither…and* instead, choice (D) contains an error and is the correct answer.

13. **C** The earlier part of the sentence uses the pronoun *one*, but choice (C) uses *you* in place of *one*. Since the two pronouns are not interchangeable, choice (C) contains a pronoun agreement error and is the correct answer.

14. **E** The adjective *eccentric* appropriately describes the noun *painter*, so choice (A) does not contain an error. The verb *helped* is in the past tense, and, since Duchamp helped to revolutionize art *in the early 1900s*, the past tense is appropriate here. The verb does not disagree with any subjects. It is also not in a list, so you do not have to check for parallelism errors. Thus, choice (B) does not contain any errors and is not the correct answer. Since *helped…by* is the correct idiom, choice (C) does not contain an error. In choice (D), the noun *developments* is plural, and does not disagree with any other nouns in the sentence. Additionally, *developments* is not the subject of a verb, so choice (D) does not contain any subject-verb agreement errors. The noun is also not redundant and, since its meaning is appropriate for the sentence, is not a diction error. Finally, *developments in* is the correct idiom. Thus, choice (D) does not contain an error. There are no errors in this sentence, so the correct answer is choice (E).

15. **B** The word *suddenly* is an adverb, and should therefore modify a verb, an adjective, or another adverb. However, in this case, *suddenly* modifies *rushing*, which this sentence uses as a noun. Since adjectives, not adverbs, modify nouns, *suddenly* should be changed to the adjective *sudden*. Thus, choice (B) contains an error and is the correct answer.

16.   **D**   The pronoun *him* is an object pronoun, but this sentence uses it as a subject pronoun, that is, as the subject of the verb *expected*. Thus, this sentence contains a pronoun case error. To see the error more easily, use the drop test by removing the words *and I* from the sentence. If you use the drop test, you're left with *the party was still more enjoyable than him expected*. Now it's easier to see that you need *he expected* rather than *him*

17.   **B**   Use *when* to refer to a time. Since this sentence does not explicitly refer to a time, you need *without*, rather than *when not*. Thus, choice (B) is the correct answer.

18.   **E**   The adverb *enthusiastically* modifies the verb *sing*, and is therefore correctly used. The verb *sing* is in the present tense, and agrees in tense with other verbs in the sentence such as *march* and *crush*. The verb *sing* is also plural, and therefore agrees with the plural subject *members*. Finally, *sing* is not in a list, and so does not need to be parallel with other verbs. Thus, choice (A) does not contain an error. *Before* is the correct preposition in this case. The plural pronoun *they* replaces the plural noun *members*, and is in the correct case. Thus, choice (B) does not contain an error. Since *onto* is the appropriate preposition here, choice (C) also does not contain an error. Finally, since *where* appropriately refers to a place—*the field*—choice (D) does not contain an error. This sentence does not contain an error, so the correct answer is choice (E).

19.   **C**   The pronoun *their* is plural, but the only noun in the sentence to which it can refer is the singular noun *dog*. Thus, choice (C) contains a pronoun agreement error, and is the correct answer.

20.   **E**   In choice (A), the conjunction *whether* appropriately introduces the first of two alternatives, so choice (A) does not contain an error. The adverb *solely* correctly modifies the verb *were*, so choice (B) does not contain an error. The conjunction *or* is appropriate, since the correct idiom is *whether...or*. Thus, choice (C) does not contain an error. In choice (D) the verb *were...inspired* is in the past tense, and therefore agrees in tense with the other verbs in the sentence and does not create any subject-verb agreement errors. Additionally, the phrases *were solely the result* and *were actually inspired* are parallel in form, so choice (D) does not contain a parallelism error. This sentence does not contain any errors, so the correct answer is choice (E).

21.   **B**   Use *less* to compare two things; use *least* to compare three or more things. Since this sentence compares Aurélien's new apartment to the other apartments he has rented in the city—and he has rented a total of four apartments—this sentence should use *least* rather than *less*. Thus, choice (B) uses the wrong adjective, and is the correct answer.

22.   **B**   The verb *have become* is plural, but the subject of the verb is *telegraph*, which is singular. Thus, choice (B) contains a subject-verb agreement and is the correct answer. Correctly written, the choice would read, *has become*.

23.   **E**   The preposition *for* is the appropriate preposition in this case, so choice (A) does not contain an idiom error and is not the correct answer. The adverb *most* correctly modifies *disheartening*, and, since there aren't any other disheartening moments being discussed here, *most*, rather than *more* is the correct adverb. The adjective *disheartening* also appropriately modifies the noun *moment*,

so choice (B) does not contain an error. The singular pronoun *she* unambiguously refers to the singular noun *poetess* and is in the correct case, so choice (C) does not contain an error. In choice (D), the verb *opened* is in the past tense, and agrees in tense with the other past tense verbs in the sentence, as well as with the subject *she*. Finally, the verb *opened* is parallel in form with the verb *found*, so choice (D) does not contain a parallelism error. Since this sentence does not contain an error, the correct answer is choice (E).

24. **C** The verb *have decreased* is plural, but the subject of the verb is *number*, which is singular. Thus, choice (C) contains a subject-verb agreement error and is the correct answer. Properly written, this choice should read, *has decreased*.

25. **D** As it is currently written, this sentence compares how focused employees are at home and *the office*. However, this sentence needs to compare how focused employees are at home to how focused employees are at the office. Thus, correctly written choice (D) would read *than they are at the office*. Since choice (D) contains a comparison error, choice (D) is the correct answer.

26. **B** Here, the pronoun *who* turns the sentence into an incomplete thought. If you remove the word *who*, then the sentence is properly complete. Thus, choice (B) contains an error, and is the correct answer.

27. **B** The pronoun *them* is plural, but refers to *the golf cart*, which is singular. Thus, choice (B) contains a pronoun agreement error, and is the correct answer.

28. **B** The phrase *while building it over the course of several centuries* is a modifying phrase, and must modify whatever comes right after the comma. However, *the palace* appears right after the comma. Since the palace is the thing that was built, and not the person or persons who did the building, this sentence contains a misplaced modifier. Changing choice (B) to *it was built* would change the modifying sentence so that it would then describe *the palace,* the item that the phrase should describe. Thus, choice (B) contains an error, and is the correct answer.

29. **C** The word *affect* is a verb, and means "to influence." However, *effect* is generally used as a noun, and means "a result." Since the meaning of the sentence calls for a verb that means "to influence" rather than for a noun that means "a result," choice (C) contains a diction error and is the correct answer.

30. **D** In the original sentence, the pronoun *they* does not clearly refer to any other plural noun in the sentence, and is therefore an ambiguous pronoun. Eliminate choice (A). Choices (C) and (D) also repeat this error and are therefore incorrect. Choice (B) begins the sentence with *Although*, thus turning the sentence into an incomplete thought. Therefore choice (B) is also incorrect. Choice (D) fixes the error in the original sentence and is the correct answer.

31. **E** The sentence in question explains who studies biodiversity: *wildlife scientists, climatologists, and biologists*. Paragraph two discusses evidence relating to Bigfoot sightings. Since sentence 3 does not relate to any information in paragraph two, you would not want to place sentence 3 at the beginning of paragraph two. Eliminate choice (A). The word *Additionally* would suggest that the information in sentence 3 is a continuation of a thought discussed in sentence 2. However, sentence 2 discusses the fact that Bigfoot may still exist, and therefore discusses topic unrelated to sentence 3. Thus, choice (B) is not the correct answer. Since the paragraph is already discussing biodiversity on Earth, the words *on this planet* are redundant and make the sentence unnecessarily wordy. Eliminate choice (C). Since *include* and *are* mean the same thing in this context, choice (D) does not improve the sentence in any way, and is incorrect. Sentence 3 does not relate to anything in either the sentence before it or the sentence after it, and therefore contains irrelevant information. The best option is simply to delete the sentence, so choice (E) is the best answer.

32. **B** In the original sentence, the verb *was…claimed* is in the past tense, and does not agree with the present tense verb *supports*, which appears later in the sentence. Thus, choice (A) is incorrect. Choice (B) fixes the error by using the present tense verb *believe*, and does not introduce any new errors, so choice (B) is the correct answer. Choice (C) introduces the pronoun *they*, which does not refer to any specific plural nouns elsewhere in the sentence, so choice (C) is incorrect. Choice (D) is unnecessarily wordy in relation to choice (B), so choice (B) is a better answer than choice (D). Choice (E) uses the pronoun *you*, which does not match the voice used in the rest of the paragraph, so choice (E) is incorrect.

33. **E** The third paragraph discusses both the 1924 attack and the 2007 photograph, and in fact discusses the 1924 attack first, so choice (A), which discusses only the photograph, would not be an appropriate transition. The third paragraph focuses on those who do not believe that Bigfoot is real, so choice (B) does not agree with the third paragraph and therefore would form a poor topic sentence for that paragraph. Since nothing in either paragraph discusses the types of species which Bigfoot may attack, choice (C) introduces irrelevant information and is not the correct answer. Paragraph three does not discuss the difference between the 1924 sighting and the 2007 sighting—it merely focuses on the fact that there are those who are skeptical of both. Therefore, choice (D) also introduces irrelevant information and is not the correct answer. Choice (E) introduces the idea that not all people accept the evidence provided in paragraph two, and uses the word *however*, to indicate a contrast between the ideas mentioned in the second paragraph and the third paragraph. Since paragraph three focuses on those who do not accept the evidence provided in paragraph two, choice (E) forms an excellent transition between the two paragraphs and is the correct choice.

34. **D** Sentence 10 discusses those who are skeptical of Bigfoot's existence, while sentence 11 discusses those who believe in Bigfoot's existence. Since the two sentences contain contrasting ideas, you need a contrasting transition word to connect the two sentences. Choices (A), (B), (C), and (E) all use same-direction transition words, and are therefore incorrect. Choice (D) uses the change-of-direction transition word *however,* and is therefore the correct answer. The paragraph does use the

term *Sasquatch*, but knowing where the word originated does not contribute to the meaning of the paragraph, so you can eliminate choice (B). Choice (C) also introduces information about Richard Dyer, but this information does not clarify any statements in the final paragraph. Thus, choice (C) is not the correct answer.

35.   E   The final paragraph does discuss Richard Dyer's experience, but where the experience occurred is irrelevant to the rest of the information in the paragraph, so you can eliminate choice (A). Since choice (D) provides no information about the results of the four formal studies that it mentions, it does not clarify any information in the final paragraph, which focuses on reasons that believers in Bigfoot still have cause to be optimistic. Choice (E) explains why Dyer's experience might provide believers in Bigfoot with hope: If Dyer conducted DNA tests on his specimen, and those tests cannot be faked, then this particular experience might not be the result of a hoax. Thus, choice (E) is the correct answer.

About the Authors

Brian Becker has been working with The Princeton Review since 2005, and he has contributed preparation materials for the ACT, SAT, PSAT, and the GRE Subject Test in Literature. Brian is currently completing his Ph.D. in English at Rutgers, The State University of New Jersey, where he specializes in American Literature from 1865 to 1945 and in pedagogies of writing. Brian enjoys reading, traveling, writing, and playing squash.

Clarissa Constantine began teaching Princeton Review SAT classes in 1999 while she was working toward her Bachelors of Music in Music Production & Technology from The Hartt School at University of Hartford. Since then, she's added ACT, GRE, GMAT, LSAT, MCAT Verbal, TOEFL, SSAT, ISEE, and ASVAB to her bag of tricks, and teaches and tutors students both in-person and online. Furthermore, Clarissa is also a Master Trainer for the SAT, ACT and TOEFL. When she's not involved in education or music, Clarissa can probably be found training for her next half-marathon or spending time with her husband, Joe, and their Chocolate Lab, Sammy.

Lisa Mayo has been working with The Princeton Review since 2004 and teaches test-taking techniques for the SAT, ACT, GRE, GMAT, LSAT, MCAT Physics, and SAT Subject tests. She graduated from Smith College and has a B.A. in Physics. When Lisa is not in the classroom or writing test questions, she enjoys traveling, reading, and snorkeling.

Steve Voigt started teaching for the Princeton Review in 2004. He has taught and tutored hundreds of students for the SAT, ACT, GMAT, GRE, ISEE, SSAT, PSAT, and SAT subject tests. He is also an SAT Master Trainer, and since 2008 has been instrumental in developing the Princeton Review's SAT and PSAT instructional materials. After nine years in New York City, Steve is happy to be living in Virginia's Shenandoah Valley with his wife, dog, and two cats. In addition to his work with the Princeton Review, he is an adjunct professor of music theory and composition at James Madison University.